The Sociology of Work

The Sociology of Work

An Introduction

KEITH GRINT

Polity Press

First published 1991 by Polity Press
in association with Blackwell Publishers
Reprinted 1992, 1993, 1994

Editorial office:
Polity Press, 65 Bridge Street,
Cambridge CB2 1UR, UK

Marketing and production:
Blackwell Publishers, the publishing imprint of Basil Blackwell Ltd
108 Cowley Road, Oxford OX4 1JF, UK

Basil Blackwell Inc.
238 Main Street,
Cambridge, MA 02142, USA

ISBN 0–7456–0606–7
ISBN 0–7456–0607–5 (pbk)

British Library Cataloguing in Publication Data
A CIP catalogue record for this book is available from the British Library.

Library of Congress Cataloging in Publication Data
Grint, Keith.
The sociology of work: an introduction/Keith Grint.
p. cm.
"First published 1991 by Polity Press in association with Basil Blackwell" – T.p. verso.
Includes bibliographical references (p.
ISBN 0–7456–0606–7 (hard): – ISBN 0–7456–0607–5 (pbk.):
1. Industrial sociology. 2. Work. I. Title.
HD6955.G75 1991
306.3′6–dc20 90–1290
CIP

Typeset in 10 on 11½pt Times
by Colset Private Limited, Singapore
Printed in Great Britain by T.J. Press, Padstow, Cornwall

Printed on acid-free paper

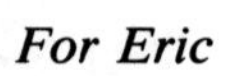

For Eric

Contents

Acknowledgements

Like all books there are many voices in this one, even if there is only one author. My first and greatest debt goes to Eric Batstone whose friendship, humour, and guidance inspired me to write this. I am also greatly indebted to Toni Batstone for her encouragement and support when the days were darkest. Many people have suffered from various forms of the ideas in here, perhaps none more so than the undergraduates and postgraduates on the industrial sociology and industrial relations courses at Brunel, and I would like to thank them for their forbearance, perseverance and good humour. Amongst those who have read drafts I would like to express my particular gratitude to John Banks, Gerhard Baumann, Willy Brown, John Burnett, Jon Clark, Eric Hirsch, Jim Tomlinson and Steve Woolgar; everyone makes mistakes but all those in here are mine. Many others have discussed ideas with me, or allowed me to steal them, or generally kept me sane, and among these I would like to thank: the Department of Human Sciences and the Centre for Research into Innovation, Culture and Technology (CRICT), Donna Baston, Norma Bowes, Marjorie Bunn, Jack Crittenden, Duncan Gallie, Jas Gill, Peggotty Graham, Richard Jenkins, Ronnie Johnson, Dion Lamkin, Leslie Libetta, Bob Looker, Janet Low, Sharon Macdonald, Peter Seglow, Roger Silverstone, Sylvia Walby and Jackie Woolgar. David Held at Polity Press kept faith with me and, with Bob Looker, stimulated my interest in the world of academia. Steve Woolgar ensured that the time expended on 'London waiting' between Oxford and Brunel was never wasted. Finally, I would like to make a special mention of Sandra, Katy, Beki and Kris for all the jokes, for reminding me about the significance of the domestic sphere, and for persistently demonstrating that there are more important things in life than work.

All extracts from the work of Eric Batstone are reproduced by kind permission of Toni Batstone.

All extracts from HMSO publications are reproduced by courtesy of the Controller of Her Majesty's Stationery Office.

List of Tables

List of Figures

Preface

This book has its origins in the untimely death of Eric Batstone in 1987. Eric had been my doctoral supervisor at Nuffield College, Oxford and a close friend. Some time after his death, when Toni Batstone and I had plucked up enough courage to clear his office, I came across his lecture notes for the industrial sociology course he taught at Oxford and mountains of related material. I owed, and still owe, a great personal debt to Eric, and Toni and I decided it would be a fitting tribute to him to combine our respective lecture notes on industrial sociology and develop them into an introductory text. I don't think Eric ever intended such a publication - he was always too busy developing new research ideas to concern himself with such a project - and had it not been for his death I would not have embarked on the endeavour. By April 1988 I was in a position to inaugurate the writing and began to delve into the enormous literature that any introductory text requires. By December 1989, with the first draft complete, I already had severe doubts about the joint authorship. Not only was it extraordinarily difficult to interpret what Eric would have thought about fields that he had not previously written about or discussed with me, but there were substantial differences of opinion between myself and the texts left by Eric. Furthermore, as the writing progressed it became clear that the original focus on industrial sociology was too narrow for my concerns about the nature of work, and that the amount of material I had been able to use from Eric's lecture notes was very small. After discussions with those closest to Eric's work (Toni Batstone, William Brown and Duncan Gallie) the decision was made to change from joint to single authorship. The book, therefore, does not reflect his views. It is, however, dedicated to his memory and without his friendship, guidance and example it would not have been written.

Preface

[illegible]

Introduction

This book concerns work. Work occupies a substantial proportion of most people's lives and has often been taken as a symbol of personal value: work provides status, economic reward, a demonstration of religious faith and a means to realize self-potential. But work also embodies the opposite evaluations: labour can be back-breaking and mentally incapacitating; labour camps are punishment centres; work is a punishment for original sin and something which we would all rather avoid – something which was, to quote a woman munitions worker in the Second World War, 'the blank patch between one brief evening and the next' (Mass Observation, 1943: 43).

The ambiguous nature of work is a central theme running through this book. Rather than restricting the review to paid labour, and concentrating upon male factory workers as much of industrial or occupational sociology does, it considers work in a rather wider perspective which includes unpaid domestic labour, which highlights the links between the sphere of employment and the domestic sphere, and which incorporates the notions of ethnicity and gender as well as class. Inevitably, an introductory text of this type can barely skim the surface of most of the debates here and I have not attempted to provide a comprehensive introduction to all forms of work in all varieties of society throughout all known periods of time. Instead, I have selected substantive fields that I consider significant and attempted to illustrate these both with conventional material and with some rather less traditional. Since an underlying theme of the approach is the complexity and differences which exist at work, rather than the uniformities, the selection of substantive fields and source material is inevitably asymmetrical: it is, for example, because I dispute the allegedly archetypal significance of the male factory worker isolated from his domestic world that the book looks beyond him to female domestic workers, to eighteenth-century sailors and to twentieth-century women civil servants for the evidence. By definition, therefore, I miss out far more than I consider, but my intention is both to introduce the sociological world of work and to undermine some traditional myths, rather than to provide the definitive account of typical work – whatever that might involve.

Although introductory texts are, by their very nature, overviews of broad areas I do not think this means the book should avoid pursuing particular and explicit theoretical lines with regard to the current orthodoxies of the day. Each chapter has its own specific perspectives to engage with but perhaps I should acknowledge an overriding engagement with four areas.

First is the denial of the superordinate position of class at the expense of gender, race and ethnicity, and the concomitant denial of the supremacy of the labour process separated from home and all else. The spheres of work, employment and home are all necessarily intertwined and to separate them as if they could exist independently is to misconceive the complex reality of work and misunderstand the significance of the relationships which it embodies. Moreover, to decant elements of social groups or individuals into categories like class, gender and ethnicity is to imply that individuals interpret the world through a single lens. If, on the other hand, individuals and the social groups they engage with are considered as heterogeneous constructs, for whom the world is perceived through a multifaceted lens, then we should concern ourselves with the fragmentation of work experience. Rather than puzzling over the 'failure' of the working class to develop a solidaristic political organization we might instead puzzle over why any collective organization exists and persists. In sum, what may appear to one person or analyst to be a self-evidently important social cleavage may not be interpreted as such by another.

The second issue is the polarization of organizational features into social and technical, with either the former or the latter being endowed with determinate qualities. Adopting the Actor Network approach, I argue that it is the mixture of human and non-human elements which generates significant resources, though how these 'alloys' are deployed is determined not by the content but by the interpretative actions of various agents within the network.

The third line I wish to pursue is that work is itself socially constructed and reconstructed. This implies that much of what we take for granted as inevitable or technically required or economically determined should be subjected to the most vigorous of critiques: if work is socially constructed then it is contingent and requires perpetual action by agents for its reproduction – it does not just happen but has to be brought off. Relatedly, whereas it is common to differentiate the moral economy of the pre-capitalist period from the market economy that displaced it, I argue that the moral and social aspects of work are still an essential component. To believe that contemporary employment is configured and constrained only by appeals to the rationality of market forces is to misconstrue the nature of work. If workers seek pay rises in line with inflation, rather than company profitability, or decry the disproportionate but performance-related increases of directors' salaries, then the market model can explain these only by asserting the irrationality of such workers; but if we retain the notion of work as a social and moral sphere, as well as a market sphere, then workers' actions become not irrational but rational from a different perspective. This does not mean that morality displaces market rationality and it would perhaps be more appropriate to consider the two as resources which different groups draw on to legitimate their particular campaigns at specific locations in space and time.

Fourth, and as an underlying feature of the above three issues, this book proceeds from the assumption that the world of work is one actively constructed through the interpretive acts of agents involved. Here, then, we should leave the world of 'objective' analysis, of certainty and predictability, and replace it with one constructed by indeterminacy, contingency and alternative perspectives. What is important in attempting to explain the world of work is not what that world *is* but what those involved in it take it to be. In short, what counts as 'work', what counts as 'inevitable' and what counts as 'rational behaviour' does not lie within the object or the phenomenon itself but within the social relations and interpretative processes that sustain it.

Chapter 1 sets out to discuss this indeterminacy by establishing the enigmatic essence of work. It begins by noting the significance of any activity being labelled as work in so far as an evaluation may be placed upon such an activity. What appear to be identical activities very often embody widely contrasting norms of behaviour such that the same 'work' of individuals in war and peace may be either 'heroic' and 'bestial' depending on the social circumstances and relations under which they are undertaken. This equivocal feature of work is highlighted by focusing upon non-Western and historical approaches to work. It then moves on to consider the consequences of attempts to persuade workers that their efforts were either sanctioned by God or an essential element of their humanity or a necessary means to buy their way out of the hell they found themselves in. The chapter finishes by looking at informal work, particularly domestic labour and unemployment, through which the nature of work as a social construct is re-emphasized.

Chapter 2 explores the historical dimension of work in radically different societies. From Roman Britain to the Luddites to nineteenth-century textile factories and beyond I argue against any reduction of work to a single form and illuminate the moral economy of pre-capitalist work relations on land and at sea. Noting the occupational diversity that also typifies British industrial experience, I consider the redistribution of domestic labour and influence at home which accompanied the industrial revolution, and the consequential disappearance from visible paid employment by the majority of married women, especially the middle class, during the Victorian era. This is linked to the activities of the early trade unions which, in conjunction with the paternalistic concerns of the state, coerced women out of many areas of skilled employment and attempted to corral them within the home. Finally, I trace the rise of women's employment through the advance of clerical labour and the two world wars to a point where, despite patriarchal influence, the beginnings of wage equality at work were established.

Chapter 3 moves from the substantive field of historical work to the theoretical endeavours of the historical 'gang of three': Marx, Weber and Durkheim. While noting the limitations of such classical approaches, especially the gender-blind or patriarchal influences of all three, each has something in particular to offer our contemporary analysis of work though none individually nor all three together provide anything like a coherent account of work. They are, then, important but flawed foundation stones rather than the adumbrations that merely need to be fleshed out.

Chapter 4 switches from the historical to the contemporary and delves into the complex world of the modern organization and its multitude of competing perspectives and analyses. Running through most of the major alternative interpretations of organizations and underlining what I consider to be their major problems, I explore the possibilities offered by the most recent advances in related areas: post-modernist theory and Actor Network theory. Drawing primarily on the latter, I develop an analysis which demonstrates the difficulty of separating human from non-human facets of organization and how such alloys of human technology can be captured and deployed by various contending groups within organizational settings.

From here the book moves on to review the three aspects of social stratification which I consider to be most important: class, in chapter 5, gender in chapter 6, and race and ethnicity in chapter 7. I begin by considering the relative weight given to class rather than occupation and to income rather than wealth, and pose some doubts as to any universal assumption about the role of employment in accounting for life chances. I then move on to examine the form of work activity most closely associated with class action – the strike. Noting the essentially organized nature of such action, I throw doubt upon the class orientation of most British strikes, though I emphasize the recalcitrance that appears to typify many British workers. Finally, some time is spent examining the labour process debates, and I emphasize the problems of an approach that systematically devalues all but the class issues and denies the necessary links between the domestic and the non-domestic spheres of work.

This linkage is continued in chapter 6 on gender, patriarchy and trade unionism which explains the various theoretical interpretations of gender inequalities and poses an alternative in which individuals are reconstructed as composite and heterogeneous embodiments of class, gender and ethnicity, rather than as discrete elements of each. Thus women and men do not experience work just through their specific gender, nor just through their differential class, nor through their ethnic group, but all three simultaneously. Using this model I examine the contemporary evidence of women at work, detailing the quest for equal pay, the advances and retreats of professional women, and the part played by trade unions in the subordination of women.

Chapter 7 considers the third of my three forms of social stratification, race and ethnicity. It looks first at alternative theories of inequality and progress to consider the wider issue of labour market influences. Again, the brief perusal of the empirical evidence suggests that we cannot consider ethnic minorities as a single group but reconceptualize them through the specificity of their ethnicity in conjunction with their class and gender. Following this, a number of different aspects of the connections between ethnicity, race and the labour market are covered, in particular the role of ethnic businesses, the value of anti-discriminatory policies and legislation and the role of management, especially in recruitment. Finally, the part played by trade unions in the persistence of racism at work is assessed before reviewing the comparative experiences of minorities in the USA and Britain.

The final chapter, chapter 8, switches from the social to the technical aspects of work but only in order to illustrate the problems of demarcating one from the other. Through a review of the polarized arguments of technological and social determinists I argue that both approaches misconstrue the nature of the relationship between human and non-human elements at work: technology-less work systems are usually as unproductive as human-less technologies. Only when we conceive of the two features of work as intimately related in a creative 'alloy' of both can we begin to explain the nature of work properly. This is supplemented by a brief review of the two most recent attempts to propel the complex and uncertain world of work into a future of radical difference and stark simplicity: the 'post-Fordist' and the 'technocracy' debates. Maintaining a healthy scepticism of such revolutionary changes, on both theoretical and empirical grounds, I conclude that neither new nor old *universal* patterns of work exist: diversity rather than universality remains the norm, and part of the reason for this remains locked into the interpretative methods by which we come to know the world of work.

1

What is Work?

Who first invented Work?
Charles Lamb, letter to Barton, Sept. (1822)

Introduction

This chapter demonstrates the difficulties of delineating the world of work from the sphere of non-work and argues that no unambiguous or objective definition of work is possible. Work tends to be an activity that transforms nature and is usually undertaken in social situations, but exactly what counts as work is dependent on the specific social circumstances under which such activities are undertaken and, critically, how these circumstances and activities are interpreted by those involved. Whether any particular activity is experienced as work or leisure or both or neither is intimately related to the temporal, spatial and cultural conditions in existence. This does not mean that the search for the meaning of work is the equivalent to the quest for the Holy Grail, nor that one person's definition of work is as influential as any other. Rather, it implies that we should consider the past and present definitions of work as symbols of cultures and especially as mirrors of power: if what counts as work is glorified or despised or gender-related, then the language and practice of work allows us to read embodied fragments of wider social power. For example, to be categorised as 'unemployed' today not only signifies the historically atypical creation of a formal division between the economy and the polity, employment and work, but also embodies the significance attached to one particular facet of contemporary Western social life. Unemployment is not a category that would be recognized outside a very limited slice of space and time; that it is today, and that the label is crucial to the status of the individual, tells us as much about the kind of society we inhabit as about the kind of individual stigmatized.

To illustrate the indexical nature of work, this chapter considers contemporary Western definitions of work and compares these to non-Western and historical forms before silhouetting radical critiques of, and contemporary orientations towards, work. It then moves on to a brief analysis of two substantive fields traditionally excluded from the study of work to illustrate the effects of such traditions: domestic work and unemployment.

Problems of Definition: What is Work?

It is more than just a pedantic requirement that this chapter begins by trying to answer the most basic of questions: what is work? One of the ways of distinguishing between them is via Arendt's (1958) opposition between 'labour' and 'work': labour is bodily activity designed to ensure survival in which the results are consumed almost immediately, work is the activity undertaken with our hands which gives objectivity to the world. A major difficulty with Arendt's approach, however, is that in many industrial societies very little activity generates products for immediate consumption, whereas in some hunter-gatherer societies very little activity generates material artefacts that give objectivity to the world. Perhaps more conventionally, work has been imputed with transformative capacity – an activity which alters nature – while an occupation is something which locates individuals within some form of market (Brown, 1978: 56). Yet those who are unemployed, that is no longer within the labour market, very often consider themselves as retaining whatever notion of occupation they previously had, so that the status of occupation, perhaps, may be divorced from the practice of that occupation; but neither the status nor practice of an occupation are the *sine qua non* of work.

Is work, then, simply that which ensures individual and societal survival by engaging with nature? Certainly, all societies have to engage with nature to ensure their survival but are activities which are not essential to societal survival (Writing sociology texts?) non-work? What is objectively essential to societal survival anyway, and is this the equivalent of individual survival? It is surely significant that the work of slaves, often derided as mere 'labour', may be critical for the survival of society yet simultaneously effect the exclusion from society of the very same slave and possibly result in her or his death. Moreover, if by work we embrace all social activities that are in some way transformative of nature, do we end up with a set of activities too broad to be of any value; if everything is work can anything be leisure or rest? Clearly, as Garfinkel (1984), Silverman (1970) and Giddens (1979) *inter alia* have maintained, since social reality has to be worked at – that is it has to brought off by knowledgeable agents who sustain meaningful interchanges with each other – it could be asserted that every human activity is work, in which case the sociology of work ought to become the sociology of everything. Again, if everything is work then the label is significant in demonstrating the importance of human processes of interaction; but unless we wish to impose our sociological conception of work as all human activities on to the populace we wish to study, then we should beware of assuming that what we think of as work is objective: to impute our own meanings into the language and practices of others is precisely to miss out on the significance of the social aspect. It is because the meanings secreted within and expressed through work are so variant that our conventional model of work as paid employment should not be taken as 'normal' (see Joyce, 1987). After all, if language is indexical, as the ethnomethodologists and others maintain (Sharrock and Anderson, 1986: 42–3; Woolgar, 1988), then the word 'work' cannot have an objective and transcendent meaning. Rather, the language and discourse of work are symbolic representations through which meanings and social interests are constructed, mediated and deployed. In short, the meanings of work do not inhere within the practices of participants but are created, challenged, altered and sustained through the contending discourses: if particular forms of activity are represented through discourse as valued or valueless then the activities themselves take on such characteristics for those appropriating such a discourse. For example, whether one regards domestic activities as 'work' or 'leisure' or 'drudgery' or something else entirely does not depend upon the activities but how we read such activities through the appropriate lexicon. It is not that the activities remain the same but that our perspectives are different: we can construct the activities only through the perspective. In effect, we do not 'see' the same activities.

The state often appears to have a definitive answer to the conundrum of meaning: the population is divided between those who are 'economically active' and those who 'economically inactive'. But the definition of activity here relates very closely to the formality of employment: if people are paying tax and insurance etc., they are working; if they are not they are not working. We might question whether such formality is the best way to define work when so many people, especially women with domestic responsibilities, appear by this definition to spend so long doing nothing. Equally significant, this model of work reflects the emergence of a perspective in which the economy gradually appears as the foundation stone of Western society and concomitantly the sphere of work assumes a discrete existence (Godelier, 1980). As Dumont (1977) has argued:

> The modern era has witnessed the emergence of a new mode of consideration of human phenomena, and the carving out of a separate domain, which are currently evoked for us by the words *economics*, *the economy* . . . It is conventional, and not too arbitrary, to take the publication by Adam Smith in 1776 . . . as the birth registration of the new category . . . the mercantilists of the seventeenth and eighteenth century mingled the phenomena we classify into *political* and *economic* . . . in the Indian civilization, while the political had been distinguished from and subordinated to the religious, the economic was never conceptually detached from the political.(1977: 33–4)

This 'triumph of economic ideology' in eighteenth-century Western Europe not only attacked assumptions that citizens had social and political rights that stood outside and above the realm of the market place, it also embodies the state's desire to classify citizens first and foremost as economic rather than political agents. The evaluative connotations of this relationship are nicely captured in the convention that political demonstrations and marches may be acceptable 'providing they do not interfere with people's legitimate business'. In effect, economic action *qua* 'going to work' is normal, political action *qua* participating in a protest march is abnormal.

But does this dismemberment of social activities help or hinder us in the quest for the meaning of work? Even if we try to escape the definitional problem of 'work' and nestle in the blanket security of 'employment', the barbs of ambiguity are wont to spring up through the cover: is the distinction between work and employment one of payment? because many activities can be subsumed under both labels. Is the distinction one based on formality? because a whole panoply of activities that are not conventionally considered as employment actually occur not so much 'under' the conventional economy but through it. In other words, although commentators like to categorize some activities as belonging to the informal or black economy rather than the official economy, it would appear that no clear cut binary division exists. We have economically inspired activity that occurs along a continuum rather than being situated in either one or another clearly marked category: formal and informal (Harding and Jenkins, 1989).

In general, most sociological accounts of 'work' actually concern themselves with paid employment; hence most sociology of work has actually been industrial sociology or the sociology of employment or the sociology of occupations. Industrial sociology, the sociology of employment and the sociology of occupations are wide and important fields of interest in and of themselves, but employment *qua* full-time wage labour through an occupation within an industrial setting has been a common phenomenon only in a very restricted window of space and time; i.e., the last two centuries of a minority of nations (Brown, 1988: 33). In fact, one might go further to agree with Moorhouse (1987: 237) that paid work in car factories has been 'elevated to an iconic status such that labour on the track or line became, somehow, the explicit or implicit model of what most modern work is like, or would soon be like'. This book, like the work of Moorhouse, is iconclastic in intent; it does not reduce the sociology of work to industrial sociology or the sociology of occupations and employment but argues that they are all aspects of the sociology of work.

In some senses work is the opposite of leisure: it is something we have to do, something we may prefer not to do and something we tend to get paid for. But we must also eat and drink without considering this as work; we usually have to go shopping but this is not conventionally recognized as work, though, as with much domestic labour for those undertaking it, such activities can be extremely arduous. Moreover, there are very few activities undertaken outside a pecuniary relationship which do not also occur inside one. Washing, ironing, breastfeeding, childminding, cooking and a hundred other such domestic activities all exist as unpaid and paid labour, though the correlation between paid labour and work normatively configured as 'valuable' or 'real' is not coincidental.

Nor can we distinguish between work and non-work on the basis of non-work being leisure: for some people playing sport is an occupation not a leisure activity while for others the enforced 'leisure' of unemployment turns the freedom of non-work into a nightmare of perceived worthlessness. Even for those who are employed it is not always clear how work and leisure can be separated. Loudon's review of work on South African farms suggests that for white farmers the social system requires the conflation of activities: 'Where sport and leisure activities are crucial factors in defining membership of a local community and also provide a setting for the informal exchange of ideas and information, farming as a way of life involves no clear separation between non-work and work' (Loudon, 1979: 129). Nearly two centuries earlier, the Quaker business community also managed to combine work and non-work into a seamless web of people and processes, for this 'group with the greatest overlap between kinship, friendship and religious community . . . often combined religious missions with commercial travelling' (Davidoff and Hall, 1987: 216).

In different segments of space and time the activities we may refer to as relaxations from work have been the difference between life and death: in contemporary Britain a failed crop of vegetables in the kitchen garden is a waste of time and effort but the equivalent failure in different parts of the world now or at earlier times in British history would be the end of time for the responsible gardener. Not that poor economic returns necessarily dissuade people from continuing particular forms of work. Crofting can hardly ever have been a route to economic prosperity and the rise of commercial agriculture has long since made it a marginal form of employment. Yet crofting continues because it is of great symbolic significance for those involved in it: it ensures 'the maintenance of a valued collective identity . . . through which men [*sic*] locate themselves in their cultural tradition' (Cohen, 1979: 250–1). That farming on a small scale may be considered as economically 'irrational' yet continue to involve many people is another demonstration of the incomplete dominance of economic ideology.

It is noticeable that we often avoid the term 'work' to describe activities involving children: workers, doctors, farmers and hairdressers may 'work' but parents just 'look after' children. In short, it is not just that the linguistic terms we use have some degree of ambiguity inherent to them, so that we cannot always distinguish between work and non-work; as Schwimmer (1979) reveals, for some people (in this case artists) the division is absurd. The very same term may also carry contrary meanings. 'Going to work' is one thing, having to work when you get there is a separate matter altogether. Work, then, in its physical features and its linguistic descriptions is socially constructed: there is no permanent or objective thing called work, there are aspects of social activities which we construe as work and this embodies social organization. The difference between work and non-work seldom lies within the actual activity itself and more generally inheres in the social context that supports the activity. By implication, therefore, what counts as work cannot be severed from the context within which it exists, and that context necessarily changes through space and time.

Working Beyond the Contemporary West

Clarification of what counts as work is often best achieved by pushing the boundaries of what we conventionally refer to as work to their most extreme forms. For example, Malinowski's (1984) account of the Trobriand Islanders is important in emphasizing two features: first, the irrelevance of monetary incentives in a cashless economy where social obligations to kin are the primary motive to engage in labour; and second, the seamless web which knits what we might recognize as work and leisure activities together in a social network of practices. For the islanders there is no separation between the work of gardening and the associated rituals – they are one and the same process:

> When the plants begin to grow a series of magical rites, parallel with the inaugural ones, is performed, in which the magician is supposed to give an

> impulse to the growth and development of the plant at each of its successive stages. Thus, one rite is performed to make the seed tuber sprout; another drives up the sprouting shoot; another lifts it out of the ground; yet another makes it twine around the support; then, with yet other rites, the leaves are made to bud, to open, to expand respectively. (Malinowski, quoted in Littler (ed.), 1985: 16)

Similarly, the work of Sahlins (1972) on some hunter-gatherer societies has demonstrated that the motivation to work, that is to fill up time with 'productive activities', is a distinctly contemporary Western idea, since for many hunter-gatherers 'work' ceases as soon as the minimum necessary activity has been achieved. More recently Woodburn (1980) has suggested that work-related activity is contingent on the nature of the subsistence system: most hunter-gatherers are indeed immediate consumers of the food obtained, though there are some, especially Australian aborigines, where consumption is delayed and a consequentially more formal organizational system exists to distribute and control the food. The crucial point, though, is that abundance and scarcity of food and other resources do not appear to determine the form of social organization – whether hunter-gatherers are relatively sedentary and mobile, more or less formally organized, is ultimately the result of social constructions not environmental determination. One of the main problems with trying to assess the significance of work in hunter-gatherer societies is that many of them now exist only in the most marginal lands, pushed off the most productive land by the encroaching settlers. Thus although they may now have to work rather more hours than they would like in order to secure food supplies, it does seem that working hours are directly related to such concerns and not to any standardized hours of gainful activity.

Of course, many people in the so-called Third World today appear to have little option but to accommodate themselves to the newly industrializing order, and that means maximizing their potential income by extending the working day as long as possible. Just as many pre-industrial societies seem to have operated without a clear division between work and leisure, so too life in the huge 'informal sectors' of contemporary Third World cities often obliterates the division. However, the seamless web that knits work and non-work is more pervasive because of the absence of clear cut non-pecuniary activities rather than the conflation of work and leisure. As Stalker argues: 'Work in this case is not so much what gives a meaning to life, more what makes life possible: a means of gleaning something, however slight, from a hostile environment. It has no beginning and no end. Working and eating and sleeping and childcare and everything else blend into one organic whole' (1986: 8). While the majority in Western industrial nations have or had fixed sites for employment and semi-permanent occupations and income, possibly between twenty and seventy per cent of the urban workforces in major Third World cities are informal, that is without fixed place of work, occupation or income (Rosenberg, 1986).

Some of the most poignant images of people caught in the transition between non-industrial and industrial socities are gleaned through the rhetoric of those without employment. Bourdieu's (1979) study of Algeria in 1960 highlights the conflicts as 'old-fashioned peasant' becomes transformed into 'urban sub-proletarian' and, in the absence of employment, operates as a street trader. Given the relatively insignificant sums of money earned by such practices, Bourdieu argues that such practices

> borrow their justifications from the peasant morality of the past . . . the outward appearances of being occupied are the last resort against the ultimate degradation of the man who gets others to feed him . . . activity is identified with social function and is not measured by the product in kind (still less in money). . . . Those who find themselves in a position where it is impossible to get real work endeavour to fill the abyss between their unrealizable aspirations and the effective possibilities by performing work whose function is doubly symbolic in that it gives a fictitious satisfaction to the man who performs it while at the same time providing him with a justification in the eyes of others. (Bourdieu, 1979: 41–2)

Indeed, this concern for social obligation and the creation of self-respect, from what many might regard as the worst of all possible worlds, is also recreated in the rhetoric of the 'untouchable' road sweepers and lavatory cleaners of Benares (now Varanasi) for whom work provides both identity and material reward, and facilitates the reproduction of ritual and social obligations. Moreover:

> Sweepers associate their work of sweeping with a toughness that they admire in both men and women; with drinking and eating of 'hot' substances, meat and strong liquor. Linked with this is their belief that they are hot-blooded and highly-sexed. Both men and women lay great emphasis on honour and will in defence of it fight without much provocation. . . . The sweepers' sense of identity and self-esteem comes from their style of life rather than from their work . . . the meanings [they] attribute to that work are different from those attributed to it by the larger society. (Searle-Chatterjee, 1979: 284–5)

Images of Third World urban poverty are commonplace but why do people move in from the countryside to risk this form of marginality? The major reason appears to be to improve one's life chances: casual labourers in Delhi, for example, can work for 250 days a year – twice as many as are possible in a countryside already overcrowded (Stalker, 1986). Yet we should not assume that economic desire necessarily drives out all other issues of social life. As Lal (1989) has recently argued in the case of India, the explanation for problems related to limited economic growth may not be structural rigidities and labour market distortions derived from, amongst other things, the caste system, but may more simply be that even underemployed workers are not always willing to exchange leisure time for high money incomes. Similarly, Perlman's (1976) analysis of informal workers in Rio de Janeiro and Bombay suggests that while almost half came to the city for financial reasons a similar proportion were driven by family or health reasons, though not by the attractions of the 'city lights'. Even for those towards the bottom of the material ladder the sphere of necessity, then, does not automatically invade and replace the sphere of freedom.

If some of the difficulties facing the urban poor of the Third World can be related to Western ideas of economic rationality, where do these original interpretations stem from? Some of the most enduring are from ancient Greece and many have their origins in the practices not of those undertaking the work – the view from below – but of those attempting to legitimize the view of those not engaged in it – the view from above.

Historical Rhetorics of Work: Views from Above and Below

In ancient Greek society the sphere of freedom is conventionally seen as being the opposite of the sphere of necessity, the labour of slaves being automatically associated with the latter. This did not mean that all forms of manual labour were regarded as loathsome but it did mean first, that anyone who *had* to work at an occupation all the time was ignoble, and second that the essence of ennoblement lay in the realm of politics, a realm based on, but untarnished by, the labour of other, lesser mortals (Held, 1987). In fact, while the Hebrew word for work, *avodah*, has the same root as *eved* meaning slave, the Greeks had no general word for 'work' but three particular ones: *ponos*, meaning painful activity; *ergon*, meaning task (military or agricultural); and *techne*, meaning technique. The sphere of necessity was complemented by the nature of dependence: if, as a craft worker, you were dependent on the whims of the customer, you were not considered to be engaged in truly creative activity. In fact, the element of originality imputed to skilled crafts actually declined as Greek society became more consumerist: the craft worker became the medium of the labour process not the originator (Godelier, 1980).

It is worth reflecting here on the sources of these ideas: many stem from individuals like Aristotle and Plato whose distrust of democracy was inseparable from their dislike of the labouring classes. For them, those who were dependent on others could not be free to engage in political debate, hence labour became conceived not as the foundation of the realm of politics, but as its underminer. Furthermore, Aristotle and Plato raged against democracy and labour *because* both individuals were unable to resist the democratic influence at the time. The pro-democratic forces were much more inclined to defend the status of labour – even if they left little in the way of literature to support their case (Wood, 1981). What the slaves would have had to say on the topic is even less certain. In Orwell's words:

> Civilizations founded on slavery have lasted for such periods as four thousand years [yet] the detail that frightens me is that those hundreds of millions of slaves on whose back civilization rested generation after generation have left behind them no record whatever. We do not even know their names. In the whole of Greek and Roman history, how many slaves' names are known to you? I can think of two. . . . One is Spartacus and the other is Epictetus. (1984: 232)

What passes for *the* Greek attitude to work, therefore, depends on which Greek you read and how you read the text.

The instability and metamorphosis in the nature of work represented in Greek literature is also contained in the couplets Labour/Work and Mühe/Werke, and captured in the development of the French words used to describe work. Indeed, it is striking how the words for work resonate with the twin images of forced labour and, to a lesser extent, free expression: 'Gagner' entered the language in the twelfth century from the Frankish word 'Waidajan' meaning to pillage and search for food. Until the sixteenth century two words concerned work: 'Oevrer' was a work of art but derived from the Latin 'Operarus' meaning a man of pain or affliction; while 'Labourer', to plough, came from the Latin 'Labor' or agricultural toil. These two words tended to be replaced by the single word 'Travailler', to work, from the Latin 'Tripaliare' meaning to torture using a Tripalium, a three-pronged instrument (Godelier, ibid.). The connection between work, pain and the absence of freedom is hardly coincidental.

The position of slaves highlights another significant aspect of the human condition, for this most debased form of labour still contains a quintessential aspect of social relations often ignored in contemporary debates about work: the significance of resistance. Giddens (1979: 145–50) has argued that too many conceptualizations of power take a position in which the default category is one of zero-sum: the more A gains the more B loses to the extent that many work relationships can be considered as ones of powerlessness on one side. Yet 'all power relations, or relations of autonomy and dependence, are reciprocal' (1979: 149).

That is to say, despite enormous variations in power resources, individuals can make a difference; they are not coerced into a specific form of behaviour except in a remarkably small number of situations. Even suicide can be taken as an act of defiance rather than submission to external forces. The suicides in Alicante of defeated Republicans in the Spanish Civil War, so chillingly described by Saturnino Carod, a Saragossa trade union leader, are a valuable reminder of the ultimate rebellion: 'As he stood staring out to sea, the man next to him with a cigarette in his mouth slit his own throat and crumpled on the quay. Almost immediately, word came from the other end of the port that someone he knew had shot himself. Suicides spread like an epidemic . . .' (Fraser, 1979: 503).

But such extreme forms of consummate resistance should not divert attention away from the more mundane, yet probably more significant, forms of resistance enacted by those commonly regarded as powerless – slaves. Mary Prince, the first black slave to escape from slavery under British control and publish her memoirs, provides two distinct but important lessons for a study of work. First, her recognition of the situation of slavery as being socially constructed, and therefore subject to change as opposed to natural or inevitable, is one which she gradually comes to appreciate, not one she is born with. Thus for Mary her childhood as a slave 'was the happiest period of my life; for I was too young to understand rightly my condition as a slave, and too thoughtless and full of spirits to look forward to the days of toil and sorrow' (Ferguson, 1987: 47). Second, even as a slave she manages to construct strategies of resistance that serve to restrain her owners' control and maintain her own dignity. Thus she manages to earn some money in the hope of buying her way to freedom: 'When my master and mistress went from home . . . I took in washing and sold coffee and yams and other provisions to the captains of ships' (p. 71). And she also utilizes her knowledge of the different legal systems then operating in the plantations; when her new owner in Bermuda begins to whip her just as her old owner in Turk's Island had, she repudiates his action: 'Sir, this is not Turk's Island' (p. 67). Her owner is typically abusive but appears to desist from the whipping. Ultimately, Mary's quest for freedom is linked by her owner to her indoctrination by the Moravian church, associated with Lutheran beliefs, but Christianity has not always played the role of the liberator from slavery and often interpreted work in a wide variety of ways.

Christianity originally had a jaundiced view of work: it was imposed upon humanity as a direct result of original sin and a means, therefore, to avoid the temptations of the devil and the flesh, as well as a penance.

But spirituality, not work, was the true route to salvation for Christians, at least until Lutherans, and more particularly Calvinists, proposed that work, rather than prayer, could either save your soul or at least be taken as confirmation that your soul was already saved. It was this transformative period that is critical both in the elevation of work itself, from a necessary chore to a moral duty, and, according to Weber (1978), in the augmentation of rational capitalism (see chapter 3). Yet, as Weber made clear, the fragmentation of the Christian church also facilitated the unravelling of Christianity itself. If, as the Reformation ably demonstrated, there were divergent interpretations of God, then foundational belief in any omnipotent God was subject to severe doubt. As a result the certainties of life, as constructed by the priesthood, were replaced by the uncertainties of life: life itself became meaningless without any universally accepted form of religiously prescribed beliefs. If God was dead then humanity had to construct the meaning of life for itself. Furthermore, since an appeal to God could not resolve the clash between different ideals, the very meaning of life was now considered as subjective.

The later scepticism of intellectuals like Nietzsche and Weber to the search for the meaning of life seldom seemed to have concerned the manufacturers of the Victorian work ethic in Britain, many of whom explicitly linked the duty to work to religious incantations. As the contemporary economist J.R. McCulloch put it: 'the eternal law of Providence has decreed that wealth can only be secured by industry – that man must earn his bread by the sweat of his brow' (quoted in McClelland, 1987: 184). Samuel Smiles is probably the best known early distributor of such ideas, based on his regurgitated religious maxim that 'Heaven helps those who help themselves'. The result, according to Mathias, was that 'The virtues of hard work – the gospel of work preached by Samuel Smiles – saving, thrift, sobriety became the new social imperatives dinned into the heads of the new working classes by their social betters by every known means of communication. They were enshrined in Nonconformist and evangelical doctrine' (1969: 208). What is particularly noteworthy here is that despite the popularity of this kind of rhetoric amongst certain sections of the middle class, neither the working class nor the aristocracy were universally enamoured of the sentiments. Even within the middle class the petty bourgeois and ascetic essence of Smiles never garnered total support. As Davidoff and Hall claim, at least until the middle of the nineteenth century, 'the thrusting individual entrepreneur whose only aim was profit maximization is rare in the local records' (1987: 215). At least one other middle-class Victorian crusade for work as a moral or religious duty existed, this time epitomized by Carlyle's phrase: 'blessed is he who has found work' (at least until you could afford to escape from banausic affairs (Musgrave, 1981: 62)). For Carlyle, the contemporary Victorian flight into the 'mechanical age' was a disastrous inversion of human potential, it turned work into drudgery against all rationality, for 'there is a perennial nobleness, and even sacredness, in Work . . . in idleness alone is there perpetual despair' (quoted in Clayre, 1977: 241). Or in Ruskin's equally evocative text:

> It is not that men are ill-fed, but that they have no pleasure in the work by which they make their bread, and therefore look to wealth as the only means of pleasure. . . . It is not, truly speaking, the labour that is divided; but the men: Divided into mere segments of men – broken into small fragments and crumbs of life. (quoted in Clayre, 1977: 260)

For Ruskin, Carlyle, Morris, Hobhouse and even J.S. Mill and Marx, work *should*, but self-evidently did not, provide the material base for the self-development of all. Indeed, even Carlyle rejected the 'mechanical age', not simply in terms of the impact of machinery upon individuals but also, and more particularly, because the period exuded a faith in machinery that was entirely misplaced and distorted the creative and 'dynamic' element of humanity (Carlyle, 1977). Work, for Carlyle then, was 'natural' in so far as it demonstrated the spiritual side of human nature.

The glorification of work, or the 'Gospel of Work' as Carlyle called it, found its physical apotheosis in the Great Exhibition of 1851, designed in part as 'an academy for teaching the nobility of labour' (Henry Mayhew, quoted in Brown and Clayre, 1978: 45). A symbolism not lost on an acerbic Marx who called it an exhibition where 'the world bourgeoisie . . . proudly places on show the deities it has fabricated' (quoted in Brown and Clayre, 1978: 46). Yet Marx was also fascinated by the incredible productivity and profusion of capitalism, and sought his own 'radical' gospel of work that paralleled the bourgeois version: work was the medium through which humans realized their potential and created the cornucopia of communism.

In fact, establishing the effects of such doctrines, as opposed to their mere existence, is a difficult task. If the working class were so susceptible to the Victorian gospel of work, then reconciling the manifestations of discontent and poor productivity etc. poses some severe problems. Even at the height of the Victorian period, during which work arguably acquired a moral colour in harmony with the Smilesian (Briggs, 1955: 124–57) methodological and puritanical ethics of the time, work was infested with the sinews of class. Work, conceptualized as a moral responsibility, was still only really appropriated by the middle class and despised or ignored by the aristocracy and working class alike (Houghton, 1957). For the working class work appeared more akin to a material necessity than a duty, while for the aristocracy because work was not a material necessity it was relevant only in its exclusionary embodiment: if you had to work you were excluded from the aristocracy.

The apparent juxtaposition of the aristocracy and the working class in their disparagement of the Victorian work ethic should not blind us to the antipathy existing between the two: the aristocracy undoubtedly despised the manufacturers and 'grocers' but several socialist-inspired writers had also articulated a working-class hatred of 'the unproductive classes' (Saint Simon) or 'the parasitical layers upon the broad backs of the proletariat' (Lenin). Work might be unremitting toil, and empty of the physical pleasures apparently represented, for example, in the painting of *Work* by Madox Brown, but this did not mean the aristocracy were admired for avoiding it. One of the reasons the aristocracy could avoid work was because in most Western industrial nations a very high division of labour was constructed, in which work become associated almost wholly with economic incentives and almost completely dissociated from the social relations that had entrammelled previous modes of work. Thus despite the critics from the radical left, the idle rich seldom came in for the same moral opprobrium as the idle poor. The idle rich had better things to do than work. As Veblen argued, the leisure class established an entire repertoire of behaviour that demonstrated their complete disdain for anything practical or useful (Veblen, 1899); an ethic that found great favour in the peculiarly British fascination for the cult of the amateur (Wiener, 1981; Roderick and Stevens, 1981; Elbaum and Lazonick, 1986).

While some historians have assumed that the work ethic impaled Victorian employers and employees alike (Best, 1979: 94–5), working-class autobiographical accounts suggest something wholly different. In the words of one such journeyman engineer, the surface layer of bustle and activity should not be confused for the 'inner life' of workshops where the first thing an apprentice learned was the skill of 'keeping nix': 'Keeping nix, consists in keeping a bright look-out for the approach of managers or foremen, so as to be able to give prompt and timely notice to men who may be skulking, or having a sly read or smoke, or who are engaged on 'corporation work' – that is, work of their own' (Wright, 1967: 85). This was certainly a work ethic but one which restricted, not promoted the activity of material production. Even when conditions were poor and incomes low, many members of the working class appeared to have more important things to do than work especially hard for somebody else's profits while accumulating marginal improvements of their own (Hobsbawm, 1964b). This should not be read as the incipient development of working-class socialism because, although such beliefs were present, there were also a large number of workers who appeared to accept the role of the market and the mutuality of labour and capital, albeit in a rather unequal and exploitive conjunction. As Charles Blake, secretary of the Tyne and Wear Chain Makers' Union, said in 1861:

> since the commencement of the present Union they had directed their

> attention to obtain the best wages the state of the market would allow, and to prevent employers obtaining an exorbitant profit out of their labour. Masters always had a right for a fair profit upon their capital invested, and remuneration also for their business capacity, but when trade was prosperous it was the business of workmen to see they enjoyed their share of that prosperity. (quoted in McClelland, 1987: 189)

Nevertheless, there is little evidence that, at least until very recently, work was anything other than something 'to be endured rather than enjoyed' (Burnett, 1974: 15). Writing in 1899 Allen Clarke wrote of Lancashire factory workers: 'Some few seek recreation in Sunday school work and prayer meetings, but these are the minority; the majority want stirring amusements, lively and intoxicating - something to make them forget' (quoted by McClelland, 1987: 205). As the late nineteenth-century Music-hall songs revealed, work was an evil but there was no escape from it nor from the class system, both were simply facts of life. For all that socialists tried to generate some enthusiasm for an alternative social system it would always be the case, as Billy Bennett sang:

> it's the rich what gets the pleasure,
> It's the poor what gets the blame.
> (quoted in Jones, 1983: 229)

So where did such ethics that rejected the economic rationality of capitalism come from? Partly, of course, their origins lie in the conventions of pre-capitalist and pre-industrial society where work was structured by and festooned with the ribbons of social and normative convention - work was for social as much as material purpose. Partly, though considerably later, such ethics were forged through the pens of ideologues.

Radical Approaches to Work

Although Marxist- and socialist-inspired radicals tend to dominate the literature rejecting the Victorian gospel of work, there were other, especially anarchist, denuciations of the wage labour system, such as Kropotkin's inversion of the bourgeois gospel of work: 'let us begin by satisfying our needs of life, joy and freedom. And once all will have experienced this well-being we will set to work to demolish the last vestiges of the bourgeois regime, its morality derived from the account book, its philosophy of "debit" and "credit", its institutions of mine and thine' (Kropotkin, 1983: 107). There was also an outright rejection of the universal 'myth' of work as propagated by Lafargue in his *The Right to be Lazy* (to the considerable chagrin of his father-in-law, Marx) (Kumar, 1984: 11) and put rather more delicately by Russell in his *In Praise of*

Idleness where he claimed that 'A great deal of harm is being done in the modern world by belief in the virtuousness of WORK . . . the road to happiness and prosperity lies in an organized diminution of work' (1983: 25). Yet the virtues of work were not simply a charade dreamed up by the bourgeoisie to increase still further the exploitation of the working class. From Locke's (1960: 329) theory of property, in which property could only be legitimated through its intermixing with human labour, to Hegel's discussion of the Master and Slave relationship in his *Phenomenology of Spirit*, with the concern for the significance of objectifying humanity in artefacts, and beyond to Marx's notion of 'species being', in which it only becomes possible for humans to realize their true potential through labour (*homo faber*), it had become accepted that the world of work was the central arena for social and individual development; as well as for the basic reproduction of material necessities and the satisfaction of immediate desires. In fact, Hegel's argument in his Jena lectures suggests that labour, like language, is significant in so far as it distances experience; it 'breaks the dictates of immediate perception . . . and immediate desire' (quoted in Giddens, 1982b: 150). Hegel, unlike Marx, was not concerned with the results of labour but only in the process of labour: it was not the material changes wrought in nature that interested Hegel but the fact that labour was essential to the production and reproduction of human consciousness. Thus in attempting to dominate nature, humanity realized its true self (Taylor, 1979: 50–1).

For Marx the material results of labour were significant in so far as they embodied uniquely human attributes: self-realization through work was at the heart of Marx's communist vision (Elster, 1985). Marx, while adopting Hegel's labour and interaction couplet, also subordinated the latter to the former, such that even though his empirical work paid due respect to the significance of human interaction, the theoretical primacy of labour and materialism ensured that interaction became perceived as derivative of, rather than irreducible to, labour. As a result, argues Habermas (1974), Marx saw social problems as technical problems and the ultimate aim of society as being productivist, based on an ever expanding technology of production rather than an ever expanding degree of participation and emancipation through 'communicative action' (see Giddens, 1982b).

Even Marx's primary target, economic liberalism in the guise of the utilitarians, could accept the significance of work, not in itself of course, but as a means to an end. Marx went so far as to call Adam Smith the 'Luther of political economy' because of his assertion that capital was not external to, but an expression of, the human subject (Avineri, 1968: 78). By trading off the necessary pain of work for the pleasures purchased with the material rewards, individuals could buy their way into self-realization. For Bentham, the moralistic essence of work, that is the assumption that work should provide a reward in and of itself, was rather bizarre, for the 'desire of labour *for the sake of labour*, of labour considered in the character of an *end*, without any view to anything else, is a sort of desire that seems scarcely to have a place in the human breast' (Bentham, 1977: 200–1). Adam Smith put it even more strongly, for work was actually a necessary evil, and individuals had to have some incentive to give up their leisure; that incentive was the material improvements secured through work. Thus a virtuous circle would emerge: since people could only realize their potential outside work, and since only through work could the material prerequisites for self-realization be obtained, individuals would create the very products that they would eventually consume in pursuit of self-realization. But the virtuous circle is a mirage: the utilitarian trade off between pain and pleasure, between work and leisure, signally fails in so far as those with what are commonly regarded as the most interesting jobs also tend to have the greatest access to leisure, while those with the ostensibly worst jobs are often materially incapacitated by work to the extent that they cannot possibly purchase a compensatory level of leisure. Anyway, are people actually free to develop identities through leisure patterns that are dissociated from their occupational routines? Can those with what are experienced as the most demeaning and poorest paying jobs (and they do tend to go together) really buy their way to Nirvana?

For Marx, capitalism inverted the world of work and turned it against the workers, thereby not just preventing them from realizing themselves but actually developing a system through which work became the source of anti-humanism, the origin of alienation and exploitation. Like Marx, William Morris contrasted the possibilities raised by capitalism with its technical advances: it offered the chance of reducing mundane and tedious work as well as generating enormous advances in material prosperity, but his perception was of a reality where the environment was choked with poisons, where people became slaves to, not controllers of, machines, and where starvation and poverty still prevailed. While Marx's schema for the future of society counterposed an uneasy alliance between self-managed producer units and centrally co-ordinated social planning, the material wherewithal for the communist cornucopia was to be achieved through exploiting nature and eliminating scarcity. Towards the end of his life Marx argued that perhaps individuals could only realize their self-potential outside the realm of socially organized work (Rattansi, 1982). The anti-productivist drift of Marx's apparent volte-face in *Capital*, volume 3, is worth reproducing in full:

> The realm of freedom really begins only where labour determined by necessity and external expediency ends; it lies by its very nature beyond the sphere

> of material production proper. . . . The true realm of freedom, the development of human powers as an end in itself, begins beyond it, though it can only flourish with this realm of necessity as its basis. The reduction of the working day is the basic prerequisite. (Marx, 1981: 959)

Nevertheless, the essence of the anti-capitalist alternative was a society which, freed from the constraints imposed by private ownership and the profit motive, would outproduce all previous societies. In practice this meant that the aim of Lenin, Stalin and most other Marxist leaders was not to generate a society that was more democratic than existed under capitalism, even though this may still have been an ultimate aim; but a prerequisite to this was the provision of a more productive society. Consequently, Marxism had a productivist kernel underpinning its liberatory shell: the people would be freed from want through technological advances; social progress meant material progress. It is not coincidental that one of the greatest advocates of Taylorism (see chapter 5) was Lenin (1968c: 413–46) (cf. Nyland, 1987; Kossler and Muchie, 1990) nor that what are experienced as the intrinsic satisfactions of work for the majority under state socialism appear to be as minimal as they are under capitalism (Haraszti, 1977; cf. Burawoy, 1985; Burawoy and Lukacs, 1989).

Morris, although an avowed socialist, would not have been impressed by Marx's original productivist strategy but would have been very sympathetic to his later reformulation. For Morris social progress had little to do with levels of material wealth and much to do with providing self-fulfilling work experiences, for: 'it is the nature of man [*sic*] . . . to take pleasure in his work [but] there is some labour which is so far from being a blessing that it is a curse; that it would be better for the community and for the worker if the latter were to fold his hands and refuse to work' (1983: 35). Morris not only despised capitalism with its degradation of work, he despised the results of capitalism: the degradation of the workers' minds and bodies; the domestic servants who serviced the 'parasites' of society; the marketing departments; the creators and purchasers of 'articles of folly and luxury', and the creators and consumers of 'inferior' goods. In sum, Morris despised the entire ensemble of social classes: 'a class which does not even pretend to work, a class which pretends to work but which produces nothing, and a class which works, but is compelled by the other two classes to do work which is often unproductive' (1983: 40). But what was Morris's alternative, and what role did work play within it? As a foundational social ethic Morris argued that 'No man [*sic*] would be tormented for the benefit of another – nay, no one would be tormented for the benefit of society' (1983: 42). Note here that notwithstanding the progressive thrust of Morris's views, his assumptions about the 'proper' role of women were hardly compatible with this non-tormented society. Nor, despite his concern for the beauty of nature, was he keen to work with it; rather his vision was replete with the 'conquering' of nature so popular with the rest of his more conventional Victorian colleagues. Nevertheless, Morris's vision of the future was distinct from the productivist world envisaged by capitalist and Marxists alike. Since all would be engaged in 'useful work', as opposed to 'useless toil' or idleness, the working day would be shorter, more varied and more harmonious than at present. The notion of variety is important because here Morris asserts that even skilled work can be alienating if it becomes the sole activity undertaken: just as soldering is commonly regarded as a skilled job and digging a hole is perceived to be less skilled, so soldering all day may be tedious while digging the garden twice a year can be pleasurable.

It is not just the content of the work which is critical, and it is axiomatic that there are limits to the amount of 'interesting' work any individual can hope with (Arneson, 1987) but the social relationships within which they occur are also crucial. Thus work for Morris should also be undertaken in decentralized units, in attractive surroundings where machinery would be used to minimize the duration of unpleasant but necessary labour. Work itself would then become the medium for self-realization. But what about the 'repulsive' work which even volunteers would hesitate to undertake? 'Well, then, let us see if the heavens will fall on us if we leave it undone, for it were better that they should. The produce of such work cannot be worth the price of it' (p. 55).

This overt concern for the well-being of the individual producers, rather than the necessity of 'the system', is continued in the more contemporary writings of Gorz (1982, 1985, 1989). Gorz can best be described as an heretical Marxist: he accepts the humanist critique of capitalism developed by Marx but denies the teleological assumptions surrounding the role of the proletariat and the inevitability of socialism. He is also dismissive of the productivist essence of Marxism in a way very close to Morris. On the other hand, Gorz is more concerned than Morris to retain a 'necessary' degree of advanced technology and 'other-directed' or heteronomous work, since only such a structure can provide the level of material production which we have now become accustomed to, and without which the creation of a sphere of autonomous, or 'self-directed', work would be impractical. For Gorz, therefore, as for the later Marx and aspects of Morris's writings, self-realization, the fulfilment of potential, does not occur within conventional 'work' at all but is rather associated with what we might now call hobbies or leisure activities. We have to tread carefully here: if the argument is that heteronomous work *only* provides the material basis for the real work of identity construction which can only occur outside the sphere of heteronomous work, then the argument is simply over-generalized and hence suspect. Just because many people may find working on an assembly line alienating does not mean that everyone does; to accept this is to deny the significance of the social construction of work – its meaning is socially constructed, it does not inhere within the technology of the assembly line. Nor is it necessarily the case that a variety of craft-based activities can replace the degree of self-respect which employment appears to provide. Perhaps the clearest example of this is the experience of being unemployed, where the sudden provision of time, in and of itself, is often regarded as being as much a burden as an advantage. Nevertheless, the crucial point is that to privilege work over all other forms of human activity is simply to elevate one arbitrary action over another. As Arneson remarks in criticism of any work-dominated philosophy: 'If one has a vision of one monolithic good that society ought to pursue, then institutions ought to be organized so as to render society a crusade directed at this aim. The more one recognizes diversity in human good, the more one's perfectionism will in practice approximate to a preference-respecting policy' (1987: 533).

Contemporary Western Orientations to Work

That work *has* been arbitrarily privileged over other forms of activity and discourse in contemporary Western societies has not led to any consensus about the meaning of work nor about the orientations that workers conventionally have about work. Dubin (1962), and Mannheim (1951) certainly appeared to take the utilitarian line that the absence of expectations of meaningful work was a demonstration of the acceptability of alienating work: if workers did not expect meaningful work then society had a green light to pursue the road to alienation, providing an adequate level of monetary reward could buy the necessary level of external compensation. But rather than assuming that manifestations of alienation can be taken as evidence of the impossibility of developing meaningful work it could well be argued that alienation at work only makes sense if we assume work ought to be non-alienating. Why should we experience work as alienating unless we expect it to be otherwise? (Sayers, 1988: 725–6). We do not have to accept Marx's prognosis of the ills of capitalism, nor to assume that work is *the* central life activity, to accept that work is *a* central life activity that we have learned to expect more from than most of us tend to get. Nor should we assume that because workers may be instrumental about their work that this is because they are inherently instrumental. In other words, although workers may appear to work primarily for extrinsic rewards (money etc.) rather than intrinsic rewards (job satisfaction), this is not foreordained. On the contrary, if the sociological approach to work tells us anything it is that our experiences are socially structured not 'natural' or 'inevitable'.

Argyris (1964) attempted to resolve the enigma of work meaning by arguing that people want whatever it is that the job supplies in the greatest quantity: they rationalize their position *vis-à-vis* their job. But the meaning of work for any worker is not simply job-determined. Indeed, there is considerable evidence to suggest that the links between the domestic and the non-domestic spheres are critical: workers with heavy family responsibilities tend to be more concerned with extrinsic rewards (money and security) than those without. Workers with what have come to be regarded as the most intrinsically rewarding jobs value them for just this reason (Loscocco, 1989).

The whole issue of work orientations was put on a much firmer conceptual base by Lockwood's approach (1966) in which four types of worker are identified, each with a different perspective of society. Briefly, the middle-class employees perceived society in terms of a consensually graduated status hierarchy; the deferential workers had a very similar overall picture though they placed themselves lower in the hierarchy; the traditional proletarian-configured society through a conflicts driven class model, while the affluent or privatised workers envisaged society in terms of a desocialized structure divided on the basis of money. Such variations in imagery could be related, according to Lockwood, to the nature of the work situation and the community structure in which the different types of worker were located.

Lockwood, in conjunction with Goldthorpe et al. (1968), set out to use the notion of affluent workers to test the embourgeoisement thesis which suggested that as the working class acquired middle-class levels of income they also adopted middle-class social and political habits. Using prototypical affluent workers in Luton, they selected their sample of workers in terms of technology and as producers, as well as consumers, of affluence. As they noted: 'we wished to examine the effect on workers' attitudes and behaviour of different types of production system and our choice of firms was in fact made so that three major types-small batch, large batch and mass production, and process production – were represented' (1968: 4). The concept of 'orientation to work' developed when the authors were unable to find significant differences in overall satisfaction according to the respondents' jobs. As they state:

> one very definite result emerges: that job satisfaction in terms of workers' experience of their immediate work tasks and roles cannot be associated in any direct way with job satisfaction in terms of workers' attachment to their present employment . . . the question of *satisfaction from* work cannot in the end be usefully considered except in relation to the more basic question of what we would term *orientation towards* work. Until one knows something of the way in which workers order their wants and expectations relative to their employment – until one knows what *meaning* work has for them – one is not in a position to understand what overall assessment

> of their job satisfaction may most appropriately be made in their case, (1968: 31–36)

Goldthorpe et al. go on to distinguish three types of orientation which broadly correspond to Lockwood's triple worker types. For the privatized worker with an instrumental orientation to employment the primary meaning of work is as a means to an end, work is 'labour' with ends external to the work situation; these workers are therefore calculatively involved in the firm, they do not see work as a source of self-realization nor as a site for significant social relations but as a necessary arena for the improvement of non-work opportunities (1968: 38–9). The bureaucratic worker, typical perhaps of the middle-class employee, considers employment as a service to an organization, imbuing the relationship with moral elements which blur the distinction between work and non-work. The third type of orientation is solidaristic: work is seen as a group activity and, in the deferential type of situation, means moral involvement in the firm, while for the traditional proletarians – such as the miner – moral involvement is restricted to the mining community and involves a clear distinction between 'them' and 'us'; nevertheless there is little separation between work and non-work.

Even if we can identify a worker's orientation, what does this tell us about her or his behaviour? According to Goldthorpe et al., instrumentalism tended to be associated with a pecuniary interest not just to the firm but to work colleagues too. Yet, as they accept (1968: 76–7), this does not mean that such workers are inevitably moderate in their demands and behaviour. It could well be argued that such instrumentalism poses just as high a risk to management as does the more socially or politically inspired unionism, in so far as the primary relationship between employer and employee is money; no appeals to the interests of the firm or the nation are likely to dissuade such instrumental workers from taking whatever action they feel necessary to achieve their 'just' rewards. Thus very different orientations to work may generate apparently identical modes of behaviour.

Goldthorpe et al. assert that such instrumentalism reflects the choices made by such employees who have left what they regard as intrinsically interesting but poorly paid jobs for apparently intrinsically uninteresting but highly paid jobs. This does not mean that all workers, or even all workers in Goldthorpe et al.'s Luton sample, were uninterested in intrinsically satisfying work. It may mean that the choice is so limited that we have no way of assessing any third option. That is to say, because workers under certain contingent conditions work in what they regard as well paid but boring jobs does not mean that they would not choose interesting jobs provided the economic rewards were satisfactory. Nor does it mean that jobs *are* intrinsically uninteresting – even if they are experienced as such.

The concept of orientation to work has been used widely since Goldthorpe et al.'s work: Cotgrove and Box (1970), for example, have adopted it with regards to the work of scientists, and Ingham (1970) in his comparison of small and large firms. However, the very notion of orientation to work has been subject to considerable debate. In particular, to what extent can one identify a clear and relatively stable set of worker priorities and expectations? Given the transient state of many workers, especially in the Luton sample, another aspect is critical: attitudes to work are not stable, they change as individuals change their status, their family situation, their age and their interpretation of the discourses imbricated around such categories. Indeed, a whole body of literature suggests that ideological perspectives are inconsistent with regard to the distinctions between attitudes to general principles and particular events they become involved in, as well as being internally incongruous (Mann, 1970; Nichols and Armstrong, 1976; Held, 1984). An example is beautifully captured in the words of one Jock Keenan: 'Frankly, I hate work. Of course I could also say with equal truth that I love work; that it is a supremely interesting activity; that it is often fascinating; that I wish I didn't have to do it; that I wish I had a job at which I could earn a decent wage. That makes six subjective statements about work and all of them are true for me' (quoted in Fraser (ed.), 1968: 273).

This particular issue raises the related one concerning the origin of such orientations. Implicitly, Goldthorpe et al. develop their approach through an externally generated source of orientations: orientations appear to be autonomous of the working environment; they influence, but are not influenced by, what happens at work. Can it really be the case that orientations are affected by past work experiences but not present ones? Of course, it may be that over time the maturation of orientations leads to some degree of self-selectivity, such that workers end up in employment environments conducive to their orientations, but again this is not likely for all workers nor does it eliminate the significance of work experiences. As Brown (1973, 1974) has demonstrated, the initial movement of people into work can have very powerful influences upon the later orientations to work. Alternatively, it may be that orientations of instrumental workers *are* autonomous of the work situation *because* they are unconcerned by the working environment, while the orientations of non-instrumental workers are not autonomous.

It is noticeable that most of the empirical studies are based on male workers and tend to assume that women are oriented towards the home rather than work. Such issues are discussed later in this chapter and more fully in chapter 6 but Dex's (1988) research implies two things worth bearing in mind when analysing orientations to work of men and women. First, the major differences in orientation can be explained through occupational differences rather than gender differences. Second, where gender differences appear more systematically, it is domestic responsibilities, and especially child care, which are critical.

Where it does seem to be the case that work experiences have a direct impact upon orientations is in the long-term effects. Kornhauser (1965) has noted how older workers become fatalistic over time, learning to accept the delimited experiences as inevitable and adjusting their orientations in this direction – further evidence of the socially malleable and contingent nature of our interpretations of work. Argyris (1964) has examined the development of psychological methods to cope with the perceived frustration of work but it is not self-evident that workers always learn to accept their situation. Or, to put it more graphically, in the words of a bus driver: 'I was at the ripe age of twenty five when I started with the London General Omnibus Company – I am now sixty six years of age . . . If I were twenty five years of age today, you could stick this job on the buses where a monkey is reputed to stick his nuts!' (Jones, quoted in Fraser (ed.), 1968: 217). Whatever the apparent orientations to work offered by workers, then, it is by no means clear that such attitudes operate independently of work: if work *is* experienced as boring and alienating then it would be irrational to consider that it could be self-fulfilling. Such responses are not untypical and it appears common for American workers, at least, to blame themselves for their relatively low position in the social hierarchy which ultimately leads them to cultivate and sustain very low levels of expectation. If you do not expect much from work you will not be disappointed and may, in fact, remain 'happy' with your lot (Sennett and Cobb, 1977).

But if, as Anthony argues (1977), work is, and always has been, the most boring amd mundane activity, why do so many other people appear to regard it with such high esteem? Does work exude a magic spell to enchant people? It certainly is the case that the question 'are you happy at work?' embodies so many variant interpretations as to be almost worthless. Are people who answer 'yes' (and from Labriola's survey in 1931 to Jahoda's in 1979 the majority answer has been yes) happy with the skill content of their jobs or the responsibility they can exercise or the material reward or the social relationships, or the routines and the pride engendered through being employed; in particular, are people happy *in* jobs or *with* jobs? What has to be remembered, particularly by those looking at, rather than engaging in, apparently mundane manual labour is that no job is completely bereft of skill and many embody the potential for a measure of pride that exists independently of the requirements of employers. As I. Edwards (1983) so eloquently testifies, even shovelling is an art:

> A navvy, using his shield-shaped escavating shovel in a trench with a bad bottom, does wonders, but in a long time . . . and the corporation

> employee, lifting little bits in the street, would have died of fright had he seen our shovels. . . . Patsy slung the blade of the shovel towards the heap until it touched the edge, then followed up with both knees driving hard against the back of his hands to supply the power. A quick downward jerk of the wrist loaded the shovel, it was withdrawn slightly, swung backwards as the body straightened, then delivered over the shoulder into the skip with a graceful sway and twist of the trunk . . . the shovel and its motion seemed but an extension of those long arms [it] made shovelling an art to be studied and not merely a distasteful task for the unskilled. (1983: 85–6)

Correspondingly, the richness of life evoked by Roy's (1954, 1973), and later Burawoy's (1979) and Cavendish's (1982), ethnographic descriptions of factory life is a useful reminder of the creativity of people in what they regard as non-creative jobs, even if much of the creativity is expended in activity unrelated to productive activity. But it is worth reiterating here that the satisfactions gained by these people are generated *at* work without being directly related to any particular aspect *of* work, and without being produced independently of the non-work environment. As a Ford worker explained to Beynon, there is more to work than work:

> At the end of the shift we'd run for the clock. I don't know why we did . . . it just meant we had to wait on the bus. Well one day I run to the clock, grab for my coat and it's tied up in knots. It was Clarkey. He was a strong bastard and he'd really tied it up tight. I couldn't move it. So the next day I took some boxes of those very small tacks into work. I made a tiny hole in the pocket of Clarkey's coat, tipped the tacks in and then gave the coat a shake. When he came to pick it up it was like a ton weight. (Beynon, 1975: 236)

Beyond the significance of orientations brought to work it is important to confirm the class, race and gender-based influences upon working experience. That is to say that the meaning of work may be structured by these kinds of categories more than it is by individual attitudes generated apparently autonomously. Much of these arguments form the basis for chapters 5, 6 and 7 but suffice it to say here that the vast majority of research carried out with regard to class divisions reproduces a very similar class-based level of work experience. In the USA, France, Britain, Yugoslavia and the Soviet Uinon it is the case that 'the lower we direct our attention within the occupational status scale, the more likely we are to find people deriving little conscious meaning from their work apart from the pay and security it offers' (Fox, 1976: 37). This does not mean that all manual employees all over the world have identical experiences. After all, the decisive word in Fox's text is 'meaning'. Such meanings are not determined by the task nor the job nor the technology nor even the social structures. But then neither does this imply that meanings can be imputed to invariant tasks on an individual basis. It is not that individuals all read experiences in a different way but that some readings, especially but not exclusively those provided by superordinates, are endowed with a legitimacy and import that others are not.

What counts as work, therefore, and what we take as skilled or difficult or dirty work, is inherently unstable and ambiguous. It depends upon the social relations within which it is undertaken but it may also be a contested concept within those same relations. Work is more than employment but less than all forms of social activity; indeed, employment is a form of work but not all work is employment. Where the self-description of agents' activity implies that their activity is conceived by them as work, we should take note, but the point really is not whether this or that activity is actually work, but what such activities involve, whose interpretation of the activity carries the most weight, and why this should be the case.

In the remainder of this chapter I want to explore the nature of work further by focusing directly upon two areas which, under the conventional definition of work *qua* paid labour, disappear from view: work in the informal economy, and especially domestic work; and non-work, or unemployment. The latter form of non-work is significant in so far as it highlights in stark form what work means to individuals and communities. Both these activities are often discounted in studies of work but they both act as powerful manifestations of the dominance of certain images of work. Moreover, they both signify an aspect of work which by convention is unconnected to work: the domestic sphere and the sphere of paid labour are intimately connected in a seamless web of relations. Indeed, unpaid domestic labour is an imperative element of paid labour because without the former the latter could not continue in its present form.

Domestic Labour

Although domestic labour has conventionally been associated with unpaid homework, or more appropriately 'housework', and has, therefore, been eliminated from most concerns about work until recently, it is worth noting that domestic labour also involves unpaid activities outside housework strictly defined, for example, shopping, gardening, fixing the plumbing, painting the walls, car maintenance, ferrying children to school, bearing and bringing up infants, organizing family recreation and entertainment etc. After all, who thinks having to watch endless Blue Peters, or worse, having to make all those wretched 'drawer sets' and 'gift boxes' out of battered shoe boxes without the proper glue and expensive shiny paper, does not count as hard work? Since almost every activity undertaken without payment in the home is also undertaken for money in the formal economy the distinction between work and non-work is seriously flawed.

The division is further eradicated by what Pahl (1984) calls 'household work strategies' through which the available labour within a household, rather than that available just to an individual, is the basis upon which work inside and outside the home, within and without the formal economy, is organized; though Pahl's enthusiasm for the household approach seems to submerge all aspects of individualist strategies (cf. Moorhouse, 1987).

Some assessments of the links between the formal and the informal sector suggest that as people's time in one contracts it expands in the other. Thus, in general, such models assert that as women spend more time in formal employment they spend less time in the domestic sphere, and their male partners have a related and inverted correlation (Gershuny and Thomas, 1980; Rose, 1983). Others imply that the contraction of formal employment involves the reduction of the material resources to undertake informal work so that there is a joint contraction or expansion in both sectors depending on whether the individual is employed or not (Pahl, 1984).

Concomitantly, women's work outside the home has become circumscribed by their activities within it, resulting in the construction of occupational sex-typing (Cohn, 1985; Dex, 1985; cf. Grint, 1988). Thus employment opportunities for women have historically been restricted in the main to analogous domestic activities: cleaning, cooking, caring, teaching. Despite this relationship the primary positions in such occupations tend to be occupied by men. For example, chefs, consultants and head teachers are all involved in occupations associated with domestic activities but are nevertheless normally male reserves. Relatedly, many of the jobs undertaken by women have domestic reflections which lead employers to perceive them as less skilled than jobs undertaken by men which have no equivalent domestic associations (Taylor, 1988). Men are more involved in the care of the elderly than has hitherto been recognized, and Arber and Gilbert (1989) estimate that about 33 per cent of co-resident carers are men, but 75 per cent of these look after their spouses; they are not, therefore, heavily represented amongst those looking after parents or other elderly relations.

In short, we cannot erect an impervious division between domestic labour and formal employment because they are so intimately connected and interactive. We do not have a division between work and home that is free from ideological nuances because the very model of work we operate with is a patriarchal model. It is not just that men tend to monopolize the privileged jobs and occupations; after all, there are token women in many positions of authority – so it cannot be the case that women are unable to succeed within the labour market. But the critical point is that this can only occur for individual and isolated cases if the patriarchal model of work is maintained. If employment is automatically and inflexibly constructed around a five-day week from 9 to 5 then all those involved in such employment cannot look after sick children or relatives, nor can they take them to or pick them up from schools. Hence the problem of work is not simply a definitional one, nor even a normative one, it is organizational in two senses: time and opportunity. First, unless we all decide to forgo having children we either have to reorganize employment hours to fit flexibly around children and domestic circumstances, and/or inaugurate mutiple company and community crèches etc., or maintain the patriarchal status quo. Of course, altering working hours or organizing the provision of crèches would probably not result in a sudden burst of enthusiasm for domestic work on the part of men, but it might be a first step towards the equal distribution of domestic work. Second, if women continue to remain primarily located within the worst-paying and least career-structured jobs the end result is for most women to be without an adequate wage or occupational pension; as a result the employment experiences of women have a direct bearing on their retirement experiences, dependent as they often are on meagre state pensions (Glendinning and Millar, 1988). Likewise, the significance of social networks for recruitment and promotion purposes, and the general predominance of men in these, tends to delimit the opportunities for women's employment and career development. But however important social networks are for promotional and occupational patterns, one has to beware of assuming that they are the primary route *into* employment: in 1988, for example, only 12 per cent of those seeking work actually used social networks as their primary method, 37 per cent used a Jobcentre while 41 per cent used the newspapers or other adverts (*Social Trends*, 1990: 81).

Naturally, not all women experience the same kind of restrictions: Victorian working-class women may have sought the kind of idyllic life allegedly consumed by middle-class women, with a houseful of servants and nothing but the gardening, bridge and dinner parties to organize, but few middle-class women probably languished in such a state of torpor (Davidoff and Hall, 1987: 388–96; Maynard, 1985) while many working-class women would have spent some time as a domestic servant themselves. It was not just that domestic work was regarded as unfit for men because it was low status; rather, women were regarded as inherently better suited to the creation of a domestic environment that was private, pure and moral, in sharp contrast to the public and immoral world of paid labour. Domestic work was, allegedly, a mirror image of the physically rough, dangerous and dirty world of the miner. Inevitably, class differences emerged through such gendered divisions of labour. In

1917 Elizabeth Stern, an American memoirist, recounted such class differences when visiting a school friend in a wealthier part of town:

> I could not believe that the woman who opened the door to my knock was my friend's mother. A women in *white*! Why, mothers dressed in brown and black, I always knew. And this mother sang to us. She romped through the two steps with us . . . I had always thought that mothers never 'enjoyed', just worked. This strange mother opened a new window for me in the possibilities of women's lives. (quoted in Cowan, 1983: 170–1)

Seventy years later a variety of empirical studies still suggest that women consistently undertake more work than men, in terms of hours, whether they are employed outside the home as well or not. Thus, where women take on employment, although their domestic work contracts, their overall work level increases. With average weekly hours for male employees hovering around 44 (including overtime) and for full-time women around 37 hours (including one hour overtime) (*Social Trends*, 1988, 1990), the average hours of a full-time houseworker are between 57 (Walker and Woods, 1976; Berk and Berk, 1979) and 100 (Leghorn and Parker, 1981). The everage hours of a full-time employed women are over 70, with 33 hours spent on housework. By implication, those households with women in employment are making do with marginally more than half the time full-time houseworkers spend in maintaining the house: either the former live in veritable pigsties or we have cultural expectations of cleanliness that are remarkably consistent with Parkinson's, or perhaps more appropriately Parkindaughter's, law – domestic work expands to fill the time available. As Ehrenreich and English (1979) acknowledge, there is precious little evidence that such a high level of domestic cleanliness is necessary for health purposes, though there is some which suggests that such activities are damaging to women's health. The phrase 'a woman's work is never done' says more about women's domestic responsibilities than most books on the subject.

Some feminists have argued that the solution to the problem of inequitous work loads, and the exploitation it embodies, is to secure wages for housework, and several estimates suggest that the total costs would be staggering: almost half the West German and American GNP or a quarter of the Canadian GNP (Leghorn and Parker, 1981; Goldschmidt-Clermont, 1987; *New Internationalist*, 1988). However, despite the propaganda value of such claims it is, as Gorz (1985) and Fairbairns (1988) argue, more an admission of defeat than a strategy for success since it confirms women's position within the household and acknowledges the failure to coerce or persuade men to undertake their share of domestic work.

There are counter-arguments which suggest that the sexual division of labour manifest in women's domestic responsibilities is not inequitous at all but rather a mechanism to maximize the efficiency of the household unit. Just as specialization brings efficiency in conventional capitalist production so too, the argument goes, the specialization of partners in different spheres (who does what is not critical) is the most efficient way of allocating the labour available within a household (Becker, 1985). Yet, since housework is unending, and requires more in terms of organization than specialized knowledge, it would actually seem more efficient to minimize it by both partners being employed. Moreover, if women remain in employment (even part-time) then the detrimental consequences of a career break are minimized (Joshi, 1986). Even if specialization is marginally more efficient in economic terms, the cost to women's health, and via them to their children, throws doubt on the unambiguous advantages claimed for domestic specialization. In sum, the sexual division of labour in the domestic sphere appears to be both inequitous and inefficient for the household (Owen, 1987).

Many women also tend to regard housework as intensely monotonous, yet shot through with moral attributes of cleanliness that they find difficult to ignore (Gale, 1985). For Suzanne Gail, 'Housewife':

> As I work, evangelical hymn-jingles from my carefully obliterated past well up in my mind. But I cannot achieve that degree of irony. It would be hubris, and the walls might fall in if I started chanting:
> I'm H-A-P-P-Y. (Fraser, 1968: 144)

Only cooking, shopping and childcare appear to have major benefits, though children can be both a source of disruption in themselves (as well as delight) and, at pre-school age particularly, have been associated with some mothers' mental ill-health and dependence on drugs of one sort or another (Gavron, 1968).

Despite the common assumption that some women's negative attitudes towards domestic work are very recent, research from the 1950s on has suggested that such perspectives were relatively common even then. There has, though, been a slight shift away from the assumption that married women with children should not work amongst the younger generation of women (see Dex, 1988: 25–8). Nevertheless, Britain, in contrast to many major industrialized nations, has a particularly high proportion of women who prefer to stay at home (37 per cent) or perceive their work as 'just a job' rather than a career (30 per cent) (Bartos, 1989).

Even the domestic activities of fathers, as opposed to husbands or partners, appear to be restricted in degree and kind. The involvement of women in raising children is *in addition* to their houseworking responsibilities, whereas for fathers, child raising activities are a *substitute* for housework (Maynard, 1985). Popular opinion would have us believe that households are far more egalitarian than they ever used to be, and there are arguments which assert that a form of equality does exist between men and women on a 'different but equal' basis, with the domestic jobs being gender-related (Edgell, 1980). But is there any empirical evidence for the claim, and is the division more like a gendered apartheid than an equitable division? In Oakley's (1974) research a mere 15 per cent of husbands participated in, or rather 'helped with', housework, with 25 per cent involved in childcare activities, though such help tended to be irregular and was perceived by men as a 'favour' to their wives rather than a responsibility of their own (Deem, 1985). One exception to this general norm is that men with children undertake more domestic work than men without children, primarily, it would seem, in order to facilitate their wives, or partners' employment requirements (Dex, 1988). But the 'freeing' of time through male unemployment does not lead to any equivalent increase in domestic labour by men (Hartley, 1987). Nor has there been any rapid mushrooming of the New Man throughout the West. Over the last twenty years American husbands have extended their housework by an extra nine minutes a day on average, though even this appears to be considerably more than most Italian husbands (Taylor, 1988). The most recent British study (*Social Trends*, 1989) suggests that men undertake more domestic work than women in only one area – repairing household equipment. Overall women undertake 72 per cent of domestic tasks, while they are shared equally in just 22 per cent of the cases. Morris's (1990) Anglo-American study of domestic roles provides further evidence that patriarchy is alive, well and inertial. Men generally also tend to perceive the relationship between work and family to be unidirectional: where a conflict exists between family and work the normal response is to subordinate home to work; for women the opposite appears to hold in most cases (Deem, 1985: 43). Such attitudes coexist easily with those revealed by Dex (1988: 38–9) in which almost half of wives not working argued that their husbands' disapproval of working wives was a factor in them not seeking employment.

Gender-based inequalities are not inevitable, and Soviet-dominated societies have long purveyed an ideology of egalitarianism. However, the reality has often been one that has 'allowed' women to undertake what were previously regarded as 'men's jobs' without ensuring that men undertook a comcomitant degree of domestic work. One of the consequences of this has been a rejection of Western feminist perspectives amongst some women within the recently democratized eastern European societies, and the generation of a 'return to the home movement':

> The communists said that in the first place a woman is a worker, then she should be active in political life, then in the third place have a family . . .

> add to this the time taken for shopping, then throw in the duties of childcare and housework and cooking, and it becomes understandable that women should now be wanting to slough off some of these burdens. (Redding and Leydon, 1990).

It should be remembered, though, that gender tends to interact with, rather than override, the significance of class. O'Brien's (1982) research suggests that working-class fathers perceive few contradictions between work and family, primarily because they see their role almost entirely in terms of 'the breadwinner' for whom practical activity, at least involving so called 'women's' jobs, stops once 'work' ceases. For middle-class fathers domestic responsibilities are considered as important but the demands of their professional jobs supposedly prevent them realizing much of their good intent.

Hochschild (1989) suggests that even Western egalitarian households, where domestic and occupational responsibilities are initially divided equally, tend to subordinate the domestic to the occupational if both partners are professionals. For Moore Campbell (1988), such equality often prevails at first, but once babies arrive the typical response is for the conventional gendered division of labour to reappear or for the relationship to break up. There is an irony for many men, in that it is only because they are not responsible for domestic life that they can devote themselves full time to their careers; on the backs of their partners and behind the backs of their children. Thus, it would appear that the general occupational progression of women is dependent upon the displacement of men and the latters' engagement with domestic responsibilities (Dale, 1987).

We might wish to question just how much gendered choice is involved in the issue of domestic responsibilities; will professionals who stay home to look after sick children automatically lose out in the promotion race? Certainly many professionals who claim to support equal distribution of domestic activities end up by admitting that their employers or colleagues will not countenance such demonstrations of split loyalty (Hochschild, 1989). This very notion of split loyalty is a manifestation of the significance of work: paradoxically, for nations that pride themselves on the sanctity of the family, the idea that family commitments should take precedence over commitment to the work organization clings tenaciously to the banner of treason rather than the flag of reason. Even if corporations appear to subordinate family responsibilities to themselves, have many professionals attempted to reverse that assumption? Who chooses to engage in the promotion race anyway – are the spouses or partners of professional men consulted on the likely results, and do these spouses and partners have such a degree of choice in their own activities? (J. Woolgar, 1989). It may look as though professional men have no choice, but we have to be wary of the claim to external coercion; the fallacious self-denial of freedom and responsibility, or 'bad faith' as Sartre called it, has a long and not very pleasant history.

The case of cross-class families is interesting in so far as it tends to disrupt conventional assumptions and norms of behaviour. Sweden may not be representative of most European societies, let alone anywhere else, but it would appear here that working-class wives of working-class men are the most 'entrapped' in traditional gendered domestic roles, while middle-class wives of working-class men are the least likely to be similarly snared (Leiulfsrud and Woodward, 1987) (see also Russell, 1983). This analysis also throws a rather abrasive spanner in the traditional class analysis pursued by Goldthorpe (1983, 1984b), since it questions the validity of ignoring the occupational position of women in the construction of stratification systems (Stanworth, 1984) (see chapter 6). If we continue to assume that families are the most appropriate criteria for analysing stratification systems we ignore the stratification that occurs *within* the family. This is not only with regard to the inequitous division of domestic labour but also the inequalities of other resources, especially money. There is evidence that on the basis of total income, families which would otherwise be above the poverty line actually have those resources so maldistributed that women, and sometimes children, are below the line while men remain above it (Glendinning and Millar, 1988). Relatedly, although it is assumed that the break-up of a marriage tends to lead to the collective decline in material standards for all involved this need not necessarily occur. As Brannen and Wilson (1987) argue, although the total income entering a household may fall in proportion to the absence of the male adult, the pre-existing inequitous divisions within the family may be removed to the extent that family income levels may actually rise with the removal of a husband or male partner.

It is another commonplace to assume that domestic technology has liberated women from housework. Certainly the pattern of work has changed from one where heavy and monotonous cleaning and washing was the major element to one where childcare, shopping, food preparation, cleaning and ironing are the prime elements. But as Schwartz Cowan's (1983) subtitle (*The Ironies of Household Technology*) reveals, the diffusion of household technology has done little or nothing to liberate houseworkers from the time spent in housework, even if it has limited the amount of heavy work. For example, the washing machine has not so much taken washing out of the realm of work but has ensured that we have clothes which are constantly clean. Similarly, the vacuum cleaner has not reduced the amount of time involved in cleaning the floors but led to even more time spent in ensuring ever cleaner floors; sophisticated cooking technologies and food preparation technologies lead not to the reduction in time spent preparing food but to more and more elaborate meals. In the event the time spent undertaking housework appears to rise with the development of domestic technologies rather than decrease through them (Vanek, 1974).

In conclusion, I would just reaffirm the conviction that work is not simply restricted to paid labour but note also that the subordinate and gendered status of domestic labour and its popular classification as non-work is a valuable reminder of the significance of patriarchal ideology in the evaluation of work. As a central institution of society, work, and especially domestic work, embodies forms of power that spread far beyond the limits of the factory gate. A similar argument can be made for the inverse of domestic labour as unpaid work: paid inactivity as unemployment.

Unemployment

Domestic activities fall within the definition of work appropriated here, but unemployment is axiomatically more difficult to situate. In so far as being 'out of work' but 'available for work' implies the absence of any activity that might interfere with the search for work, it cannot be defined as work. But unemployment is still critical in several senses: it marks out the conventional Western boundary between work and non-work; it poses questions about the centrality of paid labour in contemporary society; it often has catastrophic consequences for the individual and household concerned; and its definition – as those seeking work and signed on for unemployment benefit – mirrors the state-supported ideology of work as a full-time non-domestic, and hence masculine, phenomenon. Unemployment is also important in the sense discussed throughout this chapter – that work *qua* activity may well continue even if employment does not.

Just as the definition and organization of employment is socially constructed, transient (see Deaton, 1983; and Marsh, 1988a for recent changes) and often critical for the subordinate position of women at work and in the home, so too unemployment is dispersed unevenly between the able bodied and the disabled, ethnic minorities and the white population, skilled and unskilled, and north and south of Britain. For example, the highest rates of unemployment tend to be found amongst those with no qualifications, from the working class, amongst those who are chronically sick or disabled, and whose ethnic background is Pakistani or Bangladeshi. Women, especially young married women, are more likely to be short-term unemployed than men, but men, notably older men, comprise the majority of the long-term unemployed (*Social Trends,* 1990). Regional variations are also noteworthy: Northern Ireland, the Western Isles, Strathclyde, Gwynedd, Mid Glamorgan, South Yorkshire, and Cornwall are all well above the rest of the UK (*Employment Gazette*, March 1990).

Unemployment may also have considerable consequences for those who may not originally be unemployed. For example, there is a strong tendency for unemployment to run in families (White, 1983) to the extent that having the head of the household unemployed (irrespective of gender) effectively doubles the chances of the rest of the adult family being unemployed (Payne, 1987). The form of household is also significant for men in a rather different way to women: although women tend to leave employment during early child-rearing years, and their employment prospects are constrained by their domestic responsibilities, it is usually assumed that men operate independently of domestic responsibilities – though clearly dependent upon their partners' services. Yet unemployment also relates to marital status, with married men being significantly less likely to be unemployed than their single counterparts. This, it has been argued, probably reflects a number of facets of the domestic relationship: married men may have more incentive to seek or retain employment; they may be more conventionally oriented towards economic activity; and employers may prefer them since they believe them to be more constrained by the domestic commitments. In short, marriage appears to stabilize employment for men, though for young women the opposite appears to happen.

Unemployment also operates in reverse when marriages break down, such that unemployment amongst widowed, divorced and separated men is almost double that of married men (Payne, 1989). Indeed, since the first systematic studies of the unemployed in the 1930s the results have shown that for most individuals unemployment is consistently destructive, manifest in ill health, despair and chronic lethargy – symptoms remarkably similar to those related to the loss of a friend or relation (Archer and Rhodes, 1987). Two of Sinfield's unemployed respondents bring this out quite acutely:

> It was very depressing and got worse the longer I was unemployed. It wasn't so much the money or the way I felt. It was degrading . . . when you are unemployed you are bored, frustrated, and worried, worried sick.
>
> My wife is right when she said it affects me as a *man*: it isn't the money so much as the feeling men have. (Sinfield, 1985: 194)

This does not mean that all households facing unemployment by one or more of the members react in a similar way. Far from it, because the reaction depends to a considerable extent on the numbers of unemployed involved, the stage in the life cycle of a family, the extent of their social networks within the local community (Clark, 1987), and the interpretation of the phenomena by those involved. It also depends on the interaction between a whole series of features conventionally derived from employment which are no longer available to the same extent for the unemployed, such as: the opportunities to use skill, for social contact, to control one's own environment, to achieve external goals, to accumulate money for all kinds of purposes, to acquire personal security and to maintain one's own status (Warr, 1987).

The consequences of unemployment are also different depending on the class of the unemployed person. For example, Fineman (1983) suggests that the middle class suffer greater status collapse than the working class, given the former's greater personal involvement in work careers, and subsequent work in a different field or a different region may act disadvantageously towards them and their families. In the words of one 43-year-old redundant manager: 'I've been rejected for being overqualified, underqualified, too old, not enough business experience, and too much experience! I've tried everything. . . . My wife can't get used to me being at home under her feet' (Fineman, 1987: 87). The working class, and especially the young working class, are more affected by the financial consequences (Warr, 1983). For many unemployed members of the working class in zones of high unemployment the experience of unemployment is tempered by the knowledge that perhaps as many as 50 per cent of their immediate neighbours are also unemployed. In these circumstances unemployment becomes a social condition as much as an individual problem. Nevertheless, the serious and deleterious consequences of unemployment should not be minimized: instances of suicide and particularly parasuicide have some correlations with patterns of unemployment (Ashton, 1986), and it would seem that much of the strain of maintaining a family intact during periods of unemployment is borne disproportionately by the mother (Hutson and Jenkins, 1989).

Despite the mass experience of the unemployed, though, even people who self-evidently have not priced themselves out of work, and who end up as redundant through massive plant closures unrelated to their own work efforts, appear to experience unemployment as an individual not as a member of a social group. Such individualizing of what are, at heart, social problems runs against what Wright Mills (1970: 14–15) called 'the sociological imagination'. That is, the way in which 'the public issue of social structure' become perceived as 'the personal troubles of milieu'. In effect, a social problem is experienced as a personal problem and the responsibility for the issue is drawn off from the social structure and relocated within the apparent personal 'failings' of an individual, in this case a 22-year-old: 'Sometimes I feel like curling up in a corner. . . . The worst thing is when you write off and you here nothing from them. When I was first unemployed, I had a little bit of hope, but not a lot now. If you think about it too much you crack up' (Buckland and MacGregor, 1987: 187). Irrespective of whether the unemployed perceive themselves to be responsible for their own plight, it would appear that the majority of employers do. Where the cause of unemployment is redundancy, rather than anything to do with the individual's conduct, there is still a widespread belief amongst employers that particular groups of individuals have been selected for redundancy because of their work records. Such employer hostility increases with the length of time an individual has been unemployed, and although many argue that the unemployed should lower their demands and seek work of any kind, the irony is that few employers are prepared to take on unemployed workers who do precisely this, assuming that anyone that desperate must have a personal problem or have no real interest in the particular job on offer (Crowley-Bainton, 1987). The other side of this picture is that management has indeed used redundancy not just to slim down the work force but to remould it into a more malleable resource (Turnbull, 1988).

The impact of this non-sociological imagination is also critical to the response of people suffering the pressures of social problems. For example, if unemployment was experienced as the direct result of an inefficient or inhumane economic system then the unemployed and the employed might attempt to restructure the system. However, if unemployment is perceived as the fault of individuals (and there is considerable evidence to show that it usually is perceived in this way (Sinfield, 1981)), then little in the way of collective action against it is likely. After all, participation in any form of political activity is normally correlated with high levels of self-esteem and sufficient material resources to facilitate activity, not with the poverty and status disintegration that appears to be more common to the unemployed (Gallie, 1989). The disinclination of the unemployed in particular, and the labour movement in general, either in the 1930s (Croucher, 1986) or the 1980s (Forrester and Ward, 1986) to involve themselves in mass protests against unemployment is perhaps a good example of the way unemployment is experienced: it is both an individual event and, for the majority at least, probably an intermittent fate for many rather than a permanent state of affairs for a few (Marsh, 1988a). Were it otherwise the very heterogeneity and instability of the population of unemployed would act to disorganize any effective collective response; it is not coincidental that trade unions are usually strongest when their membership is permanently and securely employed in large factories, not transiently employed in isolated units. Nor is it likely that union members consider that they could affect the situation anyway – when collective bargaining is as decentralized as it is in Britain the likelihood of success of a single union's action against unemployment is strictly minimal. Deciding to forgo a wage rise in one company is not going to resolve mass unemployment; for that co-ordinated mass action channelled through the TUC in conjunction with the government is essential: the history of British labour suggests that such events are unlikely in the extreme. In effect, concern for unemployment is organizationally dispersed away from conventional collective bargaining.

Unemployment is not an inevitable consequence of organizational or economic systems; if it were, the gross international disparities highlighted by Therborn (1986) would not exist. Thus, for example, while Austria, Sweden, Norway, Japan and Switzerland have managed to ride out the economic depression of the 1980s, other nations in similar economic positions, like Belgium, Netherlands, Canada, Denmark and Britain, have literally been swamped by a veritable sea of unemployment. Disputing the assumptions that welfare systems generate unemployment, or that economic growth rates are correlated with unemployment, Therborn argues that it is the specific employment policy of each state that determines the level of unemployment. In effect, unemployment is socially or at least politically constructed, as are its effects: in Italy and France unemployment is primarily displaced on to women and the young, whereas in Britain unemployment, and particularly long-term unemployment, is almost wholly a male problem. In Austria and Switzerland it has been the policy of repatriating foreign workers which has enabled the apparent employment miracle to be brought off. Certainly technical development has not led inevitably to unemployment: Japan has the highest technological development and the lowest unemployment of the major nations. Nor does the contingent extraction of huge oil reserves necessarily soak up unemployment: the contrary experiences of Britain and Norway in this matter are useful reminders of the importance of practical policies to combat unemployment in place of market-driven spontaneous expansion. Sweden, on the other hand, has neither oil revenues nor rapid technological or economic expansion, yet it does have a vigorous and successful anti-unemployment policy (Marsh, 1988a: 353–4).

Neither are the unemployment figures simply objective measures of the numbers of people who do not have paid employment. Again, what has to be stressed is the social construction of such data and thus their susceptibility to different interpretations and manipulations. For example, although the number offically unemployed in the UK in mid 1990 stood at around 1.5 million, a series of category and regulatory changes of the last decade appear to have removed 1 million from the register without them acquiring employment. About 750,000 of these are reputed to have been 'lost' through the government's Restart Programme which involved 6 million interviews with unemployed claimants, and which encouraged the unemployed into Employment Training or into a job (only 6,000 appear to have gained a job as a result). Once these people returned to the unemployment register they were reclassified as new claimants rather than long-term unemployed. The upshot of such statistical and category massaging was the inexplicable 'loss' of 515,000 unemployed males between June 1985 and June 1988, without any concomitant rise in the employment figures. Most of these individuals appear to have been recategorized as disabled or the long-term sick (Harper, 1990). It is not only work which is socially constructed.

Yet in industrial cultures, all of which are officially dedicated to some kind of work ethic, the experience of unemployment can be one of great personal shame and guilt, irrespective of the cause or political machinations behind the figures. The experience of mass unemployment between the wars generated several arguments about the importance of perceiving it as a process which changed through time for individuals. Initially, once the shock had worn off, unemployment was regarded as a temporary rest during which the stockpile of domestic jobs could be eliminated. There followed an active phase of searching for employment during which time optimism remained high, but this was gradually eroded so that after a period of six months individuals became fatalistic about their prospects, eventually treating unemployment as a way of life rather than a transient experience between jobs (Eisenberg and Lazarsfeld, 1938; Hill, 1978; Ashton, 1986). The long-term result of this, and the equivalent today, was often regarded as debilitating to the morale of the nation: eventually an entire generation of individuals would have lived without any experience of employment and would, consequently, be incapable of pursuing a 'normal' and 'responsible' life. Such fears appeared to melt rather rapidly with the onset of rearmament in the late 1930s, and we should remain similarly sceptical about the effects of long-term, rather than permanent, unemployment (see Jehoel-Gijsbers and Groot, 1989).

What do unemployed men do when not searching for work? The evidence suggests they are not engaged in domestic labour and many prefer to maintain appearances by being out of the house during conventional working hours. What little alteration there is in terms of domestic roles is limited to a small degree of 'role renegotiation' rather than a more radical 'role reversal'; some men may 'help' a little more but the majority do not (Hartley, 1987: 133). They also fail to appear as significant moonlighters; indeed, unemployment appears to rob the unemployed of the resources and will to undertake any kind of constructive activity. Assuredly, Jahoda's (1979) studies of the unemployed of Marienthal over a vast span of time, and the more recent research of Bostyn and Wright (1987), imply that unemployment destroys the very structures that employment generates but that the employed take for granted – that is, the structures of time, routine, status and social networks. Given the excessive amount of time on their hands the unemployed ought not to be persistently late for interviews but they often are (cf. Miles, 1983); they ought to spend extra time on careful budgeting but they appear to lose interest in such details; they ought to have more time to undertake leisure activities but they seem to retreat from all such social interaction. Employment facilitates and unemployment tends to debilitate social routine and the rhythm of social life itself, but the exact nature of the impact of unemployment is a feature of the individuals themselves, rather than their collective position (Fryer and Mckenna, 1987).

Work in itself may not be the means to self-realization, nor the means to achieve sufficient wealth to compensate for what may be experienced as the alienating consequences or work, but the effects of unemployment are a clear indication that work is a central social institution and an essential part of most people's lives.

Conclusion

This chapter has concerned the problematic and complex task of establishing the meaning of work by sketching in, and drawing upon, a wide range of tasks and activities that may not normally be associated with work conceived as paid employment in the contemporary West. In essence, work is a socially constructed phenomenon without fixed or universal meaning across space and time, but its meanings are delimited by the cultural forms in which it is practised. Some cultures do not distinguish between work and non-work; others distinguish between work and leisure; still others by reference to employment as a particular category of work. Generally, work might be any form of transformative activity, but what counts as work depends upon the social context within which that transformative activity occurs. The implication is that where particular activities are relegated to the category of work or non-work then it is these categories as well as the activities which should draw our attention. What some aristocratic and anti-democratic ancient Greeks despised because it was work, and hence for them the equivalent of slavery, others heralded as the foundation stone of (male) democracy. Where Christians and capitalists alike sought to inveigle the faithful and the working class with a metaphysical zeal for productive activity, anarchists and some socialists preached the gospel of laziness or of craft skills. Indeed, even the economy as a discrete category is a relatively recent social construction – a product of Western societies whose conventional epithet 'capitalist' is yet another reminder of the form of discourse which we operate within. That individuals come to be recognised as 'unemployed' rather than as 'mothers' or 'graduates' or 'gardeners' conveys a great deal about the significance allocated to formal employment as *the* distinguishing category of social life by the state. Similarly, the notion that domestic activities do not constitute conventional work or that certain people are 'just housewives', or that universal orientations to work can be derived from the experiences of male workers, connotes a culture shot through with patriarchal mores of work. The conventional adage may be 'one man's work is another man's leisure' but it might be more appropriately written as 'one man's leisure is another woman's work'. In effect, what counts as work cannot be read off from an objective analysis of specific activities because the meaning of work is not immanent to the activities; meanings are socially constructed and maintained, they are contingently present and permanently fragile. The answer, therefore, to Charles Lamb's question 'Who first invented work?' might not be a name but another question: 'Who said the inventing of work had ceased?'

2

Work in Historical Perspective

I like work: it fascinates me. I can sit and look at it for hours.
Jerome K. Jerome, *Three Men in a Boat*

Introduction

This chapter on the history of work refrains from attempting the impossible: to cover the history of work adequately is to cover a substantial section of all human history. Therefore, what it does is illuminate some significant features by reference to multiple examples. These examples are drawn from pre-industrial, agricultural, industrial and domestic sources, as well as some which do not fit into regular taxonomies. There is no attempt to cover a representative sample, nor to describe the 'typical' work experiences of history. Indeed, the argument is that such experiences are probably rare and we seldom have the knowledge to assess what might count as typical. Thus I have drawn from sources beyond the conventional focus of 'industrial' sociology to demonstrate the limited significance of what has become perceived as the archetypal 'worker': a male craft worker in pre-industrial periods or a male blue collar factory worker in the industrial era. Since there are already several texts which focus predominantly on the historical experience of men at work (see for example, Hobsbawm, 1964a, 1984; Fox, 1985) the bias of examples here tends to be towards women. This brief synopsis of work in historical perspective is designed to highlight several critical features. First, work is a social not an individual activity – even those who work on their own do so within a socially constructed network of relations. One implication of this is that such relations can alter the very meaning of work; in particular the process of industrialization in Britain witnessed a transformation from a moral to a market economy. Yet the transformation is not one where the market simply replaces morality but rather one where the market sits on top of the moral economy. To use a textile analogy, the moral economy underlies the market economy in the way that the batik process involves a waxen base to resist areas of surface colour. The result of a batik process may provide a sheen of surface colour but the pattern is affected by the form and extent of the wax underlay. Thus, the world of work remains one that cannot be adequately explained by reference to market forces and economic rationality alone: it is quintessentially a social phenomenon, a world of symbolic representations, meanings and interpretations rather than a world of self-evident objective facts. Second, the history of work buttresses the suggestion of the previous chapter that the very term 'work' is ambiguous and transient but this is not indicative of any pluralist notions of equality: it is important not just that disputes exist about the meaning of work but also that such disputes are often resolved in favour of the more powerful. Third, some patterns of work are ephemeral in the extreme while others are notoriously inertial. Fourth, the social inequalities of work manifest in gender, ethnic and class divisions long predate the rise of capitalism and therefore pose problems for theoretical perspectives that root the generation of systematic inequalities solely in capitalism. Fifth, the image of work as separate from, and unrelated to, the home, and the associated predominance of male breadwinners, is both historically atypical and theoretically vacuous: home and the place of work have always been, and still are, intimately connected by a seamless web of social interdependence. Sixth, an appreciation of the history of work is crucial if we are not to assume that contemporary work is wholly the result of contemporary actors. What may appear irrational today, for example trade union demarcation disputes, may well reflect a pattern of work that was constructed to fulfil a real need at the time of origin, in this case the determination to remain employed by making each skill an essential part of the productive process.

In what follows I consider pre-industrial work, the transition from feudal to industrial forms of work, the significance of occupational changes, the rise of trade unions, the interventions of the state, the development of clerical labour, and the impact of the wars.

Pre-Industrial Work

Perhaps the major problem to be encountered in any historical review of work is the paucity of evidence about pre-industrial work and, by comparison, the enormous amount of data available for contemporary work. Even though we generally know very little about the working lives of the population in any epoch prior to the industrial one, as will be evident from the next few chapters, even the contemporary evidence is far from satisfactory. All that can be done is to adumbrate a skeleton of ideas and fragments of evidence rather than draw a series of definitive conclusions. Since the intention is to demonstrate the diversity of experience, as well as their social origins and forms of deployment through various discourses, such a skeletal approach should be sufficient.

If it is the case that contemporary hunter-gatherer societies are little changed from our own indigenous historical variants, then we can assume that the approach and forms of work considered in the previous chapter are appropriate. Hunter-gatherer societies are not normally encumbered by the kind of work ethics that require submission to socially constructed units of time of the 9 to 5 variety, nor do they divide up time into slices for work and recreation. Work and non-work are not so much merged together as irrelevant terms to describe the activity. Yet one of the major themes running through the approach has been to stress the continuities as well as the discontinuities across time. There is no doubt that changes occur all the time but these have to be contextualized adequately if we are to appreciate their relevance. Thus, we can only really talk about a decline in the work ethic or a rise in instrumental orientations to work if we know what existed previously, and not just a decade previously but perhaps a century or more. For example, in Britain the former Chancellor of the Exchequer, Nigel Lawson, noted in 1985 the common assumption amongst Conservatives that, as a direct result of post-war Labour policies, taxation rates had, for the first time ever, been pushed so high that they became economically damaging. Yet such concerns for work disincentives are not new: over 1500 years earlier Priscus of Panium met a Greek merchant who preferred living free amongst his previous captors (Attila's Huns) rather than under the Roman Empire because, amongst other things, the taxes were lower (Salway, 1981: 457).

Such financial calculations for work mobility in Roman Britain during the same era were no doubt irrelevant for the vast majority of the population involved. Most of them were primarily engaged in subsistence farming but there were also some specialized areas. For instance, Britain was renowned as a leading producer of agricultural commodities (cattle, hides and corn), as well as hunting dogs, timber, slaves and precious metals (Salway, 1981: 630–1). Nor should it be forgotten that the work of the Roman army and the economic viability of the Empire were intertwined in what Tacitus called the *pretium victoriae*: war was supposed to pay for itself, it was work not unlike any other in the underlying aim of securing a living, albeit through perfecting the art of killing.

The largest non-military industry for the major part of the Roman period seems to have been pig iron, which Britain was self-sufficient in by the end of the first century AD. But what is significant about this is that a mere 1500 craft workers would have been sufficient to provide the necessary labour: if iron production was the largest single industrial employer we can rest assured that the majority of the population not in the army were wholly agricultural in orientation and location (Salway, 1981: 639). That is not to say that everyone not engaged in killing people or moulding iron pigs spent all their time farming. On the contrary, a number of people were full-time potters, shopkeepers, smiths, metal and jewellery workers etc. Even the trusty British duffel coat made its first appearance under Roman rule as *byrrus Britannicus*.

Once the Roman army had gone, by the fifth century AD, Britain, like many areas of the old empire, was subject to the rapacious interests of external and internal military groups. One eventual socio-economic response to this was the system of feudalism which conjoined a method of agriculturally based production with a military protection racket. In return for resisting external threats to life and limb the military aristocracy secured the surplus from their peasants (North and Thomas, 1973; Anderson, 1974), yet such a system, although politically stable in the main, also reproduced economic and technical developments that tended to undermine, though not destroy, social and legal rigidities. In particular, the notion of property rights underwent some radical transformations, especially in Britain somewhat distanced, as it was, from the more ingrained Roman law of continental Europe. With the expansion of feudal agriculture into marginal lands, combined with fluctuating birth rates and natural catastrophes like the Black Death, the end result was declining productivity, a drastic economic squeeze on the nobility and an increasingly vociferous peasantry, eager to make the most of its new labour market strength despite its failure in revolt (Brown and Harrison, 1978: 48–71).

As the social relations between serf and master were gradually eroded in favour of economic relations, manifest in the switch from the provision of labour to the provision of money rent, so too the personal forms of authority were depleted. In their place authority relations resurfaced at the level of the state, not at the level of the local noble: the absolutist state, complete with its power to dispense privileges to local trade groups and guilds of craft workers, was born and the age of feudalism was rapidly drawn to a close; the age of market capitalism was just beginning.

But at this stage, with technological innovations minimal, most industry as such was labour intensive and, with the single major exception of woollen cloth, England in the fifteenth century was economically retarded in comparison to its European neighbours. Indeed, the great economic success story of the European medieval world was Flanders which had prove to be the single most important factor in the development of

English commerce from the twelfth to the fourteenth century (Postan, 1972: 213–16). In England luxury textiles were still surpassed by those of Italy and the Low countries; in mining and metals it was outproduced by the Germans and Swedes, and in many other things by all of these countries as well as France and Spain.

By the sixteenth century the power of the English guilds had already been largely ceded to the state and by the eighteenth century many guilds had all but disappeared (Coleman, 1975: 19–22). The state's control of working arrangements was considerable: it acted through Justices of the Peace and through legislative controls to set wages and conditions and intervened extensively in a mercantilist fashion to protect and promote native industries. Thus to help the woollen industry and its workers there was a legal obligation to be buried in a woollen shroud, and the Statute of Artificers of 1563 demanded a seven-year apprenticeship for all clothiers. The state even restricted the size of enterprises in the woollen industry: by an Act of 1555 it was forbidden for country clothiers to own more than one loom; weavers could not own more than two. One of the clearest cases which demonstrate the social or normative rather than the inevitable or natural responses of the state to industrial considerations was its reaction to technical advances prior to the industrial revolution. Gig mills, devices to raise the nap on woven cloth before shearing, were banned in 1551 to protect jobs (Harvie, 1978: 15); over two and a half centuries later, in 1813, seventeen Luddites were hanged for their part in the rebellion against the new shearing technology which the state now presumed to be inevitable and necessary (Reid, R. 1986). The attempt to replace the 'moral economy' with the 'market economy' was a transition littered with similar, if less brutal, conflicts (Thompson, 1968).

It was not until the early eighteenth century, however, that the picture began to change dramatically as the state dismantled the legal restrictions on trade and industry, and English economic production began to outpace that of its continental neighbours (Coleman, 1975). Much of this seems to have come about through the dispersal of textiles away from the town-based guilds and into the rural-based putting-out system: the original green field sites. Yet despite the critical role played by the industrial textile workers, in terms of both generating wealth and the incipient trade union movement, the significance of the town-based craft workers should not be underestimated; for the coopers, masons, thatchers, carpenters and the like survived well into the nineteenth century and formed the productive core of town life in Britain and France (Sonenscher, 1989). However, their power rested squarely on controlling a static labour market; once product demand grew incessantly, as it did from the sixteenth century in England, the guilds slowly began to disintegrate, hastened by the rural developments in textiles and the shift in state sponsorship towards the Justices of the Peace and against the monopolistic guilds.

The Transition from Feudalism to Proto-Industrialization

In England the absolutist state was remarkably short lived. Having terminated the age of feudalism it was itself subject to decline. In conjunction with the diminishing power of the crown was the associated decline of legal restrictions on trade and crafts. These lattice-like systems of property ownership and associated usufructs (rights to derive profit from land owned by someone else) were often grounded in common law and tradition but had been active inhibitors of private enterprise and capitalist market relationships (Landes, 1972). Not that the removal of such economic inhibitions had been achieved by an absolutist state. On the contrary, the British state, as a result of the civil war and construction of a constitutional monarchy, was dominated by a land-owning aristocracy not by any monarch. Moreover, this elite was directly involved in commercial activity; it transcended the distinction between landed and commercial interests rather than being swamped by the latter, and ultimately spawned an ideological system of values often regarded as instrumental in the degradation of manufacturing industry and the superordination of financial affairs (Wiener, 1981; Roderick and Stephens, 1981). But this did not mean that the political revolution of the seventeenth century resulted in a concomitant economic revolution; if anything the reverse is the case, for economic restructuring was noticeably absent (Hill, 1969: 240).

That said, economic and industrial stasis did not survive for long. One of its major underminers was the putting-out system, developed initially in thirteenth-century Flanders, but refined and expanded in England where an abundant labour supply and the difficulty of making a living as an independent farmer or weaver ensured the growth of the first proletariat of industrial (i.e., textile) workers by the end of the eighteenth century. By then, for example, master clothiers, keen to rid themselves of legal regulations on their expanding businesses, and smaller entrepreneurs and journeymen under direct threat from the new factories, combined to demand a Parliamentary enquiry into the woollen industry. Its report, in 1806, noted both the distinctions between the independent clothiers of Yorkshire and the putting-out system in the West Country, and that the latter system tended to undergo considerable bouts of unrest as technological innovation spread (Harvie, 1978). The network of medieval restrictions was much less significant for the relatively independent craft workers of Yorkshire, and Defoe writes of Yorkshire in the early eighteenth century as a veritable garden of Eden in its productivity and as a decentralized egalitarian idyll:

> this whole country, however mountainous, is yet infinitely full of people; these people are full of business; not a beggar not an idle person to be seen, except here and there in an alms house, where people ancient and decrepit and past labour might perhaps be found; for it is observable, that the people here, however laborious, generally live to a great age, a certain testimony to the goodness and wholesomeness of the country. (quoted in Reid, 1986: 5–9)

In fact, although such descriptions undermine images of generalized pre-industrial poverty, the decentralization in Yorkshire did not lead to egalitarian work relations because, as Cole makes clear, most of the craft workers were small-scale capitalists rather than truly independent (cited by Landes, 1986: 605). Nevertheless, the point made by Hobsbawm is that such a decentralized industrial structure had profound consequences for the future development of the industrial revolution and the nature of workers' reactions to it: 'Such a form of business structure has the advantage of flexibility and lends itself readily to rapid initial expansion, but at later stages of industrial development, when the technical and economic advantages of planning and integration are far greater, develops considerable rigidities and inefficiencies' (1969: 65). This point is crucial because it reflects the fundamental significance of the historical dimension: the impact of the process of industrialization was such that it becomes very difficult to understand contemporary work patterns without some historical knowledge: today's ossified work practices and productivity inhibitors may simply be yesterday's radically innovative method for achieving productivity advances.

It is also important to note that one of the most successful of the early trade unions developed in cotton where the very powerful, and male-dominated, skilled mule spinners organized both themselves, and ultimately the other cotton workers, to resist the might of the cotton masters. Whereas prior to the industrial revolution the social divisions between people were not channelled *primarily* along class-based employer/employee lines, they now tended to be. Whereas societal norms had been complex and pluralist they were now constrained by the increasing significance of a new breed of animal: capitalism (Hobsbawm, 1969: 66). As Thompson (1971) and Randall, A. (1988) have argued, the work, life and protest of much of the eighteenth century is soaked with an overarching concern, not with markets and issues of supply and demand, but with a 'moral economy' in which, however inegalitarian, relationships between social classes were at least reciprocal to some degree.

The moral framework of the combinations is well represented in the initiation ceremonies and oaths sworn by the Luddites and Tolpuddle Martyrs alike. Both groups were 'twisted in' rather than simply 'admitted' to membership. For each Luddite had to 'swear that I will use my utmost endeavour to punish with death any traitor or traitors who may rise up against us, though we should fly to the verge of existence' (quoted in Reid, R. 1986: 92). Each of the Tolpuddle Martyrs had to swear not to reveal the rules of the Union on pain of having their soul plunged into eternity (J. Marlow, 1985: 81). This moral undertone was not simply intended to deter reprobates from undermining the collectivity but also embodies a distinctive approach to working life: work was not simply an economic activity stripped of all non-pecuniary interests but a *social* activity circumscribed by custom and traditions that went far deeper that the cash nexus. Indeed, one of the reasons why the Luddites were initially so successful was that their fight was not one of skilled workers against unskilled, or even textile workers against textile machinery (much of which was not 'new' anyway); rather their conflict was, like the miners' strike some 170 years later, a strike involving a large proportion of the population of certain local communities (Reid, R. 1986; Berg, 1988). The tenacity of such communities suggests that even now work remains imbued with a moral vigour consistently misunderstood or ignored by those whose analysis of work remains restricted to the operation of market forces alone. It was a struggle of one community against another and, as such, re-emphasizes a critical theme running throughout the book: work and the domestic sphere are intimately and irrevocably linked in a web that confounds all accounts which are ignorant of it. Work was, to put a gloss on it, a way of life; an end in itself not a means to an end. A point not lost on Carlyle for whom the whole process of industrialization had split society assunder, dissolving the critical moral fabric of the community, and for whom, as for Marx, the immediate future was one of foreboding.

Yet not all employment during this transient stage towards industrialization was decentralized, home-based and ultimately threatened by technological development, even if much of it was. Mines, shipyards and mills had all been thriving non-domestic units from the Tudor and Stuart period, although even if one or two units employed hundreds, most probably had little more than a handful. Indeed, even as late as 1851 the average productive unit still only employed about 8.5 employees: the apotheosis of early Victorian industrial Britain witnessed a nation of agricultural labourers, domestic servants and small workshops, not gigantic factories filled with thousands of clone-like workers (Hopkins, 1979; Burnett, 1990). A few mines in northern England operated with hundreds of miners but many just had a handful while some of the largest single productive units were not in the private sector at all but in the Naval dockyards: by 1700 Chatham and Portsmouth employed over a thousand workers each (Coleman, 1975: 23–51). Work, then, before the dawn of the industrial factories and even well into it, was ultimately small scale, predicated on a social as well as an economic footing, and had few of the class-based antagonisms that were already being forged in the northern mills.

A useful place to assess any alleged pre-industrial homogeneity might be the largest and most expensive work unit in the Western world of the time, the eighteenth-century British Navy. Although the Civil Service employed 16,000 in 1759 the Navy had almost 85,000 officers and men (Rodger, 1986: 11, 332). Several critical aspects of this massive organization are pertinant to any assessment about pre-industrial work organizations. First, contrary to popular myth, officer or managerial control generally operated on the basis of persuasion not physical coercion. At a time when the civil land-based population had little regard for the control of the civil authorities it would seem appropriate that a similar absence of direct coercion was the norm at sea. This prescient form of participatory 'human resource management' extended to situations in which ship's captains would ask the crew whether they ought to engage the enemy or surrender:

> The *Penguin*, a twenty gun sloop, found herself chased by two French thirty-six gun frigates, which head-reached on her and ranged up on either side. Captain Harris summoned his officers and men and asked their advice whether to fight or not; they replied they would have taken on one thirty-six, but two was too much. So the *Penguin* struck her colours without firing a shot, and at the court martial Harris was honourably acquitted, as having done everything that a good officer could do. (Rodger, 1986: 237)

Ordinary seamen would also visit admirals in their homes to discuss personal grievances. This did not mean that anarchic confusion reigned supreme; quite the opposite, for the discipline of the British crews was an important factor in the victory over the less disciplined French navy, and in terms of ensuring a particular proportion of the fleet was always at sea the mid eighteenth century was more efficient than that operating during the Second World War (Rodger, 1986: 36, 229–37). Neither should we fall prey to the belief that sailors were disciplined through some patriotic duty; both sailors and shipwrights in the Royal dockyard were quite prepared to strike or petition for improvements at the very moment of war (Rule, 1988: 5). Nor was it simply the case that shipboard life, with its inherent dangers and mutual dependence, ensured that discipline would not be a problem; since the merchant navy had an alarming number of mutinies and reports of brutality it would appear that the policy of the Admiralty, in conjunction with the protection of subordinates by the King's regulations, ensured peace usually prevailed. This is important because it is an early demonstration of the mutual advantages of bureaucratic regulation: it was not that the Navy was run by rule-bound officers, quite the opposite in many ways, but the existence of a backdrop of mutually advantageous rules deterred both officers and men from adopting the violent solutions to work-based problems that plagued the merchant navy and later, after considerable changes, the Royal Navy too.

Second, the typical ship's company was not divided cleanly along class lines (though these became much more prominent as the industrial revolution gathered pace into the nineteenth century); rather the divisions were multiple, based on different forms of hierarchies, and sustained by the groups themselves rather than being forced upon them by superordinate officers. For example, not only were the officers split between commissioned, warrant and petty, but all these were associated *with* the seamen but against a whole panoply of others including the marines, carpenters, gunners, cooks, servants and (male) children (Rodger, 1986: 15–29). There were one or two women who passed as men in the Navy, the most celebrated being William Prothero, a marine aboard the appropriately named *Amazon*, but however relatively liberal the Navy was then (to the extent that it commissioned a black sailor from Jamaica in 1782), it did not open its ranks to women.

Whatever else the pre-industrial world of work in Britain was like, it certainly does not appear to have been composed of a mass of skilled craft workers, nor was it a world where employers or their agents always rode roughshod over the interests of employees or labourers. Diversity and dependence are as useful a summary of work in this period as solidarity and coercion; but the latter were certainly to become more prominent as the industrialization, and especially the development of factories in Britain, destabilized the occupational system and with it the world of work.

Factories and Technological Change

Considerable controversy exists over the role of technology within industrial development, particularly with regard to the rise and spread of factories. By convention, from Adam Smith, Andrew Ure and Charles Babbage onwards, it has been assumed that the organizational demands and economic rationality of large-scale technology simply obliterated household production and replaced it with gigantic factories. Whether the cause of technical development was economic or social, or even whether it was autonomous, is secondary to the reality of its alleged effects: the new powers of steam engines and mechanical production required factory production, facilitated the division of labour and thus demanded greater degrees of co-ordinative and controlling power on the part of the capitalist factory owner. The hierarchy of control within factories, then, was supposedly technically and organizationally inevitable; any other method of organizing production would simply have been economically inefficient and technically irrational.

This orthodoxy, which received support from Engels though less so from Marx, has been subject to attack primarily from Marglin (1982). His argument suggests that the origins of hierarchy within capitalist production lie not in the extended division of labour engendered by technical developments but in the desire for social control on the part of capitalists so that levels of exploitation could be increased. Thus factories, which were, after all, established with the kind of technology already in place in many domestic units, were constructed to maximize control; they were not the inevitable results of technical change nor were they the inexorable results of the search for simple efficiency. In effect, capitalists divided up the labour process, beyond that concomitant with any complex labour process, to fragment the workforce so that control over it was facilitated. As a direct result this fragmentation provided capitalists with a formal, and apparently technically required, role as integrator and co-ordinator. If Marglin is right then, by implication, egalitarian and co-operative work organization is possible and hierarchies, beyond some form of co-ordination system, are technically unnecessary.

One difficulty with Marglin's case is his assumption that capitalists needed to make a role for themselves. It is not self-evident why this should be so; after all, rentiers have been content to draw profits simply from their ownership of property without constructing an active role for themselves, so it is not clear why capitalists should feel obliged to do more than was required. Nor do they appear to have suffered from any crisis of legitimacy. A second issue relates to the irrelevance of capitalists: if their role was entirely specious why did workers not simply set up shop on their own without capitalists? Third, was the level of specialization really so unnecessary? If it was then there is a difficulty in accounting for the connections between those, like Wedgwood, who extended the division of labour to the greatest possible degree and those, again like Wedgwood, who were the most efficient in terms of production costs (Landes, 1986).

However, if a radical division of labour was critical to efficient production in certain forms of production this does not account for the transition to large numbers of factories. Since much domestic production adopted the latest technological and organizational forms of production before the factories spread, we need to explain why a spectacularly efficient method of production based at home spawned a transition to factory organization. The answer is probably one even the protagonists of this particular debate would agree on: domestic production of this form was *so* successful that it enabled workers to do less and less work for more and more money. As discussed in the previous chapter, there is no inherent human desire to acquire material wealth through work, instead there are culturally and temporally specific norms of human activity. If technology facilitated greater levels of income for less effort, and if the cultural norm was to minimize human labour rather than maximize human reward, then technology could just as easily serve to restrict as to expand total production. The response of merchants and putting-out capitalists was clear: to make the most of the new techniques required central and hierarchic control - workers had to be coerced to work when capitalists required them to, not when they felt like it.

Yet there appears to have been more to the success of the factory over domestic production than a concern for maximizing control. In that some production was housed in factories far sooner than others, and that some forms of manufacture remained stubbornly domesticated well into the nineteenth century, we should be wary of accepting that the issue is solely to do with control rather than control and other features. For example, it was seldom feasible to develop domestic production where the process required a large input of natural energy (as did iron), or the product was large (such as ship building), or the machinery very expensive etc. It is also clear that the technical innovations most associated with factory production were often aimed at circumventing the exclusive and, from the capitalists' perspective, profit-retarding skills of particular groups of workers.

Nor were the responses of the early nineteenth century Luddites typical of the earlier period. When the Luddites rose against the machinery they did so because their very livelihoods were threatened by it and because certain of their skills could not be taken abroad. But Hargreaves's 'spinning jenny' (1767) and the 'water frame' (1768), initially at least, soaked up surplus labour rather than posed a threat to the existent workforce and enhanced or at least retained operatives' skills. Such technical advance was often marketed precisely as a means to generate work for the unemployed and underemployed, not as a method of dislodging recalcitrant workers, hence the limited resistance on the part of the workers to these early developments. The hybrid 'mule' (1779) was rather different because it was designed on a large scale which was deemed by its supporters as innappropriate for domestic adoption and because economic conditions had worsened by this time (Landes, 1986). Likewise, Roberts's 'self-acting mule' involved the degradation of skills and the elimination of labour and was consequently resisted, not just by labour but also by many Tories shocked at the implications for the nation of such 'rationalizing' measures. For such patricians machinery was 'an insatiable Moloch [with a] heart of steel, jaws as wide as the grave, teeth of iron and claws of brass' (quoted in Berg, 1980: 265). The moral economy was not simply a dream of the working class but an element of reciprocal class relations. Similarly, technology was not axiomatically received as an embodiment of rationality by the middle and upper classes but interpreted in a variety of ways consonant with people's wider ideology.

Factory production, therefore, was not merely the result of capitalists' desire to carve themselves a role: they were probably more concerned with carving out a living than a role. Certain aspects of production were portrayed as more viable under factory regimes than situated within the domestic unit but the analysis of this development does not take place outside an arena of political life. After all, many domestic spinners and weavers soldiered on at their looms and wheels well after factories had made their product uncompetitive and their independent living precarious. For example, the handloom weavers, struggle for existence in the first quarter of the nineteenth century became increasingly difficult as wages fell (mechanization was not a major threat until around 1826), yet the number of handloom weavers actually continued to grow. As Mathias notes, it was not just economic need which maintained the family based industry but also 'the cohesion of family employment [and] . . . the values of a whole way of life' (1969: 207). The point really is how different political interests were served by the rise of factory production: you do not have to be a capitalist to recognize that extending the division of labour can be a more efficient method of production – but who benefited from this extension and who suffered form it? Moreover, how did the beneficiaries manage to win out? Such a question requires more than a concern for issues of control over the labour process and more than an analysis of the putative technical superiority of certain kinds of machinery. It requires us to look at the seamless web that the victors managed to weave between themselves and the technical artefacts, between the domestic and the factory spheres of life, and between themselves and the politics of organizational life. We also need to explain why the resistance of the factory proletariat to the expansion of capitalism, so elegantly argued by Marx, appeared to be limited to trade unionism. A major reason is the apatetic nature of this same proletariat: its form and shape changed in conjunction with capitalist developments and a homogeneous class never emerged.

Occupational Change

Although, as discussed in chapter 5, much has been made recently of the disaggregating consequences of capitalism as a once homogeneous workforce of skilled craft workers is deskilled and degraded into a myriad of occupational specialisms and statuses, close attention to the pre-industrial historical evidence suggests that uniformity was noticeable mainly by its absence. We have always to be wary of any kind of data but occupational data prior to the nineteenth century are notoriously suspect. However, a glance at figure 1 should highlight the problems of reconstructing a homogeneous occupational structure.

Although the denials of homogeneity are probably safer to make than positive statements concerning the proportion of specific groups, it is noticeable that no occupational group accrues more than 25 per cent of the total at any period covering the century up until the beginnings of the industrial revolution, though a large margin of error must be accepted even here. Prior to the beginning of the Census in 1801 very little reliable evidence beyond local examples and parish registers exists, and up until 1831 the Census itself kept little occupational data. Lindhert's (1980) scrutiny of burial registers highlights the problem of identifying the occupations of women since they were mainly identified by their marital status, though it is clear that a large proportion of women worked at home producing saleable commodities, especially textiles. In line with the concern for the interpretative approach it should also be clear that different interpretations of 'significant categories' generate very heterogeneous models of the social and occupational structure. Since women recede from view in many of these early models a model based on gender would reveal the persistent and homogeneous domination of employment by men, rather than a fragmented social structure.

Lindhert's analysis suggests a generally stable occupational structure from the middle of the seventeenth to the middle of the eighteenth century with the exceptions of an expanding agricultural and manufacturing sector and a declining group of low-income dependants. In the second half of the eighteenth century, and the beginnings of industrial revolution proper, the occupational structure alters quite markedly: manufacturing, or rather textile manufacturing, mushrooms in size, with the numbers of men engaged tripling in fifty years, while the number of weavers doubles. Relatedly, building, mining, the professions and the armed forces all expand rapidly, while the numbers of unskilled rose only marginally and agricultural employment drops to the point where, very approximately, just over a third of the population were engaged in agriculture in some form by the beginning of the nineteenth century. What is particularly significant is the point that at no time can we really talk about the work experience of the majority of the categorized population as if such a homogeneous category existed. Of course, there are large groups with similar life experiences: handloom weavers or agricultural labourers or miners etc. Indeed, it could be argued that the wives of men in such categories probably had similar lives; but none of these groups ever approximates a majority of the population: diversity, not similarity, is

Figure 1 Occupational structure of England and Wales 1688, 1759, 1801–3 (%)

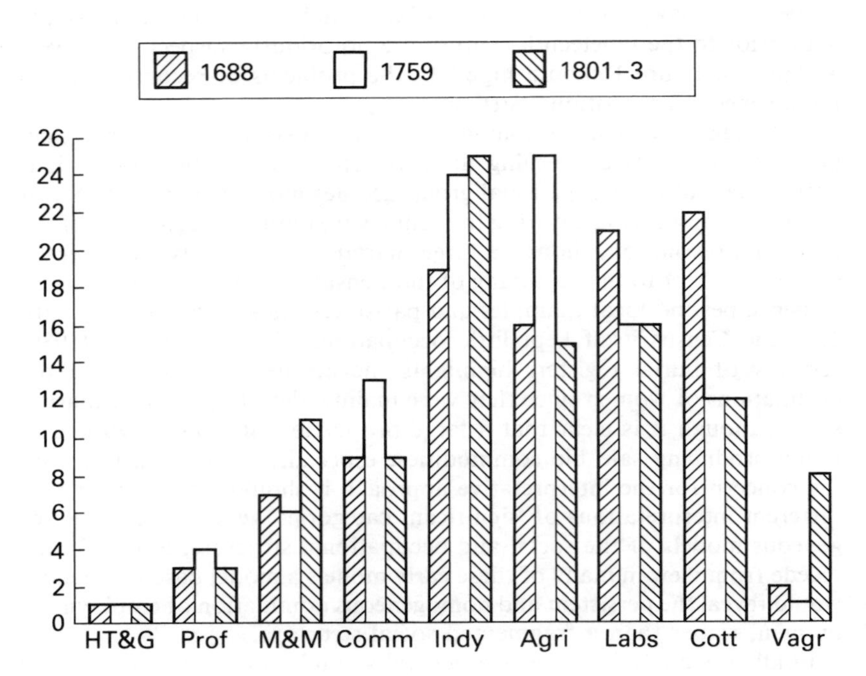

Key:
HT&G – High titles & gentlemen
Prof – Professions
M&M – Military & maritime
Comm – Commerce
Indy – Industry & building
Agri – Agriculture (freehold)
Labs – Labourers
Cott – Cottagers & paupers
Vagr – Vagrants

Note: There are significant problems with this data: domestic servants (mainly women) have been omitted; labourers are not distinguished by sector; women's occupations are rarely recorded; the figures reflect families rather than individuals.

Source: Lindert and Williamson, 1982; Crafts, 1985

probably a more appropriate universal term for describing their mode of existence.

The textile industry, with a million workers, was virtually the only one which, by mid nineteenth century, employed roughly equal numbers of men and women. It was also the largest single industry involving widespread, and occasionally very large, factories. Indeed, with the exception of some iron and coal works, cotton was virtually the only industry that was mechanized and factory based (Hobsbawm, 1969: 72) relatively early. Almost all of cotton spinning was mechanized and factory based by 1851, though weaving survived a little longer as a handloom operation. But however diverse the occupational structure of mid nineteenth-century Britain, and however limited any specific occupation might be in size and distribution, it was still the case that industry figured largest, both in terms of overall size and, equally significant, in terms of influence. Not only was industry disproportionately important in terms of its provision towards the gross national product but it was also critical in an indirect way: its absorption of labour from agriculture ensured the maintenance of a viable agricultural labour force and its manifest success in the generation of a new middle class sustained the expansion of domestic service. The middle class was by no means insignificant in numbers: in London, even before the industrial revolution, the 'middle station' as Defoe called them comprised somewhere between 20 per cent and 25 per cent of the total population (Earle, 1989).

The prototypical example of an industrial region was Lancashire, where despite the enormous importance of cotton and manufacturing the former declined through the second half of the nineteenth century while the latter was virtually static. In the country as a whole between 41 per cent and 46 per cent of the population were employed in manufacturing, mining and industry between 1870 and 1914 but it was in directly related employment that the biggest growth occurred: in shipping, services, exporting, transport and finance (Mathias, 1969: 272–3).

It is important to note too that the decline of the more traditional, that is agriculturally-based and home-located, lifestyle in Britain may not have been quite so rapid as has been previously assumed. It is common to argue that Britain's peasantry were virtually extinguished by the mid nineteenth century (Hobsbawm and Rudé, 1973; Barrington-Moore, 1967: 25–9), yet the problems of categorization in the Census obfuscate the probable persistence of the English peasant well into the nineteenth century. Even in 1851 although industrial occupations outnumbered agricultural ones it is still the case that agricultural labour was the biggest single occupation, domestic service was the second largest and building the third. In fact, the population engaged in agriculture as labourers (1.75 million, of whom 0.25 million were women mainly employed as farm servants) had been growing, albeit slowly, throughout the nineteenth century. Yet at the same time there were four times as many industrial workers of various kinds as agricultural workers, though again only a quarter of the industrial workers were employed in mechanized (i.e., steam driven) industry, including mining (Hopkins, 1979: 3). In short, no homogeneous factory proletariat existed and, furthermore, occupational divisions were seldom as clear cut as the Census data would suggest. Work for many people in the rural parts of Britain, then, and for much of the nineteenth century was still a matter of multiple rather than singular occupations. For those in urban areas the typical place of employment was more likely to be a small workshop rather than a factory of any size. There were some very large industrial centres by late nineteenth century: Swan Hunter's and Palmer's shipyards in north-east England both employed over 7,000 men (McClelland, 1987: 181). But many of the most successful manufacturing centres, rather than factories, were located in rural areas rather than urban centres; not because natural resources forced such dispersal but because social features encouraged it. That is, although we commonly consider the relocation of industry to 'greenfield sites' as a twentieth-century phenomenon it has a long history. While the original guild organization in towns acted to inhibit greater levels of production through the guild members' influence over the labour and product markets, few such socially constructed barriers existed in rural areas. Here, wages were cheaper and restrictive practices fewer; and it was here that Britain generated the domestic forms of specialization that led the rest of world at the end of the eighteenth century. As one contemporary put it: 'When Mr Arkwright established his works . . . he did not establish them where the people had been been in the habits of spinning at all; but he established them at Cromford . . . where till that time the People [women and children] had been almost wholly unemployed, except in the washing of lead' (quoted in Landes, 1986: 608). Associated with the movements to greenfield sites, of course, are movements away from previously productive areas. This is significant in so far as many popular historical approaches tend to locate the growth of industry from a general agriculture base in the north. In reality, the rise of the manufacturing north had a long history of domestic-industrial production and brought with it the decline and collapse of similar industries in the south of Britain (Berg, 1988a).

At this time, in the late eighteenth and early nineteenth centuries, the working day was conventionally at least twelve hours long, even for children (of whom there were over 50,000 officially employed full time in 1851 and still 22,000 as late as 1871 (DOE, 1971: table 102 note 7)), and accidents and physical punishment a common hazard (Ayres, 1988). Though perhaps few were as cruel as those suffered by one Robert Blencoe:

> I have seen the time when two hand-vices of a pound each, more or less, have been screwed to my ears at Lytton Mill, in Derbyshire. There are the scars remaining behind my ears. Then three or four of us at once have been hung on a cross beam above the machinery, hanging by our hands, without shirts or stockings. Mind, we were apprentices, without mother or father to take care of us. (quoted in Hopkins, 1979: 10–11)

It should be remembered though, that the long hours and miserable conditions of work in the first half of the nineteenth century were little different from those that existed in the previous century, or indeed in some places well into the twentieth century (Mathias, 1969: 203–4). Equally common, and soon to be eliminated, was the form of work group. Typically this was a small team, often family based, and clearly a derivation of pre-industrial work practices. Only in the cotton mills was team work unusual by the mid-nineteenth century (Landes, 1986), but via the 1867 Agricultural Act the gang-based system of agricultural work (involving women and children supervised by a male overseer) was finally all but destroyed when it was declared illegal to employ women or children with men in a field gang. One of the major reasons for this, as in the related Factory Acts, was the desire on the part of the establishment to buttress the family as the normal social unit: married women and children were to have no place in the public world if it threatened the cohesion of the private world. By 1871 only 15 per cent of the working population of England and Wales were employed in agriculture, and by 1911 this had dropped by half to 7.6 per cent (Mathias, 1969: 263). Naturally, as the proportion of people able to supplement their wages through the produce of their own land diminished so too did the number of workers and families who were not overwhelmingly proletarian in character. Also in decline was the number of people not subject to the discipline of the clock and free from what many experienced as the monotonous and putrefying conditions of many urban areas (Hobsbawm, 1969: 84–8; Engels, 1969a).

As table 1 and figures 2 and 3 suggest, over the period from the middle of the nineteenth to the first quarter of the twentieth centuries, the occupational structure underwent some very radical alterations. Of particular note are the ways in which over two-thirds of women are virtually eliminated from the occupational tables except in so far as domestic service, textiles, and, towards the latter period, commercial employment are concerned. Also note the devastation of the agricultural and fishing populations: down by two-thirds over a mere eighty-year spell, accompanied by the 50 per cent reduction in the clothing and textile trade over the same period. Their places are taken by a much wider variety of employment forms but especially commercial, transport and

Table 1 Selected distribution of the occupied (i.e., paid) British labour force (% of total (males and females) occupied)

	1841		*1871*		*1901*		*1921*	
	M	*F*	*M*	*F*	*M*	*F*	*M*	*F*
Public administration	0.6	0.0	0.9	0.1	1.2	0.2	2.0	0.4
Armed Forces	0.7	0.0	1.1	0.0	1.1	0.0	1.3	0.0
Professional	1.6	0.7	1.7	1.3	2.1	2.0	2.1	2.3
Domestic service	3.7	14.3	2.0	14.3	2.1	12.2	1.9	9.5
Commercial	1.4	0.0	1.8	0.0	3.7	0.5	4.7	3.0
Transport etc.	2.8	0.1	5.6	0.1	8.7	0.2	7.9	0.4
Agriculture & Fishing	21.1	1.2	14.1	1.2	8.5	0.4	7.2	0.5
Mining	3.2	0.1	4.4	0.1	5.7	0.0	6.4	0.1
Metal manufacturing	5.7	0.2	7.4	0.4	9.1	0.5	11.0	0.9
Building	5.4	0.0	6.1	0.0	7.5	0.0	4.6	0.0
Other manufacturing	3.9	0.4	4.3	0.8	5.1	1.5	5.0	1.4
Textile etc	12.8	8.1	8.4	11.2	6.0	9.8	3.7	6.7
Food & drink	3.9	0.6	3.8	0.7	4.3	1.3	1.2	0.6
All others	6.9	0.6	8.0	0.2	5.8	0.5	11.6	3.6
Total occupied %	73.7	26.3	69.6	30.4	70.9	29.1	70.6	29.4
Number (million)	6.908		11.752		16.280		19.354	

Source: Reconstructed from DOE, *British Labour Statistics: Historical Abstract, 1886–1968*, tables 102 & 103

manufacturing of all kinds. Again, what is perhaps most significant here is the heterogeneous patterning which marks out the development of industrial capitalism in Britain, as more and more old occupations were systematically extirpated.

Furthermore, we should be wary of assuming that the experiences of textile or factory operatives were typical. As has already been stressed, typicality is a very dubious word to describe the experiences of the industrial revolution just because experiences were so very diverse. Thus, although the weavers of Lancashire did witness a very rapid transition in their lives from home workers to out-putting and eventually into the mechanized factory, other areas witnessed only gradual and incremental changes to the traditional pattern of work and life. A case in point is the Birmingham tradition of small manufacturing workshops of the mid-eighteenth century which adapted to the new demands of industrial production with very little of the social or technical eruption that so bedevilled their northern neighbours (Hopkins, 1988). But such incremental change at the industrial level does not appear to have been the experience of the family and the home as the site of production.

Figure 2 Male labour force 1841–1921 (%)

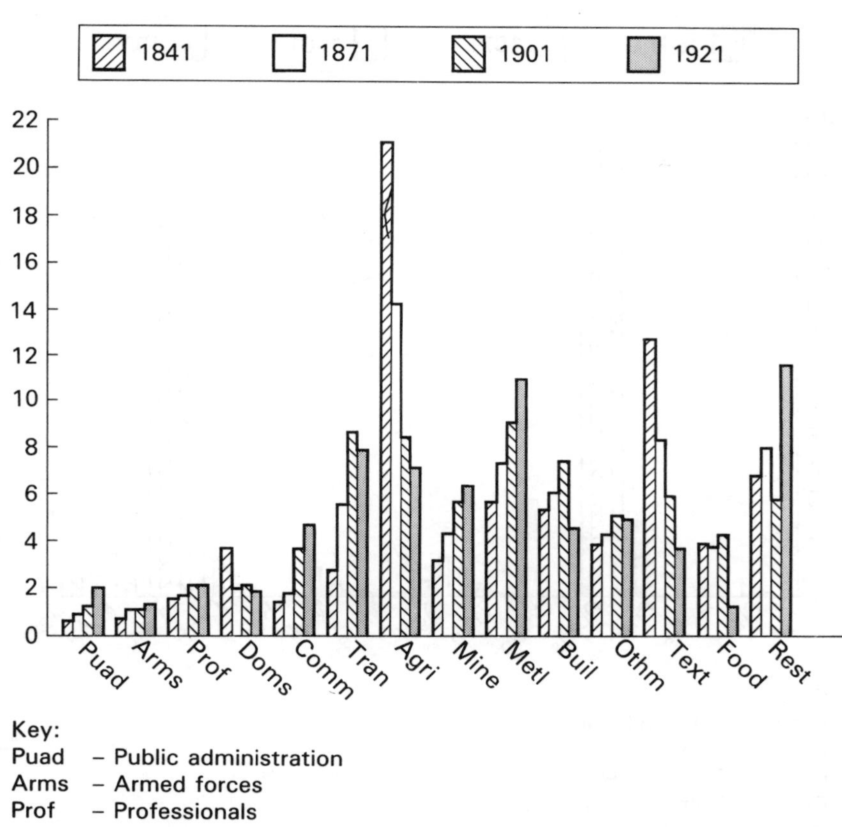

Key:
Puad – Public administration
Arms – Armed forces
Prof – Professionals
Doms – Domestic servants
Comm – Commercial
Tran – Transport etc.
Agri – Agriculture and Fishing
Mine – Mining
Metl – Metal manufacturing
Buil – Building
Othm – Other manufacturing
Text – Textiles etc.
Food – Food & drink
Rest – all others

Source: Table 1

Figure 3 Female labour force 1841–1921 (%)

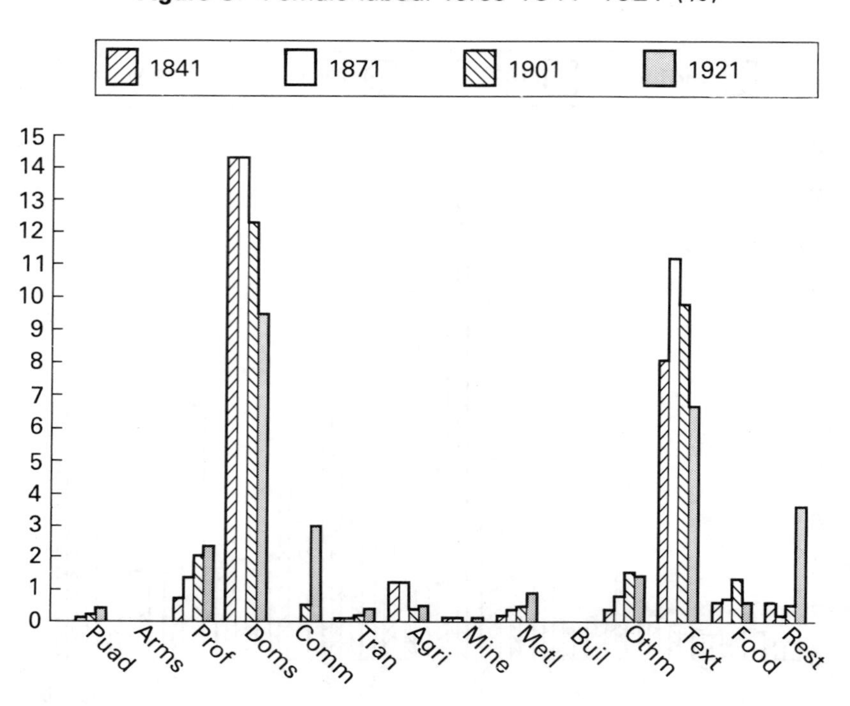

Key:
Puad – Public administration
Arms – Armed forces
Prof – Professionals
Doms – Domestic servants
Comm – Commercial
Tran – Transport etc.
Agri – Agriculture and Fishing
Mine – Mining
Metl – Metal manufacturing
Buil – Building
Othm – Other manufacturing
Text – Textiles etc.
Food – Food & drink
Rest – all others

Source: Table 1

Work, the Family and Gender

If the industrial revolution had a differentiated effect upon occupations and regions in Britain, what impact did it have upon gender and the family? In particular, did the industrial revolution and the rise of industrial capitalism segregate home from work and allocate women to the former - the sphere of the private - and men to the latter - the public arena? Answers to this question are almost as various as the patterns of wages that have existed. There is some evidence that women undertook a much greater variety of jobs before, rather than after, the industrial revolution, though there were few areas where some degree of gender-related inequality or segregation did not exist. Certainly the evidence to base any overall assessment is limited but Middleton's (1988) perusal of bonded labour in the thirteenth century reflects the importance of gender for the allocation and reward of work with a disproportionate number of women undertaking the most menial, poorly paid and domestically related jobs. Although there appear to have been few travelling journeywomen there were many female masons, carpenters and coopers - though most had faded from view by the sixteenth century (Leeson, 1980: 27). The activities of the craft guilds - the forerunners of trade unions - seem to have been exclusively male-oriented with increasingly severe restrictions on women's membership.

Yet we know remarkably little about work-related gender relations prior to the nineteenth century (Berg, 1988b: 67; Segalen, 1983) except that the distinctions drawn in the contemporary literature between domestic labour and paid work probably made little sense. Instead, it would appear that because the site of virtually all work was domestic and wage labour played a relatively small role until the nineteenth century, and because all members of the family participated in many forms of labour, work became an instrumental activity disconnected from its particular location. Thus gender-based patterns of work, and family located sites of work, are forms that pre-exist capitalism: they are not the results of capitalist-induced social change (Middleton, 1988). As far as it is possible to tell, just as women were once employed alongside men as miners so they have traditionally undertaken a considerable share of all kinds of labour, even though a gendered division of labour has always existed. A typical example is brickmaking where by tradition women made the bricks, girls transported the clay and bricks, and boys fired them in the kilns (Hopkins, 1969: 7). That is not to say that all forms of work had equal status, or that men, women and children all undertook identical work. Rather, it would seem that a hierarchy of work did exist, with men at the apex, women in the centre and servants and children at the base.

Prior to the industrial revolution there were, of course, several forms of industry but most of them were intimately related to agricultural produce: milling, baking, distilling, textiles, wood-based produce etc. Moreover, such activities were seldom undertaken by particular crafts but tended to be executed by people whose main work was directly agricultural but due to the seasonal nature of such work undertook several different occupations. Equally, the first occupational identities that were distinct from the domestic sphere of collective activity appear to relate closely to men (Middleton, 1988: 28). However, although tasks within families did appear to be gender-related, the exact patterning of task allocation varied in time and space. It should also be remembered that patriarchal control over work is not restricted to sex-segregation but encompasses the allocation of occupational statuses. Although male workers may construct innumerable strata within each occupation to provide exclusionary badges and labels, women's occupations tend to be provided with universal not variegated statuses: medical specialization may multiply in different fields and hierarchies, to the state where senior doctors lose their title to acquire the more prestigious consultants' Mr, or less commonly Mrs, but to many people all nurses – at whatever level of seniority and skill – are still 'just nurses' (Maynard, 1988).

Perhaps the clearest denial of any 'natural' form of the sexual division of labour is to note the atypicality of the male breadwinner status. For much of the industrial period since the end of the eighteenth century normative assumptions about the 'proper' role of men and women have regularly reproduced an ideology that perceives male workers to be the primary, if not the only, source of income for their families. Yet, just as the household was the site for a collective work effort so, prior to the industrial revolution, families were generally based upon multiple incomes, albeit of differential sizes. Nevertheless, it is the case that women, or more exactly married women, were systematically removed from the labour market after the initial phase of the industrial revolution. The exact timing of this fade from the labour market is itself disputed: Clark (1982) dates its origins in the seventeenth century, George (1965) places it roughly during the eighteenth century and argues that the early factory system proved beneficial to women, releasing them from the grossly exploitive domestic manufacturing system. Hill (1989) also places the change squarely in the eighteenth century but associates it with a decline in women's fortunes. Snell (1985) asserts that women in apprenticeships, later reserved for men, continued through to the middle of the nineteenth century, though it is by no means clear that female apprentices undertook the same kind of training as male apprentices. Skill, as Rule (1987: 107) notes, was usually configued (by men) as male property. Whatever the dating involved, the largest single form of employment for women for almost the entire period of the industrial revolution until the First World War was domestic service of one sort or another; initially as young unmarried farm servants living with a farm-owning family (Malcomson, 1988: 52), and later, from the beginning of the nineteenth century, as servants of the middle class (Beechey, 1986: 10). In 1911, the peak period of manual employment for men and women in Britain, and the high point for factory labour, there were more domestic servants (2,127,000) than miners (1,202,000) or the metal and engineering workers (1,795,000) (Stevenson, 1984: 183). In short, industrial capitalism not only witnessed the decline of agricultural work, most rural industry, multiple occupations and sources of income, but it facilitated the decline of the family as a collective work unit and polarized the work opportunities of men and women.

However, the polarization of opportunities did not necessarily mean the elimination of women from employment. On the contrary, the early phase of industrialization, manifest in the putting-out system, provided women with new opportunities for domestic industry, but only because of their cheap labour. Women who could work either from home or away from home in the new small factories often did so precisely because their income could be so much higher (Berg, 1985: 173). Even when the first spinning jennies were introduced towards the end of the eighteenth century, although many women were eventually made redundant through productivity advances, its initial small-scale development lent itself to cottage use, advancing rather than removing employment for some women. Only when the technology was introduced into the factories did women's wages fall in a more universal pattern. Indeed, in the 1841 Census only 6 per cent of factory workers were women. This did not mean that such women were free from the exploitation commonly associated with this period; as James Leach, a Manchester operative, witnessed: 'We have repeatedly seen married females, in the last stages of pregnancy, slaving from morning till night besides the never tiring machines and when . . . they were obliged to sit down to take a moment's ease, and being seen by the manager, were fined sixpence for the offence' (quoted in Ayres, 1988: 8).

Agricultural work seems to have been an area where both technical advances and the genderized polarization of work opportunities marched in step throughout the eighteenth century, especially with the introduction of the corn scythe which gradually replaced the lighter sickle. Roberts (1979) links this to the physical superiority of male workers, though unless it is assumed that all men were stronger than all women we should expect fewer women scythers rather than none at all. What this suggests is that male representations of what women could or could not do were more successful than women's representations; whether all men were physically stronger than all women is not what matters - which group's rhetoric is deployed most effectively is what ultimately counts. Moreover, the shift towards more intensive cereal growing, the decline of common grazing land and the loss of peasant farms also squeezed a labour force that by the nineteenth century was actually beginning to expand rapidly, adding to the pressures for employment opportunities; the fact that this employment contraction was at the expense of women merely confirms not the physical strength of men but the political and organizational strength of patriarchy (Snell, 1985). That said, it still seems to be the case that many forms of labour were generally, if not uniquely, regarded as 'men's' or 'women's' work; men usually undertook the heaviest and what was perceived to be the most skilled work of ploughing, mowing and hedging, women looked after the garden, poultry, the dairy and most of the household duties (Reed, 1984). Occupational sex segregation, then, existed earlier than the industrial revolution and laid out a pattern that was reproduced and remoulded rather than shattered by the rise of industrial capitalism: the strong links between domestic responsibilities and employment were evident in seventeenth-century rural England, early nineteenth-century London (Alexander, 1976), and still abound today.

Whatever the rules and ruses developed by men to exclude women from the most preferential jobs, there were serious barriers to such strategies. As late as the middle of the nineteenth century the putative male breadwinners in Scottish manufacturing towns could often provide no more than between one-third and two-thirds of the family income (Holley, 1981). This wide disparity is important because it reflected the distinction between 'respectable' and 'unrespectable' families: those which included a skilled worker could survive on a single income providing it was consistently available and providing children could add supplementary income. But where the primary income generator was categorized as unskilled the family as a unit had no option but to engage as many of their members as possible, critically including the mother, in as many forms of employment as practical. The inability to survive without recourse to the earnings of married women denoted the badge of poverty in most parts of the country; for married women to *have* to work became less respectable as it became less common.

There were cases of women undertaking all jobs by convention executed by men, but they were atypical and more often than not related to the inheritance of an occupation or business through the death of a women's husband or father; few women appear to have initiated occupations conventionally associated with men (Berg, 1988b: 83). It is perhaps not coincidental that where the laws of inheritance have been fashioned to ensure male predominance, the perceived threat and atypicality of women inheriting their husband's property appears to have been one of the factors associated with the accusation of witchcraft in late seventeenth-century New England (Karlsen, 1988). Equally patriarchal were the assumptions that jobs biologically restricted to women were the source of disease or evil; for example wet nursing, which may have involved up to a quarter of all Parisian babies in the middle of the nineteenth century, was sometimes held responsible for spreading venereal disease (Fildes, 1988). There are several points in this historical development at which pecuniary and moralistic rationalizations of patriarchal interest are woven together in a seamless web to support not so much the interests of capital as the interests of men. But there are other times in which the thread of this patriarchal web is often spun into the adornments of trade unions.

The Rise of Trade Unionism

The origins of British trade unions lie in the original guild system, and the beginnings of British guilds can be traced back to the first century AD in the emergence of at least five *collegia* or associations, one of which was the *collegium fabrorum* (the guild of smiths) operating in Chichester (Salway, 1981: 659). Contrary to popular opinion, the first recorded instance of a strike was not amongst the Brigantian miners of what is now Yorkshire led by Athurus Scargillus but actually Hebrew brickmakers in Egypt in 1490 BC (Webb and Webb, 1919: 2). But the more recent development of guilds only really becomes confirmed in 1383, when the Corporation of the City of London prohibited them, though the prohibition seems to have been ineffective for a strike by the London guild of cordwainers is recorded five years later. By the eighteenth century guilds for all kinds of crafts which had been commonplace were in decline but it should be remembered that these were combinations of entrepreneurs and 'master' craft workers rather than manual workers (Webb and Webb, 1919: 14–16).

The early British unions of the eighteenth century appear to have initiated a pattern of unionism still extremely influential today: they were craft-based, sectionalist, decentralized, highly democratic and successful (Fox, 1985). There are certainly several records of their vigorous defence of interests which included pitched battles with other groups of workers, and it is quite possible that their very success undermined the more radical political movements of the period (Dobson, 1980; Christie, 1984). Since the early nineteenth century witnessed the return of radical sentiments it may be surmised that the suppression of unions was not a coincidental phenomenon. Yet despite their apparent illegality many unions, or combinations, particularly skilled ones, continued to operate with some degree of success faced by the kind of employers for whom pragmatic rather than ideological hostility was the norm; where this failed, bargaining by riot sometimes succeeded (Hobsbawm, 1964a: 5–22). Certainly there was little unmediated connection between market position and employer response: labour and product market conditions were important, but seldom determined employers' responses to the early nineteenth-century unions. Indeed, many capitalists in the first half of the nineteenth century looked to the state for a resolution of their labour problems rather than attempting to stamp out or accommodate unions in their own factories. However, many capitalists simply refused to negotiate at all with unions, not so much because of the unions' radical claims, which were few anyway, but because of the symbolic power of such combinations. At a time when moral panics over subversion of the state were commonplace and when workers were wholly excluded from the democratic system, such as it was, many capitalists appeared to have assumed that all unions, *qua* class organizations, were a fundamental and unequivocal threat to the status quo. Indeed, since those capitalists who did articulate a philosophical position generally appeared to assume a paternalist explanation of workers (as irrational and misled children) without recourse to paternalist policies (e.g., employer built and controlled housing and education etc.) it was self-evident to them that unions were not merely subversive but thoroughly irrational and transient. Not really until the mid nineteenth century did employers begin to consider seriously the possibility of an accommodation with unions and a method of controlling the workforce that did not rest primarily upon physical coercion (Haynes, 1988). Even then, once the demands of trade unionists spread beyond the workplace to include electoral demands the greatest fears of the establishment resurfaced. In the words of Robert Lowe MP speaking in the Commons in 1866:

> I shall not refer to the subject of strikes, but it is, I contend, impossible to believe that the same machinery which is at present brought into play in connection with strikes, would not be applied by the working classes for political purposes. Once give the men votes and the machinery is ready to launch those votes in one compact mass upon the institutions and property of the country. (quoted in Bagwell, 1974: 35)

But the state was seldom directly implicated in the control of trade unions. Despite the tyrannical implications of the Combination Acts of 1799 and 1800 it was still the case that, then as now, much of the initiation of proceedings against combinations had to begin with the employer and, just as today, the state began to distance itself from the regulation of wages, preferring to allow the market to determine due rewards. But the Acts were not simply confirmations of tradition for they made combinations, rather than the activities of combinations, illegal, and, perhaps more significantly, the 1799 Act prescribed penalties not for specific occupations but for the class of 'workmen'. Social class, rather than occupational strata, now became an overt form of categorization, institutionalized in the new legal framework (Orth cited in Rule, 1988: 12).

Equally significant was the repeal in 1813 and 1814 of the apprenticeship clauses of the Statute of Artificers (1563) which forbade journeymen's organizations from restricting the labour market via lengthy (e.g., seven-year) apprenticeships, and confirmed the revocation of wage setting by Justices of the Peace. From then on the full force of the 'free' market was to prevail as the state withdrew from certain regulatory practices (Moher, 1988). In reality many journeymen's organizations retained their apprenticeship regulations, often by reconstructing them along more informal lines (Rule, 1987: 100; McClelland, 1987) but such tight worker control over labour was seldom achieved again (Leeson, 1980). The alteration in the rules of work was experienced by many workers, especially craft workers, as a violent and shameful assault upon their 'right' to exercise their skills. Skill was not just a means of carving out a living and a market niche, it was regarded as a 'property' from which, like other forms of property, certain rights and responsibilities accrued to the owner and were protected by the state. In the words of the watchmakers in 1817:

> the apprenticed artisans have collectively and individually, an unquestionable right to expect the most extended protection from the Legislature, in the quiet and exclusive use and enjoyment of their several and respective arts and trades, which the law has already conferred upon them as a property, as much as it has secured the property of the stock-holder in the public funds; and it is as clearly unjust to take away the whole of the ancient and established property and rights of any class of the community unless at the same time, the rights and property of the whole commonwealth should be dissolved, and parcelled out for the public good. (quoted in Rule, 1987: 105)

Not surprisingly, when these combinations of artisans were faced by the new legal restrictions, the technical innovations that threatened their very livelihood, and a steadily growing labour force desperate for work, disputes were common and violence not unknown, though much of it was directed against other workers rather than employers.

Despite the legitimation of restricted forms of trade unions after the repeal of the Combination Acts in 1824, the very impotence of individuals and most unions to resist the onslaught of capitalism in the first third of the nineteenth century seems to have ignited the movement towards a wider, more politically aware, alternative: Owenism and the Grand National Consolidated Trades Union (GNCTU) of 1834. Ultimately, the collapse of the GNCTU and the débâcle over the Tolpuddle Martyrs deflated the radical shift and inaugurated a movement towards more 'respectable' unionism, epitomised in the New Model Unionism of the Amalgamated Society of Engineers, formed in 1851. This respectability, however, did not imply submission to managerial control even if it did embody a vigorous hostility to the political intent of syndicalism or socialism. As Rule argues:

> it is a fact of very great significance that British trade unionism has a long history which began before the era of the factory and the formation of the modern proletariat. . . . To its craft origins must be attributed British unionism's distaste for industrial unionism; its adherence to job demarcation and the closed shop and, not least, its willingness to contest the employers' right to manage in matters of recruitment, working practice and wage forms. For all that its distaste for 'foreign' socialism has seemed a matter for congratulation to some, the British trade union movement has, in important respects, been the least accommodating to the capitalist economy. (1988: 22/2)

It is also noticeable that unionism remained the preserve of skilled male workers in the main, and that exclusionary practices against women and unskilled men persisted and indeed strengthened throughout most of the nineteenth century: the generation of a homogeneous class-based labour movement was, with the exception of the early 1830s, never likely (Sykes, 1988; cf. Foster, 1974; Behagg, 1990).

This heterogeneity should not be interpreted as providing support for individualism at work. Just because many British workers did not heed the call of the socialists does not mean that they fell for the opposite Victorian ethic of work (see chapter 1). The habit of taking 'St Monday' off work did not die with industrialization and such reinterpretations of time by employees persisted throughout the nineteenth century (and could well be argued to persist now), despite the alleged advance of the clock and employers' time as against the natural rhythms of pre-industrial work (Whipp, 1987; cf. Thompson, 1982). As Harry Pollitt recounted, at the turn of century – when British shipbuilding productivity was superior to all others – the boilermakers' return to work after a holiday was highly contingent on a scientific experiment involving the eldest picking up a brick and declaring: ' "Now lads. If t'brick stops i' th'air, we start; if't brick comes down, we go whoam'. I do not remember any occasion on which we did not go whoam' (quoted by McClelland, 1987: 197). It may have taken another thirty years for American consultants like Mayo to recognise the significance of social norms in restricting output (see chapter 4) but what Lenin called 'trade union consciousness' has a long history:

> Self-seeking individuals who declined to observe the customs of the trade met with the sanctioning disapproval of their comrades. Offending compositors found their type had been mixed by the 'chapel ghost'. Deviant cabinet makers found the loss of their tools attributed to 'Mother Shorney'. . . . Liverpool shipwrights who took more than their share of

> work were 'drilled': that is, their fellows refused to work with them for a period of time thereby preventing them from working. (Rule, 1987: 112)

For the major part of this entire period what evidence we have suggests that male workers, and their collective organizations where they existed, were generally hostile to unskilled workers, to non-unionised workers, and to competing unions (McClelland, 1987). They were also antagonistic towards female workers, despite the history of women's participation in industrial action against exploitive capitalists and new technology (Berg, 1988b: 75/88).

The general hostility of trade unions to women was almost universal: the Mule Spinners Union struck over women workers from 1810 and banned them from membership in 1829 (Berg, 1987: 80); the Amalgamated Cotton Spinners Association, for example, admitted female members from 1837, but its predecessor – the Cotton Spinners Union – had argued at the repeal of the Combination Acts in 1824 that women should not be allowed to take men's jobs because 90 per cent of women had only themselves to support, and to provide such jobs and money to women would mean that 'the reins of government are broken and the excited feelings of youth and inexperience let loose upon the world' (Hunt, 1981). This fear was echoed half a century later in 1875 when, at the newly fledged TUC, Henry Broadhurst noted that one of the functions of trade unionism was 'to bring about a condition . . . where wives and daughters would be in their proper sphere at home, instead of being dragged into competition for livelihood against the great and strong men of the world' (quoted in Turner, 1962: 185). The moral threat to patriarchal control seems to have been as important as the economic competition, and the two developments became entrammelled in the male spinners, vigorous and successful attempts to retain the most skilled and the supervisory positions within most textile factories for men (Walby, 1986a: 99/100).

This differentiation between the skilled and unskilled positions was influential later when technological advances in the shape of various forms of spinning mule began to threaten the employment of spinners: since the mules could not, initially at least, reproduce the more skilled aspects of spinning it was only the women representing the less skilled spinners who were under direct threat (Chapman, 1972). Spinning is a notable example because for the whole of the eighteenth century the textile industry was the largest form of manufacturing and it was dominated by women and children. By 1833, however, the workforce was split almost equally between adult males, adult females, juvenile males and juvenile females (Hammond and Hammond, 1949: vol. I, 36). Spinning, then, was an atypical industry in terms of the number of adult women employed and their location within factories, but spinning unions were not unusual in their patriarchal concerns: in the latter half of the eighteenth and early nineteenth centuries women were forced out of work by the Spitalfield silk weavers, by journeymen bookbinders, by the Stockport Hatmakers, by the Mule Spinners Union and by London tailors (Berg, 1988b: 68–77). By 1886 the results of this consistent onslaught against women were clear: only one per cent of women employees were unionized (Hunt, 1981); in comparison the male figure was approximately ten times this (Salamon, 1987: 559). In fact, the oldest durable union for women only appears to have been the Edinburgh Upholsterers Sewers Society, formed in 1872, though there were several earlier short-lived attempts, especially in the textile industry (Boston, 1987: 19), such as the West of Scotland Power Loom Female Weavers Society, established in 1833 (Bagwell, 1974). By 1875 several small women-only unions flourished in London including the Women Bookbinders, Upholsteresses, Shirt and Collar Makers and Dressmakers (Webb and Webb, 1919: 336), and in the same year Emma Paterson became the first woman delegate to the TUC. The real turning point for women, though, was probably signalled by the strike of women and girls at the Bryant and May match factory in London in 1888. Aided by Annie Besant, the strike garnered support from the unskilled workers, especially the Dockers and Gasworkers, who went on to admit women to membership. By 1914 women's union destiny had risen to 10 per cent while men's had climbed only to 23 per cent (ibid.).

It is worth noting at this point that the forms of work-based resistance to capitalism and patriarchy were not restricted to activities undertaken *within* the orthodox system. Although not many alternative communities sprang up in the nineteenth century there were some. These ranged from the barely disguised paternalism of Titus Salt's Saltaire community to Robert Owen's New Lanark (Morton, 1962), through to the more radical self-organizing communities such as Whiteway Colony in Gloucestershire. In the Whiteway Colony, for several decades from the end of the nineteenth century, an anarchist group provided not just a non-capitalist form of work community but one that attempted to pursue a non-patriarchal one too. It clearly had some success, ensuring that the women members undertook work which conventional society regarded as strictly male; however, it would appear that it was women's roles which expanded to encompass all activities while men's roles remained more or less static: women undertook men's jobs but seldom the other way round (Hardy, 1979: 201–2).

Yet, however implicated trade unions and trade unionists were in the employment-based discrimination against women, many of the most salient barriers to gender equality at work were erected not by unions but by the state.

State Intervention and the Factory Acts

If we can provide some sort of answer to the issue of *when* women, that is primarily married women, were segregated away from the labour market and restrained within the home this does not provide us with the definitive reason for such a development. Nor, indeed, is it the case that women became economically inactive just because their presence within the increasingly large-scale manufacturing industries was continually reduced (Pahl, 1984). Although it may seem more than coincidental that the rise of capitalism and the decline of women's employment opportunities occur with a remarkably parallel progression, in fact the progression is not parallel, nor is the connection self-evident. Since women tended to be cheaper than men to employ it would seem more logical to assume that the new factories would be staffed by women and children, rather than men. Of course, many of them were until the various Factory Acts began to delimit the extent of women's and children's labour. In themselves, the legislative restrictions on women's and children's labour embodied both progressive and regressive aspects: to prevent the gross exploitation of children and limit the hours of work was and is clearly a progressive move – as witnessed by the rage expressed by a reactionary employers' representative writing to Sir John Cam Hobhouse, who was responsible for introducing it:

> The first and immediate consequences of limiting the age of children employed, to 'under 9 years' will be to throw out of employment all that class of hands. This is perhaps the most cruel stroke to the poor man which could be inflicted . . . this threatened invasion of the rights of the parent over the child [is] an infringement of the liberty of the subject, and a direct violation of the homes of Englishmen. (quoted in Ward, 1970: 141–2)

Indeed, it is crucial to note just how innovative such legislative restrictions were, not so much in themselves, because state controls proliferated under the pre-industrial mercantilist economy, but rather in the protection of child labour. As George (1931: 132–3) argued, what was revolutionary about the factory system was that for the first time child labour came to be seen as inhumane; prior to this most children had worked at home as mini-adults with little public concern as to their welfare. Some Tories in the Commons were shocked at the very sight of women and children labouring in factories, others were shocked merely because it occurred outside the home for the first time (Berg, 1980: 264). Again, this development should be seen as a reminder of the resilient moral economy: market forces alone would have stripped work from expensive men to cheap children and women but the moral economy that supported the partriarchal family was a critical resource in the demise of employment for married women and children.

Relatedly, the dawn of the factory age was not interpreted by all as one of dark satanic mills and therefore as a problem. It was also perceived not just as a method of acquiring a fortune for the owners but as a means of relieving unemployment, of improving desultory working-class moral habits, and of infusing some level of education (Gray, 1987). The factory presented inconsistent symbols of light and dark, solutions and problems – it was a very different beast for very different people, and it was an apatetic beast whose form altered as groups using particular forms of discourse sought to represent it in their own language, notably the moral economy versus the market economy. But even privileged modes of discourse do not always prevail. The first English Factory Acts, in 1802, 1819 and 1847, which restricted the hours of children and women, seem to have been ignored by many factory owners (Hammond and Hammond, 1949: 35), partly because so few inspectors were appointed to enforce them, and partly, perhaps, because so few adult women were actually covered by them. For the latter part of the nineteenth century most female employees were the daughters of agricultural labourers and were themselves domestic servants; a family-related pattern that long predated the rise of factory capitalism and was outside the scope of the first Acts. As Pahl put it: 'perhaps the best way to view women's employment in the nineteenth century is as the employment of *daughters* but not mothers' (1984: 64). As late as the 1920s about a quarter of all teenage girls were in residential domestic service (Ellison, 1989).

The restriction on women's labour simultaneously limited employer exploitation and ensured the predominance of male workers in the most skilled areas. Humphries (1988) insists that the interests of male workers were coterminous with those of working-class families since the elimination of women ensured the maintenance of a family wage for male breadwinners, rather than subsistence wages for all. Nevertheless, many families did not have breadwinners, many male workers did not have dependants, and a very large proportion of working-class families were still reliant upon multiple incomes (Harrison, 1984: 302), so this proclass/family argument is dubious. It still does not explain why capitalists should acquiesce in the 'artifically' high wages for men, particularly when women were conventionally regarded as far less prone to trade unionism than men (Grint, 1988). After all, industrial capitalists were seldom philanthropists so why should they concern themselves with the consequences of their action; providing a labour force could be recruited why limit profits by paying for men? Certainly there is evidence that families, rather than individuals, formed the basis of many work groups, especially in areas like the potteries where the family provided the bridge between the world of work and the world of home: the mechanism for training, recruiting and disciplining (Whipp and Grieco, 1983). Barret and McIntosh (1980) suggest that the moral qualms of bourgeois philanthropists, concerned with the potential disruption to family life initiated by working wives, in conjunction with the material and patriarchal interests of male workers, is a more powerful explanation of the success of the factory legislation; an argument further elaborated by Walby who resurrects the significance of the Tory–Whig division (1986a: 108–34; cf. Gray, 1987). And it should not be assumed that all factory owners were divorced from the moral implications of their position: many were profit maximisers but many were intent simply on sustaining their position in society (Gray, 1987).

Nevertheless, the instrumental alliance argument should not blind us to the limitations of the parliamentary aspect. First, the sparseness of the inspectorate meant that many factories were able to circumvent the law. This was not the only reason for the absence of prosecutions: although the Workshop Regulation Act of 1867 covered most domestic workshops it did not cover those containing just a husband and wife. Moreover, even where women were illegally exploited by their husbands in larger workshops it was, as an inspector of 1889 put it: 'not usual to proceed against a man for overworking his wife' (Hopkins, 1979: 59–62, 105). Second, the impact of legislation on women was contingent on their activities prior to the legislation. In mining, for instance, although women were prohibited from underground work by the 1842 Mines Act its impact was regionally dispersed: from then on men replaced women, boys and girls in areas like the east of Scotland where previously women had supplied a third of the adult labour (Ayres, 1988: 52–5), and monopolized the more lucrative jobs in the West Riding of Yorkshire, Cheshire, south Wales and some parts of Lancashire. But in other areas its impact was negligible: for example, women had not been employed in Lancashire east of Manchester for some time, and had been all but absent from the pits of north-east England since 1780 (Hammond and Hammond, 1949: vol. I, pp. 39/40). Third, and crucially, female factory workers represented only a minority of female employees; small workshops were exempt from the legislation, as were all shop assistants, casual and unskilled workers, all home workers and, of course, all domestic servants (Best, 1979: 138). Fourth, even when prosecutions against owners were brought, the courts were keen to exploit all possible loopholes to facilitate the employer's escape from justice (Ayres, 1988: 46). What may have seemed a good example of various dualist theories, where the power of bourgeois philanthropy operated in conjunction with patriarchal trade unions, actually seems to be very limited because such a small proportion of women were covered by the Acts. This is significant because the focus on the import of the Factory Acts replicates the distorted lens of much conventional industrial sociology: factories were a minor part of the world of work in the middle of the nineteenth century, just as they are now, yet what happens within factories often seems to be taken as the model for all work experience.

Finally, it is worth reaffirming that patriarchal interests did not simply win out over the interests of capital. Women were forced out of many occupations both by the legislation and by male workers but there were many forms of employment where male interests were not sufficient to eject women and some forms of mechanization developed in conjunction with, rather than at the expense of, women (Berg, 1987: 88).

The Factory Acts are also significant in generating further doubts as to the coherence of capitalism and patriarchy. The liberal state had apparently ridden roughshod over industrial capitalism and, ostensibly, over its own philosophy of laissez faire. Yet the factory legislation facilitated the legitimacy of the government and the factory system in the communities where it was designed to operate; it was 'an important symbol of 'industrial legality' and reciprocity between employers and workers' (Gray, 1987: 177). Laissez faire was qualified by patriarchy rather than removed by it. Although the legislation cut into the economic profits of industrial capital, it did so to prevent an abuse of laissez faire. As Peel himself argued: 'it is not desirable that the state should interfere with the contracts of persons of ripe age and sound mind' (quoted in Taylor, 1972: 44). This underlines the inferior status of adult women as well as children, and rewrites rather than undermines the rules of laissez faire (Perkin, 1969: 439). The legal inferiority of women was also manifest in the transference of all property to the husband upon marriage; a situation that included the sale of wives by their husbands which, though untypical, was not confined to the fictional pages of Hardy's *The Mayor of Casterbridge*. On the contrary, as late as 1840 newspapers could still be found recounting stories like the following: 'On Saturday week, a fellow named Gibbon sold his wife to a country fellow for 2s 0d. The latter was proud of his purchase, while the woman cried with joy at getting release from her master' (quoted in Hopkins, 1969: 203). Such gender-based legal inequality prevailed until the Woman's Property Act of 1882.

Even when women had been removed from the mines the intervention of the state often had unintended consequences and should remind us of the problem of reading historical change as the functional result of capitalist, or for that matter patriarchal, developments. For example, the 1860 Mines Act provided for checkweighmen to alleviate the industrial unrest generated by suspicions of fraud by the mine owners. Yet the provision of these 'neutral' figures actually provided protection for a post which later came to be associated with the leaders of the miners' unions (Ayres, 1988: 51). Moreover, even though legal restrictions on women's employment facilitated patriarchal control over some sections of the labour force, the domination of employment by men had much more to do with the expansion of the engineering and metalworking industries, in conjunction with the growth of mining and transport systems etc., for it was in these areas that employment grew most rapidly in the second half of the nineteenth century (Harvie, 1978: 36).

In sum, the Factory and Mine Acts were passed not so much as a result of the interaction of the discrete forces of capitalism and patriarchy but by the internecine conflict of unholy alliances of groups within both comprising: men as workers, men as bourgeois philanthropists and men as Tory landowners etc. That is, not only is the alliance of forces a congealing and unstable mass but the individual components are themselves heterogeneous composites not single elements (see chapter 6).

Occupational sex-segregation is considered in chapter 6 but it is important to note that discrimination against women also occurred within occupations that were not so strictly sex-segregated. One of the most important of these was clerical work, particularly within the largest single employer of clerical labour until after the Second World War, the British Post Office.

The State and the Development of Clerical Labour

The Post Office was, in sharp contrast to the textile industry, one of the very few employers of self-allocated middle-class women. Women were first recruited into the Post Office through the nationalization of the telegraphic companies in 1870 and were employed throughout the organization except in the male-reserved areas of sorters and postmen (cf. Walby, 1986a: 150). Typically, men monopolized the most desirable positions and duties within clerical work generally and the Post Office in particular, but within the latter, the separation of men and women also necessitated distinctive career structures with consequential openings for women as superordinates over subordinate women. Some of the advantages of separate career structures for women were lost when gender-specific offices and departments were desegregated but this movement towards homogeneous conditions of service ultimately resulted first, in the termination of the marriage bar in 1946 and second, in the acquisition of equal pay by women in the Post Office main grades in 1961.

The reproduction and eventual overturning of pay inequality resulted from a rich and contingent concoction of influences, but broadly speaking it was male workers' opposition which inhibited equal pay, and their instrumental and rather deceitful 'support' for it (on the grounds that it would deter management from feminizing the labour force further) which removed the major obstacle. Walby (1986a: 154) argues that the hostility of male clerks was actually circumvented by employers channelling new female labour into new segregated sub-groups which did not threaten existing male areas. This argument may have some validity in the field of engineering but in the Civil Service and Post Office, the new all-female writing assistant was in fact both the only example and one comprising a minimal proportion of clerical employees. The fact is that after the 1926 General Strike débâcle for the labour movement, the management of the Post Office and the Civil Service was able to ride roughshod over the exclusivist interests of male workers; conflict was not avoided so much as met head on and overcome (Grint, 1986: 268–95).

Although equality of conditions or career potential is still not evident within the Post Office, equal pay for most major grades was a movement that began in 1919 and achieved a considerable degree of success by 1961. This does not mean that male workers in the Post Office and Civil Service were the harbingers of the new egalitarian man, but it does imply three things: first, patriarchal interests are not omnipotent; second, labour market pressures can prove superior to such forces; and third, the state is not an unambiguous servant of capital or patriarchy but has a sufficient degree of autonomy to deflect – if not stop – the influence of both.

Underlying and shaping the state's complex position regarding women was a tightening labour market in which female clerical labour was increasingly difficult to recruit: between 1911 and 1951 female clerical workers increased sevenfold, and less than 5 per cent of this increase was due to the feminization of clerical labour, that is the displacement of male clerks by female clerks. An increase in the demand for clerical labour per se, which was filled by women, was the main explanation of the huge upsurge in female clerical labour (Joseph, 1983: 87); as the size of business enterprises grew and the division of labour intensified, white-collar labour became progressively more important (Abercrombie and Urry, 1983). Also, and very significantly, the state as an employer was influential in stimulating the expansion of white-collar labour, particularly in the first majority Labour administration after the Second World War, and in setting the standards required for all employers. In effect, its public presence and status as a public employer eventually exhausted its power to resist the limited flood tide of equality ninety years after women had first entered state employment in any substantial numbers (Grint, 1988). That most women have still not achieved the levels of wage equality acquired by women in the Post Office, Civil Service and teaching profession back in 1961 also underlines the importance of an employer that was not subject to the direct machinations of the competitive market, in so far as maximum profitability was not required. Yet is was subject to them in that to fulfil the political obligations of the government a tight labour market had to be eased apart by increasing labour rewards. Just as the respective genders seldom form cohesive fronts so too employers are internally differentiated.

Women, Work and War

Labour market pressures were also responsible for the greatest ever acceleration of wages and conditions of work for women – the experiences of the two World Wars. On both occasions women in many of the nations involved (with notable exceptions such as Nazi Germany) were recruited to undertake all, or virtually all, the activities vacated by men at the front. On both occasions the state called women to undertake their patriotic duty in the munitions and armaments factories, on the farms and railways and in the shipyards. In Britain the dangers of military defeat were self-evident, the concerns of trade unions equally so: under the 1915 Treasury Agreement, the 'dilution scheme' – which 'diluted' skilled jobs – and the later Munitions Act, the compromise between the major unions and the government entailed women 'dilutees' taking what had previously been exclusively men's jobs only on condition that they were restricted to war work, paid the wages of skilled men and would be removed from their temporary positions at the termination of hostilities (Braybon, 1981). Very few women were recruited by male-based unions during the First World War, and although strikes were actually common throughout the period some of the largest were the direct result of infringements of the restrictions on dilutees. In the engineering and printing industry, and the Post Office, the evidence suggests that management was much more willing to concede to union threats based on the demands of male privilege than on demands based on class privilege (Walby, 1986a: 162; Grint, 1986: 437–62; Zeitlin, 1985: 216). That is, male privileges could be protected but rises in wages or increasing democracy were vigorously resisted. Yet even this statement is capable of two interpretations: either managers conspired with workers to keep women out, or class interests were more important than patriarchal ones.

In fact, neither of these is accurate: no patriarchal conspiracy was necessary because hostility to women at work was a normative convention of most men not a sinister secret; it was part of the male representation of the moral economy. Second, the comparison of class and patriarchal interests is illegitimate. Comparing a quantitative change in labour costs is not the equivalent of undermining a patriarchal system any more than it can be compared with ceding control to the workers. Thus a more realistic comparison would be just that, i.e., one where the prize and penalty is worker's control or patriarchal control. In short, union demands for taking over the factories, or even wage rises that threaten the survival of the factory, are obviously a direct threat to the preservation of management; but union demands for the continuation of male privileges are, for male managers, just an economic cost; for women employees the privileging of class over patriarchal interests is reversed. This implies not just that the hierarchy of influences is contingent upon the position of those affected (and therefore neither capitalism nor patriarchy can occupy an objectively superordinate position), but that the agents involved are not men or women first and capitalists or workers second (or vice versa) but male capitalists, female workers etc. The analysis therefore requires us to consider human agents as composite and heterogeneous entities, not unitary homogeneous entities, nor even entities with dualist features (see chapter 6).

Indeed, one can go further than this to say that heterogeneous composites rather than binary composites are likely. For example, in the Post Office case male managers who were likely to supervise women and men on the sorting office floor were often much more apprehensive about, and therefore hostile towards, women employees than their head office superiors whose interests lay in the financial benefits of feminizing the workforce. Concomitantly, the attitude of women depended not just on their gender but on their class and future prospects. Such prospects were themselves constrained by the official 'marriage bar' which forbade the employment of married women in the Civil Service from 1876 to 1946 (see Grint, 1988). Middle-class women, who perceived their future to lie in marriage, appeared concerned that they should give up work on marriage and 'retire' to the home. Working-class women supported the marriage bar because the associated marriage gratuity was their only chance to save enough capital to set up home. But for those women intent on remaining single and making the Post Office a career, the marriage bar sloughed off the great percentage of competitors for promotion. The marriage bar may have been a patriarchal institution but women interpreted it in several different ways and had their own reasons for supporting, or at least acquiescing to it (Grint, 1986). In sum, if we simply adopt gender or class based models of work then the contingent complexity of social relations becomes more opaque not more transparent.

In Britain, at the end of the First World War, the returning men from the front and the economic decline effectively ensured the dispersal of women from areas of declining demand, such as engineering, ship building and agriculture. Women had been particular effective in farming where the Women's Land Army, in conjunction with the Corn Production Act of 1917 which guaranteed high prices and stable markets, had rescued farming from the oblivion to which it had fallen (and with it the agricultural unions: Pretty, 1989) since the last quarter of the nineteenth century (Pagnamenta and Overy, 1984: 195–6). The reversal of this long-term decline in agriculture, under pressure from foreign competition, did not survive the war; as James McIver remarks in *Akenfield*, when he arrived in East Anglia in 1932, 'what a scene we found . . . Dereliction' (Blythe, 1969: 316). Clerical work, however, remained relatively buoyant and the numbers almost static, especially in the south east. Not that this reflected the eclipse of patriarchal concerns. Many attempts to extend the marriage bar were made, and they were particularly successful in the depressed textile industries of the north (Walby, 1986a: 180–1). The government also restructured its unemployment legislation to discourage women from seeking work, and Britain's leading trade unions were notably absent in the movement for equality that, ironically perhaps, began to gain ground during the inter-war period (Boston, 1987: 258–9). Nevertheless, two very significant achievements were made between the wars: in 1918 women over 30 with some property won the vote and in 1928 all women over 21 achieved suffrage on equal terms with men. Whether these compensated for the restriction of opportunities within the labour market is the subject of some dispute. Certainly the middle-class 'housewife' appears to have been the ideal which many women were encouraged to follow (Samuel, 1983a, b); and Roberts (1982) asserts that even working-class married women perceived their liberation to be away from, not towards, paid employment. Those married women who did undertake paid work often appeared to have little choice in the matter. This need not undermine perspectives concerned with the patriarchal advantages of restraining women within the home; it simply confirms the importance of ideological aspects and the flexibility of attitudes to work.

During the Second World War women were once again drafted into previously 'male' occupations, although not immediately. When the war effort did require extra labour the government went beyond the confines of tradition to encourage married women into the factories by, amongst other things, providing a level of nurseries and crèches that, limited though it was, has never been achieved since. In fact, Britain's mobilization of its female workforce was unsurpassed by other nations, but the control over wages ceded to the trade unions through Bevin's insistence effectively ensured that the movement towards equal pay remained stillborn; aided, no doubt, by a series of strikes against equal pay by men, the most infamous being at Rolls Royce, Glasgow in 1943 (Smith, 1984). Equally, or rather unequally, the engineering unions went out of their way to inhibit the employment of women until they were reluctantly forced to accede to a reality not of their making or choice (Lewenhak, 1977).

The ambiguity surrounding the role of women in wartime was not limited to the engineering union. On the contrary, the government itself appeared caught between the need to mobilize all available labour for the war effort and yet simultaneously retain the conventions of family life. The immediate solution, which prevailed through to 1941, was to call married women into the factories and on to the land but demand that they made their own provision for child minding. Even at the height of the war effort, in 1943, the government still only provided sufficient nursery places to accommodate one quarter of the children of women war workers. This difficulty, combined with the escalation of rationing and its associated phenomenon of queuing, pushed absenteeism so high that the government was eventually coerced into constructing a solution. It was typically minimal and based on self-help; women were encouraged to form 'neighbourhood shopping leagues' and granted unofficial leave to do their shopping. When this failed the government dreamed up another diversionary tactic – they readjusted the hours women were allowed to work to facilitate their double roles as mothers and employees (Summerfield, 1985).

Thus women entered the dawn of the post-war period much as they had entered the dawn of the industrial revolution; they took primary responsibility for domestic arrangements and undertook similar activities to men. The major differences were that most income-generating activities took place outside the home and women's occupational equality was generally perceived to be limited to the duration of hostilities. Also of significance, and perhaps an appropriate way to end this chapter on the history of work, the attitudes of the women working in wartime Britain are remarkably resemblant of many of the attitudes that have already been observed in the more contemporary period discussed in the previous chapter. Thus the *War Factory*, a Mass Observation study of the Second World War, reported a persistently low morale and complete lack of interest in anything connected to work despite its military significance and the nature of the threat facing the country. Work may have been indistinguishable from non-work for many hunter-gatherers; work may have been shot through with moral threads and traditional streamers for many pre-industrial and industrial workers; but for British women undertaking mundane but urgent assembly work in the 1940s work was not even primarily a means to an end, it was 'the blank patch between one brief evening and the next' (Mass Observation, 1943: 43). Eighty years earlier a favourite tale of the travelling journeymen of England was that relating to a workshop owned by one Davy Robinson. To ensure that his employees did not dawdle he prowled round his workshop 'shabbily dressed' and caught a new employee staring into space. ' "What are you looking for?" demanded Robinson. "Saturday night, you old varmint!" replied the man . . . Davy took to his heels and ran up to the shop, shouting out to his foreman, "Mills, Mills, here's a fellow looking for Saturday night, and it's only Thursday morning! Sack him! sack him!"' (Wright, 1867: 102).

Conclusion

Trying to summarise the experience of work over several millenia is one of my more difficult tasks. There is self-evidently so much material to cover that no text of conventional size would be able to deal adequately with the complexities of the situation. However, this chapter has been written on the assumption that some knowledge is preferable to complete ignorance, especially if to understand the present we have to situate it against the past, and it has tended to concentrate upon women to balance out the conventional preference for male history. The limited history that has been covered, focusing as it does on Britain until 1945, suggests that the complexity of the experience of work defies any simple assumptions about the significance of work or its relationships to non-work or its role in the development of modes of subordination and superordination. What perhaps can be salvaged from the past is not an objective model of what work has always been like, nor what it should be like, but rather a conclusion that illuminates the significance of the social. Work has been the medium of such a variety of forms and contents that its very diversity undermines universal propositions about work. While not wishing to argue that the history of work reveals an infinite anarchy of interpretations, such that work has been all things to all people, I would argue that work, like other institutions, is inherently and irreducibly constructed, interpreted and organized through social actions and social discourse. The implication of this is that no 'natural' form of work exists and no inevitable or necessary attitudes towards work are inscribed in the human psyche. The history of work suggests that the very meaning of work is something which has to be worked at; what is crucial is which individuals or groups or states secure the resources to have their own interpretation of work accepted as the legitimate interpretation. But control over the language of work does not ensure control over subordinates; the language of free markets and economic rationality may have gradually provided the dominant form of discourse through the process of industrialization but the prior moral economy of work remained to confound the capitalist visionaries. The pre-capitalist moral economy was not dismembered but overlain by the market economy where it served as a resource for all groups involved to legitimate their collective resistance and advance. Of course, whether such groups were successful or not is a separate issue: representing an issue as moral rather than economic does not guarantee that such representations are accepted. For example, many women and colonized peoples have resisted the representations of work made by men and colonizers, claiming the latter to be specious and unjustifiable; many such resisters found their cases 'not proved' and lived out their lives in poverty and slavery. Indeed, it is because of such historical acts and processes that contemporary work embodies lineages of the past: work today is not a prisoner of the past but it is a bruised descendant.

3

Classical Approaches to Work: Marx, Weber and Durkheim

And the Gods of the Copybook Headings said:
if you don't work you die.
Kipling *The Gods of the Copybook Headings*

Introduction

This chapter considers the classical approaches to work through the ideas of the 'gang of three': Marx, Weber and Durkheim. Marx, Weber and Durkheim are usually portrayed, in both an academic and a political sense, as being situated at alternate corners of a triangle: while Durkheim focused on, and sought to extend, social solidarity, integration and control, Marx concerned himself with social fragmentation, disintegration and conflict and Weber developed his theory of rationality and bureaucracy. Durkheim was of a social democratic orientation though he was seldom directly involved in politics except in the case of Dreyfus and in a more diffuse way as the supporter of the Third Republic against the vicissitudes of the French church and military. Marx, of course, was a revolutionary who railed against capitalism and actively promoted its overthrow. Weber, on the other hand, was a conservative liberal, anxious to preserve both the freedom of the individual and the sanctity of the German state, though his success as a sociologist was in sharp contrast to his failure as a politician. Both Marx and Durkheim adopted structural arguments that delimited the influence and impact of individuals upon society and social change. The structural approach of Durkheim was, in fact, far more rigid and consistent than that of Marx. Part of Durkheim's rigorous adherence to an anti-individualist methodology (as distinct from his support for ethical individualism) relates to his overarching concern to legitimate sociology as an academic discipline within French universities, in contrast to other social sciences, particularly psychology. For Marx, the issue of academic advancement was never pre-eminent and always subordinated to the needs of the proletarian revolution. Furthermore, Marx's arguments are neither simple nor coherent, and tensions between his early and late works, as well as between his theoretical and empirical texts, are discernible. Weber's individualist sociology was clearly demarcated from the approaches of Marx and Durkheim though, like the former, Weber's work does not form a coherent whole but is rather a collection of disparate, and sometimes incompatible, themes and ideas.

Marx and Capitalism

Alienation, Labour and Humanity

This is clearly not the place for a thorough review of the various interpretations of Marx (see Callinicos, 1983; Giddens, 1971; Kolakowski, 1978; Elster, 1985; Roemer (ed.), 1986) and the discussion will be limited to the essential features for our particular concerns.

One of the most significant distinctions between Marx and Durkheim lies in the former's disavowel of industrialization as the primary explanatory axis of society. Certainly, Marx considered industrial society to be both progressive in comparison to agrarian societies, and a necessary stage for the eventual triumph of human freedom, but the mainspring of this social formation was not the industrial process but its capitalist pattern. It is capitalism which is important because only capitalism, rather than industrialism, carries within it the seeds of its own destruction and the adumbration of what, to Marx at least, appeared to be the single viable non-exploitive alternative: communism.

Essentially, Marx's argument is that the human species is different from all other animal species, not because of its consciousness but because it alone produces its own means of subsistence (1970, 1975). This uniquely human attribute also provides the medium through which individuals can realise their true potential as humans: in short, the arena of productive activity, the world of work, incorporates the secret of human nature. But why does capitalism, rather than industrialism, deny humanity its quintessentiality, its 'species being'? Well, Marx is careful to distinguish between 'objectification' and 'alienation'. Objectification is the product of human labour on raw materials; it embodies the producer's creativity and yet remains separate from the producer. Thus some form of production is essential to humanity both in providing the material structure of social life and in facilitating the self-realization of individual potential. However, where the system of production is capitalist, that is where the means of production are owned by a minority, where the majority own only their labour power, and where production is for profit through a commodity market, the result is not objectification but alienation. Hence, the unique quality of human beings – their ability to produce their own means of existence, to actualize and realize their true, creative capacity through labour – is stultified and indeed inverted through capitalism.

Marx broke down the formulation of alienation into four conceptually discrete but empirically related spheres. The first facet of alienation is derived from the absence of control by the producer over the product. In the absence of control the product reduces, rather than expresses, the producer's humanity, and simultaneously sustains alienation by buttressing capitalism. The more workers expend themselves at work the weaker become their prospects of self-realization. Since products are designed and produced as profit maximizers, rather than for the satisfaction of human needs, capitalists are also alienated by capitalism but, since they gain materially from it, their alienation remains unconscious. The second aspect of alienation stems from the ever-increasing division of labour. This fragments the productive process into meaningless, and ostensibly unrelated, tasks such that the general orientation of labour to work is not one of creative liberation but instrumental and 'forced' labour. Note that for Marx this meaninglessness is an inherent feature of capitalism; for Durkheim the same meaninglessness is a transient phenomenon related to the pathological division of labour, not capitalism per se. The market economy and commodity exchange comprise the third facet of alienation, for they turn every productive group into competitors, setting individual against individual and reducing the social relations between people to economic exchanges of commodities. Finally, Marx asserts that the mindless repetition that typifies work under capitalism blurs the distinction between humanity and animality by destroying the creative content of production. In effect, objects designed for use by humans are transformed via the capitalist mode of production into commodities that dominate humans.

It is clear from this argument that Marx would have had little time for the assertions of Durkheim concerning the importance of *extending* the division of labour; the problem for Marx was how to reintegrate disparate skills, not how to further differentiate between them. As he wrote in *The German Ideology*, the division of labour ensures that each

> has a particular exclusive sphere of activity, which is forced upon him and from which he cannot escape. He is a hunter, a fisherman, a herdsman,

> or a critical critic, and must remain so if he does not want to lose his means of livelihood; while in communist society . . . it [is] possible to hunt in the morning, fish in the afternoon, rear cattle in the evening, criticize after dinner, just as I have a mind to, without ever becoming hunter, fisherman, herdsman or critic. (1970: 54)

Paradoxically, towards the end of Marx's work, in the third volume of *Capital*, he reconsidered this whole issue and argued that rather than human self-realization being necessarily limited to the realm of labour (and hence the need for multi-skilled individuals), the realm of human freedom actually existed: 'beyond the sphere of material production' (1981: 959). In sum, while Marx's early criticisms of the capitalist division of labour are similar to Durkheim's interpretation of the pathological division of labour, Marx's early alternative is for the reintegration of skills, while Durkheim's is for the expansion of specialization in line with individuals' 'natural' propensities. However, while Durkheim's position remains at this level, Marx's entire approach is reconstructed in his later work through the assumption that the arena of labour is no longer the sphere of freedom but remains the sphere of necessity, even under communism; true freedom occurs outside, not inside, the realm of labour (cf. Rattansi, 1981; Gorz, 1982, 1985).

Does this suggest that Marx accepted alienation would remain as an unfortunate but necessary aspect of work even under communism? This is difficult to say since Marx says so little about the future structure and form of communism, but there does seem to be an underlying contradiction within his criticism of alienation under capitalism. This does not concern the issue of operationalizing the concept of alienation: since, for Marx, alienation exists wherever capitalism exists, then the absence of empirical data concerning alienation is irrelevant. If alienation is not defined by the subjective experiences of workers but by the objective existence of capitalism, then the apparent satisfaction of workers at work is a manifestation of the depth of their alienation not their freedom from it. In fact the concept is one unsuited to empirical investigation.

Beyond this issue, though, is the problem of whether unalienated production is feasible. It is already apparent that Marx changed his mind on the importance of the sphere of production for individual freedom but without specifying the reasons for this switch. One unarticulated difficulty with Marx's early assumptions about unalienated production is the tension that remains between a productive system democratically controlled by the producers and a social system democratically controlled by its citizens. Since there is no logical reason to suppose that the interests of producers and citizens exactly coincide then the wishes of one or the other must prevail: society is either 'worker-controlled' or 'citizen-controlled', it is not self-evident how it can be both. Of course, some *degree* of both is plausible but Marx does not consider such a compromise and anyway this would necessarily imply that a degree of alienated activity remains. This is important because some Marxist approaches to the world of work embody a critical approach to capitalist methods that implicitly assume a utopian alternative. That is to say, that all the apparent or imputed ills of industrial society may be heaped upon its capitalist foundations when they may well be the effects of industrialized productive methods. This, of course, is precisely the issue dividing some of Marx's ideas from Durkheim's. It is also relevant to note here that contemporary green approaches to industrial society are seldom axiomatically compatible with Marxist approaches, and while Durkheim's can hardly be considered as a green perspective, given his enthusiasm for industrial growth, Marx does not fit easily in the founder's chair either (Spretnak and Capra, 1985).

Exploitation and the Capitalist Labour Process

If Marx's conceptualization of the alienating consequences of capitalism is both tension-ridden and at least partially flawed, his arguments within his later works, notably *Capital*, move from the field of philosophy to economics: from alienation to exploitation. What unites the early and late Marx is both the critical attacks upon capitalism, and, more importantly in this context, his focus upon the world of work as crucial to the explanation of social conflict and social change. It is crucial because *inter alia*: productive activity distinguishes humans from animals; it provides the medium for self-realization; under capitalism it distorts that very process; as a result of this distortion it generates social conflict; and, ultimately, it creates the means for the destruction of capitalism and the development of communist society – the revolutionary proletariat. What is significant in this for the sociology of work is not simply the focus upon work but the assertion of an inherent spawning of conflict between opposing interests and the concomitant requirement for methods of capitalist control.

How does Marx arrive at the conclusion that work in capitalist society is inherently conflictual and requires forms of industrial coercion? In brief, he begins by accepting Ricardo's (1951: chapter 1, section 1) argument that the exchange value of a product is determined by the quantity of labour necessary to produce it. An earlier argument by Locke (1960: 329) had similarly argued that property could only be legitimated through the intermixing of labour. However, neither Ricardo nor Locke confronted the possibility of exploitive wage labour because both argued that the rewards of wage labour were exactly equivalent to the value of labour added to the product. Where Marx differed was in his assumption that the very existence of the profitable employment of wage labour implied a disjunction between the exchange value of commodities and the exchange of labour for wages. Hence exploitation, the disequilibrium between work and wages, engendered by the relationship between employer and employee, must exist. Indeed, recognition of exploitation can only be evaded by assuming that the rewards of labour are exactly equivalent to the value of that labour added to the end product. Marx's position is that while it is labour that determines the exchange values of commodities, the exchange of labour for wages is not reciprocally balanced. In fact, what is exchanged is not labour at all, but labour *power*: the capacity to work. Thus while orthodox accounts regard labour as just one more commodity, and therefore encapsulated within simple exchange relations, Marx asserts three counter-points: first, labour is not just an inanimate commodity and cannot therefore be reduced to simple exchange relations; second, the commodity exchanged – labour power – is not the equivalent of that entering the labour process – labour; third, that the consumption of labour power does not take place within the sphere of circulation, or market, at a fair exchange, but within the sphere of production, the 'hidden abode of production', under conditions of gross inequality (1954: 172). This obscuring of exploitation made it appear 'natural and inevitable' while Marx regarded it as merely temporary and socially constructed.

It was this 'hidden abode' that both distinguished capitalism from prior social formations and resulted in the conflicting and contradictory interests of employers and employees. Under feudalism the surplus produced by the peasantry was appropriated in kind by the ruling class: 'surplus labour' was visibly exploited. But under capitalism the surplus produced by the proletariat and appropriated by capitalists, 'surplus value', was invisible exploitation that occurred through the labour process itself. In effect, the difference between the workers' wages and the value of their productive activity provided the surplus value, which, when realized in commodity exchanges, became transformed into profits; since the exchange involved in wage labour was inequitable, the relationship between capital and labour was exploitive.

Four points are noteworthy from this analysis. First, despite its poor utility as a price theory (for it implies that inefficiently made commodities with considerable labour costs are exchanged at higher prices than those with lower labour costs), Marx's labour theory of value does have considerable merit in demonstrating that the relationship between exchanges, prices and values is not merely a quantitative economic one, but embodies social relations too. Second, because the capitalist only purchased the potential for labour, not a predefined quantity of products or effort, some mechanism of managerial control was essential in transforming labour power into labour. Third, because the wage labour relationship was inherently exploitive, the interests of labour and capital are considered to be necessarily antagonistic. Indeed, it is because the sphere of work generates exploitation not self-realization, and because this sphere is potentially the embodiment of all that is uniquely human, that Marx, and most Marxists, regard the exploitation based on class to be more important than exploitation based on gender or ethnic origin etc; a point of considerable controversy. Fourth, Marx's analysis suggests that because capitalism is a system grounded in the imperatives of economic competition, the administrative machinery and policies of capital are determined by these market forces not by the individual wishes of capitalists: thus the motivations of individuals are irrelevant (1954: 555).

Using this framework Marx then distinguishes between three types of production: co-operation, manufacture and machinofacture. There is some doubt as to whether Marx considered these three within an evolutionary, or an analytic, typology but the controversy need not detain us here (Berg, 1979: 110; Friedman, 1977: 13, 19). Under co-operation a simple division of labour ensured a greater quantity of production and merely the 'formal subordination of labour'. That is, although labour was bound to work exclusively for capital, because it was excluded from ownership of the means of production and could not consume the commodities it produced, none the less it retained a degree of independent power. This power was founded upon the irreplaceable skill that provided the material base for labour's control of the labour process; capitalist control was therefore restricted to the economic sphere. While the technological apparatus of production remained relatively simple and static, any increase in exploitation invariably manifested itself in the guise of expanding 'absolute' surplus value – by lengthening the hours of work, for example. With 'manufacture' the beginnings of the 'detail labourer' appear as the pre-existing 'natural', or social, division of labour into different trades is systematically extended such that each worker produces only a fraction of the total product. This stage also witnesses the growth of factories, as workers are brought together to facilitate the necessary reintegration of the specialized skills of the 'collective labourer' in the beginnings of the 'specifically capitalist mode of production' (Brighton Labour Process Group, 1977: 10). At this juncture machinery is introduced, initially within the parameters of 'manufacture' and ultimately this develops into 'machinofacture' and the 'real subordination of labour'. Under this, any remaining element of control by the workers over the labour process is dissolved, and they are collectively reduced to mere appendages of machines (Marx, 1954: part IV).

The reverberations of this development set the scene for Marx's subsequent analysis. First, deskilling becomes a universal phenomenon that simultaneously turns the workers into 'crippled monstrosities', cheapens labour, inhibits workers' upward mobility and homogenizes them as a class, uniting them in their exploitation by, and opposition towards, capitalism. Second, a wage hierarchy is established to fragment opposition to capitalism. This implies, paradoxically, that deskilling is not a comprehensive effect, and thus real subordination can never be achieved completely. This is inevitably the case since, as Marx argues elsewhere, coercive economic laws that force capitalists constantly to revolutionize the technology of production also require the development of new skills with their consequential leverage over the labour process (1954: 331–8). Third, technology facilitates the breaking of strikes, immunizes production from the problem of labour turnover, concentrates decision making, and most importantly, the physical control of labour itself is no longer derived from any legal, moral or economic force alone but is actually inscribed upon the productive process itself. Fourth, because of the greater technical efficiency of new machinery, the labour time necessary to produce commodities is decreased through a rise in the production of 'relative surplus value'. And finally comes the 'creation of that monstrosity, an industrial reserve army kept in misery in order to be always at the disposal of capital' (1954: 457).

A particularly striking motif running through Marx's analysis here is that of autonomous technical development, where technology itself inaugurates various forms of social change and, in some senses, can be used as a measure of social development; a productivist perspective directly opposed to the contemporary green view but symmetrical with capitalist, social democratic and conventional Marxist, and especially Bolshevik, attitudes to economic growth (Anthony, 1977: 138–45; Sirianni, 1982: 245–60).

It is also apparent that Marx appears confused over the role of management within advanced capitalist factories: at one point he considers them to be inherently authoritarian as they strain to retain control of an evermore belligerent workforce, yet since control is inscribed into the technology of production at this point it is difficult to see the necessity for such control strategies. This assumption of increasing despotism is not simply an empirical issue but actually manifests a political lacuna in Marx concerning the issue of 'freedom' in free wage labour. According to Marx this freedom is merely freedom to sell labour power and freedom from having anything else to sell; it is, therefore, a bourgeois sham. But, as Giddens (1981: 220–6) has argued, the freedom of free wage labour also implies that labour cannot be physically coerced into work and is thus free to organize resistance through trade unions etc. Of course, Marx recognized the existence and importance of trade unions and in his empirical works, such as the analysis of the British Factory Acts, was clearly aware that the alleged despotism of the factory was heavily circumscribed by forces other than those directly devolved from capital itself (1954: 264–80). Nevertheless, Marx does systematically underestimate the possibility that management may also need to organize consent as well as coercion (Burawoy, 1979: 27).

The reconceptualization of capitalist management as necessarily involved in consent construction also suggests that Marx's zero-sum theory of power is inadequate: while the interests of labour and capital are not coincident, the assumption that they are irreconcilably, and diametrically, antagonistic is misleading. Part of the explanation for the difficulty with Marx here lies at the level of analysis: while Marx's theory concerns the irreconcilable interests of social classes at a macro-level, this abscures the very real way in which, at the level of the enterprise, the interests of employees and employers may be very tightly intertwined. Marx's constant reassertion of the salience of class interests at the macro-level makes the theory particularly difficult to apply to discrete empirical cases (Tomlinson, 1982: 11–46).

Capitalism and Class

This difficulty is exacerbated by Marx's dual theory of class. His concept of classes, which perceives them to be aggregates of individuals in the same relationship to the means of production, does not change: all owners of capital are capitalists, while those who own only their labour are proletarians. However, Marx does provide contradictory statements as to the historical development of the class structure: in *The Communist Manifesto* (Marx and Engels, 1968: 41–5) the class structure is polarizing; in the *Theories of Surplus Value* (1969: 573) the middle classes are expanding and consolidating their intermediate position. Exactly which of these theories is the one Marx would have preferred is difficult to say, for his work in this area effectively ended just as he was about to embark upon a major study of class. Nevertheless, it is appropriate to reiterate the point that Marx was not a reclusive academic but an active revolutionary, and the Manifesto was written as a polemical call to the barricades on the eve of the 1848 revolutions, not a scholarly text. Once the 1848 revolutions had failed Marx obviously had to reassess his assumptions and, in the light of more detailed empirical work, seemed to distance himself from the early claims to class polarization.

Rather more important than the nature of empirical trends is the radical breakthrough contained within Marx's theoretical approach to class. The innovative nature of Marx's theories actually lies not with the descriptive value of his analysis but with the causal explanation; in particular, Marx differentiates himself from the contemporary 'revenue' theories of class. These revenue theories took the levels and origin of income, and symbolic reward derived from the market, as the criteria for class construction, not the pattern of ownership of the means of production. But, argued Marx, this implied that the market itself was a pre-existing, natural, and therefore neutral, feature of society. For Marx, nothing could be further from the truth because the market itself was constructed upon the pre-existing relations of ownership and non-ownership of the means of production. It was not that the market had no impact upon the class structure but that the market was generated by a particular class structure. In turn, this meant that equality of opportunity in the market was not as significant as, and was actively undermined by, pre-market inequalities. Moreover, Marx's primary criticism of capitalism was not that it created an inegalitarian society; all societies would be inegalitarian to some extent. In the first phase of post-capitalist society, or socialism, Marx argued that rewards would have to relate to effort, not need; in the second, or communist, stage a form of positive discrimination would prevail where rewards were distributed according to need, not effort. Neither of these stages is inherently egalitarian. Rather, Marx's claim was that capitalism was inherently alienating and exploitative. Hence, to increase the level of rewards or even to provide equality of opportunity, does not, in itself, eradicate alienation or exploitation; thus a class structure of exploiters and exploited remains impervious to the manipulation of levels of material and symbolic reward. In political terms this meant that trade union actions to secure employment or boost wages and conditions did nothing to root out the cause of the proletariat's condition, it simply provided a temporary anaesthetic for the symptoms of spiritual degradation and material poverty.

This qualitative gulf separating the two major classes also explains the antagonistic, rather than simply competitive, relationship between them. This does not mean that mortal combat was a pervasive feature of the relationship, because although the system was inevitably exploitative, as already discussed, the system also obscured the reality of exploitation through the opaqueness of the labour process. Consequently, Marx distinguished between a class 'in itself', where the objective conditions generated a class, irrespective of the attitudes of the members, and a class 'for itself', where the objective conditions facilitated the creation of a conscious solidarity amongst a class in opposition to another class. Exactly how this revolutionary class consciousness is generated is the subject of considerable controversy (Giddens, 1973: 112–17), but basically Marx assumes that class consciousness corresponds to the stage of material production such that: 'it is not the consciousness of men that determines their being, but, on the contrary, their social being determines their consciousness' (1973a: 504). This can be interpreted to mean either that class consciousness is *determined* by material forces or that it is *constrained* by them. Either way it is still the case that Marx sees consciousness as being more influenced by social being than vice versa. This correspondence principle is, then, associated with the revolutionary activities of the proletariat, though the link between an ideology controlled by the ruling class, which facilitates the manipulation of the proletariat through false consciousness, and a revolutionary class of proletarians, freed from the taint of capitalist ideology, is a leap of imagination as much as anything else, as Lukács (1971) and Lenin (1970) implicitly suggested by their own attempts to resolve the practicalities of revolutionary action. What neither Lukács nor Lenin does, of course, is to question the general theoretical approach of Marx: the primacy of economic relations. As a result, economic exploitation at the point of production is ensconced as the critical field for social analysis and political activity. In effect, class conflict predetermines all other forms of social conflict, in particular that based on gender, ethnic or national considerations. Concomitantly, the elimination of class conflict, in theory at least, simultaneously destroys the material base for these other social conflicts to the extent that the institutions necessary for mediating various forms of conflict are unnecessary. In political terms such an interpretation induces the 'end of politics': an apparent utopia that actually germinates the seeds of dictatorship (Held, 1987; Johnston, 1986; Polan, 1984).

Conclusion

In terms of the sociology of work the impact of Marx is considerable: his illumination of the essentially political nature of the employment relationship and the material base for industrial conflict still supplies one of the elementary building blocks for an analysis of employment. However, the exclusivist approach to economic exploitation at the point of production precludes, or at best subordinates, both analysis of the links between home and work, and forms of exploitation other than those based on class. In short, what Marx helped to do was stimulate the very idea of a sociological approach to work but delimit the scope to the sociology of the factory. Finally, following Merleau-Ponty, we should treat Marx as a classic: an intermediary we need if we are to progress beyond him. Even if we do reject his ideas we can only go beyond him *because of them*, rather than in spite of them.

Durkheim and Industrial Society

Emile Durkheim's contribution to the sociology of work is fundamentally derived from *The Division of Labour* and his discussion of 'anomie'. Written as his doctoral thesis, at a time when sociology hardly existed in

France, *The Division of Labour* grapples with the issue of social solidarity and cohesion during a time of rapid social and economic transition. In essence, Durkheim suggests that the popular assumptions of the time concerning the imminent collapse of social life, in response to the ever increasing division of labour and general urbanization of life, were not just exaggerated but actually wrong. Thus, although Tonnies claimed that modern society was disintegrating under the transition to industrial life, represented by the transition from *gemeinschaft* or 'community' forms of society to *gesellschaft* or 'societal' forms representing mere 'associations' where solidarity was disintegrating, Durkheim retorted that rather than being dismantled, solidarity was simply being reconstructed in a different form. Similarly, while Simmel (1971) asserted that the intensity of nervous stimulation in modern urban society was such that individuals would be forced to retreat into their own private worlds, Durkheim argued that modern industrial society actively freed people from isolation by inducing mutual dependence through the increasing division of labour.

Even Spencer, whose optimistic approach to social change through evolutionary development Durkheim would have partially accepted, failed to recognize the critical significance of the social nature of life. For Spencer the free reign of egoism and laissez faire propagated, by means of natural selection, the best of all possible worlds, but for Durkheim only collective solidarity and morality could furnish the necessary foundations for individual freedom: ethical individualism not psychological egoism was the key to progress for Durkheim, and this key lay buried within the increasing division of labour. Of course, Durkheim recognized the difficulty of reconciling the apparent impending decline of moral order at the turn of the century; an atavistic response to the problems of change which he loosely labelled 'anomie': a situation where the prevailing morality disintegrated to leave an anarchy of selfishness, rather than a pluralism of difference. However, this was a temporary problem for the future held out the prospect of combining individualism *and* social solidarity.

In sharp contrast to what Durkheim perceived to be the reactionary perspectives, he regarded pre-industrial social solidarity to be derived not from the liberatory aspects of any mythical independent yeomanry, but from the rather suffocating effects of uniformity of experience and thought. In such cultures individuals were integrated into society through the *collective conscience*, but that very integration was at the direct expense of individuality. This symmetry of life Durkheim called *mechanical solidarity* in contrast to the *organic solidarity* manifest in the contemporary individualism engendered under the increasing division of labour. There is, then, no necessary correlation between increased specialization and decreasing solidarity, though Durkheim maintained that 'abnormal' forms of the division of labour still persisted and brought with them problems for the production and reproduction of the necessary degrees of social solidarity. Of these abnormal forms two were particularly important: the 'anomic' and the 'forced' division of labour.

The anomic form referred to the meaninglessness of work: a transient form generated between the collapse of mechanical solidarity and the creation of organic solidarity. During this phase new norms of behaviour had yet to be diffused throughout society and were exacerbated by the apparent de-skilling of work manifest in the factory system where workers were constrained to meaningless operations on products that they could hardly envisage and for consumers they would never know. As the norms of behaviour spread, and what Durkheim believed to be the unbridled anarchy of the free market dwindled under social regulation, the anomic division of labour would disappear. However, Durkheim also warned that mere construction of consensually grounded goals and meanings without the concomitant provision of opportunities to achieve such goals would extend the period under which anomie prevailed: an interpretation of industrial, and for that matter social, life which was to prove influential in the ideas of some of Britain's foremost scholars of the industrial scene over sixty years later (Fox and Flanders, 1969). Indeed, in the second edition of *The Division of Labour* (1902) Durkheim's optimism about the spontaneous generation of a normal division of labour had been replaced by his assumption that 'corporations', or occupational associations that bridged the gap between trade unions and employer associations, would form a prerequisite mediating institution between individuals and the state. This is important because Durkheim's suggestion is that without some form of institutionalized dispute resolution at work, anomie is likely to prevail.

The forced division of labour occurred when existing patterns of inequality failed to mirror what Durkheim took to be the normal or inevitable distribution of personal inequalities. Thus, the advantages of the normal division of labour would be found 'only if society is constituted in such a way that social inequalities exactly express natural inequalities' (1933: 377). Durkheim, then, was not an egalitarian but a supporter of meritocracy induced, amongst other things, by the eradication of personal inheritance. As he put it: 'there cannot be rich and poor at birth without there being unjust contracts' (1933: 384). His assumptions about 'natural' inequalities do have to be critically assessed: he regarded industrial workers as more intelligent than farmers, and men as more intelligent than women, using the flimiest of empirical evidence. He also assumed that the gender-based domestic division of labour was a good example of the social harmony generated when social inequalities were allowed to mirror 'natural' inequalities. Yet the 'naturally' affective functions of women and the 'naturally' intellectual functions of men also provided a case where Durkheim's own uncertainty about gender relations provoked the beginnings of a critique of patriarchy. For: 'Although by constitution woman are predisposed to a life different from man . . . if these differences make possible the division of labour they do not necessitate it . . . for specialized activities to result they must be developed and organized' (1933: 264–5). In short, Durkheim suggests that only when 'predispositions' are buttressed by social organization do they become enacted.

Both meaninglessness and unjustifiable inequalities pose threats to the cohesion of contemporary society but few of the orthodox solutions to these issues satisfied Durkheim. The laissez-faire approach of free marketeers simply compounded the difficulties generated by both issues: inheritance was buttressed by liberal notions of individual freedom and the same philosophical position undermined any attempt to construct *social* norms that would regulate individual behaviour by providing regulated codes of conduct. In reality, argued Durkheim, such egotism posed a very grave threat to society since it stimulated individual desires and greed that were uncontrollable because they were inherently infinite. Only social regulation provided the resolution of social problems but this does not imply that Durkheim was favourably inclined towards Marx's ideas. Although a professed socialist, Durkheim considered the methodological assumptions of economic determination in Marxism to be overly restrictive, while Marx's solution to the crisis of capitalism was too dependent upon the state and yet paradoxically too limited in its concern for regulation. That is, he argued that, first, the state was too far removed from the everyday experience of individuals and hence mediating organizations or corporations would form the primary mode of social organization. Second, Marx's assumptions about the determining role of the economy prevented him from assessing the need for all institutions to be regulated, not just economic ones. It was, therefore, morally grounded and socially regulated institutions coupled with an ever widening division of labour that facilitated the development of individual skill which would ultimately create the future utopia: evolution not revolution; regulation not anarchy; solidarity through individualism and mutual dependence not conformity through uniformity.

Equally important here, it should be noted that Durkheim's critique of scholars and contemporary society that he regarded as reactionary was aimed not at the essence of capitalism but at industrialism. It was the case that Durkheim railed against the injustice of private inheritance and the inequities of unjustified inequalities but, although he died only a week after the Bolshevik revolution in Russia and had, therefore, no experience of state socialist states, he had little doubt that a revolutionary approach to social change, of the kind envisaged by Lenin and Marx, would fail to resolve the problems facing society. Certainly, Durkheim was no lover of capitalism but the transcendence of the ills of capitalist societies had to be through the forces unleashed by industrialization embodied in the division of labour, not through the political machinations of a minority of self-appointed, professional revolutionaries. Industrialization had spawned the promise of salvation and simultaneously generated some very unhealthy reactions, but the remedy lay in reconstructing the pattern of the original seed, not in the destruction of the soil. For Weber, however, as indeed for Marx, the original pattern displayed fault lines that boded ill for the future.

Weber

The third member of the founding 'gang of three' was Max Weber. His work is often assumed to be a dialogue with the ghost of Marx, though most of his dialogue was with contemporary Marxists rather than with the works of Marx himself – many of which were not published during Weber's lifetime. Weber's contribution to the sociology of work lies in several rather disparate fields: first, his theory of social stratification; second, his interpretative methodology; third, his arguments concerning the rise of rationality, the nature of bureaucracy and the form of bureaucratic control. In some sense all three substantive areas embrace criticisms of Marxist perspectives.

Class and Stratification

It has also to be stated that there is much of common belief between Marx and Weber. In terms of Weber's approach to social stratification it is apparent that both accepted the significance of property ownership: it was for Weber the 'basic category' and determinant of class position. Yet, argued Weber, Marx was wrong to assume that the different components of stratification – in particular class, status and party – were necessarily coterminous when, in Weber's view, they were actually contingently related. This contingent aspect also extended to Weber's analysis of the relationship between class position and class consciousness. Rather than assuming that a proletariat without class consciousness must be suffering from the delusions of false consciousness, Weber asserted that the complex, multi-dimensional and cross-cutting nature of social stratification necessarily inhibited the acquisition of class consciousness. Much more likely was the creation of status groups with a degree of political or corporate consciousness that would thrust them to the forefront of political activity. This fragmented stratification system, in conjunction with the essentially subjective nature of understanding, meant that the proletarian revolution predicted by Marx was extremely unlikely.

But what was the theoretical premise upon which Weber launched his critique of Marx? Well it is closely associated with the revenue theories that Marx was so disparaging about: for Weber, a class existed when a number of individuals had a significant component of their life chances determined by their power within an economic order (1978: 302–7, 926–39). This indicates that classes are unambiguously economic and closely related to, if not identical with, market situations. Weber then goes on to distinguish between three types of class: property classes, commercial or acquisition classes, and social classes. Note here that, because Weber relates class to market situation, anyone without access to the market is restricted to a status group not a class; thus slaves, individuals with unpaid domestic duties, and even the long-term unemployed, are written out of Weber's class analysis and relocated within the status system. It is also evident that Weber provides no theoretical criteria for distinguishing between classes but simply assesses the general empirical distinctions of occupations; as such there can be no theoretical limit to the number of classes which exist, for there are as many classes as there are different occupations. The details of these groups need not detain us here but it is significant that Weber explicitly denies a link between property classes and political consciousness: property classes are, in this sense, non-dynamic. This is self-evidently counter to Marx's arguments and can hardly be considered as evidence of the importance Weber allegedly allocates to this 'basic category'.

Weber's third form of class, social class, is occupationally based and distinguishes between the Working Class of labour sellers; the Lower Middle Class of small shopkeepers etc.; the Intelligentsia with little property but technical qualifications; and, finally, the Privileged Class who owe their superordinate position to property ownership or education or both. Weber actually doubts whether many identical class situations exist but insists that all are derived from market situation. Thus, in the absence of materially resemblant situations, there is little possibility of collective class action. This is not to say that Weber refutes all possibility of class action but he does reject Marx's argument that seems to impute interests to social classes. In contrast, Weber asserts that the actual interests of specific classes must be studied empirically and this requires a distinction between two forms of social action: communal action, such as that undertaken by trade unions in defence of sacked colleagues, and societal action designed to reconstruct the general distribution of life chances, such as that manifested by socialist political parties. This distinction is significant because Weber locks the likelihood of social action to the transparency of the connections between the causes and the consequences of the class situation. Not only does a group have to be collectively aware of its unjust situation, but it also has to be in a position to resolve the perceived problem. For these reasons Weber believed that groups like trade unions in factories, where the physical constraints of production facilitated union organization, leadership and control, were best placed to demonstrate class-oriented social action.

Nevertheless, Weber generally assumed that, outside periods of economic or political crisis, class action would be minimal. Instead, the norm would be action undertaken by status groups. Status, the distribution of social honour or social esteem, despite its tendency to correlate highly with class, was not determined by it, nor was the influence unidirectional. In fact, Weber argued that because markets were determined by impersonal forces, status considerations were of high value within capitalist societies. Usually status was determined by lifestyle, formal education, and hereditary or occupational prestige. Status groups were not indentical with class groups but Weber believed that the greater homogeneity of status groups provided them with a stronger claim to social action. Furthermore, this homogeneity was actively reproduced by the exclusionary practices of members. A difficulty here is differentiating status from class: indeed, since the correlations between the two are usually so close it could well be argued that class provides the material wherewithal for the provision of status symbols. Thus status may not be as independent of class as Weber maintains. On the other hand, it would seem that in some circumstances status is more influential than, and independent of, class. For example, it may well be the case that membership of an ethnic minority or gender group is more influential for the determination of life chances than class position. In sum, it may be that in some circumstances class is more relevant as the explanatory variable, while in other circumstances status orientations are crucial.

Weber spends little time in analysing the position of women through the category of status group, even though it clearly lends itself to such an interpretation. In fact, like Marx and Durkheim, Weber was generally uninterested in women's subordinate position at work or in society generally. Although relatively liberal in his support for the political emancipation of women in Germany, Weber, like Durkheim, regarded them as 'naturally' fitted for domestic responsibilities and failed to link the patriarchal domination of employment organizations with the patriarchal construction of society. Such a lacuna necessarily leaves Weber's corpus of work, like that of Marx and Durkheim, significantly flawed.

The final aspect of Weber's trilogy of power was the party. While classes fought over economic issues, and status groups contested the distribution of social honour, parties – which were oriented towards the acquisition of social power – operated at all levels and across all boundaries of class and status. The actual divisions between all three are notoriously slippery, though Weber implies that parties attempt to reconstruct the status quo, while class and status groups generally reflect the status quo.

Methodology

It is important to remember at this juncture that although Weber often wrote in terms of such collectivities as classes and status groups etc., he categorically denied the structural approach of both Marx and Durkheim, which seemed to him to relegate the role of the individual to the proverbial cog in a giant wheel. In contrast, Weber argued that all social collectivities and phenomena had to be reducible to their individual constituents: only individuals thought and acted; no group mind or behaviour existed above and beyond the sum of individuals' thoughts and actions. This assumption was critical because Weber's approach posits that individual interpretation was an inherent aspect of human knowledge. As such, sociology became a study of social collectivities explicable only through individual interpretaion, and, moreover, a distinction had to be drawn between externally visible 'behaviour' and 'action' that required interpretation of intentions. Weber did not argue that intentions always led to specific outcomes but he did assert that identical forms of behaviour could be based upon divergent intentions. This 'interpretative method' or *verstehen* was clearly different from the observational methods used by 'natural' science, primarily because sociologists, and social scientists more generally, faced a thinking subject whose subjective understanding was the secret to explaining action. Perhaps one of the clearest examples in this field is the distinction between wandering around town as a pleasurable experience during a vacation, and undertaking exactly the same 'behaviour' as an expression of boredom through unemployment. The difference between leisure and unemployment is difficult to explain at the level of observation and requires interpretative understanding for a more convincing analysis.

Inevitably this approach has its own difficulties. In particular the approach is conditional upon individuals being consciously aware of what they are doing. Interpretative understanding also depends upon a level of a priori understanding that Weber himself limits to a rather restricted vision of 'normality'. That is, Weber argues that sociologists can only interpret behaviour in so far as it is within the sociologists' sphere of normal action and behaviour. Quite where this leaves the anthropological approach to alien cultures is uncertain since to treat all aspects of culture as 'alien', that is requiring interpretation in the first instance, is something which Weber's method cannot accommodate.

Weber also distances himself from the more positivist approaches of Marx and Durkheim on the issue of external, objective reality. Durkheim, especially, laid great emphasis on the objective nature of external reality and its impact upon individuals but Weber, while accepting the existence of regularities in the social world, denied the presence of social 'laws'. Hence Weber's creation of the 'ideal type': a theoretical abstraction, an artificial and one-sided extrapolation of important traits or characteristics that simultaneously suppresses unimportant traits. This ideal type was neither ideal nor typical. That is, it was not ideal in any evaluative sense, since Weber's argument seeks to extrapolate significant existing realities, rather than impose normative or projective forms. Indeed, Weber was very suspicious of those who sought to impose their own truth upon others since he regarded reality as ultimately meaningless, and thus no moral position could be scientifically accredited; though he was a staunch defender of liberalism and the interests of the German state. Nor was an ideal type typical because it did not represent any norm or average form but merely a one-sided exaggeration. Its use, then, was purely as a heuristic theoretical device to facilitate the measurement of reality and the comparison of empirical forms.

Capitalism and Rationalization

Despite Weber's scepticism concerning any transcendent meaning to life or any historical patterns to it, he was convinced that contemporary society was increasingly grounded in the symbolic and material advance of rationality. What did he mean by this term? The principle physical manifestations took three related forms: capitalism, rational jurisprudence and bureaucracy. However, the essence of the concept consisted of three facets: secularization, calculability and the growth of ethics orientated to means, not ends. The rise of rationality meant, in short, the decline of magical interpretations and explanations of the world, and the gradual elimination of all mysteries, as science exploded more and more mythical assumptions. It also meant the replacement of 'affective' and 'traditional' action with 'rational' action: we no longer undertook activities because that was how things had always been done, nor because we had emotional reasons for doing it. Instead we did things because we calculated that the benefits outweighed the cost, or because we assessed the action as the most efficient way to achieve our goals. Human actions were also constrained by rational rules now. Not that they had previously been completely unconstrained but historically the rules guiding us had been religious or derived from the force of tradition. Now we obeyed rules because they appeared to be built upon rational principles and common sense, and the foremost example of this form of authority was, of course, bureaucracy.

Weber was clear that bureaucracies pre-dated the rise of capitalism, notably in the 'patrimonial' bureaucracies of the Roman, Byzantine and Egyptian empires. But these were not structured around the rational principles of free contract, fixed salaries and delimited spheres of competence. Though Weber never formally defined bureaucracy he did provide an extensive analysis of the necessary principles of legitimacy, authority and selection. It is not essential here to repeat Weber's description of the principles at length (see Albrow, 1970: 40–5; Beetham, 1987; Pollitt, 1986), but the crucial elements involve: an abstract, legal code of conduct; individual spheres of competence structured within a hierarchy of offices; the non-ownership of offices; selection and promotion through qualifications and proven ability; fixed salaries, and a pension and security of tenure for all office holders (Weber, 1978: 217–21). The essential points of bureaucracy, then, are twofold. First, it was 'legal' in that it operated on the basis of procedures that could be adjudged correct or otherwise through resort to a body of rules by those subject to its authority. Second, it was 'rational' because it operated on the principles of expert knowledge and calculability.

It was upon these twin foundations that bureaucracy began its allegedly inexorable rise to power, though Weber limits the utility of bureaucracy to the requirement for legal rational administration rather than the desire for a universally efficient form of administration. In fact, Weber was by no means oblivious to the potential distortions likely to befall organizations administered through bureaucracies, particularly where red tape or sectional control undermined their rational hierarchical control in the interests of the whole. Yet a whole series of empirical case studies has suggested that the existence of rules does not determine their execution, nor are subordinates unaware of the value of utilising rules to protect themselves from superordinates, either through control over upward flowing information or by failing to select appropriate rules in 'working to rule' (Merton, 1957: 50–4; Crozier, 1964: 187; Batstone, 1979: 262; Mitchell and Parris, 1983).

Clearly, then, Weberian bureaucracies are not simply the harbingers of top-down omnipotent control but, rather, they bring in their wake problems of control as well as enabling powers. In sum, bureaucratic control does not appear to be unambiguously effective. It is, however, not part of Weber's claim that the legitimation of authority through bureaucratic administration is, by itself, sufficient for the control of subordinates (cf. Littler, 1982: 37). Weber, like Marx, actually assumed that industrial control in market economies required an essential degree of economic need as well as normative acceptance of a work ethic and bureaucratic authority. The main reason for such a panoply of control measures lies in the expropriation of the workforce (including management in some circumstances) from ownership of the means of production. This expropriation is deemed necessary because individual control militates against co-ordinated social production, and because managerially controlled enterprises offer stricter controls over recruitment, discipline and investment (Weber, 1978: 130–7, 152). It has to be admitted, though, that Weber also accepts that the strongest incentive to work is individual ownership and control, though producer co-operatives avoid the contradictory interests that inhibit production in conventional capitalist enterprises.

Weber's explanation for the rise of capitalism in the West is closely related to the generation of new modes of work incentive. As made clear in the previous chapter, work patterns tend to be governed by normatively inscribed human needs. Since human needs are socially constructed they are also transient and flexible; thus pre-capitalist working hours were often far more limited than those which currently exist. Weber claimed that the inauguration of a new attitude to work, the generation of cultural change in which work became a means of demonstrating godliness, was linked to the rise of Calvinism and that this cultural change was associated with the rise of rational capitalism itself. Capitalism, in some form, had probably always existed *qua* 'booty capitalism' practised by hundreds of invading armies etc., or in the form of 'pariah capitalism' in which an alien group provided financial assistance to those groups prevented from such activities by their cultural or religious beliefs. The early Christian outlawing of money lending and the proximity of Jewish money lenders to Christian businesses is one such example.

Rational capitalism, however, is associated with the Protestant arm of the Christian church, and Weber sought an explanation in the beliefs and actions of Calvinists in his work *The Protestant Ethic and the Spirit of Capitalism* (1976). With the Calvinist doctrine of predestination, manifest in the acquisition of a state of 'grace' by the chosen few, Weber argued that the orientation of Calvinists to work was quite different from their Catholic or non-Christian contemporaries. While Catholics, according to Weber, believed they could secure their place in heaven through, amongst other things, 'good works' on behalf of the poor on earth, Calvinists believed that their predestined future left them with no means of knowing or altering their ultimate destination. This uncertainty led Calvinists to search for signs of 'election' by God and to assume that worldly success could be taken as a manifestation of 'grace', though obviously not as a means of achieving 'grace'. However, although Calvinists were now persuaded that material success, including business enterprise, was something that should be pursued with all possible vigour, their ascetic lifestyles prevented them from consuming the results of material success. Thus Calvinists were coerced by their beliefs into reinvesting their profits rather than dissipating them in consumptive behaviour. The result was the establishment of a group of people with radically new work ethics: they had to work, literally all hours that God sent, to demonstrate their state of grace but because they were forced to reinvest almost all their profits they very quickly became evermore successful capitalists. Of course, the development of rational capitalism had not been their intention; they intended to serve God but ended up serving mammon. Indeed,

Weber's thesis of rationalization is again brought into play as the very material success of capitalism gradually undermines the Calvinism, and eventually Christianity, which was associated with its birth. The word 'association' rather than 'cause' is significant here because it is not clear whether Weber's argument suggests that the cultural changes inspired by Calvinism were causally associated with the rise of capitalism or just contingently related through the 'elective affinity' between the two phenomena (Parkin, 1982). Either way, Weber's point is that the generation of rational capitalism, contrary to Marx, cannot be explained through wholly material and structural forces.

Inevitably, Weber's claims have been subject to considerable attack and equally determined defence (Marshall, 1982; Ray, 1987). First, his evidence of the actual behaviour of Calvinists is drawn primarily from the ideas of Baxter, a Calvinist preacher, rather than from an empirical investigation of Calvinist capitalists. Second, the earliest examples of rational capitalism are not restricted to Calvinist or even Protestant nations, with some Calvinist countries, such as Scotland, failing to 'take off' and some Catholic nations, such as Belgium and several Italian city states, being amongst the market leaders. Third, it is not self-evident why Calvinists, faced with the salvation anxiety, should adopt material success as the manifestation of grace: charitable acts have a much stronger tradition in early Christianity than making money has. Fourth, the ascetic lifestyles of Calvinist capitalists face a significant problem because the system is dependent upon non-ascetic consumers. Either the only Calvinists who were ascetic were the capitalists or large-scale trading with non-Calvinist nations must have sprung up to accommodate the flow of commodities. Indeed, this regional aspect is also important in highlighting the point that most of the successful early capitalist economies were geographically beyond easy control by the Catholic church (Mann, 1986).

Whatever the problems of Weber's interpretation of the significance of cultural features for the generation of rational capitalism it remains a crucial work in its innovative approach and its suggestive interpretations of material change. For our purposes it appears to be a flawed but innovative account of the significance of interpretative sociology, the role of cultural factors and the development of work practices that continue to demand our contemporary concerns: why do people enagage in such apparently irrational work patterns? If the work ethic doesn't exist how do we explain the almost compulsive work behaviour of some? Like Marx and Durkheim, Weber stands as a critical figure in the development of the sociology of work and his heritage of writings on rationalization, bureaucracy, and the significance of the individual as an interpretative actor whose actions often have unintended consequences, are a mainstay of contemporary approaches.

Conclusion

The three founders of the sociology of work all continue to have their contemporary adherents and detractors. Durkheim's moral concerns proved crucial to the development of work in mainstream industrial relations in the early 1970s and, as discussed in the previous chapter, the moral economy continues to pervade the market economy, making predictions about human action based on amoral, economically rational behaviour less than convincing. Perhaps where Durkheim has been most vigorously criticized has been in relation to the allegedly cohering effects of an extended division of labour. Neither Marx nor Weber nor the mainstream of managerial theories which are considered in the next chapter support Durkheim on this point: dependency does not generate mutual solidarity. For Marx, the division of labour generated the opposite social phenomenon: class conflict. Marx's fascination with class, conflict and the labour process formed the basis for the most popular new approach throughout much of industrial sociology from the late 1960s through to the current period. However, although it spawned a complete school of thought in the labour process tradition (see chapter 5), its limitations became more evident as the approach attempted to explain all manner of social phenomena directly through the prism of class. Finally, Weber's theories of rationalization and bureaucracy have never been far from those analysing the trend towards larger and larger organizations or indeed from the apparent movement towards more flexible work organization patterns today. Again, though, Weber's over-rationalized approach underestimated the significance of destabilizing and sectional forces within work organizations. Had Weber adopted his own interpretivist methodology more widely in his organizational studies perhaps some of these shortfalls would have been attended to. Despite all these problems it is still the case that future research in the sociology of work will continue to adopt and adapt the ideas formulated by the 'gang of three', though probably not with the level of uncritical appreciation that has sometimes appeared in the past. In contemporary arguments there is much more concern for issues that none of these three considered crucial: the relationships between genders and ethnic groups; the significance of the links between the sphere of employment and the domestic sphere; and the role of social forces in the construction, as well as the deployment, of technology. Only a very thin slice of the classical approaches has been discussed here. Where, exactly, the ideas and values of these three founders of the debates appear today, and why a more disparate network of approaches has taken us beyond their original analyses, will be considered in the next four chapters.

4

Contemporary Theories of Work Organization

'Our sentence does not sound severe. Whatever commandment the condemned man has disobeyed is written upon his body by the Harrow. This condemned man, for instance' – the officer indicated the man – 'will have written on his body: HONOUR THY SUPERIORS'

Kafka, *In the Penal Settlement*

Introduction: Organizations, Bureaucracies and Professionals

Organizational theory is a discipline in itself with a consequentially huge corpus of literature and research. A single chapter cannot hope to do justice to the complexities of such debates and it will, therefore, seek to highlight some of the major distinguishing themes. Readers interested in a fuller and more systematic approach should attempt the following: Handy (1985); Morgan (1986); Clegg and Dunkerley (1980); Burrell and Morgan (1979); Reed (1985); Alvesson (1987); Rose (1975); Salaman (1979); Silverman (1970); and Donaldson (1985).

The bewildering variety of organizational approaches often seems to obfuscate the explanations of organizational behaviour rather than clarify them. Addressing such problems, some authors (e.g. Burrell and Morgan, 1979) have argued that each approach or paradigm should pursue its own path in splendid isolation. Only in this way will the messy effects of compromise be avoided, clear insights into organizations be achieved and, most critical of all for them, what they call 'radical organizational theory' be able to survive the imperialist intentions of others. Yet it is not self-evident that the greatest intellectual advances can be made by choosing to ignore the criticism of those from different perspectives, and it would seem more likely that it is the clash between approaches, rather than the accretion of evidence from within discrete approaches, that will prove more heuristic.

A different procedure is suggested by Bernstein (1983) and supported by Reed (1985) in so far as a pluralist approach should be used which seeks to generate common ground, where possible, by reconciling differences through debate. This need not degenerate into a theoretical approach that lacks any form of critical edge and it does at least assert that an arena of commonality can ensure mutual enlightenment rather than isolated blindness. Unfortunately, Reed does not take us beyond a plea for pluralism so we are still unable to progress beyond a basic level of tolerance. Before embarking on the systematic analyses of the various approaches considered in this chapter, it is important to reconstruct the historical origins of the general substantive field of research: formal organizations.

Formal organizations, most of which are bureaucratic to some degree in that they are grounded in formal rules and a hierarchy of offices, are typically associated with problems of scale. In small organizations formal rules and a complex division of labour may be unnecessary. Thus, small-scale capitalist organizations were, and still are, often controlled by a single entrepreneur, and democratic or participatory organizations may be organized informally with rotating co-ordinators to avoid institutionalizing hierarchies of power. Bureaucracy may be avoided, then, for both economic and political reasons. However, once organizations expand beyond the point at which personal control or direct democracy is unproblematic, the general tendency has been to introduce some degree of bureaucratic control. This is not to say that democratic control of large organizations is impossible, as Michels (1949) claimed, but it is nevertheless notoriously difficult to develop properly and may require some degree of bureaucratization in order to ensure stability (Pollitt, 1986).

The relationship between the problems of scale and the advantages of bureaucracy usually ensured that the earliest forms of bureaucracy, as we have already noted in the previous chapter, emerged in either state-related organizations like the military, the Civil Service, state industries etc., or in religious organizations. In Germany, for example, an extended division of labour and its associated administrative hierarchy operated within monasteries and the sixteenth-century workhouses, developed to re-educate the criminals and beggars of the time (Kieser, 1989). In Britain the Civil Service, and particularly the Post Office, spawned the first large-scale non-military organization based on strictly demarcated offices, meritocratic career structures and rationalized systems of control. The preconditions for such a bureaucratic expansion are a necessary level of literacy which can provide recruits familiar with filing systems and accounts, a sophisticated money economy and an urbanized, and organizationally rich, society. Yet, as Stinchcombe (1965) has argued, even then the process of bureaucratization tends to be a two-stage affair. First, a bureaucratic administrative system of files and accounts is introduced and only after this is there a separation of ownership from immediate (day to day) organizational control. However, there is more to the growth of bureaucracy than determination by size alone: diversifications of products and services are also critical features, for the economic stimulus to diversification necessarily implies a diversified managerial and administrative structure (cf. Fletcher, 1973). Such linkages between diversification and bureaucratic growth have been well documented both in the USA (Chandler, 1962) and the UK (Channon, 1973). Perhaps the clearest examples of the ultimate result of such growth and diversification amongst work organizations are the multinational corporations, and it is significant that these manage to create not just employment opportunities for the host nations and problems for national sovereignty (Held, 1989) but also manage to remain extremely centralized in terms of administrative control (see Lash and Urry (1987) and Harvey (1989) for a discussion of contemporary capitalist organizational trends at the national and international level).

Another aspect of the development of bureaucracies is the rise of the professions. It is important to remember here that organizational members may have interests in the expansion of their own profession or group which are independent of the assumed purposes of such organizations. Thus, for example, the classic arguments concerning the nature of the managerial revolution by Berle and Means (1968), Burnham (1962), and Dahrendorf (1959), in which a new profession of managers allegedly displaces the entrepreneurial capitalists of a previous era, are just one form of the professional 'capturing' of organizations (Scott, 1979, Johnson, 1972: Larson, 1977: Nichols, 1969; Reed, 1989). As Perkin (1989) has recently demonstrated, professionals in Britain approached the status of a fourth class through the period of the twentieth century, though their interests in corporatist administrations have fallen somewhat into disrepute after the Thatcher administration began to split public from private professions.

Organizational theories, despite their current diversity and proliferation, can, for the sake of understanding, be reduced to a position along two interlocking axes: the determinist - interpretativist axis and the technocratic - critical axis. The former axis distinguishes between those approaches which stress the scientific and objective way in which organizations can be assessed, often relating specifically to underlying structural conditions and requirements (e.g., market imperatives, rational decision making, efficiency etc), from those approaches which focus on the indeterminate and contingent nature of reality, the significance of human interaction, the unintended consequences of human action, and the influence of interpretation. The technocratic–critical axis represents what may be called the political continuum. At one extreme, the technocratic pole, there are those approaches often developed by business consultants for whom organizational theories are essentially pragmatically oriented tools for the improvement of organizational efficiency. Within this perspective the impact upon the lives of organizational members or the wider society is subsidiary at best, and irrelevant at worst, to the need to maximize profits and efficiency. At the other extreme, the critical pole, are radical explanations of organizations and behaviour within organizations for whom the social effects of the organization upon its members and the society within which it operates are more significant than the question of profits or efficiency. The Critical side of this axis tends to encompass most conventional sociological approaches to organizations in that they are crucially premised upon explanatory accoúnts, rather than accounts which are primarily designed to improve or 'rationalize' organizations in some way. Of course, rationalizing organizations implies a high degree of knowledge surrounding the nature of organizations but this, in turn, begs the question of interests. In short, if 'improving' an organization requires mass redundancy, does this not rather suggest that improvement is defined solely in the interests of the owners and controllers rather than the entire body of employees or members? It is not necessary to label non-technocratic organizational theory 'radical organizational theory' as has become popular recently, since this implies that explanation is determined by political preferences. To admit to the inevitability of political bias is not the same as accepting that explanations may be accounted false simply by reference to their origins rather than their content. Thus, the knowledge that authoritarian control over organizational subordinates often generates counter-productive hostilities and conflicts does not require a radical perspective but rather a perusal of the experiences of such organizations.

What follows is another way of considering the relationships between various forms of organizational theory along the grid below. The interpretation of where the theories lie is clearly subject to dispute, nevertheless the claim is not that this is the best way of illustrating the types but that it is a heuristic way for our purposes. Since I have grave doubts about the validity of some of the claims of the perspectives, particularly the claims to 'scientific status', I have allocated them according to their professed claims, rather than their practices. Thus, for example, the human relations approach is located in the technocratic–determinist corner even though the interpretation here suggests that the practice of human relations approaches is far more contingent than its supporters claim. What is striking about the grid is the paucity of approaches that lie in the determinist–critical corner: if something is regarded as inevitable there is probably little incentive in generating an explanation or focusing upon organizational effects.

The interaction of the two axes of organizational approaches is represented in figure 4.

Figure 4 Organizational theories

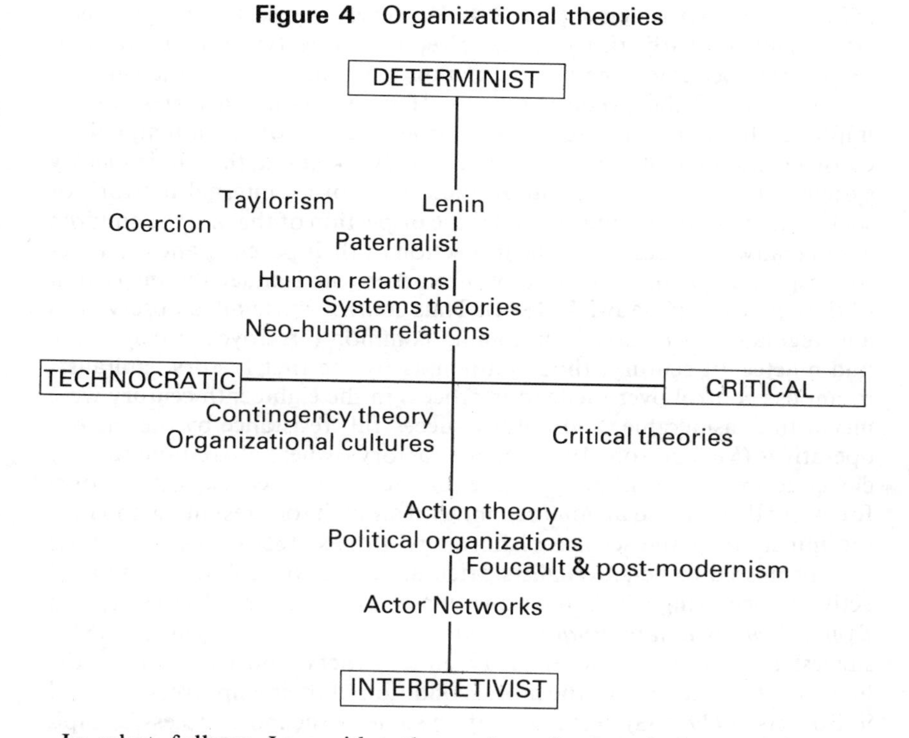

In what follows I consider the various facets of these theoretical approaches to organizations, attempting at the end to provide the outline of the Actor Network perspective, drawn from the sociology of science, which promises to circumvent some, at least, of the major problems in the preceding designs. In the first section I consider the earliest forms of organizational theory and practice in the modes of control attempted by the early factory capitalists: philanthropists and misanthropists alike.

Factory Management: Coercion and Paternalism

Historically speaking, most early (i.e., late eighteenth-century) British factory entrepreneurs did not seem unduly concerned about how their organization should be managed; provided it was profitable and the employees kept working there was little to be done in the way of improving the organization, let alone studying its workings. Not that things appear to have changed very quickly: in Houser's studies of American managers in 1924–5 very few had any information or apparent interest in what the employees thought of managers or how this might affect productivity (Jacoby, 1988). However, where labour problems erupted in the early factories there tended to be two rather different responses: coercion – the most common reaction; and paternalism.

Since one of the primary objects of constructing factories was to improve discipline through observation many owners attempted to construct a system of self-coercion; as Chadwick noted, the whole factory system was designed to maximize the effects of an internal network of social controls: 'the young are under the inspection of the old; the children are in many instances under the inspection of their parents, and all under the inspection of the whole body of workers, and under the inspection of the employer' (Chadwick, 1842). Thus control via detailed observation and regulation was already becoming common (cf. Joyce, 1980) in the mid nineteenth century, though attempts by the first factory capitalists to impose control over the labour process in the eighteenth century were met with considerable, and initally successful, resistance by the factory operatives (Malcomson, 1981). Some factory owners altered the factory clocks to extract even more sweated labour from their exploited workforce and then sacked anyone caught with a watch for presuming 'to know too much about the science of horology' (Miles, 1850). Many of those who professed to be paternalists often appeared to wash their hands of activities occurring within their own factories and mines. As the *Reports from Commissioners Enquiring into Children's Employment* (1843) suggests: 'there is not one in fifty mine owners who cared about the housing and education or the moral condition of their employees' (quoted in Roberts, 1979: 183). Yet it was often some of the most successful capitalists who were keenest to enforce strict disciplinary codes, banning late time keeping, drinking, swearing and mere talking. As Pollard (1965) argues, the vast majority of the earliest capitalists, faced with horrendous problems of control, and saturated with the belief that the labouring class were beyond moral improvement, let alone moral incentives, tended to resort to the traditional methods of coercion (fines, beatings or dismissal) or an occasional and very atypical reward. 'Rule 11' of one Manchester factory summed up this coercive approach: 'If any hand in the mill is seen talking to another, whistling or singing, [he] will be fined sixpence' (quoted in Ayres, 1988: 8). Some 'masters', such as Robert Blincoe's were undoubtedly sadistic: 'we beat only the lesser, up to thirteen or fourteen . . . we use a strap' (quoted in Pollard, 1965: 219). The factory owners were not alone in treating their employees harshly. John Bolling, a cottonmaster, resisted such beatings but still had trouble with children running away from work: 'The other day there were three children run away; the mother of one of them brought him back and asked us to beat him; that I could not permit; she asked us to take him again; at last I consented, and she beat him' (op. cit.). Other control methods included piece work (developed originally in northern lead mines in 1688) which accounted for almost half the payment systems of cotton mill workers in 1833, and which suggests that the traditional concern of labourers to earn just enough to provide for their customary level of subsistence was already breaking down.

The other kind of response to labour problems (the paternalist), was to assume that perhaps the workers were human after all and might actually respond better to a rather more gentle form of persuasion. As Josiah Wedgwood admitted: 'Our men have been at play four times this week, it being Burslem Wakes. I have roughed and smoothed them over, and promised them a long Xmass, but I know it is all in vain, for wakes must be observed though the world was to end with them' (quoted in Pollard, 1965: 214). Yet even Robert Owen's great experiment in paternalist organization, Harmony Hall, was premised on detailed control of members' behaviour, dress and furniture (Hardy, 1979: 54). This concern for detail was not dissimilar to the 'silent monitors' used in his New Lanark factory where workers had their previous day's work rate translated into a coloured mark and displayed above their machine. Similarly, the other paternalist capitalists, such as Crowley, Wedgwood, Marshall et al., all attempted to reconstruct the morality of the new working classes by delimiting the availability of drink, free time, and self-indulgence (Pollard, 1965: 213–31).

Both coercive and paternalist responses were technocratic in the sense that the intention was to raise productivity not consider whether factory capitalism was an inherently problematic method of organizing production. But the paternalists were, nevertheless, critical of the brutal methods often used to coerce workers, not just because such methods bordered on the immoral but also because they seemed counter-productive. Both methods also sit within the determinist side of the vertical axis: both implied that through the correct application of specific forms of encouragement or violence, productivity could be maintained or increased. The possibility that organizations were inherently unstable social forms, for which no permanent or scientific strategy of control existed, did not figure high in these approaches.

Exactly why the first century of the industrial revolution had produced such a phenomenal growth in industrial organization and such a dearth of organizational theory is difficult to say. Pollard's (1965: 292–301) argument is probably as accurate as anyone's: first, the major problems facing capitalist organizations in this early period were perceived as external not internal. Obviously, worker discipline and organizational structures were obstacles to success, but the crucial issues as far as the capitalist entrepreneurs were concerned were often considered more significant, such as whether a road could be built to move the products or whether the labour supply would continue etc. Second, organizations were dominated by individual entrepreneurs and owner managers for whom the thought of delegating responsibility to a 'professional' manager was probably anathema. Third, the dominant ideology amongst organizational controllers was, for the most part, one that imbued labour with a sullen recalcitrance such that the 'solution' to organizational problems was obvious: more control, discipline and coercion, even if it had to be legally constrained; more importantly, more machinery to embody the mechanical discipline that was regarded as so much more effective than personal control.

Three quarters of a century after the government commissioners were complaining about the level of employer indifference to the well-being of their employees, little seems to have changed with the exception, perhaps, of the Quaker employers, Rowntree, Cadbury and Lever, who argued vociferously for a direct connection between employee welfare and company prosperity. Their paternalist intent strayed well beyond concern for training and health within factories and moved into provision of entire communities like Cadbury's Bournville and Rowntree's New Earswick at York, the latter still very much a model Quaker village in the significant absence of pubs. Such major organizational innovations were not intended to ensure that the workers' places in heaven were secured but to maximize productivity through humanitarian and moralising strategies of control. As such, they can be regarded as technocratic and deterministic in that they believed human nature and the capitalist system determined the best form of organization. Such examples of direct employer intervention over the entire lives of their employees were rare. What were increasingly visible, though, were moves in this direction by the state, first in terms of compulsory education. Later, after the débâcle of the Boer War, during which time over a third of the recruits were rejected as medically unfit, and in conjuction with Booth's and Rowntree's poverty reports and the muscle flexing of the labour movement, further advances were made by the state towards the provision of improved health, welfare and later insurance (Hopkins, 1979).

The interests of the state in the mechanisms of organizational efficiency accelerated under the direct stimulus of the First World War, as the provision of manpower and munitions for the front forced the government to intervene directly in the management of industrial organizations. One result of this was the Industrial Fatigue Research Board, set up to investigate and promote mechanisms of efficiency at work, including the utility of rest, working hours, ventilation and lighting systems. By the end of the war, and under the guidance of Myers, the orthodox explanation for worker (mis) behaviour had switched from a physiological to a psychological causal analysis. Just as Taylor had argued that jobs and individuals should be matched, so too Myers, then heading the National Institute of Industrial Psychology, argued for vocational guidance to facilitate the individual requirements of specific workers and particular jobs. Moreover, where problems still manifested themselves, the cause was likely to be the disharmony between the personality of the workers and the work situation in which they found themselves (Rose, 1989). Myers, then, believed that work provided more than economic rewards and, in particular, it provided the means through which individual instincts could be gratified. Where work organizations were not constructed to provide such facilities, or worse, where they compounded otherwise minor mental or emotional instability, seriously maladjusted workers would result (ibid.). This approach was yet another in the technocratic mould: the problem was not really how you explain organizations or whether organizational life was inherently damaging to health but how organizations could be made to operate more efficiently.

Taylor's approach (see chapter 5) conceived of personal health as identical with organizational efficiency. When Taylor began to develop his approach to incentive schemes and the wider issues of scientific management at the end of the nineteenth century, there were several rather distinctive facets that set it apart from the earlier modes of control. First, rather than assuming that all employees were universally similar, Taylor argued that individuals were differentially endowed and therefore, in the interests of efficiency, jobs and workers should be matched in terms of necessary skills and intelligence required. Second, Taylor advanced the claim of control through expertise rather than property rights. It was the case that engineering had already begun to make claims towards a professional status in Britain in the first half of the nineteenth century but even here the movement was minimal and, outside of engineering, although well-defined groups of managers existed there was no managerial profession as such (Pollard, 1965: 159–88).

The impact of Taylorism upon capitalist organizations is the subject of much dispute (see chapter 5), but one of his greatest admirers was Lenin. This may seem paradoxical in the light of the latter's political critique of capitalism but there are several points to remember. First, like Taylor, Lenin sought a 'scientific' solution to the problems of production and argued that Taylor's objective methods could be separated from his political ends. Second, Lenin's aim was not to develop a network of interacting autonomous units of production controlled by their own workforces but to institute a centrally controlled system of production that would unleash the potential hitherto inhibited by the capitalist quest for profits. Thus productivity was essential to the Bolshevik utopia because only when a cornucopia of production had been achieved would the conflicts generated by shortages be abolished. Hence, nothing that inhibited the drive to industrialize and outproduce the capitalists could be tolerated – including workers who still clamoured for 'outmoded' independent trade unions: since capitalism had been abolished, with the elimination of private property, all resistence to the 'Workers' State' must be counter-revolutionary. Lenin's approach to organizations, then, reproduces many of the assumptions of Taylor but under a new perspective. Organizations are not essentially political bodies embodying conflicting interests but merely neutral mechanisms for achieving the consensually agreed goal – greater levels of production for the benefit of all. Thus Lenin sits uneasily midway along the technocratic–critical axis and halfway into the determinist camp. He was axiomatically critical of all capitalist organizations but argued that the problem lay in the issue of ownership not control: once the capitalists had been removed then rational organizations of the type avowed by Taylor could equally well serve the communist state.

Lenin's position is, to say the least, ambiguous. His arguments in *State and Revolution* suggest that organizational control would rest with local soviets but in almost all his other work control is restricted to the Bolshevik party 'on behalf of' the working class. His admiration for the technocratic essence of Taylorism was clear:

> The Taylor system, the last word of capitalism in this respect, like all capitalist progress, is a combination of the refined brutality of bourgeois exploitation and a number of the greatest scientific achievements in the field of analysing mechanical motions during work. . . . We must organize in Russia the study and teaching of the Taylor system. (Lenin, 1968c: 413–14)

Rational organization for Lenin, then, was not a matter of interpretation any more than Marxism was a partial perspective – both represented the truth and both represented the only permanent solution to the contemporary organizational problems of capitalism. Given Lenin's previous insistence on the ineradicably capitalist nature of the state (1968b), and the need to dismantle it completely, his assumption about the neutrality of work organizations is astonishingly naive, and a disaster for the future direction of the Soviet state.

The Soviet experiment in atheist government was heading back down the road of the time and motion expert, having expropriated the capitalists and therefore apparently solved the problem of the alienated worker. Across the Bering Strait American capitalists were heading in a rather different direction towards the same goal: the maladjusted worker was about to make another appearance, this time not in a solo part in a psychological drama written by Myers, nor in a collective polemic directed by Lenin, but as part of small and irrational team production.

Human Relations and the social group were about to be written into the folklore of industrial and organizational sociology.

Human Relations

Although, as we shall see in the next chapter, Taylorism faced stiff opposition from workers, managers and the American state, the movement towards a more scientific assessment of organizations in the USA did continue in particular enterprises, though without the kind of national research centre as provided by the National Institute of Industrial Psychology in Britain. One of the more enlightened businesses interested in experimental research was the Western Electric Company's Hawthorne plant at Chicago (Roethlisberger and Dickson, 1939), where 29,000 employees, representing sixty nationalities, produced telephone equipment for the Bell system. There is some doubt over exactly who was responsible for the research, and the part played by Mayo, but this has only marginal significance for our purposes (Rose, 1975: cf. Smith, J.H. 1987). What is more important is to note that although the motivational models eventually developed from the Taylorist and human relations schools were very different, the former being *homo economicus*, as opposed to the latter's *homo gregarious* (and Marx's *homo faber*), the technical features of Taylorism did not necessarily contradict the social implications of human relations; they were both technocratic in orientation with the human relations approach being more critical only in so far as it rejected Taylorist models of organizational efficiency: social interaction not money was the primary motivator at work.

There were obviously some tensions between them, besides the different motivational theories, and one was whether to facilitate or outlaw social groups, but the two were not diametrically opposite. It could be argued that the two models are linked in a more direct way, in so far as the results of Taylor's extension of the division of labour and its consequential destruction of 'inherent' interest for workers, left the human relations approach to pick up the prices and compensate for the loss of alleged intrinsic job interest with social stimulation. In this vein Sievers (1984) argues that motivation becomes an issue only when meaning is eliminated from jobs. There are three related problems with this. First, it still poses a romantic notion of work; that is, that at some indeterminate time all jobs had intrinsic interest. Second, it also misdirects attention wholly on to the job itself, when the situation within which the job is executed is also important in defining the nature of that intrinsic interest. Third, activities do not have 'intrinsic' interests in the sense that they can be objectively assessed in isolation from the person undertaking the job: job 'interests' are what the worker derives through interaction with materials etc., they do not sit 'within' materials waiting to be released. Thus it is the interaction and the interpretation of that interaction which should be considered in establishing forms of job interest. To take an example, building a television may be experienced as intrinsically interesting or inherently tedious but which of these is the case depends not upon the task of building but the interpretation of the builder and the persuasive powers of those attempting to make the task appear interesting or tedious.

Such interpretative concerns were not regarded as problems for the Hawthorne researchers, and the initial experiments, begun in 1924 in conjunction with the National Research Council of the National Academy of Sciences, assessed the conditions of work, monotony and fatigue, particularly in response to lighting variations. However, the results appeared so mystifying that Roethlisberger, from Harvard Graduate School of Business Administration, in association with Mayo (also from Harvard), and Dickson from the Hawthorne Employee Relations Department, set up a series of further experiments that were to take until 1932 to complete.

The 'illumination experiments' suggested that 'efficiency increased more or less continously . . . but not as a sole function of illumination' (Roethlisberger and Dickson, 1939: 14–15). Indeed, the lighting of one group was systematically lowered such that only when the workers could not actually see what they were doing did the productivity rate stop rising and begin to fall. Finally, the lighting system was left stable while electricians merely pretended to increase or decrease the lighting. Although the workers praised the 'brighter' lighting, and complained when it got 'darker', no actual change took place and productivity remained stable. The conclusion which the department came to was basically one of perplexity, at which point they called in the Harvard academics. Over the next few years the experiments changed from lighting to include, amongst other things, variations in work rates, rest pauses, payment methods and hours. The Relay Assembly Test Room experiments involved selected groups of six women and their variations in output were charted by a single observer. Once again, productivity increases were recorded that bore markedly little connection to specific forms of variation in inputs. Two other experimental groups were inaugurated but these were discontinued after conflict developed both within the groups and between them and the rest of the workforce.

Ignoring the problematic results of these two latter groups, and the forced removal of two of the original six women in the first 'successful' group, one conclusion is of great significance: the work group was responding not to variations in conditions etc., but to the very fact of being treated as an experimental group with consequential high status. Moreover, they actually appeared to be reacting in the way they thought they were supposed to react: what became known as the 'Hawthorne Effect'. Although Roethlisberger and colleagues played this down (1939: 526–31), it was very significant for the time and motion studies then developing under Taylor's scientific management because it implied that observation of workers would not necessarily provide an accurate account of what normally happened. Instead, the very act of observation would alter the activity being measured. Hence, although the human relations school considered themselves to be within what has been termed the deterministic axis, their 'science' of measuring human behaviour actually appeared much more like a game of estimation.

Clearly, not every group could be so treated but the major conclusion of the research team themselves was to be more significant in the resolution of organizational problems: the experience of working in a closely knit social group was, in itself, a direct boost to productivity. Second, although officially just an observer, the recorder had become a 'surrogate supervisor' acting on behalf of the work group. The implication of this was that supervisors would play a crucial role in mediating between the demands of the company and the desires of the worker group. Third, and relatedly, the productivity increases provided evidence of the 'latent energy' which work groups normally withheld through what the team called their 'non-logical sentiments' but which could only be released through the right kind of management. Fourth, despite the radical implications of the assessment there were many issues that remained problematic. In particular, did solidaristic work groups necessarily cohere in the pursuit of objectives that the company found acceptable? or did the troublesome elements in the experiments suggest that group solidarity was, if not inherently problematic as Taylor argued, at the very least a double-edged sword? For all the claims of 'social integration', what the human relations school were really talking about was 'social engineering': another form of technocratic theory and practice.

The first practical response of the company was to investigate in more detail the nature of company morale and the role of supervision, since this seemed to be a critical feature of sustaining efficiency. Consequently, the next stage of the experiments involved interviewing some 1,600 employees over the winter of 1928–9. The results suggested that the research programme itself was having beneficial effects on the morale of the employees, and the interview schedule was expanded to include 10,300 employees in 1929 and 21,126 in 1932. Subsequently, the general economic collapse led to massive redundancies and the interview programme was wound down. Nevertheless, the data, which in 1929 alone included 40,000 comments, was utilised in a series of supervisory training schemes. Employees' complaints were also channelled back to the appropriate department and the researchers spoke of the cathartic effects of employee interviews. As the report noted: 'it was thought that many adverse attitudes had been improved by these emotional "abreactions" which the interviews afforded' (Roethlisberger and Dickson, 1939: 228). Yet the interview schedule was not regarded as a success, and one of the reasons may well be that it highlighted a strong link between attitudes to work and the wider social attachments outside the plant, especially the early socialization of individuals, which the company were powerless to affect. Here, then, we can perceive an incipient critical approach to organizations but one which was ultimately stillborn: the employment situation cannot be analysed solely by reference to itself – the links between the domestic and the employment situation are critical.

The final stage in the research programme was aimed at a detailed investigation of a small group, using anthropological methods to try and ascertain the 'more subtle and spontaneous aspects of the employees' social organization' (p. 376). This involved a group of fourteen men being closely observed for six months between 1931 and 1932. No environmental conditions were altered in this Bank Wiring Observation Room experiment but a rather complicated group bonus scheme was introduced. In the event the group appeared to limit their production to their group interpretation of 'a good day's work': 'the bogey'. This social norm did not just restrict the maximum output but ensured a minimum output too, as well as involving the fiddling of output records to maintain the norm. Where such norms were threatened, enforcement was usually restricted to verbal encouragement or threat: one of the inspectors who insisted on accurate recordings of work left after being threatened with a 'a punch in the nose'.

In fact, one of the issues that became clarified later was that few of the workers really understood the group incentive scheme. The report concluded that the men were operating along non-logical sentiments and that, however problematic this was for increasing organizational efficiency, it clearly demonstrated the significance of the informal organization of work. Equally significant, the research had revealed the power of the 'logic of sentiments' as opposed to the 'logics of cost and efficiency'. Workers were stimulated by sentiments such as 'fairness' and the 'right to work', while managers and supervisors were more likely to be more concerned with the 'logics of cost and efficiency' because of their 'particular concrete situation' (p. 565). Management's, and particularly personnel managers', skill lay in channeling the logic of sentiments so that it paralleled, rather than contradicted, the logic of cost and efficiency. It was Mayo, rather than Roethlisberger and Dickson, who interpreted this in Durkheimian fashion as the call of the isolated individual to be bound into the collective; to replace the traditional bonds of community, now disrupted by the ever increasing division of labour, with the new sinews of socially manipulated work groups. The integration of the individual through her or his subordination to the group, controlled and facilitated by expert managers, was the way forward. More alarmingly, Mayo linked the non-logical sentiments of the mass into a blend of elitist social engineering in a way that mirrored some of the fascist ideas then sprouting in Italy and Germany. Conformity to elite-inspired norms was the normal path for the mass of non-rational subordinates in organizations who would only become anxious if left to decide for themselves. In short, although the attitudes of the workers appeared unpredictable, this merely made the task of the manager more concerned with rooting out such contingencies and ensuring the direction of organizations could be determined by expert managers. Conflict and disharmony were not examples of inherently conflictual situations but of maladjustment; as Nik Rose argues: 'The minutiae of the human soul . . . had emerged as a new domain for management . . . management could represent its authority as neutral, rational and in the workers' interest' (1989: 71, 2). Ironically, it is dubious whether management actually needed to: the world-wide inter-war depression, and in Britain the catastrophe of the General Strike, probably ensured that few employees were willing to question too cloosely the legitimacy of their bosses' claims to authority on the basis of expertise.

In America the pattern of counselling set up in Hawthorne and repeated elsewhere eventually led to a massive government intervention to sustain employee morale. By 1945 over 20 per cent American psychologists were engaged directly in such efforts (Jacoby, 1988: 78). However, the end of the war left the new school of human relations experts to pick up the pieces just where they had fallen before the war.

Neo-Human Relations

With the cessation of hostilities some of the ideas relating to the significance of social cohesion and the processes of the unconscious were fused in a new model of human relations on both sides of the Atlantic: by 1954 over 40 per cent of large US companies had introduced mass attitude surveys of their employees (though by 1981 this had barely changed to 45 per cent). Even General Motors was caught up in the enthusiasm: in 1947 it introduced a competition amongst its employees for the best essay in response to the question: 'My Job and Why I like it'. Most of the surveys were conducted without union knowledge or approval (Jacoby, 1988: 79–84). One branch of this eventually surfaced as socio-technical systems from the psychoanalytic interests of the Tavistock Institute of Human Relations, which is discussed in chapter 8. The other branch, and the one more directly derived from the technocratic pragmatic of Mayo et al., began by rejecting the simplistic models of human social behaviour drawn by the early Human Relations studies. The human model now moved from *homo gregarious* to *homo actualis* (Managerialist): self-actualization, courtesy of the management, was the new order of the day, but the day remained technocratically organized and the arguments retained the air of a scientifically determined model rather than a sketch drawn around the interpretive actions of humans.

As McGregor, one of the leading lights of the neo-human relations school, concluded on the activities of the inter-war period: 'during this period the human side of enterprise has become a major preoccupation of management. The lot of the industrial employee . . . has improved to a degree which can hardly have been imagined by his counterpart of the 1920s . . . *but it has done all these things without changing its fundamental theory of management*' (1984: 325) (original emphasis). McGregor's complaint was not that management had simply been technocratic or instrumental in its adoption of humanistic policies. On the contrary, his concern was that many of the humanistic schemes, like 'permissive management', 'industrial democracy' and organizational 'peace' were simply unworkable; they were pendulum reactions to the previously autocratic methods of control. Neither worked, but human relations had established one possible alternative organizing principle to overt coercion: integration through self-actualization. Moreover, 'the model of the successful manager in our culture is a masculine one. He is not feminine; he is not soft or yielding or dependent or intuitive in the womanly sense. The very expression of emotion is widely viewed as a feminine weakness that would interfere with effective business processes' (McGregor, quoted in Basoux, 1987). The current vogue for intuitive thought and 'responsive' management, heralded by the likes of Peters and Waterman which I discuss below, could not be a better example of an apparent managerial inversion that leaves the technocratic status perfectly intact.

McGregor argued that traditionally firms were organized along what he termed Theory X principles: first, that most people had an inherent dislike of work; second, because of this, coercion of some variety was necessary to ensure compliance at work; third, most people preferred to be controlled than to have autonomy. This drew loosely on Maslow's (1943) motivational theory, which asserted that a hierarchy of needs existed with the physical needs at the base, moving through safety, love, esteem and ultimately self-actualization. In essence, McGregor asserted that Theory X neglected the dynamic nature of human needs, for as economic rewards satisfied material needs, so other, higher, needs were ignited and a concomitantly higher form of motivation was necessary. Thus, motivation becomes increasingly difficult because Theory X firms have no provision for coping with the new, higher needs of contemporary workers. McGregor argues, paradoxically, that the very success of capitalist management in the provision of high living standards undermined the only motivator it had consistently used: when nobody starved any more the provision of wages, in itself, was of little motivational value. But this is to assume that, at a given level, material demands stop rising, and also that universal human needs exist rather than, as discussed in chapter 1, needs which are socially and culturally constructed and hence transient.

The problem, as far as McGregor sees it, has a parallel with the pattern of human socialization. Adopting Argyris's (1957) notions of child/adult responsibilities, he notes that whereas individual development is premised upon the gradual accretion of responsibilities, organizations adopting Theory X principles provide only the very limited responsibilities associated with childhood: the result is childish behaviour by adult employees frustrated at their treatment by the employers.

Theory Y attempts to resolve these motivational and behavioural problems by generating a radically different set of basic assumptions: first, work is not disliked by everyone; second, coercion is not the only motivator; third, it is possible to provide organizational goals that fulfil the highest motivator - self-actualization; fourth, responsible behaviour is a result of trust, and the avoidance of responsibility is a reaction to experiences that deny responsibility; fifth, creativity is widely dispersed throughout the population, even if few jobs require it (p. 326–7). McGregor concludes that management's task is to develop 'integrating' organizational procedures through which individuals can realize themselves through achieving organizational goals, that is the goals as specified by management. It is significant, then, that McGregor's schema is axiomatically technocratic; it is little more than sophisticated social engineering. The concern is not with creating a society in which individuals can realize themselves but with redeveloping managerial strategies, such that the latent energies so dear to human relations approaches can be directed more accurately towards managerially defined goals. Only if employees' goals coincide with managerial goals can they legitimately be pursued within the context of the organization.

Equally technocratic, and also mildly deterministic, are the ideas of another of the neo-human relations school, Herzberg (1966). His argument is similarly locked into motivational theories and reworks the problems of hierarchy of motivation into a dualism: hygiene and motivational factors. Hygiene factors, like the conditions, material rewards and security of work, are negative motivators in so far as their absence decreases productivity while their presence is merely the pre-condition for higher productivity. This has to be achieved through the positive motivation factors, which are symbolic and psychological rather than material, like status, advancement, intrinsic job interest etc. It is not clear why a dissatisfactory job content should not be considered an element of the hygiene side, since this appears elsewhere to decrease levels of productivity (Lawler, 1973). In short, the new human relations may appear to have been sculpted from the clay of self-actualization rather than the old model of group relations but the original mould was still struck in technocratic bronze. Self-realization was only thought viable via the managerial route to organizational success.

What were the effects of this reworking of human relations? After all, although the general concern for social underpinnings and motivational complexities of work were irredemably technocratic and managerialist in origin and orientation, the ideas might have been suggestive enough to introduce in and of themselves. The point that work cannot eliminate underlying contradictions of interest, and therefore can never be totally harmonious, should not have worried hard-headed personnel managers eager for a long-term solution to the problem of worker motivation. So what happened? Again, we have to make a clear distinction between developments within organizational theory and the common experiences of organizations: while academics and consultants battled away with their pens and clients, the reality of organizational life took a rather different turn. The apparently terminal crisis facing British industry at the time these works were published in the 1960s, wracked as it appeared to be by unofficial industrial action and declining efficiency, tended to smother the search for radical, let alone ostensibly humanist, personnel strategies. Batstone (1988: 60–4) makes clear that although British personnel managers developed from the oppositional poles of welfare work and conventional management, by the time the neo-human relations material was available, the technocratic or orthodox management proxy role had already won out over the softer welfare approach. British management was then, as it had always been and predominantly still is, relatively unconcerned by labour relations or personnel issues that affect organizations: finance and fire fighting seem to be the twin pillars of interests (ibid., pp. 64–71).

In many ways this may seem counter-productive to organizational efficiency but the hard-nosed British approach may be very practical. After all, despite claims to the contrary (Blumberg, 1968), there is precious little unambiguous evidence of a direct link between job satisfaction and work performance (Kelly, 1982), even if there is some for a link between dissatisfaction, absenteeism and labour turnover (Lawler, 1973). Moreover, it may be that managerial concern for ensuring harmonious social relations at work actually inhibits the time available for work concerned with improving products, acquiring customers and suchlike (Zaleznik, 1989). As Drucker noted forty years ago: 'the main function and purpose of the enterprise is the production of goods, not the governance of men. Its governmental authority over men must always be subordinated to its economic performance and responsibility'

(Drucker, 1951: 81). It should be noted, though, that many of the neo-human relations approaches may be more viable in the USA, where the limited nature of public health care and welfare makes in-house schemes more attractive to employees than they would be in Britain (Sloan et al., 1987). Yet it remains an irony in both countries that despite a succession of analyses that fail to establish this causal link between morale and productivity, most managers, most of the time, appear to believe there is one (Jacoby, 1988: 88). It is this kind of faith that has aided the generation of a new form of 'organizational fundamentalism': organizational culture.

Organizational Cultures

The assumption that management is merely the pursuit of rationality implies that rational choice, or as management gurus prefer to call it, strategic planning, is the solution to organizational problems. Yet the necessarily interpretative, contingent and discontinuous nature of business life makes such strategic planning today – and its progenitor, Fayol's functional structure and planning – utopian ideals. As Mintzberg has suggested, 'we have no techniques for predicting discontinuities, we can only extrapolate' (1989). Such extrapolations can become less contingent, according to the faithful of the organizational culture school, if we are able to analyse the culture and ensure it corresponds to organizational strategy. In short, organizations work best where members' and organizations' beliefs, actions and goals are mutually compatible.

A primary extrapolation from the work of this culturalist approach is derived from Durkheimian concerns for organizational solidarity through ideological consensus and from Mayo's postulations on the intimate links between the emotional needs of individuals and the organizational need for integration. Typically the approach is interpretative to the extent that organizations are free to interpret and develop a specific form of culture, though it should be noted that many of the 'best seller' approaches to the culture of success tend to assume that senior management's articulation of their company culture is identical to the actual culture itself – assuming that only one culture exists (Carroll, 1983; Alvesson, 1987). In fact one of the basic problems with this entire approach lies in its technocratic design: it is intended not so much to explain what the contemporary culture of an organization *is* but what it *should be*. Thus it operates along a pragmatic, if not a utopian, line of operation: changing the organization in a direction designed to facilitate efficiency rather than accounting for the current form of culture and assessing its significance. This is also problematic in that it may well persuade managers to act *as if* the preferred cultural attributes already existed, such that the acting out of a cultural myth becomes the organizational reality. Unless we really believe that all organizations claiming to be excellent are just that, then we should be wary of many such culturalist approaches. The current trend in which corporations formalize their cultures through explicit statements, which members are supposed to read and inwardly digest, implies that such formulations *create* cultures as much as *reflect* already existing ones (cf. Lorsch, 1986; Hassard and Sharifi, 1989).

A less manipulative approach to the significance of organizational cultures is provided by Handy (1985). He distinguishes between four types: power, role, task-based and person. Power cultures are symbolized by a concentric ring or web where key individuals radiate power from the centre and rely upon trust not rules for their control over the organization. Role cultures are typically to be found in bureaucracies; they exude rationality, specialization, procedures and rule following. Task cultures are primarily job or project oriented, represented by matrix organizations where flexibility and decentralized control prevails. Finally, person cultures exist where the individual is the focus of the organization, and Handy argues that while this exists within families, communes and small groups its significance is limited within conventional business organizations. Precisely how these various cultures evolve is related to the interrelationship between six major influencing factors: history and ownership, size, technology, goals and objectives, the environment, and the people. Generally speaking, Handy argues that the larger an organization, the more routine its environment, and the more interdependent and expensive its technology, the more likely it will be to adopt a role culture. Where the technology and environment changes rapidly and where the goals of the organization are rapid growth, then a power or task-based culture will tend to predominate. The result is that 'different cultures call for differing psychological contracts, and that certain types of people will be happy and successful in one culture but not in another' (Handy, 1985: 204). Culture, in this perspective, then, becomes the glue holding an organization together; it is the Durkheimian social cement without which no social group can exist.

However, rather than taking culture as the glue holding the organization together, it might be more appropriate to regard it as the result of social action. That is, culture does not cause people in organizations to act in specific ways, rather culture is generated by certain individuals defining some forms of action as representative of the 'official' organizational culture. A consideration of two of Handy's cultural types will suffice for my purposes here: role culture and power culture.

Power culture exists where organizational power/control is in the hands of an individual or a small elite: in Handy's phrase 'This culture depends on a central power source, with rays of power and influence spreading out from that central figure' (1985: 189). In short, a leader's power causes others to act. Yet when such a leader does 'exert power' it is subordinate others, not the leader, who engage in action. If the subordinates do not act then the leader has no power; only as a *consequence* of subordinate actions can leaders be deemed to have power. Thus power is a consequence of action, rather than a cause of action. This shift from the 'principle' of power to the 'practice' of power, as Latour (1986) calls it, also implies that subordinate action occurs only through the interpretation of self-advantage by the subordinate. In turn, it is likely that the command of the leader will become distorted through what Latour calls the 'translation' process: not only are leaders dependent upon their subordinates but a subordinate's translation of the edict may well prove to be a distortion of the leader's intention. The implication of this for Handy's power culture model is that rather than the rays of power spreading out from the centre to the periphery in a determinate and unmediated fashion they are both highly contingent and the subject of constant interpretation and renegotiation. Such a revision enables us to cope rather better, for example, with some of the radical changes in the recent political history of Europe. The position of east European communist leaders and their structures of power did not change dramatically between 1988 and 1989 but the willingness of the subordinate population to obey them certainly did: their former power was a consequence of the populations' subordination not a cause of it.

The second of Handy's types, role culture, is epitomized by rule-based action – a bureaucracy. In theory, once we know the rule the action is determined by it. But again, this implies that the culture explains the organization. However, rules are inherently ambiguous: there can never be enough rules to cover every contingency nor are rules self-explanatory – we need rules to explain which rule to apply and to interpret the meaning of each rule *ad infinitum*. It is for just this reason that 'working to rule' – which should mean working as effectively as possible – leads to the development of grossly inefficient working practices. Rules, then, may be conceived of not as determinants of action but as post hoc rationalizations, as resources to justify action already taken. Again, the implications of this interpretative approach are profoundly disturbing to any assumption that role cultures provide for rule-bound behaviour.

This does not mean that analysing culture is an unimportant aspect of organizational theory, though it could be argued that the entire technocratic approach is of greater importance as a manifestation of dominant culture than any inter-organizational differences which may appear to exist (Alvesson, 1987: 213). Analysing the sellers of cultural excellence also provides insights into organizations and organizational consultants; but believing what organizational consultants claim, without assessing their empirical evidence, is tantamount to establishing a new school of organizational thought: what might be called the HLS (Hook, Line and Sinker) perspective. Relatedly, we should acknowledge the implication of adopting organizational myths as a symbol of corporate culture. As Bowles (1989) argues, such organizational myths embody attempts to generate an organizational belief system not too distant from those previously erected by religious groups: the myth of the corporate executive who subordinates everything to the greater good of the corporation acts both to inspire resemblant behaviour and to inculcate a body of executives whose allegiance is close to that of religious disciples. It may well be that few blue- or white-collar workers are drawn into the same level of 'dependence', despite (or perhaps because of) the best efforts of corporate managers to instil enthusiasm through company songs and collective company physical jerks, but the allegiance or pragmatic acquiescence of these groups may be acquired through other means. Just as dominant ideologies are crucial for the dominant, not the dominated groups (Abercrombie et al., 1980), so too the proselytizing essence of corporate enculturers is aimed primarily at corporate controllers not employees.

Perhaps the clearest British example of this recently was provided by the speech of Peter Morgan, Director General of the Institute of Directors's 10th Annual Conference (27 February 1990). Here Morgan stressed not just the reduction of the country to 'UK PLC', and national success to the gross national product, but constructed images of the Thatcherite enterprise culture as one bespattered with militarism. Directors are 'heroes of the enterprise culture' leading their 'soldiers in a global economic war . . . the battle for Britain' where our poor educational system means that 'we confront panzer divisions with the home guard'. The articulation of a power culture may be clear but are such bellicose demands active shapers of organizations? A hefty dose of scepticism is a useful antidote: self-appointed heroic leaders whose army actually resembles a motley group of old men with sticks rather than the SAS have probably received too many head wounds in previous fights.

Critical Theories

At the critical pole of the technocratic – critical continuum, towards the opposite end to the organizational cultures school discussed above, lie a collection of theories labelled critical theories. Whereas the organizational culture approach tends to assume that efficiency and rationality are uncontestable concepts that are axiomatically linked to the pursuit of a managerially inspired culture, the critical approach denies the rationality of the entire framework of capitalism. Much of the original work was undertaken by Marcuse (1964, 1969), and his starting point is one which situates capitalism itself as a form of 'technological rationality'. Technological rationality represents an instrumental and technologically determined approach to life and nature; all human problems are perceived as reducible to technological solutions with the result that what little debate exists focuses not on the ends of human society but the means to achieve a pre-given, normative end: the expansion of capitalism. Thought, under advanced capitalism, then, becomes one-dimensional, that is non-critical: it takes for granted that we should organize social institutions such as work in a way calculated to exploit, rather than nurture, natural resources; it takes for granted that there is no alternative to the status quo: organizations are, therefore, perceived to be 'naturally' hierarchical and authoritarian. Moreover, the system becomes self-reproducing in so far as it swamps all potential criticism in a sea of commodities: the 'good life' can be measured in the ownership of an ever increasing supply of material goods, not an ever increasing degree of self-actualization and democratic control over society.

Habermas (1970, 1971), the other major theorist within this approach, argues that human activity can be differentiated into 'purposive rational' action or work, and 'symbolic interaction' or 'communicative action'. The former is concerned, amongst other things, with material production which is based upon technical rules, while the latter is concerned with social and cultural life governed by socially constructed norms. According to Habermas the two different systems of thought become conflated to the extent that the critical aspects of symbolic interaction become subsumed under the purposive-rational systems. In other words, and translating these ideas very loosely, the critical aspects of organizational theory become suppressed by the technocratic aspects.

Neither Habermas nor Marcuse was overtly concerned with analysing individual organizations per se, and much of the recent work most directly related to this form of approach has been undertaken by Burrell and Morgan (1979), Clegg and Dunkerley (1980) and Alvesson (1987). Perhaps the most useful summary can be constructed from the model provided by Alvesson in his 'Six Theses for a Critical Organization Theory' (1987).

First, there is a permanent source of tension in organizations between two contrasting rationalities: technological rationality seeks to maximize resources and minimize shortages; its opposite (which Alvesson calls 'practical reason') seeks to maximize freedom and minimize repression. Second, the dominance of technological rationality over the operational process corresponds to the interests of the predominant social strata. Third, technological rationality involves an ideology that systematically distorts the reality generated by itself. Fourth, an organizational practice which corresponds to the mental make-up of humans as well as to the interests of the majority must break with the supremacy of technological rationality. Fifth, business organizations etc. are instruments for reproducing technological rationality which, in turn, they depend on. Sixth, the functioning of organizations must be comprehended within the compass of that rationality which dominates the given historical and social context.

Several features of this list call for comment. The first point is accurate in so far as a tension does exist between differing rationalities. However, it is questionable whether just two rationalities are involved here. There is a considerable amount of empirical evidence to suggest that many people operate with multiple and internally conflicting rationalities such that the manichaean 'either or' model of Alvesson may be a useful way of posing the extreme opposites but should not be taken to represent the two oppositional empirical norms (Mann, 1970; Held, 1984). Second, the correspondence between technological rationality and the dominant social strata should be seen as something which needs to be permanently reproduced, a contingent issue, rather than something which is itself taken for granted. That is not to say that the technological rationality of the dominant social group is permanently threatened but it is the case, for example, that the recent popularity of green issues poses a considerable threat to them. Third, the distorting effects of the ideology of technological rationality are undoubtedly influential but do not appear all-encompassing. If they were, then green politics would never emerge and the very idea of critical organization theory would have been still-born. Fourth, claims about the mental make up of humans and the unarticulated interests of the majority should always be treated with considerable caution. If, as argued in chapter 1, the needs of humans are socially constructed rather than innate dispositions, then such claims cannot be justified. Indeed, such claims are, like Marcuse's critique, a direct mirror image of the technocratic arguments: managerialists would have us believe that the interests of all society are exactly equivalent to theirs, some critical theorists would have us believe that our interests are being misrepresented by the managerialists - but not by critical theorists.

In sum, the critical theorists' criticisms of technocratic theories highlight the distortions and misrepresentations of human interest as reducible to the interests of managers. But equally problematic are the attempts by some critical theorists, and for that matter all other attempts, to impose or impute a set of universal interests upon humanity.

Systems Theories

Around six years before Marcuse was to decry the absence of critical thought and the suppression of conflict in capitalist society, Dunlop was attempting to ensure that the fledgling discipline of industrial relations strenuously avoided any mention of the conflictual approach which he perceived to be rampant amongst industrial sociology at the time. It is ironic that while some of the critical theorists also decried the movement towards systems or wholistic models of society, one of their number, Habermas, was himself to adopt and adapt systems theory to his own radical ends.

It has long been a tradition within many fields of study to explain phenomena through 'analysis', that is breaking up the whole into discrete elements for the purposes of clearer argument. One particularly successful movement in the opposite direction - towards a synthetic all-embracing theory - was 'systems theory'. Although elements of such an approach have been around from the beginning of the twentieth century, the first systematic approach was that of Bertalanffy in a series of articles in the 1950s and 1960s (1981). However, the more conventional route of systems theory into the sociology of work and organizations has been, paradoxically, via the work of Dunlop (1958). Dunlop adopted the Parsonian convention that rule-bound behaviour was the key explanatory category, and that these rules encompassed all major actors within the industrial relations system: unions, management and government. In turn, these groups are locked together by a normative consensus which, amongst other things (technology and markets), assumes that power analysis is beyond the scope of industrial relations theory (Roche, 1986). As Roche makes clear, not only is the removal of power a debilitating elision, but there is no reason why rule making cannot exist outside a normative consensus. Indeed, it could well be argued that the reverse applies since a consensus implies that rules are less necessary, at least in any overt or coercive form, while disagreeements may require precisely such a form of constraint via rules if the disputes are not to lead to serious conflict.

Systems theory asserts that it is the relationships and interactions between elements which explain the behaviour of the whole. Indeed, the systems approach is not only technocratic in its denial of conflicting ideologies and material interests but also deterministic in its pursuit of the correct prediction of behaviour through an analysis of organizational rules. Closed systems, such as central heating systems, are virtually internally self-regulating, and all the elements are mutually dependent. Open systems, however, are necessarily dependent upon the wider environment with which they interact. Hence, open systems are less stable than closed systems even though an explanation of the behaviour of the whole is still dependent upon the relationships between the sub-systems. For example, the behaviour of an organization is not wholly dependent upon the character of the director or the movements of the markets but on the way all the elements of the system interact with each other and in relation to the external environment.

Systems theorists, in their pursuit of wholistic explanations, have often tended to mirror the conservative emphasis of evolutionary theories which highlight the significance of organizations and individuals reacting to, rather than actively constructing, their environment. That is, if organizations are merely reactive to changes in environments then they have little capacity to change radically in any proactive stance: they cannot change themselves except in so far as environmental change demands specific and functional forms of evolutionary change. However, not only is the evolutionary, environmental and functional emphasis misplaced – because social institutions can actually generate their own environments or at least change them as well as being changed by them – it is also inherently flawed because functionalism inverts the logic of cause and effect by assuming that effects lead to causes (see Giddens, 1977; Craib, 1984). In fact, the conservative label is not necessarily deserved. Even if most systems approaches have been concerned to explain how disequilibriums need to be resolved in favour of organizational equilibrium there are several writers whose interests lie in a much more radical development. Thus the works of Habermas (1970), Wallerstein (1974, 1979) and Baumgartner, Burns and DeVille (1979) can all be categorized as radical systems theorists.

Four forms of criticism tend to be mounted against systems theory. First, it reifies organizations. That is, it imputes animate needs into inanimate objects. To assert that an organization needs to find an equilibrium implies that organizations have needs. But organizations are merely legal institutions, they have no existence beyond their human members whose relationships bind an organization into existence. Thus, when we talk of organizations 'needing' something we really mean that some or all of the human elements of an organization need it. Furthermore, we usually mean that the human actors in control of the organization, the ones who articulate and represent allegedly organizational needs, are the ones whose needs are really being demonstrated.

The second and related criticism of systems theory concerns the nature of organizational stability. Even if we accept a degree of dynamism into the equilibrium it is still doubtful whether most organizations are stable across time. A mere reference to the British economy in the 1980s would suggest that given the manufacturing collapse of the 1979–82 period, the stock market seesaws of October 1987 and 1989, and the record levels of bankruptcies, new businesses and mergers, the last label to describe the system as a whole, or the individual system elements, would be 'stable'.

Third, systems theories, at least within the organizational field, tend to take an ahistorical perspective. That is to say, they take for granted the prior development of systems and sub-systems to the extent that historical imbalances of power between groups, for example, are irrelevant to explaining their contemporary relations. This is akin to arguing that the present position of women in work organizations has nothing to do with their historically generated subordination. Obviously, not all systems theorists are guilty of this misunderstanding of the significance of history (Wallerstein's (1974, 1979) world systems theory being soaked in historical argument) but many of the pragmatic accounts are.

Fourth, the essential thrust of systems analysis is towards the development of integration and consensus. The explanation of disintegration and dissensus, therefore, requires some form of pathological or dysfunctional argument. Yet, as we shall discover below, it may be that disintegration and dissensus are the norm rather than atypical; for humans may thrive not on uniformity but disunity. If this is the case then the whole foundation stone of conventional, that is conservative, systems theory is subject to a terminal form of cancer (Cooper, 1986).

Systems theory, then, at least in its traditional conservative form, represents an approach that appears to be inherently deterministic and generally, though not wholly, technocratic. On the other hand the assumption that the links between ostensibly unrelated phenomena and institutions need to be assessed, that such a system may be inherently unstable, that it has a history, that little consensus exists, and that rules are resources for, not determinants of, action, all have some role in the development of Actor Networks which are discussed later. The idea of an interlocking system is not inherently flawed but the practical adoption of such an idea within conventional systems theory is. It was from just this latter kind of complaints that contingency theory developed.

Contingency Theory

Contingency theory has probably proved to be the most influential of all organizational theories – at least until the organizational culture approach hit the bookstores. Its origins lie in the work of Burns and Stalker (1961), Lawrence and Lorsch (1967), and the Aston Studies (Pugh and Hickson, 1976). It was overtly technocratic in approach and attempted to reduce the infinity of information implied in the systems approach down to a manageable level. It did this by focusing upon a delimited number of specific management problems, such as the management structure, the issue of leadership, organizational bottlenecks etc. Such problems and their appropriate solutions were regarded as contingent upon a small number of variables.

There was not a 'single best way' to resolve organizational problems but then neither did management have the freedom to do whatever it liked. The label 'contingency' does not imply an increasing level of freedom for actors, based upon the significance of the interpretive act, but actually seeks to eliminate such 'freedom'. In the words of Greenwood et al.:

> Contingency theory rests upon the assumption that organizational characteristics have to be shaped to meet situational circumstances. The extent to which any organization secures a 'goodness of fit' between situational characteristics and structural characteristics will determine the level of organizational performance. (quoted in Lee and Lawrence, 1985: 38–9)

Where the contingency approach is most vulnerable to criticism, and why it sits very close to the determinist line, is in its construction of independent variables. This is most clearly shown in Woodward's (1958) account of organizational performance amongst manufacturing plants in the south-east of England. Woodward argued that although some degree of contingency existed, in so far as managers could choose between different forms of organizational structure, only those which chose the most 'appropriate' structure – as determined by the technology of production – were likely to be successful. Thus contingency does not really relate to unrestricted choice nor to the level of uncertainty. In fact, the argument is one which attempts to remove contingency by specifying the conditions under which the success of particular organizations can be determined. Similarly, Lawrence's and Lorsch's (1967) argument focuses on the way the internal structure of a manufacturing organization is determined by the level of contingency which exists in the product market: the higher the level of product market uncertainty the greater the need for a flexible, or 'differentiated' internal structure.

However, the most meticulous contingency study, and the one which best illustrates its problems, is the Aston approach of Pugh and Hickson (1976). This study distinguished between a sequence of independent variables – such as the pattern of ownership and control, the size, goals, technology, location, resources and level of interdependence with other organizations – and a series of dependent variables. These included the division of labour, level of bureaucratization, the extent of the formalization of communications, and the centralization and shape of the power structure. The relationship between the independent and the dependent variables was analysed through a stream of (mainly) quantitative data which suggested that size, technology and location were the three most significant factors affecting organizational performance. Yet, for all the effort and claimed 'objectivity' of this approach it is not self-evident that the choice of variables was objectively well founded, nor what exactly the statistical correlations were supposed to mean (Lee and Lawrence, 1985: 47).

The critical issue here is the meaning of 'contingency': although the label is used freely, it would appear that the element of contingency is directly related – in fact determined – by variables which are independent of the organization. Thus it would seem that environmental factors actually determine the nature of the organization; albeit the specific organizational structure is contingent upon the exact mix of environmental influences. In short, human actors appear to play little part in much contingency theory (cf. Donaldson, 1985). It was for this reason that some academics began to explore the value of a perspective that rescued the subjective and active side of organizations from the clutches of the determinists; this was to be the action approach.

Action Theory

While systems theorists attempted to model some of their ideas on the natural sciences, and especially the deterministic engineering model which has adopted the systems approach most fully (Open Systems Group, 1981), other organizational sociologists were moving sharply in the opposite direction: towards a model where contingency, not determinism, was the 'default' category. In practice, action theory tended to remain in the province of sociology while contingency theory sprouted amongst the organizational behaviourists and the business schools.

One of the most notable attempts to develop such an alternative in the sociology discipline was Silverman's (1970) pursuit of an action theory drawn from the combined works of Weber, Schutz and Berger. Silverman argued that the social sciences were different orders of subject matter and thus, although the approach of both should be rigorous, their methods would be necessarily dissimilar. In particular, sociology was concerned with understanding rather than observing behaviour – the distinction being critical in so far as it is meanings which define social reality rather than social reality being self-evident through observation. Such meanings were, in themselves, liable to degenerate and therefore required constant reaffirmation in everyday actions. Thus, social reality did not just happen but had to be made to happen. The implication of this was that through social interaction people could modify and possibly even transform social meanings, and therefore any explanation of human action had to take into account the meanings which those involved assigned to their actions. For example, whether failure to obey a superordinate's command was a manifestation of worker militancy, misunderstanding or just the beginnings of deafness depended not so much on what bosses or researchers 'saw' happen but what the worker involved meant by her or his action. Of course, misunderstanding of the meaning of action was also possible, so that the ultimate result of the interaction may not have been willed by any of the participants.

Roy's ethnographic approach to work is a classic landmark in this form of sociological investigation, and it is his factory-based 'banana time' (1973) which most clearly demonstrates the way social reality is constructed and interpreted by the actors involved. In particular, Roy himself demonstrates the significance of interpretation rather than simply observation since, initially at least, the actions of his work colleagues appear completely spontaneous, irrational and bizarre. Each day Roy witnessed one of his workmates (Ike) steal another's (Sammy's) banana:

> Each morning after making the snatch, Ike would call out, 'Banana time!' and proceed to down his prize while Sammy made futile protests . . . he never did get to eat his banana but kept bringing one for his lunch. At first this daily theft startled and amazed me. Then I grew to look forward to the daily seizure and the verbal interaction which followed. (Roy, 1973: 211)

Only when he understands what the behaviour means to the workers, how they make sense of their lives through their actions and routines which structure the working day, and how they interpret the world, is Roy able to provide a satisfactory explanation of group interaction.

A further implication of the creative essence of such an approach is that social relations between superordinates and subordinates are not simply explained through the powerlessness of the latter. Since almost all aspects of social relations are necessarily reciprocal there are few situations where individuals can categorically be said to be powerless (Giddens, 1982a: 197–200). Obviously, where one individual is tied hand and foot and about to be physically exterminated by another, the former is powerless; yet, as argued in chapter 2, even slaves have some element of power because their relations with slave owners are not determined by the apparently objective situation. If slaves can sometimes manipulate situations to their advantage then we can be sure that subordinates in rational (i.e., rule-bound) organizations have access to many more power resources. This is not to say that a pattern of pluralist equality prevails in most work organizations, the point is merely that subordinates are not powerless. Perhaps the best example of how individuals in an apparently hopeless situation can carve out some measure of autonomy is Goffman's analysis of patients' behaviour in mental institutions (1961); an image more popularly revealed in Jack Nicholson's portrayal of a mental patient in the film *One Flew over the Cuckoo's Nest*. The nature of this unofficial bargain between subordinate and superordinate is also captured in the model of 'negotiated order' developed by Strauss et al. (1963), in which apparently intransitive structures of social life are actually the contingent subject of constant renegotiation. Here, then, actors' perceptions and their negotiations actively shape the social structure.

It could be argued that Strauss's approach is too restrictive in its assertion of the role of negotiations, rather than too expansive. That is, once limits are placed on the elements within the organization which are subject to negotiation then the crucial consequence of human interpretation is diminished. For example, while Strauss might want to limit the negotiated features of a hospital organization to the interactions of the humans involved, the interpretative approach would want to include the technical forms as well. For example, the technical limits of beds per ward or the technically determined capacities of various forms of medical technology are taken for granted by Strauss, but the interpretative approach would subject both these to the critical influence of human interpretation: what counts as the maximum ratio of beds per ward? and what forms of rhetoric have persuaded actors that such a ratio is the maximum viable? who decides that specific machines can only be operated in particular ways since other ways may be equally viable?

Political Organizational Theories

The concern that action theories, although obviously not technocratic in the sense of contingency theory, nevertheless tended to fall into a subjectivist approach that eliminates the institutionalized aspects of inequalities of power in work organizations, generated the search for yet another alternative. In turn, this led to a conjunction of rather disparate approaches that have been concentrated here under the admittedly cumbersome label 'political organizational theories'. One strand took off under the auspices of Child's (1972) 'strategic choice' model in which the elite or dominant coalitions of managers took positive *action* to ensure their interests prevailed over all others. Lee and Lawrence (1985) draw upon the essentially political nature of organizational life, its innate contingency and the value of various strategies of influence to go well beyond Child. However, it would seem that in their desire to escape from the determinism of other models there is little room left for any analysis of the relationships between these human actors and the material and technological systems with which they interact. Thus power networks are restricted to social networks, rather than networks of human and non-human 'actors' (Lee and Lawrence, 1985: 143–4).

Probably the clearest account of a political model is that enunciated by Salaman (1979, 1984), though the original ideas are closely associated with Fox (1971, 1974, 1976). Salaman argues that the labour process orthodoxy, which held sway over much of academic industrial sociology for over a decade (see chapter 5), distorts the reality of work by focusing upon class to the exclusion of the more pervasive and significant aspects of work structuring: social relations. Social relations do not exclude class relations but the opposite often tends to hold, such that Marxist accounts of work organizations are partial. In its place Salaman argues that a model comprising the following should be adopted.

First, organizations should be deemed political organizations: they are structured by power relations. The implication of this is twofold: class relations are just one form, albeit an important one, of power relations and we should therefore seek out other forms, such as gender or ethnic relations etc., which may prove to be as important as, if not more significant than, class relations. The establishment of workplace relations is therefore an empirical question rather than a theoretical one, though it is taken for granted that such workplace relations will be patterned. It also denies the managerialist approach which suggests the organizations are neutral instruments for universally agreed purposes. On the contrary, organizations embody and actively reproduce the forms of social inequality that prevail in the wider society.

Second, organizations are not free floating bodies but locked into a wider, and again political, environment. Thus whatever goes on within organizations has to be explained partly as a reflection of the organization's environment. This means that we need to go beyond Marxist explanations that reduce causes to the structural requirements of capitalism and look at the complexities of organizational life rather than the simplicities. This does not mean that we should ignore the essentiality of capitalism, but this thirst for profit, while important in any account of organizations, is not sufficient in itself. Indeed, for those public organizations ostensibly beyond the conventional market imperatives a whole sequence of problems may arise that demonstrate the difficulties of assuming the issues are wholly capitalist in origin (Seglow, 1983; Batstone et al., 1984).

Third, Salaman argues for the significance of identity and the part played by organizational life in the construction of both personal and group identity. Frequently this is intimately connected to the patterning of differentiation discussed above, for the development of identity may often be forged negatively through the exclusion of others rather than positively through the creation of personal or group characteristics. Again, like the work of Lee and Lawrence (1985), a major issue with this neo-Weberian approach is the extent to which it encompasses the seamless web of relationships, not between human actors but between human actors, material and technological artefacts. The significance of human actors appears to have been rescued only to leave them bereft of a critical aspect of their character and influence: technology. Before we explore this, however, we need to develop the penultimate approach to organizational life represented by Foucault and post-modernism.

Foucault and Post-Modernism

Foucault's approach locates him firmly against much of the organizational approach discussed so far. While the writings of the classical school of organizations, such as Fayol, Urwick and Taylor, their human relation opponents, and even their radical critics like Habermas, tended to see organizations as the actual or potential epitome of human rationality, Foucault and the rest of the post-modernist tradition (e.g. Lyotard and Derrida etc.) regard organizations as more akin to defensive reactions against inherently destabilizing forces (Cooper and Burrell, 1988). Thus, where modernists perceive history as the gradual promotion of progress, reason and rationality, post-modernists perceive no such progressive intent or reality. In terms of the axes of determinism and interpretivism the post-modern tradition is firmly towards the end of the interpretivist pole.

The organization, and particularly the modern corporation, embodies for the opposing camps a useful example of opposition. For modernists the rationality of organization, complete with computer-aided decision making, speaks to the future enlightenment of the world. But to post-modernists the very same organization threatens humanity with totalizing control derived not only from its spreading tentacles of material and ideological control but from the nature of its legitimacy. That is to say, that the modern organization's claim to legitimacy rests in its claims to represent rationality and future progress. Naturally, not all modernists are of the same faith: Habermas's ideals are to return human organizations to the consensually constructed control of their human participants, whereas Bell's are much more limited to the development of rational organization. But where they both meet is in the belief that reason can promote human progress.

Another feature of differentiation between the two camps lies in the conservative modernist assumption that organizations tend towards certainty, stability and consensus; the post-modern assumption is that instability, uncertainty and dissensus are the norm. The latter is particularly important for organizational analysis for it implies that differentiation is not merely a contingent reaction to a specific mode of organizational life but a necessary feature of social relations. Accordingly, difference is, as Nietzsche argued, not one feature of social relations but the active force underlying them.

The uncertainty of social life is taken further by Derrida (1973, 1978) in that organizations are construed not as mechanisms to advance human control but processes to hide the very uncertainty we live in. This suggests that while labour process theorists are locked into an assessment of managerial control mechanisms, the post-modernist approach denies the plausibility of any group being 'in control'. To be in control presumes a rational intent and means to effect such intent but neither of these can exist within the post-modernist approach. In short, post-modernists start from the assumption that organizations are the results of reactive processes, attempts to delimit the disaggregating reality of everyday existence. The very uncertainty and fragility of social life becomes a stimulus to construct reality-distancing mechanisms: organizations are façades constructed not to advance human control but to obscure the reality that we have no control. In turn, this reproduction of the practices that sustain the precarious, but taken for granted, nature of the world ultimately prevents us from recognising the nature of the social world (Knights, 1989). Since some (post-modernist) people are self-evidently not taken in by this mirage (otherwise they could not describe it as such), the modernist alchemy must be less powerful than either side claim.

Language is another critical medium of distinction between modernist and post-modernist approaches: for the former, language is usually regarded as the neutral carrier of information - a transparent mechanism for carrying the meaning of an organization. For the post-modernist, and particularly Derrida, language does not carry the meaning so much as provide the means by which meaning can be imposed upon or constructed into an organization. Meaning, then, does not reside in an organization and await the researchers' 'discovery' but is something the researcher imputes to an organization. Hence Derrida's concern that research should endeavour to 'deconstruct' what are taken for truths by demonstrating the essential ambivalence of language and therefore, in this instance, of organizations. By implication writing, or in Latour and Woolgar's (1979) approach an 'inscription device', should be regarded as a means by which control may be formalized: the wall chart of organizational hierarchies is not a description of reality but an attempt to create the same (see Cooper, 1989).

Foucault's (1977, 1979; Sheridan, 1980) relevance to organizational theory lies in several related spheres. First, he argues that contemporary society is, and therefore presumably contemporary organizations are, maintained not by any consensus nor by the overt coercion of the state's judicial system but rather by the covert systems of bodily surveillance and discipline which are built into the framework of organizations. Thus, like prisoners, workers must always be visible to their controllers and the minutiae of daily life is legitimately ordered and observed from above and written up, not into personal details but into bureaucratic case notes. Subjectivity is systematically shredded by the organization, and a model of normality is reconstituted from the elements; anyone deviating from this model is the subject of further dissection by society's human scientists - the self-appointed judges of normality.

Foucault's major importance here lies in the notions of power articulated by his network model. Power is a semi-stable network of alliances but for Foucault the centre of concern is the human subject rather than the organization. Subjects are constructed by power but do not 'have' power. Power, then, is not the property of any individual or group, still less can it be discovered lurking in structures. While traditional theories of power, for Foucault, suggest that its origins lie in the state, its direction of flow is downwards against subordinates, and its essence is negative, he argues that this is to misunderstand the power-soaked nature of all social life and its constitutive force. Power, then, should be configured as a relation between subjects: the micro-physics of everyday life. It is 'capillary power'; it is exercised '*within* the social body, rather than *above* it' (1980: 39). Not all subjects are equal within the network of power relations which defines them. On the contrary, the resources of power are unequally distributed and this inequality is often buttressed by the strategies employed by resource rich subjects.

This does not mean that subordinates are helplessly caught in the web of power for the very indeterminancy of social life suggests that resistance and dissensus are ever present. Yet, for Foucault, the demonstration of resistance is merely a functional facilitator of greater subsequent discipline: only if resistance constantly tests the deployment of discipline can discipline be improved and secured (Burrell, 1988). Moreover, although all organizations are not akin to prisons, as Foucault suggests with his image of society as an extended Panopticon, it is still the case, Burrel argues, that as individuals we are never free of some form of organization. In this sense our lives are lived out within an incarcerated world that, with the ever-increasing expansion of computer networks and electronic surveillance, promises to claw tighter at the lineaments of the subject. This 'disciplinary power', which subjugates specific individuals (prisoners, workers, etc.), is distinguishable both from 'bio-power', in so far as the latter focuses upon the general population and subjugates it through the mechanisms of normalization such as sexual norms, and from prior forms of sovereign power. Thus during the eighteenth century the (French) state shifted its method of control from one of absolute terror, based in physical torture, to disciplinary power, based in prison-grounded regimes of institutional routine and the development of normative schemas of deviance. But the diffusion of power from the sovereign was not a strategic development as much as the result of other power centres developing their own forms of discipline. Factories, churches, schools, hospitals were all imbricated in the construction of 'normal' behaviour patterns that served to discipline the population and it is worth pointing out that if the disciplining effects of one, say education, facilitated the control of factory proletarians this was not, according to Foucault, because the factories needed such additional resources. Indeed, Foucault's argument is that the disciplinary method has its origin not in the pecuniary hands of capitalist factory owners but in the disciplinary hands of prison and asylum controllers.

Much of Foucault's and the other post-modernist writers' approach is fruitful in the different light it sheds on organizations. In particular, the contingent nature of organizations and notion of power as a web within which all are held, are useful counterthrusts to the determinist and technocratic approaches of many managerialist and, indeed, orthodox Marxist approaches. However, there is a tendency to eliminate the superordinates in the desire to paint a picture of society like a prison in which even the prison authorities are entangled by, rather than in some semblance of control over, the web of power relations. To argue that prisoners' resistance is merely functional to the development of greater disciplinary powers is also unnecessarily determinist: the history of prisons – as the 1980s in Britain are ample witness – is not one of ever decreasing prisoner resistance as each eruption merely facilitates its own elimination. Foucault might have regarded the spate of prison riots in Britain in previous years as functionally necessary to eliminate further resistance of that kind; the £60 million rebuild of Strangeways prison after the 1990 riot suggests otherwise.

Actor Networks of Organizational Power

While conventional social network approaches might explain the length of the Strangeways' disturbance through an analysis of the characters involved, it seems clear that the materials and technology involved (physical barricades, food supplies, and strategic control over the roof) are critical elements too. The Actor Network model (Callon, 1986; Latour, 1988; and Law, 1988), which is principally aimed at explaining the development and stabilization of forms of technology, is particularly useful in this and other organizational contexts. Fundamentally, the approach suggests that power depends upon the construction and maintenance of a network of actors; crucially, and contrary to the implications of Clegg's (1989: 202–7, 225) otherwise useful review, these networks involve both human and non-human 'actors'. Perhaps 'elements' rather than 'actors' might be considered a better description here since it avoids the reification implied by non-human actors. But the approach is constructed on the premise that we should avoid the conventional distinctions between human and non-human elements and should talk instead of the 'heterogeneous entities that constitute a network' (Bijker, et al., 1987: 11). That is, we should consider the unity of human and non-human actors in terms of a seamless web as Hughes (1979) calls it or 'heterogeneous engineering' in Law's (1986) case. The implication of this is that organizations should not be perceived as, or explained through, the activities of humans alone but through the alliances of human and non-human actors. These non-human actors may, for example, take the form of technology or material facets of institutions – buildings etc. For instance, it would be erroneous to consider the antics of a maniacal driver in terms of the driver or the car, or even the driver as a discrete unit and the car as a discrete unit. Rather, we should note the imperceptible network that links the two together: only when the driver is one *with* the car does the maniacal driver really exist.

When we consider the force of this approach with regard to organizational issues we have to seek out the alliance or networks that initiate and maintain the superordination of individuals or groups over others. Moreover, we should remember that many actors that are locked into networks exist outside the particular organization. For example, managerial networks rely not just upon the expertise of fellow managers and the control over material resources within the enterprise, but also the resources of the legal system (the police, the courts, the prisons etc.) and the domestic supports which are invisibly meshed into the organization's disciplinary mechanisms. Similarly, those scientists allegedly isolated from the rest of the world in their quest for knowledge are actually highly dependent upon a large array of supportive networks outside the laboratory (Latour, 1987: 145–76).

It is now possible to see the power of reification: where Actor Networks manage to construct a system that incorporates not just non-human actors but actually makes them appear independent of social aspects then the entire network becomes stronger. To clarify this point, it is not that the transport system or social inequality are both inevitable or that they can be explained as wholly technological or social phenomena. Rather, they are constructed through networks but they gain in obduracy if they can be made to appear natural or inevitable: once reified they resist attempts to deconstruct them (Woolgar, 1990). Skilled workers, therefore, maintain their position through networks that include union organization, control over specific forms of skill and machinery, and restrictions on recruitment etc. Relatedly, the network that binds women into employment is notoriously fragile and is constantly undermined by the state's refusal to establish universal crèche facilities and paid leave for family illness etc.

The means by which such networks are constructed is divided into 'moments' whereby allies are recruited in such a way that the solution to their own problems only appears viable through the network, and the point at which the network itself becomes differentiated from others through the mobilization and categorization of members. In Latour's (1986) terms, organizational power does not emanate from the leader(s) at the centre in a diffused mode but is the result of subordinates' translative action (see above). Hence we can shift analysis away from the problem of subordinate resistance to the problem of subordinate compliance. This shift from the 'principles of power' to the 'practices of power' is an essential aspect of the Actor Network model and operates as a valuable caution against those determinist accounts that explain organizations by concentrating on the formal organizational model itself rather than on the interpretative practices of humans in association with non-humans.

What should equally be stressed here is the fragile and transient nature of such networks and, implicitly therefore, the constant need for the network to be reproduced. Networks do not maintain themselves, even though a viable method of extending the time span of a network is to inscribe it in material form. For example, Latour (1988) notes how the radical Paris government built its subway bridges too small to allow the coaches of the private railroad companies to pass through, thereby ossifying its contingent political control into a concrete embodiment. As Latour concludes:

> They shifted their alliance from legal or contractual ones, to stones, earth and concrete. What was easily reversible in 1900 became less and less reversible as the subway network grew. The engineers of the railway company now took these thousands of tunnels built by the subway company as destiny and as an irreversible technical constraint. (1988: 36–7).

Conclusion

This chapter has covered a large number of approaches to, and perspectives on, organizations. In adopting a particular form of differentiating between the various theories through the organizational grid, the chapter has highlighted the twin axes [technocratic – critical and determinist – interpretivist] which are a heuristic way of structuring the alternatives. One axis concerns the degree to which the theories take the status quo for granted as self-evidently the best way to organize society. At one end of this pole, the technocratic end, lie pragmatic, business-oriented approaches which seek to confirm, reproduce and improve the 'efficiency' of contemporary work organizations. At the other, critical, end of the pole are theories which focus not on the pragmatics of organizational improvement but on the explanatory analysis of organizations: the questions concern the ways by which organizations cohere and work, not whether this or that method might improve organizational performance. The other axis distinguished between determinist and interpretivist approaches. The determinist approach implies that certain socio-economic or material structures or independent variables determine organizational form, at least in the long term: organizations may exist in opposition to the 'requirements' of their environment or variables but those that do not restructure in accordance with such forces are likely to wither. At the opposite end of this pole lie the interpretative approaches which deny, at their most radical, the determining influence of either social or technical aspects. For these approaches the significance of human and non-human components lies not in any imputed capabilities but in their construction via the interpretative processes of actors and the generation of persuasive representations of organizations.

5

Class, Industrial Conflict and the Labour Process

Work is the curse of the drinking classes.
H. Pearson, *Life of Oscar Wilde*

Introduction

This chapter assesses the merits and problems of contemporary accounts of three closely related facets of work: class, industrial conflict and the labour process. It argues that although class is a critical issue it is not the only one, nor is there any unmediated connection between class position and class action: gender, ethnic and occupational divisions, mediated by the interpretative processes of individual and social interaction, ensure that heterogeneity not homogeneity is the historically constructed norm at the level of social groups and individuals. This does not mean that society comprises a mass of unrelated and discrete individuals, rather it implies that where cohesive groups exist they have to be produced and reproduced by their members – they are not inevitable products of material divisions. Relatedly, individuals can be considered as heterogeneous composites: they are not, for example, women, and black, and working class – as if these three facets exist independently of each other – but black, working-class women whose life chances are affected by these multiple and fused categories (this heterogeneous model is discussed more fully in the following chapter). Since, however, such patterns are socially and historically constructed they are neither natural nor inevitable – but they are typical. The significance of class is highlighted by the discussion of industrial action which considers the relationships between class and strikes and between the domestic and employment spheres. Finally the ghost of Braverman is raised within the labour process debate, which embodies one of the most popular class-based analyses of work, but it is raised in order to bury it properly, rather than to praise it.

Theoretical Approaches to Class

While many Marxists and radicals have concentrated almost wholly upon the theoretical intricacies of the labour process and attempted to consider recent changes in work in terms of the labour process concepts of deskilling and degradation etc., others have pursued the more conventional sociological questions concerning the nature and patterning of inequalities and the relationship between work, employment and social stratification. The analysis of class and social stratification has spawned entire libraries of sociological work in themselves but there is no attempt to regurgitate this here (see Giddens, 1973; Goldthorpe et al., 1980; Goldthorpe and Payne, 1986; Martin, 1987; Abercrombie et al., 1988; Heath, 1981). Rather, the necessary empirical data will just be adumbrated to draw out some significant links between the major forms of class inequality and work. Inequalities associated primarily with gender or race are considered in the following two chapters.

For most Marxists, class is defined so widely in direct relationship to ownership or non-ownership of the means of production, and encompasses so many widely variant occupational groups (to say nothing of the gender and ethnic divisions), that the relationship between class structure and class action tends to be either transparent or completely obscured. When it is the former the class appears to take action as a result of its objective position *vis-à-vis* the capitalists; when the latter occurs, through the ideological chicanery of the bourgeois media and superstructural apparatus, the class allegedly lapses into inaction or intra-class hostility. The possibility that occupational divisions may form the material basis for competing interests within the working class, or that the relations are actually very complex and opaque, or that the existence of exploitive relations do not, in and of themselves, imply any corresponding level or form of political or class consciousness, appears of marginal significance to this general approach. Yet if the evidence of working-class politics generally is anything to go by, the effects of the labour process are not simply homogenizing and radicalizing in many circumstances but are often fragmentary in material and ideological terms. Under this more complex approach to the nature of class and the labour process it becomes possible to accommodate otherwise incongruent manifestations of 'false consciousness', such as the alliances of farm workers and landowners against industrial interests (Howkins, 1985: 130–53). Furthermore, where the relationship between employer and employee is not directly one of capitalist and proletariat, as in the state sector, the implicit correspondence between class position and class consciousness is even more problematic.

The retreat from the complexities thrown up in any attempt to relate objective class position to subjective class consciousness led Poulantzas (1978) to argue that only the direct producers of surplus value are proletarians, that is, only propertyless producers; white-collar workers are relegated to the realms of the petty bourgeoisie. But while this may delimit the extent of apparently false consciousness, it does so only by marginalizing the majority of the working class itself. Wright (1978, 1985) argues that while Marx's dichotomous model is inadequate, Poulantzas's approach takes the problem even deeper. Wright's solution to the problem of why occupational groups appear to have so little relationship to the class structure is to develop a model of 'unambiguously' bourgeois and proletarian classes separated by several ambiguous or contradictory classes based on different modes of exploitation. Briefly, Wright argues that individuals may occupy exploitative positions if they have ownership of capital assets or they control organizational assets or they possess the requisite skills and credentials that allow them to exploit those without such characteristics. Yet this still presumes that the working class, however defined, has an imputed real interest determined by its class location. Such 'real' interests are confounded by the point raised above that the labour process does not just generate homogenizing experiences and interests and is unlikely, therefore, to provide the foundations for universally collective real interests, let alone an alternative social system. Again, the claim is not that the labour process does not generate specific collective material grievances and power resources to resolve some of them, but that it does not generate *universal* effects upon, nor provide for the *universal* interests of, the working class.

The limitations of Weber's stratification model, with its potentially unlimited patterning of class and its dislocation from the 'situated market', have already been noted in chapter 2. The market in capitalism is not the sole origin of inequalities but both an effect and medium of property inequalities that are independent of the market. But it is the case that Weber's differentiated approach to stratification facilitates the introduction of variables such as gender and race as independently constructive of social structure, rather than as derivative of class as the orthodox Marxist position presumes.

One of the most significant attempts to go beyond the limitations of both Marxist and Weberian approaches to stratification has been the theory of structuration developed by Giddens (1973, 1984) (see also Cohen, 1989, and Held and Thompson, 1989). Giddens attempts to explain how 'economic relationships become translated into non-economic social structures' (1973: 105). He distinguishes between two forms of class structuration: 'mediate', which form the links between the market and the structured system of market relations, and 'proximate', the immediate, localized factors that affect and shape class formation. The distribution of mobility chances is a primary example of the mediate interventions which either hinder or facilitate the 'reproduction of common life experiences over generations' (ibid.). Such mobility chances are greatly influenced by 'market capacity' of which Giddens discusses three types: ownership of the means of production; possession of educational or technical qualifications; and the possession of manual labour. Three sources of proximate structuration are significant: the division of labour within the enterprise; the accompanying authority relations; and the influence of distributive groups (such as housing location). This complex of mediate and proximate structuration factors advances a class structure that is itself internally differentiated along systematic patterns, though not in direct response to each and every form of inequality. Thus, class or stratification structures require empirical analysis and cannot be read off from particular sets of economic conditions, either of ownership or authority relations. For example, it is evident that the authority relations within state socialist factories were, and where they persist probably still are, very close to those in operation within some areas of contemporary European or North American societies, yet the patterns of property ownership are very dissimilar.

Class, Wealth and Income

Social class is not just a fixation of sociologists: it has both a subjective resonance with most of the population and undeniable material consequences. The vast majority of the British population think that class is an inevitable feature of British society, can place themselves in the class structure, and have difficulty locating themselves within any other social category (Marshall et al., 1988). This in itself reinforces the imperative consequences of acknowledging the socially constructed nature of the categories: other categories can be devised (race, gender, age, religion etc.), and each categorization results in a different perspective on the social structure. But social class does not exist independently of our perspectives on society – it is a means by which we develop such perspectives.

This is reflected in some of the most recent academic developments in the field of employment which have been less directed by the class motif than is usual, though there has also been a resurgence of class-based studies which have generally taken a dual path. On the one hand there are accounts, such as Gallie's (1989), which consider the evidence for the growth of an underclass, below the conventional working class. On the other hand, there are orthodox Marxists (Wood, 1986; Cohen, 1987) who have resisted the attacks of feminists and other radical non-Marxists, and have reasserted the central significance of class, and indeed employment, against the 'rainbow' alliance arguments of the new social movements (Mouffe, 1979). Let us first set out what contemporary empirical evidence there is for these arguments.

Perhaps the first thing to note is the significance of the split between inequalities constructed through earned income and those based upon the ownership of wealth. Wealth is generally more significant than earned income in so far as the basic patterning of inequalities is concerned, reflecting the significance of non-work factors in the construction of class structures and life experiences. For example, while most of the labour process theorists concern themselves with mechanisms and levels of control and exploitation at work, it is now clear that factors external, but nevertheless related, to work may be more significant than those inside work, at least in terms of social stratification. As an illustration, using the conventional occupational division from A to E, it is currently the case that the bottom two categories visit their doctors almost twice as much as the top two categories. The Ds and Es are also more likely to suffer from more breathing problems, digestive problems, high blood pressure, rheumatism and arthritis than any other group (*Observer*/Harris Poll, 18 February 90). Similarly, the poor are more likely to develop cancer than the rich and less likely to survive once a diagnosis has been made (Kogevinas, 1990).

Class is also directly related to a system of wealth distribution through taxation policy, which, from 1911 and most particularly since 1946, has been almost wholly progressive, at least until 1979. Whether capitalists, and any wage earners for that matter, have become personally richer or poorer has often been related more closely to taxation policy than to the level of economic exploitation at the point of production. Indeed, it is not coincidental that by far the richest sector of the bourgeoisie throughout the nineteenth century was not the factory capitalists of the north but the landowners and the commercial and financial capitalists of the south. Not until the collapse of land prices and the political developments of the late nineteenth century did industrial capitalism generate large numbers of overtly rich individuals (Rubinstein, 1988).

As mentioned above, one of the problems with arguments centred wholly on activities concerning employment is that although income from employment is clearly crucial to the life chances of most people, it is also the case that a large number of people at the bottom of the income pyramid depend on state support not earned income, while a small number at the top of the pyramid secure their life experiences through unearned income. Thus while employment still remains significant for class structuration, some of the inequalities that prestructure employment-related inequalities have little to do with employment themselves. For example, it is still the case that inherited wealth and class position play a major role in deciding who controls the major industrial and business concerns not just of Britain but of Europe too (Marceau, 1989). And even though income derived from such control may be considerable, it is quite often dwarfed by the income and power generated by inherited, and in this sense unearned, position (Shoard, 1987).

Estimates of wealth ownership are notoriously difficult to verify, often very dated, and not helped by the actions of the current British government which has reduced the data collection facilities concerning the distribution of wealth. For example, although the government's own *Social Trends* for 1989 carries a report of the percentage of the adult population owning shares for 1988 (21 per cent), the figures for wealth ownership do no go beyond 1985. These data are reproduced in table 2.

Between 1924 and 1972 in Britain the share of wealth owned by the richest 1 per cent and 5 per cent of adults fell by around 4 per cent each decade, a phenomenon common to most capitalist nations (Wolff, 1987). Since 1979 this trend has ceased and, as a result of the 1988 budget, the trend has now gone into reverse, thanks to 40 per cent of the tax handouts (£1,750 million) being channelled towards the richest 10 per cent, while a mere 10 per cent went to the poorest 50 per cent (Brown, G. 1988). In fact, the top 1 per cent got more than the bottom 70 per cent (Naughtie, 1988), and since 1979 24 per cent of income tax cuts have gone to the richest 1 per cent, and 38 per cent to the richest 5 per cent, leaving 17 per cent for the bottom half of the population (Huhne, 1988b). If pensions are included in the data, the top 5 per cent own 25 per cent of the total, whereas the bottom 50 per cent of the population have seen their share drop from 17–21 per cent in 1979 to 15–19 per cent in 1985 (Stark, 1988; Huhne, 1988c). Despite the obvious decline in the wealth ownership

Table 2 Personal wealth distribution among adults of marketable wealth in Britain (%)

	1938	*1966*	*1979*	*1985*
Percentage of marketable wealth owned by:				
Most wealthy 1% of adults	55	33	22	20
5%	77	56	40	40
10%	85	69	54	54
25%	*	87	77	76
50%	*	97	95	93

* Not available

Source: Inland Revenue statistics (1988)

of the top 10 percent since the beginning of the century, the spread of wealth has tended to remain within the top 25 per cent of the population and provides a considerably distorted distribution figure, showing just how important income, rather than wealth, appears to be to the bottom 75 per cent of the population. The conventional perspective on employment which is deflected away from the social elite embodies two different facets then: for the elite, employment-generated inequalities may well be secondary to wealth-generated inequalities, whereas for the vast majority of the population income is the crucial variable. It should not be assumed, though, that the impact of wealth and income redistribution has affected the mass of employees uniformly: between 1979 and 1988 the net earnings of the top 10 per cent of non-manual workers rose by 41 per cent in sharp contrast to the net incomes within the bottom 10 per cent of manual workers which rose, on average, a mere 1.7 per cent (Milne, 1989).

These polarizing tendencies are reproduced in the differential patterns of social mobility. Very roughly it would seem that something like one third of all men end up in a different class from their fathers, though the main cause of this movement has been the restructuring of the economy with an expanding professional or service class, rather than a more meritocratic society. This is evident from the greater proportion of upward over downward mobility (Heath, 1981; Goldthorpe, 1980; Goldthorpe and Payne, 1986). However, despite the fact that Goldthorpe's data take no account of women's mobility chances, it is clear that the chances of working-class male mobility have polarized so that although such individuals now escape their background upwards in greater numbers than ever, a large proportion are also likely to fall downwards into the ranks of the so-called underclass of unemployed. For example, of British men aged between 20 and 34 in 1972 with working-class backgrounds 16 per cent rose to the service class and 60 per cent remained in the working class. But by 1983 of men in the same age category 22 per cent had risen to the service class, 40 per cent were stable but 11 per cent were unemployed and half of these were unemployed for over a year. As Goldthorpe and Payne conclude, the return of mass unemployment (and at the time of writing (May 1990) it looks like returning again), has raised the stakes for the working class (1986: 18–20).

It should go without saying (but Goldthorpe's concentration on men suggests that it does not), that within the gross class-based disparities of income there are differential patterns within individual family units: the distribution of income and domestic work between men and women, and between adults and children, can make nonesense of apparent levels of family affluence (see Bott, 1971; Brannen and Wilson, 1987). None the less, whether a family has adults in employment or not usually remains paramount to the generation, if not the internal distribution, of income. Table 3 shows the official distribution of original and final income (i.e.,

Table 3 Distribution of original and final income (quintile groups of households) (%)

	Bottom 20%	*Next 20%*	*Middle 20%*	*Next 20%*	*Top 20%*
original 1976	0.8	9.4	18.8	26.6	44.4
final 1976	7.4	12.7	18.0	24.0	37.9
original 1983	0.3	6.7	17.7	27.2	48.1
final 1983	6.9	12.2	17.6	24.0	39.3

Source: *Social Trends*, 1986

before and after state redistributions via the social security and taxation systems).

Although tables 2 and 3 are not strictly comparable, it should be clear that, first, income inequality is not as wide as wealth inequality, though the top 20 per cent still take almost half the original income; second, that while the original income of the bottom 20 per cent is almost negligible, and shows a dramatic collapse since 1976, their final income is much more respectable (though still barely half of the income of the next quintile). In fact, in April 1990 the British government admitted its data were suspect, and subsequent reanalysis suggests that rather than the bottom 20 per cent securing an 'final' increase of 6.7 per cent between 1981 and 1985 it actually grew by merely 2.6 per cent (*The Guardian*, 24 April 1990). A major implication of this is that employment, and the inequalities of life experiences and reward associated with it, may be negatively salient only for the bottom quintile. That is to say, it is because a large proportion of the worst off either do not have employment or cannot undertake it for some reason, that their situation is so dire. For this group, *pace* Marx, it is not the exploitive and alienating consequences of employment in a capitalist society that is the problem, it is *not* having employment in the same society that is the problem, or at least not having the income normally associated with full-time employment.

Class, Occupation and Inequality

One of the greatest myths of conventional industrial sociology relates to the putative preponderance and typicality of factory workers. In fact, during the Victorian heyday of manufacturing, broadly the second half of the nineteenth century, not only did the percentage of the population engaged in manufacturing actually fall (from 33 per cent in 1851 to 31 per cent in 1881) but the fastest-growing income generator was not manufacturing and mining, nor trade, but actually income from abroad (Best, 1979: 99–100). At the height of the manufacturing era around 1911, for example, there were 2.1 million (female) domestic servants as opposed to 1.2 million miners, 1.8 million in the 'metal bashing industries', 1 million in clothing and textiles, 1.2 million in transport, 0.7 million in 'commercial occupations' and 0.4 million in the professions (Stevenson, 1984: 183). In short, no universal work experience ever reconstructed the working class into a homogeneous mass, and even if many were employed as manual workers in factories their experience was never typical. Yet it must be remembered that while employment may not have been the universal cohering agent that has been claimed, neither should external factors that have combated the fragmentation of working-class experience be omitted. In particular, this involved the role of community cultures and organizations: the co-operative movement, political parties, self-help groups, public houses, sporting associations etc., all of which have acted as centrifugal forces in a world of work where centripetal powers of occupational differentiation were always omnipresent. From the German working class during the imperial era (Geary, 1987), to eighteenth-century factory operatives in the British industrial revolution (Cunningham, 1980), working-class culture has spawned a web of supportive institutions and practices that have gone some way to compensate for the disjunctures in working-class experience induced through different forms of employment.

This decline in the significance of manufacturing employment has continued apace, from about 7.5 million employees in the UK in the early 1970s to just over 5 million by 1990. In contrast, non-manufacturing employment has risen from 14.5 million to 17 million over the same period, with services employing over 15.4 million (*Employment Gazette*, March 1989, April 1990; *Social Trends*, 1989). To get an overall picture of who does what, Table 4 shows the distribution of employees and self-

Table 4 Employment: workforce (as at September 1989 adjusted for seasonal variation) (thousands) Total potential workforce 28,650,000

	No.	*%*
Males	12,006	52
Females	10,887	48
All	22,893	
Self-employed	3,276	12
HM Forces	308	1.1
Training etc.	477	1.8

Source: *Employment Gazette*, April 1990

Table 5 Distribution of employment (as at September/December 1988). Total = 25,404,000

Employment	*No.*	*%*
Agriculture, forestry & fishing	322,000	1.3
Coal, gas & petroleum extraction	163,000	0.6
Electricity, gas, energy & water	280,000	1.1
Metal manufacture, ore & mineral extraction	422,000	1.7
Chemicals & artificial fibres	346,000	1.4
Mechanical engineering	711,000	2.8
Office machinery & electrical engineering	726,000	2.9
Motor vehicle & parts	234,000	0.9
Other transport equipment	225,000	0.9
Metal goods	290,000	1.1
Food, drink & tobacco	533,000	2.1
Textiles, leather, footwear & clothing	505,000	2.0
Timber, furniture, rubber, plastics	532,000	2.1
Paper, printing & publishing	484,000	1.9
Construction	994,000	3.9
Wholesale distribution & repairs	1,246,000	4.9
Retail distribution	2,106,000	8.3
Hotels & catering	1,155,000	4.6
Transport	914,000	3.6
Postal services & telecomms	459,000	1.8
Banking, insurance & finance	2,499,000	9.8
Public administration	2,018,000	7.9
Education	1,594,000	6.3
Medical, health & veterinary	1,277,000	5.0
Others	1,652,000	6.5
HM Forces	315,000	1.2
Training	386,000	1.5
Self-employed	3,016,000	11.9

The different total from the previous table is a result of the different dates for data collection and because some figures are not seasonally adjusted.

Source: *Employment Gazette*, March 1989

employed etc., followed by Table 5 showing the industrial breakdown of employees.

Several aspects of this occupational distribution are worth highlighting. First, the highest single group is not metal-bashing manual workers but the self-employed (*Family Expenditure Survey 1988* (1990)). Second, all the sectors with over one million employees are outside the traditional stereotypes of work: the financial sector, retail and wholesale goods, hotels and catering, and the public-dominated sectors of education, health and administration. Not only is the world of work a great deal more than the world of employment but the sphere of employment is not the universal sphere of the factory: sellers and scribblers not packers and bashers are the archetypal workers of today if such archetypes do exist. Even here it is the great diversity of occupational experience, not the universalism of a single labour process, that predominates, an issue of fundamental importance to the models sociologists have used to analyse work at the point of production.

Table 6 concerns the distribution of people in employment by gender and broadly defined occupation. Even accepting a substantial degree of error in the data, they are significant in suggesting several influential points. First, the large proportion of the population – almost a third – within the managerial and professional occupations. Second, roughly a further quarter of the population are in non-manual occupations and less than half are engaged in any form of manual labour. Third, although the gender division is ostensibly relatively small within the management and professional field (see chapter 6), it is very large elsewhere, with women dominating the non-manual sector and men the manual sector.

In terms of the inequalities earned from employment it is important to note that several different criteria are significant. For example, in 1988, within the manufacturing industries the average weekly earnings of full-

Table 6 Occupational analysis of people in employment by gender (spring 1989)

	All thousands	%	*Men thousands*	%	*Women thousands*	%
Management and professionals	7,856	31	4,841	33	3,015	27
Clerical and related	4,004	16	731	5	3,273	30
Other non-manual occupations	1,935	7	866	6	1,069	10
Craft etc. inc. foremen	4,035	16	3,616	25	419	4
General labourers	165	1	148	1	17	0
Other manual occupations	6,952	27	3,837	27	3,115	28
Inadequately described	536	2	435	3	101	1
All occupations (inc. self-employed)	25,483	100	14,474	100	11,009	100

Source: *Employment Gazette*, April 1990.

time manual males was £206.80, but non-manual male employees in the same industries earned an average of £229.10. The equivalent wages for women were £121.20 and £161.60. Self-evidently, then, the differentials between occupational groups as well as between men and women are considerable. If we compare men's and women's hourly earnings rather than weekly pay, to eliminate the bias in favour of male earnings through overtime, hourly pay for male manual workers in the manufacturing industries (excluding overtime) was £4.52, for non-manual male workers it was £7.44. For female manual workers it was £3.09 and £4.27 respectively. In terms of all industries and services the differentials are very similar and can perhaps best be represented by the following ratios:

1 The hourly earnings of a full-time male manual worker is, on average, 58 per cent of his non-manual male colleague.
2 The hourly earnings of a full-time female manual worker is, on average, 66 per cent of her non-manual female colleague.
3 The hourly earnings of a full-time female manual worker is, on average, 71 per cent of her male colleague.
4 The hourly earnings of a full-time female non-manual worker is, on average, 62 per cent of her male colleague.
5 The hourly earnings of all full-time female workers are, on average, 75 per cent of their male colleagues.
(*Employment Gazette*, March 1989)

In sum, inequalities are at their highest between male manual workers and male non-manual workers and at their lowest between female manual workers and male manual workers. Once more the apparent simplicities of class-based, occupation-based or gender-based inequalities are confounded by the complexities of the actual situation. This does not mean we should abandon the analysis of stratification and its significance, rather it means that we should tread warily and seek to establish the particular components of each stratification pattern through an empirically based analysis not through a theoretical perspective that terrorises, instead of interrogates, the data.

Finally, with regard to the underlying concern of this chapter in class inequalities, it is worth reiterating the major points of this section: first, that gross inequalities do exist both between and within classes. Second, that these inequalities are themselves meshed with gender-based inequalities, which are discussed in more detail in chapter 6. Third, and relatedly, some of the most important inequalities are produced and reproduced outside the employment arena, either in the home or else via the state's taxation and social security policy. Do the difficulties raised in relation to the modelling of class facilitate an explanation for the reluctance of trade unionists to engage in revolutionary action against capitalism?

Class, Trade Unions and Revolution

It is certainly the case that few writers have claimed a specifically hallowed place for trade unions and their members in the struggle against capitalism, except perhaps the anarcho-syndicalists around the first quarter of this century (Hinton, 1973; Holton, 1976; Miller, 1984; Joll, 1979; Sirianni, 1982; Spriano, 1975; Gluckstein, 1985). Marx was initially convinced that trade unions would be able to resist capitalists and boost the wages and conditions of their members. But this would merely be attacking the symptoms of the capitalist malaise and would do nothing to surmount capitalism itself. The issue was not one of inequality, then, but exploitation and alienation that only the elimination of capitalism could resolve. However, once the trade unionists realized this, Marx assumed they would channel their energies away from the industrial battle and towards the political war through revolutionary parties.

Engels (1969b), after Marx's death, became more and more pessimistic about such a scenario and, on the basis of the British experience, argued that the workers had themselves become bourgeois. They, or at least the aristocracy of labour (the most skilled, rewarded and organized section), now had a direct interest in the maintenance of the capitalist system having been bought off by the profits of imperialism. Lenin pushed this argument to its furthest point, denying the possibility of trade unionists ever achieving class, that is socialist, consciousness unless it was brought to them by radical intellectuals from the bourgeoisie (1970, 1978). Others have taken the opposite stand with regard to the aristocracy of labour, believing it to be the most radical rather than the most reactionary (Pelling, 1968; Gray, 1981; Geary, 1984; Bonnel, 1984; cf. Hobsbawm, 1964a; Foster, 1974). But it is not just leftists that have denied the possibility of radical trade unions though, for writers of variant political persuasions have said more or less the same (Webb and Webb, 1920; Perlman, 1949; Flanders, 1965; Lane, 1974; Currie, 1979; and Gorz, 1982). Even the most sympathetic writers prefer to discuss the political intentions of trade unions in terms of ambiguous support of, and opposition to, the status quo (Hyman, 1971: 50–3; Anderson, 1977).

Kelly (1988) is the latest, and perhaps the most optimistic, Marxist to argue that trade unions still embody the potential for radical politics. This reaffirmation of Marx's original sanguine belief in trade unions is premised on three assumptions: first, workers' material interests are incompatible with those of capitalism; second, class mobilization is only likely in response to these interests; and third, the pursuit of these interest may, in itself, facilitate the development of socialism. Kelly is right to assume that the interests of capitalists and workers do not coincide, in so far as the former are responsible for, but not usually concerned with, exploitation, unemployment, and alienation. But this does not mean that workers have an objective class interest in socialism because it is not self-evident how universal class-based objective interests can be established or legitimated, and because it is not clear exactly what socialism actually comprises. In the absence of an effective, efficient and liberatory theoretical model of the socialist alternative (let alone a working model) such arguments assume that the problems of one regime necessarily imply support for another; they do not. But Kelly is right to reject the mechanical interpretations of class consciousness. It is indeed the case that consciousness exhibits both long periods of somnambulence and brief episodes of radicalism, and therefore Kelly's support for Luxemburg's thesis is accurate: there are cases when economistic strikes flow over into political battles, when strictly militant action is transformed into radical action, albeit often unintentionally. But, as Kelly himself notes, such actions are rare in themselves (see Harman, 1982: 147–51), they tend to be significant only within general crises rather than being significant in and of themselves, and the two examples he chooses (Italy 1922, and Chile 1973) illustrate a real problem: if the mass of the population is working class and their interests are served by socialism, then something other than popular support will be necessary to carry through a radical transition to socialism. Indeed, Kelly undermines his own belief in mass support when he ends with a quote from Fox who notes that: 'if successful revolutions depended on mass understanding . . . the world would have seen few indeed' (Fox, 1985: 122, quoted in Kelly, 1988: 304). Or, as Mann put it: 'perhaps a genuine Leninist dictatorship of the proletariat *is* the only revolutionary way out of the impasse . . . a coup d'etat carried out during a period of social confusion in the name of the proletariat or – and this is more likely – a Fascist coup to forestall the latter eventuality' (Mann, 1973: 73).

British Trade Unions and Labourism

It may well be rather less exciting than revolutionary action but it is nevertheless the case that 'labourism' – the pursuit of reforms within the existing forms and methods of parliamentary government and conventional collective bargaining – appears to be the overwhelming form of working-class response to capitalism, at least in Britain, so far. Labourism has already spawned a literature of its own (see: Fox, 1985; Saville, 1973; Kynaston, 1976; Hobsbawm, 1984; Kendall, 1969; Miliband, 1972; Cronin, 1984; and Hinton, 1983), and only the skeleton of the argument will be provided here. Briefly, then, labourism is explained through four interrelated spheres.

First, the patterning of actual, if discontinuous, rises in real living standards for the majority of the British working class, at least after the middle of the nineteenth century, undermined the logic of revolutionary collective action. In effect, the very success of trade unions displaced the concern for control over the productive and political process towards one enclosed by the economistic rewards that capitalism could more readily accommodate. Concomitantly, it could be argued that revolutionary unions, at least those in non-revolutionary situations, are manifestations of weakness not strength (Crouch, 1982: 137–8). The only major exception to this general pattern was just after the First World War, but living standards never fell as sharply in Britain as they did in other European nations where social unrest reached a scale not witnessed since the upheavals of 1848 (Geary, 1984: 134–78; Gallie, 1983: 224–51; Sirianni, 1982: 311–56).

The second factor is the occupational heterogeneity of the British working class that was mentioned above. Of course, such a fragmented pattern is not unique to Britain, and this goes some way to explaining the general absence of revolutionary actions by the working classes of capitalist nations, but perhaps the most notable point is exemplified by reference to the diffference between British and Russian history. At the point of gravest economic and political tension (roughly 1917–21 in many capitalist states) the Russian working class was relatively small, faced with a situation that was deteriorating very rapidly and showed no prospect of improving, and free from the institutionalized structures of conventional reformist political parties and trade unions. Such organizations existed but, given the autocratic history of Czarism, they had never developed as in Britain nor was it clear how such reformism could possibly solve the crisis. Thus without the 'disadvantages of advancement', to invert Veblen's phrase, the Russian working class constructed industrial, rather than craft, unions which generated support for class policies not sectarian policies (Smith, S. 1981). In contrast, Britain, and to a lesser extent Germany, had already constructed a system of trade unionism based on craft and led by reformists (Fox, 1985). It was not that such leadership betrayed the masses so much as that this form of trade unionism was interpreted by those involved as the more appropriate in the circumstances of their initial development; it then enwrapped itself in the carapaces of institutional privilege to develop the social rigidities so well analyzed by Olson (1982). As Gramsci argues, against the paranoiac implications of Trotsky's permanent betrayal thesis (which suggested that all labour defeats could ultimately be placed at the door of class traitors amongst the leadership), trade unions are constructed through, and reflective of, capitalism. The world of trade unions and the world of employment are not automatically conducive to class solidarity and is more likely to feed the sectionalist and sectarian ideologies upon which capitalism is founded. The road from sectionalist to class politics is necessarily elusive not self-evident; whilst trade unions *may* be socialist subjectively they are objectively capitalist (Gramsci, 1978: 76). This does not mean that trade unions axiomatically operate against the interests of their own weakest members, even if they may act against the interests of other workers and other capitalists. On the contrary, because the very nature of bargaining conventionally assumes a 'collective' format, unions often enact the 'sword of justice' whereby the weakest member is protected by the combined strength of the mass. For example, although the differential between skilled and unskilled workers has hardly changed in a century (reflecting to some degree the reproduction of the differential by unions), there is evidence that where unions operate, narrower sex, race and occupational differentials persist (Metcalfe, 1989). Of course, unions are not alone in maintaining the level of inequality: in 1889, when 'reliable' earnings figures were first published in Britain, the top fifth of the workforce received 43 per cent more than the national average while the bottom fifth received 31 per cent less. A century later the top fifth were 15 per cent *better off* in relative terms while the bottom fifth were 15 per cent *worse off* in relative terms (Horrie, 1989).

Third, while the leaders of the Russian trade unions and political parties were generally radical, if not revolutionary, the leaders of both the British trade unions and the Labour Party which grew out of the trade unions were generally reformist and, initially at least, of liberal rather than socialist persuasion. As such, the birthmarks of the unions upon the fledgling Labour Party remained etched indelibly upon the carcass of the mature movement. There were challenges to labourism, such as syndicalism, guild socialism and the Communist Party but they remained marginalized by the pre-existing power and success of the labourist position (Martin, 1969; Grint, 1986; Taylor, 1982; Kitching, 1983; Tomlinson, 1982).

None the less, there is no necessary connection between reformist trade union leaders and oligarchical control, nor between radical leaders and democratic control. As Zeitlin (1982) has argued, trade union bureaucracies are often defined so that radical local leaderships are outside the boundary wall and in some mysterious way perfectly aligned with the 'real' interests of the membership – which are seldom those pursued by the national leadership. Yet there is precious little evidence that, irrespective of the representative nature of the national leadership, local radicals are perfectly in tune with their members. Rather than having a division between the bureaucracy and the rank and file (led or at least represented by the radical local leaders) it is more appropriate to consider the division to be between (at least) two elites: a radical local elite and a reformist national elite. Moreover, if the actions of the rank and file are studied closely it is just as likely that they are as conservative and sectionalist as their leaders are alleged to be. If the masses are constantly betrayed or misled by their leaders one wonders not only how they could be so stupid as to re-elect them, but also how the future worker- or citizen-controlled decentralized society can be left safely in the hands of such a manipulable mass. The alternative is to assume, not that leaders are trustworthy and faithful to the ideals of the members, but that those which stray too far from the straight and narrow either lose support or members.

Fourth, and finally, labourism's success relates to the activities of the state. It should become clear from the discussion of the labour process below that conflict is generated at the point of production through the contrasting and conflicting interests of individuals and groups. Most of these conflicts become manifest as economistic desires of one form or another but the resolution of these conflicts in 'political' or 'economic' arenas, and through radical or reformist methods, depends to a large degree upon the presence or absence of collective bargaining. That is to say, where conflicts generated at the point of production can be resolved at the point of production through the bargaining of unions and employers then the conflict tends to remain contained and a disjunction is erected between industrial and political actions. By and large this is how British industrial relations have been constructed, with the activities of the state (at least until 1979) remaining in the background. This does not mean that collective bargaining operates autonomously of political interests nor does it exist within the arena of equal parties so beloved of pluralists, but it does mean that conflicts can be dispersed before they build into political movements with serious implications for the legitimacy of the state. This has been particularly significant with regards to the antecedent industrialization of Britain which provided for a generally buoyant economy and hence faciltated the buying-off, rather than the suppression, of working-class discontent through the raising of living standards. In contrast, where 'legitimate' collective bargaining has not been possible, either through state action or inaction, for example in France until relatively recently or pre-Weimar Germany, Francoist Spain, Czarist Russia or communist Poland, the result has often been the adoption of more radical and political strategies. Thus, just as democracy has often resulted from a realization by the authorities of the consequences of denying a legitimate voice to the population, so too trade unionism has often been tolerated by employers and the state for equally instrumental reasons (see Rustow, 1970; Therborn, 1977). But the legitimation or toleration of class-based trade unions by the state and employers, while it may have diverted pressure away from direct political challenges to capitalism or the state, has not ensured the creation of a quiescent workforce: industrial conflict is as much an inescapable element of work as collective forms of worker organization.

Class and Industrial Action

Class conflict *qua* industrial action has been the focus of a considerable amount of debate within the sociology of work (Hyman, 1972; Batstone et al., 1978; Durcan et al., 1983; Shorter & Tilly, 1974; Cronin, 1979; Gouldner, 1954; Eldridge, 1968; Edwards, 1981; Batstone, 1985; Jackson, 1987). However, almost all of this has been concentrated upon industrial action *qua* strikes; the number of studies about absenteeism, sabotage, working to rule etc. – that is, 'cut price' industrial action as Flanders (1970: 112) called it – is small in comparison (cf. Hudson, 1970; Brown, 1977; Batstone et al., 1977; Dubois, 1979; Edwards and Scullion, 1982). In itself this is an inversion of the probable occurrence of strikes and non-strike action: less than a third of manufacturing plants typically experience strike action by manual workers in any two-year period yet almost half may suffer some other form of industrial action (usually an overtime ban or work to rule) (Brown, 1981: 81).

Strikes, according to the Department of Employment – the central institution for the collation of strike data in Britain – are defined as: all stoppages of work due to industrial disputes involving ten or more workers and lasting for at least one day. Where the aggregate days lost exceed a hundred working days a strike is included in the data even if it fails to count under the preceding criteria. Whether this measure is an accurate reflection of strikes in British industry is difficult to say. Brown (1981) estimates that since Britain has historically been particularly affected by short and small-scale stoppages, especially in manufacturing industry, as many as half the actual strikes may be missed. It is, however, more conventional to assume that the statistics cover around 66 per cent of the total numbers of strikes and 95 per cent of the days lost. The disparity really relates to the ease with which long stoppages are recorded and the difficulty of accounting for the lightning strikes that appear to persist in particular industries, for example car manufacturing.

Most of Britain's strikes have tended to be unofficial, though with the Thatcher government's legislative changes there has been an initial swing towards official strikes and most recently of all a swing back to unofficial action. This most recent movement has clearly been in response to the legislative restrictions on official strike action, and the unofficial actions on the London Underground, British Rail and London buses in 1989 (Beavis, 1989; Kemp, 1989) were just the latest attempts in a long history of industrial action that seeks to circumvent what the strikers perceive to be restrictive legal controls. The unofficial element is significant in so far as two countries may have identical strike data but the one where 'lightning' unofficial strikes are most prominent may suffer the greatest economic damage. The Donovan Commission (1968) was broadly in agreement with this short strike/high damage analysis, though Turner (1969) suggested that the impact of short strikes tended to be limited to the enterprise directly affected, while long strikes had far-reaching consequences for industry as a whole. Since then there have been important changes in the occupational sources of strike action with the heavy manufacturing industries being replaced by more white-collar and service sector strikes. The Donovan Commission is also important in so far as it highlighted the 'British disease' with the number of working days lost per year hovering around 4 million. The disease promptly developed even more symptoms with 1979 accumulating 29 million days lost and the miners' strike of 1984 itself resulting in 22 million days lost. Yet it is worth noting that the current blue rinsed claims of an emasculated union movement are based on data that demonstrate a reduction by half in the number of strikes but simultaneously a number of days lost that is the equivalent of the era when the British disease came to the public's attention. As the government has already shown in many areas, statistics are inherently pliable. The raw data are reproduced in table 7.

To make interpretation of this data a little easier, figure 5 compares the number of strikes, the numbers of strikers and the number of days lost for the entire period. Three points are worth highlighting. First, the decline in the number of strikes and days lost predates the Thatcher

Table 7 British strike statistics (annual averages)

Year	*No. of Stoppages*	*Workers involved*	*Working days lost*	*No. trade unionists*	*Trade union density (%)*
1895–99	777		7,470,000	1,701,000	11
1900–04	484		2,888,000	2,004,000	12
1905–09	445		4,204,000	2,336,000	14
1910–14	932	993,250	16,120,000	3,480,000	20
1915–19	890	1,060,600	10,378,000	5,792,000	32
1920–24	857	1,061,000	30,277,000	6,316,000	35
1925–29	393	472,000	13,207,000	5,062,000	27
1930–34	412	289,000	3,980,000	4,578,000	24
1935–39	863	359,000	1,938,000	5,671,000	29
1940–44	1,491	499,000	1,813,000	7,581,000	38
1945–49	1,881	507,000	2,235,000	8,901,000	43
1950–54	1,701	584,000	1,903,000	9,500,000	45
1955–59	2,530	742,000	4,602,000	9,722,000	44
1960–64	2,512	1,499,000	3,180,000	10,010,000	44
1965–69	2,380	1,213,000	3,920,000	10,291,000	44
1970–74	2,884	1,567,000	14,039,000	11,380,000	49
1975–79	2,310	1,658,000	11,663,000	12,763,000	53
1980–84	1,363	1,297,000	10,487,000	11,775,000	50
1985–89	890	783,000	3,939,000	10,611,000	46

Source: H. Pelling, 1976; Bain and Price, 1980; Salamon, 1987; Jackson, 1977; *Employment Gazette* (various)

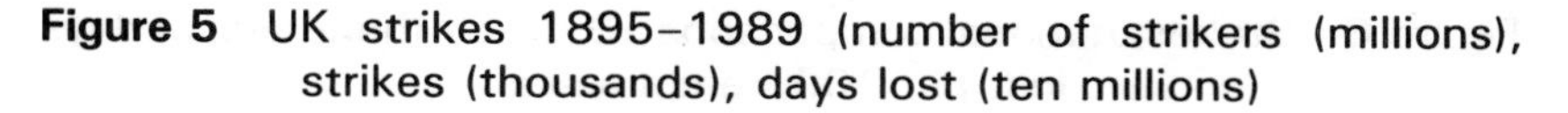

Figure 5 UK strikes 1895–1989 (number of strikers (millions), strikes (thousands), days lost (ten millions)

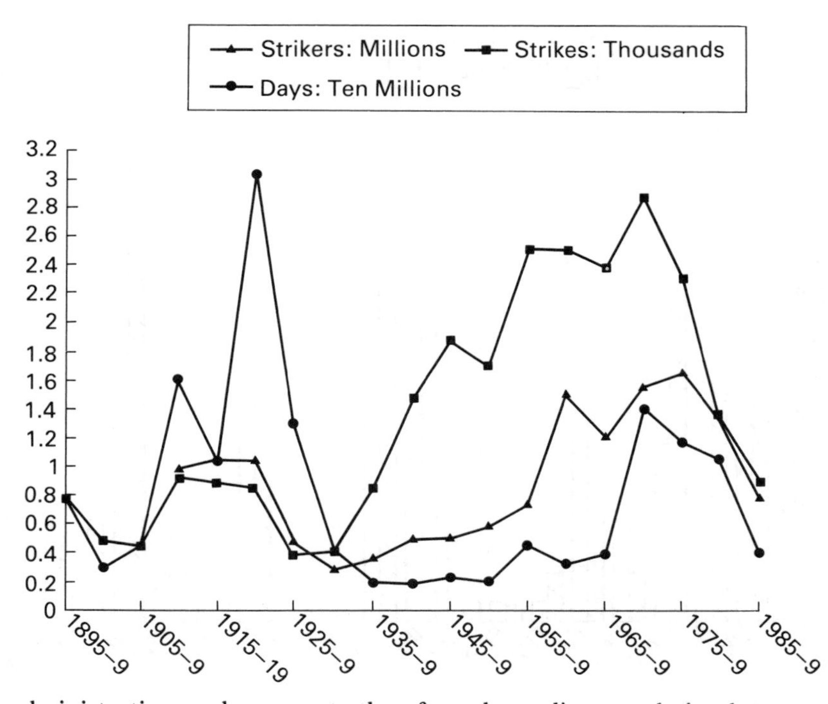

administration and may not, therefore, be a direct and simple consequence of the latter's actions. Second, strike indicators tend to correlate with general economic activity, rather than political administrations. Third, current trends do not demonstrate an industrial quiescence previously unknown. Indeed, when the data for international comparisons are procured it would seem that, with the exceptions of Denmark, Finland and New Zealand, all the major Western societies have witnessed parallel declines in strike activity (Brown and Wadhwani, 1990). This is graphically illustrated in figure 6.

It is important to note here that the strike data concern internal features not external effects. Even when the media consider the impact of strikes in terms of 'lost production' it is not always an accurate assessment since much production can actually be 'saved' through overtime or higher subsequent productivity etc. Strikes are also more significant where they affect other production. For example, a strike in a manufacturing plant operating within 'just in time' procedures, where stock levels are minimal, can be more effective and affective than where the more conventional 'just in case' procedure operates and stocks include high levels of

Figure 6 Strikes, national comparisons 1978–87 (hundreds of days lost per 1000 employees)

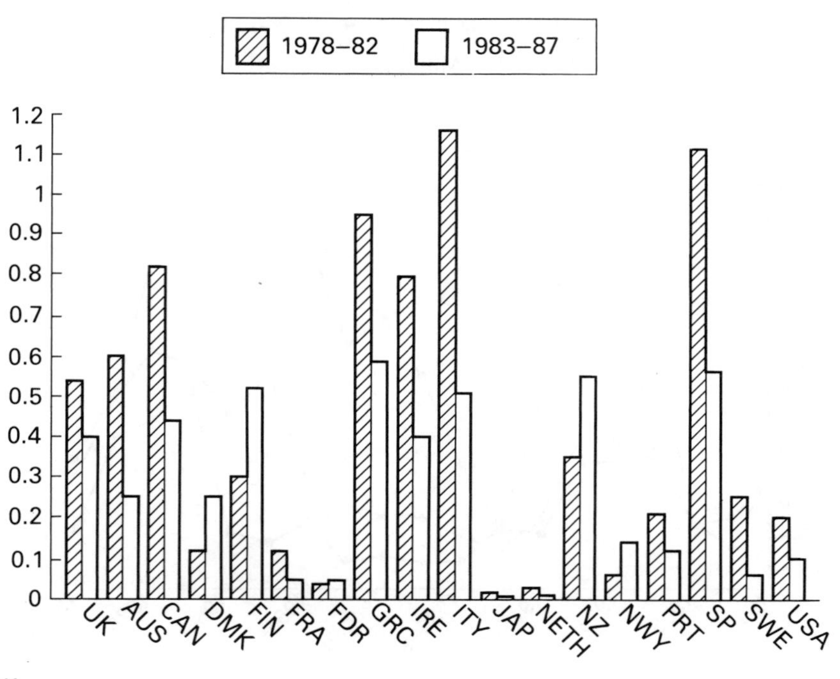

Key:
UK – United Kingdom
AUS – Australia
CAN – Canada
DMK – Denmark
FIN – Finland
FRA – France
FDR – West Germany
GRC – Greece
IRE – Eire
ITY – Italy
JAP – Japan
NETH – Netherlands
NZ – New Zealand
NWY – Norway
PRT – Portugal
SP – Spain
SWE – Sweden
USA – United States of America

Source: Brown and Wadhwani, 1990

reserves – just in case a shortage occurs. Perhaps more important is the disproportionate influence strikes seem to have on the media rather than in industry itself. For example, as Durcan et al. note, production lost through strikes is negligible in comparison to total production (about 0.25 per cent) (1983: 426), in comparison to the time lost through unemployment (about 6 per cent) (1983: 404) and, at least in Australia, in comparison to industrial accidents (Dabscheck and Niland, 1981). Indeed, even when strikes apparently reached their nadir, in 1987, it is still the case that for every three days lost through strikes there are two hundred lost through absenteeism (Cornelius, 1987). Physical illness is a significant factor: in 1988 there were 46 million days lost through back problems alone: almost twice as many as lost in the miners' strike (NBPA, 1989). It might also serve as a useful illustration to know that the average employee has been involved in less than three hours of strikes in each year of the last ten years. In the 1970s the average was four hours a year; whereas the 1960s, the origin of the British disease, involved an average of three hours. Only the second and third decades of this century have involved more action per employee, with the 1920s marking the peak at one day's strike per year. Whichever decade is chosen the actual period spent on strike by the average British employee is minimal.

Relatedly, it is not the case that strikes are axiomatically indicative of union strength. Some clearly are, but several recent strikes have been concerned with last-ditch defences rather than in pursuit of an expanding orbit of control or reward. Hence the absence of strikes may well be a demonstration of union strength not weakness. For example, Swedish unions have low levels of strikes but relatively high levels of material reward and influence over management. Similarly, there are few strikes amongst workers within small plants, but this represents the common weakness of labour in such situations not their strength or satisfaction (Rainnie, 1989). Relatedly, despite the decline in the number of strikes in Britain since 1979, real wages have kept ahead of inflation and productivity, with the pay of unionized plants possibly being boosted by between 8 per cent (Jowell, et al., 1989) and 10 per cent (Metcalfe, 1989) in Britain, 4 per cent in Switzerland and 26 per cent in the USA. Of course, some of this pay inflation is a consequence of skill shortages, especially in the south-east of England, but nevertheless a union movement that had ostensibly been tamed should not be in a position to secure inflationary wage rises, nor require the further legislative constraints being considered in 1990. It is also true that during periods where product market competition is intensifying many manufacturing firms are not in a position to risk all by the pursuit of macho management policies; a reason, no doubt, for the relatively minimal use of such Thatcherite policies outside the public sector (Batstone, 1988a).

The British strike data are limited to industrial disputes; political strikes are excluded from the data, though precisely what counts as a political strike is unclear (Hain, 1986). For example, the 1974 strike by dockers for May Day to be declared a public holiday was included as an industrial dispute while the AUEW strike against the sequestration of its funds by the Industrial Relations Court in the same year was excluded as a political strike. In fact, three one-day strikes in 1971 against the Industrial Relations Bill involved twice as many strikers as were eventually included in the strike statistics for that year but they were discounted as political strikes (Silver, 1973). It could well be argued that strikes for higher wages during a period of incomes policy are action against the state and therefore political, as indeed might be all strikes within the Civil Service. Similarly, all strikes could be considered as political in so far as they embody aspects of power that are inherently political, albeit not necessarily party political. For example, Batstone et al.'s (1978) analysis of strike situations suggests that part of the motivation for strike action lies in the struggle for control between employers and employees. Where managers are perceived to be acting beyond the limit of their legitimate authority a strike becomes political because it concerns authority relations, but this need not develop into either party- or class-based politics. Rather, such conflict concerns *factory politics*, a dispute about control over the labour process which is as likely to be sectional as universal in origin and effect.

The collection and definitions of strikes are very varied across time and space. In Britain the three main indices are the number of stoppages, the number of workers involved, and the number of working days lost. Most of the data is obtained through the voluntary self-reporting of action by employers, while in West Germany employers are legally obliged to report the number of days lost. However, the German statistics do not record the number of strikes and the Americans have recently altered their criteria for a strike from at least six strikers involved to at least 1,000 strikers involved. It is estimated that this order of redefinition will remove 96 per cent of the actions previously regarded as strikes, an action which makes them of 'little analytic value' according to Edwards (1983a), though the more recent reanalysis by Garen and Krislov (1988) is markedly more optimistic about the utility of the new data. Other problems for the comparison of data include the absence of a threshold for inclusion in the French, Italian and Belgian statistics as well as the changes that occur in the definitions over time. This obviously poses considerable difficulties but, providing the definitions remain the same over the time period in question, significant trends between countries across time can still be compared.

Predictions of strike rates, as manifestations of wider social conflicts, have varied widely, from Marx's assumptions about the ever-increasing intensity of industrial conflict within capitalism to Kerr et al.'s (1960) polar opposite position, whereby the capitalist and communist worlds converged and industrial relations became institutionalized and civilized. A further alternative is Dahrendorf's (1959) hybrid theory in which conflicts based on class are replaced by conflicts grounded in authority. None of these prescriptive perspectives appears to have been realized: there may well be patterns within strikes but they are seldom unilinear. The actual study of strikes has been as varied as the patterns: some have pursued a single strike while others have analysed broad comparative trends. Within both forms of study the focus has often ranged between the causes of strikes, the process of strike mobilization and variations in the propensity to strike. In short, the topic is enormous, but one of the most important aspects to bear in mine when considering strikes is the historical patterning that tends to occur, often in conjunction with business cycles and other related political developments.

Accounting for Industrial Action

The first thing to consider is attempts to explain *why* strikes occur. It is common to delineate three variant explanations: social disorganization or breakdown; frustration and communication; and conflicting or contradictory interests. The disorganization model is often linked to long-term trends and individual case studies: industrialization leads, in a pattern derived from Durkheimian perspectives, initially to the breakdown of consensus, although the institutionalization of collective bargaining ultimately rebuilds the consensus (Kerr et al., 1960). Alternatively, the structure, technology or management patterns are radically altered, leading to some form of temporary moral disequilibrium (Gouldner, 1954; Warner and Low, 1947). An immediate question for the disorganization theories is: 'can they account for the disorganized environments that do not lead to strikes?' For example, in the Warner and Low case the observed disorganization at work had been preceded by a long-term community and industrial disorganization so that it is not self-evident what sparked off the specific conflict.

The second strike model relates to frustration and problematic communications. Quite often these accounts minimize the explanations of the strikers involved and seek out what they regard as the more compelling reasons, such as the extent of effective channels of communications to diffuse work-based frustration (Scott and Homans, 1947). The frustration model implicitly embodies an unmediated connection between frustration and action, yet it seems much more likely that between frustration and action lies a critical variable – organization (Shorter and Tilly, 1974: 338). In fact, Shorter and Tilly reproduce the same structural approach they criticize in Scott and Homans, arguing that wage demands are not so much the causes of strikes as the symptoms of deeper problems. Yet if wage demands are not causal variables one then has to explain why so many strikers appear to be so easily misled while their academic interpreters alone are capable of establishing their true motivations. This does not mean either that dissatisfaction with wages is sufficient to generate a strike nor that all strikes are about wages. If, as suggested in chapter 2, the moral economy continues to pervade work then many so-called 'economically irrational' strikes are being analysed through the wrong perspective: moral principles are not lost in work.

There is, in fact, considerable controversy as to whether strikes over wages are actually economically rational in so far as the wages lost through striking are seldom made up by any increases gained through a successful strike. Skeels (1971) argues that strikes are *initiated* through decisions that are economically rational but they may continue beyond the point at which they become 'self-financing'; though since one can never be sure what would have happened if strike action had not occurred (i.e., wages may have dropped dramatically), scepticism of such economic analyses should remain. On the other hand, strikes can impose severe financial penalties upon strikers right from the very beginning of their action (Gennard, 1977; Durcan and McCarthy, 1974). Whatever issue or issues the strike concerns, the way in which they become legitimated as justifications for strike activity appears to depend crucially upon the action of particular members of the workplace organization (Batstone et al., 1978), and inevitably entails some aspect of the wage-effort or reward-deprivation bargain (Baldamus, 1961). The implication of this is that the strike situation is seldom static and is generally subject to negotiation and redefinition. This does not mean that strike situations are completely random: although variations between and within industries do occur it is nevertheless the case that different industries appear to be associated with different forms of industrial conflict (Knowles, 1952).

The third approach identified is in terms of conflicting or contradictory interests. These arguments tend to derive from Marxist analyses of economic exploitation and alienation, but the wage-effort model of Baldamus is equally relevant: since the labour contract seldom specifies the exact amount of effort required for a particular wage it is in the interests of employers to maximize the effort of employees and in the interest of employees to minimize effort. Yet neither model can explain the timing or vigour of particular strikes: if the interests of workers and managers are permanently opposed why do strikes only break out occasionally? One could resort to the conventional Marxist default category of false consciousness, but aside from the implicit arrogance of this explanation, which sometimes reserves true knowledge for the educated elite of Marxist intellectuals, it is not clear whether all strikes that do break out are manifestations of 'true' consciousness, nor why they break out at all. This is not to dispute the attempts by the state and management to distort the picture of reality presented to the workers but it does deny the unfailing success of this ruse.

While all three 'universal' models are unsatisfactory, other studies have striven to demonstrate the value of organizational facilities to the generation of strikes, and the process by which the institutionalization of industrial relations leads to a decline in strike rates. One of the classic arguments in this vein is that of Kerr and Siegel (1954) who attempted to explain the inter-industry propensities to strike which were common across a number of countries. The focus of their explanation lay in terms of the most strike-prone industries being those in which workers constituted an 'isolated mass'. High strike proneness, they argued, was associated with single industry communities, little occupational differentiation, geographical or social isolation from the wider society, and group cohesion. These factors were seen to influence the disposition of workers to strike and their ability to strike. Strikes were interpreted as 'colonial revolts' in so far as they were attacks upon authority far removed from the work place, and operated as substitutes for occupational and social mobility as well as the general build-up of social tensions. However, such groups could strike only because of their group cohesion and, relatedly, their isolation from broader social pressures.

The Kerr and Siegel hypothesis has been subjected to numerous criticisms, not least that the empirical evidence does not fit their theory (Shorter and Tilly, 1978; Edwards, 1978, 1981; Jackson, 1987, 1987). But the important point here is that they bring into account an organizational variable – a necessary mediation between dissatisfaction at work and strike action. Shorter and Tilly (1978) have also pursued this institutional theme with regard to French strikes, arguing that union strength is a necessary precondition of strike action, though it must be said that the causal direction may well be the other way around. That is, as in so much of social science, the correlation between two forms of activities does not specify the direction of the causal relationship. In this instance it could be argued that strikes lead to union strength rather than vice versa.

This kind of approach is extended by the institutionalization of conflict argument of Ross and Hartmann (1960), in which the organizational development of unions and collective bargaining leads to a decrease, nay the 'withering away', of strikes. They identify four broad patterns of strike activity. The first of these is the north European (mark 1) pattern, covering countries like the UK and West Germany. Here strikes involve few members and last only a relatively short period of time. The north European (mark 21), or Scandinavian, model reveals minimal member involvement but long-lasting strikes, while the Mediterranean–Asian pattern (France, Italy, Japan and Australia) has the opposite, that is to say high levels of involvement by members but short strikes. Finally, the

North American pattern has fairly high levels of involvement in long strikes. Ross and Hartmann attempt to explain these patterns by looking at the configurations of variables rather than single variables in isolation. These variables include first, the stability of the labour movement, in terms of its age and membership, both of which serve to reduce conflict; the longer a union has been in existence the more likely it is to have established a *modus vivendi* with the employers, and the more likely it is to have secured the interests of its members. The second variable focuses upon leadership conflicts in the labour movement, in terms of factionalism and rival unions on the one hand and strength of the communist groups on the other. Both weaken central leadership, and therefore the less united a union movement is the more likely it is to promote conflict. Third, the status of union management relations, manifested by the degree of acceptance of unions by employers and the consolidation of bargaining structures, reduces conflict; the more egalitarian the union/employer relationship the less likely are strikes. Fourth, strikes are reduced where a Labour Party is a potent force, and particularly where it is in office, since it can achieve workers' aims through political means, thereby reducing the potential resource implications for workers and buttressing the Labour Party. And finally, conflict may be reduced where the state actively intervenes in industrial relations and has its own dispute-resolution policies to minimize industrial disruption. Where all five features were present, Ross and Hartman argued that strikes would 'wither away'.

Perhaps the first point to make is that the analysis was developed between 1948 and 1956 and since then conditions in many places have altered radically on several occasions. In short, a central enigma still remains: do strong unions become strong through striking and are their current resources so strong that striking becomes unnecessary?

For Shorter and Tilly's (1974) French study the issue is crucially one of control over power resources, and this control is regarded as a precondition of collective action. Thus conflict is most likely when control over such power resources becomes subject to movement, i.e., when opportunities arise and when the organizational 'latticework' is sufficient to transform individual perceptions of opportunity into collective action, and in particular into working-class action.

Cronin's (1979) approach reintroduces workers' expectations linked to the patterning of economic 'long waves', but although his analysis appears to explain certain periods of strike explosions it cannot explain others. Korpi and Shalev (1979, 1980) attempt to fill this sort of partial analysis by arguing that the shifts in the distribution of power affect not only the chances of successful industrial action but also the assessment of rewards. Yet, because there is a lag in the relationship between the distribution of power and its effects on aspirations there may well be periods when power resources do not match aspirations and strikes may either fail or fail to materialize. Furthermore, the results of any conflict themselves often lead to the institutionalization of class conflict in collective bargaining and working-class political parties; thus as the labour movement grows it tends to transfer interest away from the industrial scene to the political. This approach fixes attention upon the level of working-class mobilization (defined as the level of unionization and support for left political parties) and the degree of control it has over government. Hence, in Norway and Sweden the labour movement has achieved a high level of mobilization and relatively stable political control and the result is low levels of industrial action. In contrast, Britain has a high level of labour mobilization but only sporadic political control with the consequence that conflict is high. France also has a high strike rate because of the limited influence of the left in the political sphere. In sum, where social democratic governments achieve power, and most decisively where they implement social democratic policies that favour the working class, strike levels will fall.

The superficial similarities with the Ross and Hartmann approach are, of course, striking, though Korpi and Shalev are keen to note their distancing from any structural approach: for them the structures of power resources etc. merely provide the preconditions or potential for certain forms of action and limit the viability of others. However, to explain why certain actions occur requires an analysis of the actions of individuals and groups who must mobilize the resources and turn the potential into reality. Equally relevant, one should acknowledge the import of wider economic preconditions for strike action: if the material resources for some form of compromise simply do not exist then strike action is unlikely to occur and even less likely to succeed where it does occur. Korpi and Shalev certainly seem to assume that wherever strike action does occur it implicitly embodies the political unity of the working class, and they consequently fail to consider the possibility discussed earlier that the labour process itself generates disunity as well as unity amongst the workers. In particular, one might note here that the institutional features of industrial relations, notably the forms of collective bargaining, may themselves be influential in determining the success of class-oriented union policies: where bargaining is decentralized it is enormously difficult to construct and reproduce a co-ordinated wage policy that protects the interests of the weakest as against those of the strongest.

The most institutional argument remains that of Clegg (1976) who claims, from his analysis of six countries, that strike patterns can be explained primarily by reference to differences in the nature of collective bargaining. For Clegg, plant bargaining leads to large numbers of official strikes while regional or industry-wide bargaining leads to a smaller number of strikes but a larger number of strikers. Where a sophisticated disputes procedure exists, such as in Sweden as opposed to France, then the number of strikes is likely to be lower. Similarly, the limited number of disputes in West Germany can be associated with the labour courts and work councils which act as institutional defusers of industrial conflict. Nevertheless, the critical aspect for Clegg is the level of bargaining, and where decentralized bargaining occurs, inter-union rivalry and unofficial action are most likely.

There are clearly limits to Clegg's argument and he acknowledges several of these. First, to focus the research upon the influence of collective bargaining structures begs the question of their origin: is it the level of bargaining which is significant or the forces that spawned the particular level and form of bargaining? Second, the data is drawn only from countries with collective bargaining but many others do not have this, even if they do have trade unions. To what extent, then, can his arguments be extrapolated? Third, his data may explain long-term trends but it has considerable difficulty in accounting for short-term variations. Fourth, as several studies have suggested, the very act of changing the form of collecting bargaining may in itself have no impact upon the overall levels of industrial action (Edwards and Scullion, 1982), and may actually stimulate unrest through the disequilibrium introduced (Hyman, 1972). This is clearly evident in the explosion of strikes that usually accompanies the termination of an incomes policy or, as the National Power Loading Agreement (NPLA) of the miners showed, displacing the locus of collective bargaining may simply shift the level of conflict in parallel to the level of the bargaining: in this instance from a multiplicity of short pit level strikes to infrequent but very damaging national stoppages in association with the move from pit level bargaining to national bargaining. Thus, in 1956, ten years before the NPLA, almost 80 per cent of all strikes in Britain were in coal mining. Four years after the agreement, in 1970, a mere 4 per cent of strikes were in mining (Allen, 1981: 90). Yet this movement did not, ultimately, undermine the expressions of conflict in the mining industry but merely served to redirect them into the national explosions in the mines in 1972 and 1974, and more recently of course, in 1984. As Krieger concludes: 'for the first time the interests of the face worker and of the miner working elsewhere below ground were linked, since all their wage rates were covered by a single comprehensive agreement' (1984: 268–9). In itself the preponderance of miners' strikes in the statistics at both the unofficial and the official end of the spectrum, from the lightning walk-out to the 358 days of the last national stoppage, should alert us to the problem of using such aggregated strike data as clear indicators of industrial passivity or unrest in the wider economic environment. Until very recently the strike picture has been dominated by five industrial areas: mining, the docks, shipbuilding, car manufacturing, and iron and steel. In 1979 over half of the days lost were derived from a strike by engineering workers; in 1980 the national steel strike accounted for three-quarters of the days lost; whereas the miners' strike of 1984–5 was responsible for 83 per cent and 63 per cent of the days lost in the respective years (*Employment Gazette*, July 1988: 374). All of these have either suffered a slimming down that approximates industrial anorexia and/or a lengthy strike followed by relative passivity. Yet in 1987, over two years after the collapse of the national miners' strike, 30 per cent of the total number of stoppages were still associated with the mining industry. More significantly still, 10 per cent occurred in the fields of public administration and education and a further 10 per cent in communication industries (*Employment Gazette*, July 1988). Although some major industries and their unions have clearly been devastated during the last decade, other, newer industries and unions have sprung up to fill the gap.

Similarly, it has to be accepted that even where models of strike explanation appear to account for activity within certain periods of time this does not imply the universal utility of any model across space and time; the level of political and economic contingency is simply too high for any universal model to cope with (Davies, 1979; Edwards, 1983b). Nor is there any unmediated connection between patterns of union strength and strike activity: as the power workers have consistently demonstrated, unions in strategic positions of power do not have to strike to persuade management to provide relatively high incomes. In fact, it is Clegg's later work (1979: 274–7) which establishes a further particular link between decentralized bargaining and wildly fluctuating incomes in strike-prone industries, though as Edwards (1983b: 223–4) points out, such material frustrations do not in and of themselves lead to high strike rates; for that a strong union organization must exist. But strong unions are themselves dependent upon a cohesive community that exists beyond the bounds of the factory gates or the mine. Not only have strikes tended historically to relate to communities where the domestic/work boundary is ambiguous, such as pit and fishing villages, but even the longest mass strike in British history, the miners' strike of 1984–5, was critically reliant upon the action of autonomous women's groups in sustaining the communities through their collective ideal.

In Batstone's (1985) analysis, it seems more appropriate to assume that strike rates rise with the following features. First, an asymmetrical relationship between the union and its bargaining structure; that is, where the organizational strength and the bargaining institutions do not coincide. Second, where the political left is disunited such that there can be little prospect of a left government gaining and holding power, and introducing pro-labour policies. Third, where the union is in a monopoly position so that its action will not lead to an immediate loss of membership elsewhere. Fourth, where there is a wide degree of variation between blue- and white-collar workers, between men and women, and between workers and managers. Yet although these macro-level analyses are important they seldom explain the way the structural limitation and opportunities they illuminate become realized or missed by those involved on the shop floor. In short, are strikes generated purely by socially structured conditions or do social actors play a significant part in bringing them off?

One of the major problems with answering this question relates to the way strikes have become symbolic of heroic resistance by the labouring masses against the exploitive forces of capital on the one hand, and the greedy and political machinations of an unrepresentative, extremist and bullying minority on the other hand. The former analysis usually considers strikes as spontaneously constructed manifestations of structural inequalities and exploitation. The latter analysis disavows the structural approach altogether and focuses almost wholly upon the personalities and personal whims of the strikers, and particularly the strike leaders who appear to have a charismatic appeal capable of inducing blind obedience from otherwise rational workers (see Turner, 1963; Hyman, 1972: 106–39). Yet the purely individualist approach cannot explain the frequency and social patterning of strikes, while the strictly structural approach systematically fails to explain why similar structural conditions produce dissimilar strike results.

An attempt to trace the process by which the potential for strike action becomes realized is made by Batstone et al. (1978). The perspective used here is one in which the organization of strike action is considered as an active social process in which the unsystematic discontent of the rank and file is channelled and controlled by certain of the shop stewards. This channelling and articulation of grievances is developed through 'systems of argument' or 'vocabularies of motive', to use Wright Mills's phrase, and the study illustrates the way the 'leader' shop stewards actively mould shop floor opinion, and are courted by management because of their leadership abilities. This moulding process, however, is intimately related to the direct experiences and perceptions of the workers involved; opinion can be moulded but it is seldom successfully manufactured *de novo*. Other 'populist' shop stewards are mere mouthpieces of the rank and file, subject to their capricious changes and thus generally limited in their influence with workers or managers, amongst other things because they lack the influential network of social relationships which sustain the 'leader' stewards in power. This is not to say that 'leader' stewards lead their members continually into conflictual situations; unless these bring positive results on every occasion such a strategy would soon prove self-defeating. Nor is this to suggest that the rank and file are infinitely manipulable, they are clearly not; the refusal of strikers to return to work despite the request of their stewards and the refusal of workers to accede to the advice for a strike by stewards are clear demonstrations of the limits of leadership in such inevitably contingent situations. It is because work relationships are permanently renegotiated, at least to some extent, that strikes are necessarily difficult to predict. Thus even allegedly structural features/determinants of work are themselves open to renegotiation, as the reconstruction of union organization in the wake of the unofficial strike at Pilkingtons demonstrated (Lane and Roberts, 1971). Nevertheless, given the necessary preconditioning organization underlying the vast majority of strikes it is questionable whether many spontaneous strikes are actually unorganized (Batstone et al., 1978: 222).

As Batstone et al. conclude:

> Structural factors may foster conditions which make strikes easier, but at the same time strikes and other forms of collective bargaining, along with many other factors, may change those factors. Moreover the nature of worker organization may change quite rapidly while the process of mobilization for strike action is by no means a certain one. . . . An understanding of the phenomenon of strikes may start from an awareness of the subordination of the worker, but it has to go further and recognize the complex historical interplay between structure and consciousness as mediated by organizational processes. (1978: 223)

Now it is clear that no direct correlation between union organization and industrial militancy prevails: some of the strongest unions in organizational and strategic terms have a record that displays none of the strike actions commonly associated with powerful groups (for example the electricity supply industries). Organization, therefore, provides the means to develop militant strategies but also a level of institutionalization that may either negate the necessity for strike action or actually demobilize the membership.

The debate over the value of a reformist strategy within trade unions has been long and relatively acrimonious (Pfeffer, 1979; Herding, 1972; Hyman, 1989: 149–65; Kelly, 1988: 147–83; McIlroy, 1988: 127–57; Batstone, 1988: 72–119) in a way not dissimilar to the equivalent argument within the realms of socialist strategies (Turner, 1986; Jacques and Mulhearn, 1981; Buick and Crump, 1986; Coates and Johnston, 1983). In essence, trade union organization, in association with the institutionalization of conflict expressed through collective bargaining and shop stewards' organizations, legitimates the expression of conflict but simultaneously constrains its expression through agreed channels. Thus unions achieve a stake in the system's survival both because of the substantive benefits accrued and through the legitimacy afforded to it. Such institutionalization for radicals inevitably degenerates into bureaucracy with the Michelsian consequences of oligarchical control replacing representative democracy. Certainly the recent period has seen the development of management-sponsored shop steward organizations, often at the expense of the full-time union officials, but the evidence for their 'betrayal' of rank and file interests is sketchy and it is not self-evident why the rank and file would allow their interests to be supplanted by such renegades. It is much more likely that most 'institutionalization' of industrial relations can be explained through the mutual recognition of, and desire for, some form of incomplete but necessary accommodation between labour and capital rather than through union sell-outs or quiescence. Because the accommodation is incomplete, in terms of procedural and substantive features, no permanent consensus can prevail. Indeed, the very agreement itself provides for yet further disagreements in so far as rules and regulations appertaining to agreements are seldom self-explanatory. It is, as Mann (1973a) has noted, pragmatic acquiescence not ideological accommodation that explains the development of collective bargaining. It is also a precondition of pragmatic acquiescence that the material basis for this is reproduced: without a permanent, if erratic, rise in living standards the primary mechanism for workers' 'allegiance' to their employer would surely wither and the labour process become the locus of ever-greater levels of industrial conflict. But is the labour process as critical to the sociology of work as Braverman and labour process theorists maintain?

Marx, Taylorism and the Capitalist Labour Process

Much of the contemporary interest of Marxists and radicals in the issues of labour and industrial control is derived in some way from the seminal work of Braverman: *Labor and Monopoly Capital* written in 1974 Braverman reopened a concern of Marx that the critical area for explaining social conflict and control was the labour process itself: the place where commodities were constructed and developed by mixing human labour with raw materials. It was the exploitative and alienating essence of the labour process under capitalism which made the system inherently flawed for Marx, and thus necessitated its complete destruction through revolutionary action. With the failure of such action in Russia to bring about the communist utopia, and more particularly the failure of revolutionary action in Western Europe, Western Marxists, especially those in the Frankfurt school of critical theory, began to explore the issues of capitalist culture and ideology in an attempt to account for these failures (Jay, 1973; Held, 1980). More orthodox Marxists, however, remained wedded to the notion of economic determinism–the inevitable working out of economic contradictions within capitalism which would eventually lead to communism irrespective of the activities of social actors *qua* revolutionaries (McLellan, 1980). Neither of these two alternative assessments of the situation required attention to the point of production, and Marxist interest in work and employment itself generally waned. There were, of course, radicals working in the area of work, for example C. Wright Mill's 1951 study of white-collar workers in the USA, and several historical studies with radical origins (Cole and Postgate, 1938; Thompson, 1963) but the overwhelming proportion of studies of contemporary work bore little affiliation to any form of radicalism let alone Marxism, and were perhaps closer to the liberal managerialist position adopted, and indeed epitomised, by Kerr et al.'s *Industrialism and Industrial Man* (1960).

Braverman himself saw his work as developing the expansion of Marxist theory in the field of capitalist economic development, particularly that undertaken by Sweezy (1942) and Baran and Sweezy (1966). While they had concentrated on macroeconomic 'laws' of accumulation etc., Braverman wanted to bring the focus closer to the shop floor to what he considered as the structurally determined imperatives of managerial control, its effects upon the workers themselves, and the dynamic and immanent process of deskilling and degradation that he believed underlay the progression towards monopoly capitalism. Braverman's initial challenge to the claims of what he regarded as capitalism's apologists was to refute the simple connection between broad changes in the occupational structure and an increase in individual skill levels. For Braverman all such developments have to be situated against the actual content of the jobs in question, rather than their occupational labelling, and the background of the nineteenth-century craft worker who combined a wide range of knowledge and skills so that levels of individual discretion, autonomy and control were high. For the capitalist the problem of work is the problem of managerial control: how can managers ensure the maximum degree of effort for the minimum amount of reward? The solution to the problem, as perceived by Braverman following Taylor, is through extending the division of labour, separating the conception of work from its execution, and deskilling the workforce. This will, in theory at least, provide not only for higher levels of productivity and cheaper labour, but also for more compliant labour. Thus the labour process itself becomes divorced from the skills of the labourer and, therefore, from the control of the labourer.

Such a managerial philosophy Braverman saw most clearly in the ideas of F.W. Taylor. When Taylor began work in the USA at the turn of the century, subcontracting was still the predominant form of labour organization, though most firms appear to have been relatively indifferent to the methods of labour control (see chapters 2 and 4). However, the increasing competition, and the developments in trade unionism at the time, pushed some into searching for alternative methods of control.

In Britain one route, taken most conspicuously by the Quaker chocolate manufacturers Cadbury and Rowntree, was a system of benevolent paternalism but others preferred a more direct method of labour control, and it was this which Taylor provided. Having worked as a labourer, clerk and machinist himself, Taylor was well aware of the problems of production at the level of the shop floor and argued that three specific reasons were evident: first, management lacked the knowledge to maximize production–their ignorance left them at the mercy of workers' wisdom; second, the workers themselves had a rationale for restricting output–the real fear of underpayment or redundancy; third, the existing payment system lacked a sufficiently sophisticated incentive scheme. Taylor castigated management, not the workforce, for these problems and insisted that they drop their conventional 'rule of thumb' schemes and appropriate his 'scientific management' techniques. These involved several discrete changes, especially technical improvements to the machinery, but more significantly they concerned the extension of the division of labour to the extent that each task was fragmented into its smallest constituent units which would be timed and measured. A piece rate system that was individually not collectively organized (to avoid encouraging collective action and trade unions) was also essential, and this must involve accelerating rewards and punishment as the (high) targets were under- or over-shot. The jobs would be deskilled, both to further facilitate the employment of cheaper labour and to eliminate the restrictive practices then employed by employees on the basis of their monopoly over knowledge. Some of these restrictive practices, or 'natural soldiering' as Taylor called them, were related to what he regarded as the laziness inherent to human nature and could not therefore be completely eliminated. It could, though, be contained by the provision of economic incentives - the primary stimulus to work as far as Taylor was concerned. But 'systematic soldiering', i.e., that which was 'artificially' constructed and maintained by collective action, resulted from the poor supervision and problematic incentive systems that actually discouraged maximum efficiency.

Taylor's approach, like his overall philosophy, was deeply imbued with pretensions to a scientific status, and most systematic experiments were undertaken with an immigrant called Schmidt, whom Taylor believed to have the mentality of an ox, though since Schmidt was also engaged at the time in building his own house, there must have been some remarkable oxen in the States at this time. Through the close monitoring of Schmidt's work practices in shovelling pig iron, including rest times, operating methods etc., Taylor managed to persuade Schmidt to increase his productivity by 400 per cent, in exchange for a wage increase of 40 per cent. *Homo Economicus* had arrived: by the adoption of science Taylor had demonstrated the essence of his policy: 'there is no question that when the work to be done is at all complicated a good organization with a poor plant will give better results than at the best plant with a poor organization' (1903: 62). Taylor's method, then, was not so much technical as organizational and psychological: scientific management involved both an organizational and mental revolution. The barriers between worker and employer would be broken down by demonstrating that through applying his scientific principles work would become more efficient and therefore all would benefit in the increasing levels of material rewards. Of course, since the method was scientific there could be no bargaining involved; worker resistance to management may have been rational when management was irrational but under the new scheme all would gain so all resistance was irrational. The system, however, was not constructed to provide satisfying work for all; work was about the acquisition of material rewards not individual or social satisfaction, and the way to maximize rewards for all involved was to increase the division of labour (in management too), match the ability of the worker to that required by the job, use the cheapest form of labour, and adopt intensive training methods (Noble, 1974: 276).

In fact, until 1911 most of Taylor's practical work was carried out within union-free or weakly unionized plants, while the American Federation of Labour (AFL) initiated its anti-scientific management campaign. Within weeks of its first major implementation, in the state-owned arsenal at Watertown, a strike broke out, and, following a full investigation by a House of Representatives Special Committee in which widespread malpractices and arbitrary rather than scientic applications were uncovered, Taylorist methods were banned from all arsenals, Navy yards and, from 1916 to 1949, from all government-funded operations (Noble, 1977: 272; cf. Nyland, 1987).

Taylor's unpopularity was not limited to the unions and US government: despite Taylor's previous position as president of the American Society of Mechanical Engineers (in 1906) they refused to publish his *Principles of Scientific Management* on the grounds that it was not scientific. Supporters of the general movement towards a more scientific approach to management attempted to compensate for several of his most blatant errors. Chipman argued that worker consent to any development was as crucial as the scheme itself; Gantt emphasised the error of punishing low performance through Taylor's differential piece system and the need to rely on rewards in the light of the 'human factor' at work; a movement taken further and more successfully by Frank Gilbreth, and more importantly by Lillian Gilbreth, in their fusion of industrial psychology and scientific management. For Taylor it was enough that he had demonstrated the rationality of his system to the workers; for Lillian Gilbreth managers had to persuade workers that the system was rational, not simply impose it. Frank Gilbreth was more influential in reorienting scientific management towards the labour unions in a positive light. Indeed, once Taylor was dead, and with the unions involved in the war effort, a reapprochement between the AFL and the scientific management school was eventually constructed during the 1920s. By this time Taylorism had been overshadowed by the rise of corporate liberal management: human engineering not mechanical engineering was the result (Noble, 1974: 276–8).

In sum Taylorism, despite the assumptions of Braverman, had only a limited influence upon the USA. The surveys by Nadworny (1955), Nelson (1974), Ozanne (1979) and Goldman and Van Houten (1980) can demonstrate only minimal involvement outside the areas where Taylorism was outlawed and Littler's (1982: 179–85) attempt to argue that Bedauxism (see later), as a derivative of Taylorism, was influential, and therefore we should not dismiss Taylor, has very limited empirical support (see below). Outside the USA Taylorism was adopted wholeheartedly by Lenin (Traub, 1978), though even here the might of the Soviet state under Stalin failed in its attempt to achieve complete mastery of the labour process (Andrle, 1989; Kossler and Muchie, 1990; cf. Nyland, 1987). The position of Japan is very ambiguous. According to Dore (1973), Taylor's time and motion ideas were introduced in the period around the First World War, though his individual incentive scheme was ignored and the contradiction between an extended division of labour and the traditional Japanese distrust of delimited skills clearly inhibited a complete Taylorist revolution and many early Taylorist schemes were abandoned in the inter-war period (Littler, 1982: 156–8). Nakase (1979) claims that scientific management did not really enter Japan until 1927, and while its influence was limited within Japanese companies because of the different ideologies, several American-owned companies introduced it wholesale quite successfully. These were, however, to fall victim to Japanese fascism in the run up to the Second World War. Perhaps the most significant points are raised by Daito (1979): 'we have not been able to identify any firm which adopted the Taylor system in its complete form' (p. 248), and a major problem is that anything concerned with 'efficiency' was called 'scientific management'. Given the conflation of terms here it would seem that Taylorism, at least in its total form as a unique and discrete managerial strategy, rather than just one more form of an increasingly rationalized approach to management, had very limited application anywhere.

Braverman and the Labour Process

Whatever the limits of Taylorism in practice, it did not stop Braverman from developing a theoretical critique of capitalist labour processes based directly on Taylor's ideas. Once in the public arena Braverman's 'labour process' approach enrolled many Marxist and radical sociologists, and the new perspective rapidly approached *de rigueur* status for any self-respecting non-conservative academic. This section considers the essence and entrails of the labour process perspective.

Taylorism, for Braverman (1974), comprised three 'principles'. First, 'the dissociation of the labor process from the skills of the workers' (p. 113); second, 'the separation of conception from execution' (p. 114); and third, the managerial 'use of this monopoly over knowledge to control each step of the labor process and its mode of execution' (p. 119). As Braverman notes: 'the separation of hand and brain is the most decisive single step in the division of labor taken by the capitalist mode of production'. Braverman was primarily concerned with the objective conditions of work, though he makes some acknowledgement of the way in which workers are induced to accept their degradation. In particular he notes how more fulfilling ways of working are progressively eroded and relatively high wages and consumer-oriented lifestyles dissuaded workers from seeking alternatives to monopoly capitalism. In this process of dehumanization, science and technology play their roles as servants of capital, replacing human labour, and deskilling that labour which is left, whilst management becomes the receptacle of the displaced knowledge and skill. The implication of this is that management itself is restructured through capitalism: it becomes not only strengthened but also stratified. Simultaneously, the process generates new service industries staffed by even lower waged and less skilled workers than operated within the previous manufacturing sectors. Hence, office work and retailing both become areas subject to the rationalizing mayhem of scientific management in Braverman's vision. Such a vision involves wresting control from the direct producers or operatives and re-establishing it, after the labour process has been fragmented and reaggregated, under the co-ordinative control of management, much of which is inscribed with a mechanical mode, for: 'machinery offers to management the opportunity to do by wholly mechanical means, that which it had previously attempted to do by organizational and disciplinary means' (Braverman, 1974: 195). An additional effect of this new control mode is the growth of white-collar staff to maintain and analyse the increased level of data produced by the fragmentation of the labour process. But Braverman makes clear that the new black-coated or clerical worker is vastly different from the old clerk. In contradiction to Lockwood's (1958) claim, Braverman argues that contemporary clerical labour has been proletarianized, and, moreover, that management is subject to the same onslaught from the 'Babbage principle'. In sum, Marx's prognostication on the proletarianization and homogenization of the class structure (Marx, 1968: 35–46) is validated by the universal deskilling which, Braverman argues, underpins the evolution of the capitalist labour process.

But how accurate is this vision? In the years since its publication

Monopoly Capital has received a veritable avalanche of criticism from radicals and non-radicals alike (Wood (ed.), 1982; Watson, 1986; Buchanan and Huczynski, 1985), and a whole variety of critical issues has emerged.

First, to what extent does Braverman's account of the deskilling imperative rest upon an illusory base of nineteenth-century craft work as typical? It has to be said that Braverman is far from unique in his romantic notion of the early and pre-capitalist labourer as highly skilled (Wright Mills, 1951: 220; Anthony, 1977: 113–45; Sirianni, 1982: 245–60; Pahl, 1984) but this does not prevent this notion from being erroneous, for the majority of the population work was never in the rustic craft tradition espoused by the idealists (Cutler, 1978; Elger, 1982; Harrison, 1984). Nor is his concentration on skill and specialization unique: from the late nineteenth century these had been the topics of considerable dispute (More, 1980; Gramsci, 1971). In fact, most authorities on the subject after Adam Smith, irrespective of political sympathy, have accepted the logic of deskilling as both a means to cheapen labour, and as a means of wrestling control from the workforce to concentrate it within management (cf. Cole, 1955: 28), though it is far from obvious that any universal deskilling has taken place through the period of industrial capitalism (Form, 1987). Even if many jobs have been deskilled it is by no means self-evident that the experience of work being controlled through a bureaucratic mechanism or even through a machine is necessarily more degrading that control transmitted through autocratic management.

Second, to assume that work has been deskilled requires some formal definition of skill. For Braverman, skill is the equivalent of 'craft mastery' (1974: 443) but the implication of this is that skill is comprised solely of technical components which can be objectively evaluated and observed. Yet skill is socially constructed and therefore a contingent phenomenon. For example, clerical work was originally regarded as highly skilled because of the limited levels of literacy (though one must beware of romanticising about this too; see Anderson, 1976); today clerical work is merely one form of labour, rather than the pinnacle of non-managerial occupations. Alternatively, some occupations managed to retain their skilled status despite the progress of time. For example, working in the printing industry, up until the 1980s at least, has always been regarded as a skilled occupation; even mere machine watchers were paid as skilled employees. The ability of the work group to negotiate and retain the label of skill, independently of any ostensibly technically defined job content, must, then, be considered (Turner, 1962; Lee, 1982). Indeed, when occupations are labelled skilled it is not always clear whether this refers to the whole range of tasks involved in a job or just the most difficult or even the prerequisite levels of training laid down. Since trade unions have often used control over the labour market as a mechanism for protecting their own position it has been common to extend the length of training in apprentices way beyond that normally required by the particular activities undertaken as a mature worker. Thus skill should not simply be regarded as a mechanism for resisting management but also as a means by which intra-class differentials can be advanced or buttressed (Taylor, 1982; Penn, 1982; Selbourne, 1985).

The level of discretion is not an objective measure of skill either, despite Jacques's (1967: 96) arguments, because discretion is itself context-dependent not context-free. For example, it may be that machinists have close supervision and therefore low levels of discretion and perhaps low levels of skill (and the associations between gender and skill are clear indications of the social construction of skill (Cavendish, 1982; Phillips and Taylor, 1980), but post and milk deliverers have negligible supervision and thus high levels of discretion without any related boost in skill levels. Nor will reliance upon the number of rules provide a satisfactory measure of skill (Crompton and Jones, 1984: 59): pilots have more rules to follow than cleaners, and cleaners have more than artists, but there does not appear to be a concrete link between the number of rules and the level of skill involved.

We also need to be aware of the cross-national variations that undermine the significance of concentrating purely upon the point of production. For instance, British unions tend to be relatively powerful in influencing issues very directly related to the labour process itself, but relatively weak over the more general social aspects of employment, such as levels of employment, employee participation in strategic decision making etc. The opposite tends to occur within the Scandinavian countries, Austria, Belgium and the Netherlands (Batstone, 1988b: 222). This distinction suggests further qualifications of the labour process approach. Where the approach implies that control over the labour process is directly related to the power resources utilized by labour, it is clear that resources involved in the disruption of production are merely one form of resource; the two most notable other variants being the scarcity value of particular forms of skill in the labour market (Kelly, 1985) and the ability of workers to influence the wider political process (Grint, 1986; Batstone et al., 1984).

The third problem with Braverman's analysis is that though this expansion of the work relations arena is important it does not imply any correlation between employee control or influence and *class* strategies of control. While many labour process accounts appear to assume an axiomatic link between resistance *to* employers and the advance of class interests, the two are separate. The point here is that a very powerful form of worker control over the labour process implies nothing about what that control is used for. It may well be that it advances or protects the interests of those particular workers, but advancing the interests of one group of workers may be at the expense, not of capitalists, but of other, less organized, workers. Indeed, it may well be that a very powerful system of control is erected by a union leadership not to expropriate the capitalists but rather to disinherit the lay members and ensure the reproduction of union 'dictatorship'; the national Union of Seamen in the 1920s is a good example of such a misnomer as 'worker-control' (Marsh and Ryan, 1989).

The fourth critical issue is that if Braverman, and for that matter Taylor, is right about the persistent deskilling of labour than the process should lead to a homogenous population of deskilled proletarians. In reality the opposite seems closer to the truth, with ever more divisions within the working class and a persistent tendency to heterogeneity. This heterogeneity has also been accompanied (see above) by a general shrinkage in the size of the manual labour force and an increase in the proportion of professional or service classes. Notwithstanding the concern for the definition of skill it would seem that a persistent and general deskilling of the labour force is not supported by the data on the occupational structure itself, nor by such data as the responses of a recent survey on class which reported that 96 per cent thought the skill content of their job had remained stable or increased (Marshall et al., 1988).

Fifth, is Braverman's data reliable? Unfortunately not; Braverman seems to have assumed that Taylor's schema was widely adopted without resistance, such that the reorganization of the work process appears to be the result of the conscious design of management rather than the effect of multiple and contentious social relations between different groups. Even the most obvious aspect of Taylorism, work study, is currently practised by only half the work establishments considered in a range of recent surveys of Britain and they are even less common in foreign-owned companies operating in Britain (Batstone, 1988a: 193–4). Thus Braverman falls into the same delusion that befell Taylor: that there is only one best way to organize capitalist production efficiently. For Taylor this best way is simply that derived from the application of scientific principles; for Braverman it is rather the most effective way of managing alienated labour. But a single best way, however defined, could only exist if all managements were homogeneous, faced common problems, interpreted them as such, and encountered no resistance from an undifferentiated working class. None of these provisos appears to be accurate.

Within the Marxist camp Friedman (1977) most effectively disposes of the single strategy myth with his development of a continuum between 'responsible autonomy', where workers are allowed 'leeway . . . to adapt to changing situations in a manner beneficial to the firm' (1977: 78), and the more Taylorist 'direct control'. Yet this is hardly different from the development by Fox (1974) of the 'high trust/discretion – low trust/discretion' managerial strategies, nor do strategies based on notions like 'responsible autonomy' adequately distinguish between the individual control of craft workers and the collective control issued through trade unions; both may involve responsible autonomy but they are clearly not identical. Such strategies indeed are common to the whole plethora of human relations alternatives to direct control: McGregor's (1960) Theory Y; Ouchi's (1981) Theory Z; Argyris's (1964) 'self-actualizing' strategies etc. (see chapter 4). Nor is it self-evident in which direction the causal line runs; that is whether high levels of discretion operate because managers trust employees or because the strength of the employees or their particular job prevents management invoking low discretion control mechanisms (Roche, 1983).

Sixth, Braverman rightly takes Bell to task for taking Taylor's word that the arc of the swing of poor Schmidt's shovel could be scientifically adjusted when the weight was 92 lb. (Braverman, 1974: 106). Yet Braverman does exactly the same when he moves beyond his own area of experience into clerical labour. Quoting from 'A Guide to Office Clerical Times Standards' (p. 321) Braverman implies that the times taken to open drawers (centre drawer 0.026 seconds, side drawer 0.014 seconds) etc. are significant developments in the scientific management of clerical work. But how many employers are in a position to determine this? Anyway, even if they are, does this mean the drawer opening times are significant? It seems more likely that such regulations are closer to the 'mock bureaucracies' described by Gouldner (1954), and still present today in the large-scale bureaucracies such as the Post Office where times and methods for opening letter boxes etc. exist but are routinely ignored. In short, what many labour process approaches ignore is the critical role played by the interpretative processes of agents: as considered in the previous chapter, whether such rules are deployed or not depends on who interprets them and how they are interpreted.

Such apparently trivial issues are actually symptomatic of an important fixation that both Braverman and many other labour process theorists have with the very nature of employment in capitalist society. Whether the drawer opening times are a valuable aid to management depends on their utility not in facilitating control but in promoting profit. Capitalism as a system of production does not thrive on the minutiae of control, *contra* Foucault, because control has an economic cost. If an office is to be based upon the supervised opening of drawers the number of supervisors will be almost equal to the number of clerical workers. In short, such a 'perfect' control system would be financially unviable. It may well be that workers and their unions are overtly concerned with the issues of control because they are the bearers of the effects. But for employers, control is secondary, and because it is derivative the crucial issue becomes whether control systems are facilitative or inhibitory of profits. As the Donovan Commission, and several authors since (Batstone et al., 1984; Jacobs et al., 1978; Marsh, 1982; Rose and Jones, 1985) have noted, labour relations are rarely considered in strategic decision making by boards of directors and are more usually the responsibility of subordinate level managers (1968: 41–4). Therefore, the issue must be whether control promotes or undermines profits. If it is the latter then some other method of ensuring productive activity must be constructed. This may even involve areas completely outside the particular point of production, for example asset stripping or investing in fine art or playing the market or whatever.

Paradoxically, as Kusterer (1978) has argued, the devaluation of labour regulation in British management often leads to the workers being able to control the labour process specifically because management is not particularly interested in this field. It may even be that a managerial strategy needs to embody both greater levels of coercive control for some employees and greater levels of accommodation for others simultaneously. Where technical developments promote key workers to points of strategic control over an integrated production process, while others become peripheral to it, managers may need to develop internally contradictory policies in an attempt to balance the relative influence of strategically placed workers. This more complex strategy is further compounded by delineating the different interests that management has within the labour process: while senior executives may be concerned with profits, line management is more likely to be responsible for, and therefore most interested in, ensuring production schedules are adhered to – even if this involves ignoring the rules constructed to maintain control or profits.

Not only, then, does the labour process approach tend to impute a uniformity to the workers, but an invariant strategy and interest is thrust upon management too: their foremost concern is allegedly controlling a recalcitrant workforce. Thus technology becomes a means not for advancing competitive advantage, or resolving productive quality problems etc., but for controlling the workers. This may be commonplace to industrial sociologists but it appears to be closer to fiction for many practising managers themselves (Blackburn and Mann, 1979; Northcott and Rogers, 1982; Batstone et al., 1987). Of course, as Bruland (1982) and Wallace (1978) have demonstrated, technology has been used as a method for wresting the control of the production process away from the workforce, but the point is that technology is not *just* a control mechanism, and even when it is intended as such this does not imply either that capitalism is the victor of the struggle, or alternatively that the working class is the victor. It may well be that sections of the workforce, especially white, male, skilled workers, are more likely than any other working-class group to retain at least some semblance of autonomy (Lazonick, 1979).

This universalist essence of the labour process theorists reappears between the wars in the guise of Bedauxism, a form of neo-Taylorism that allegedly swept to prominence so that by 1939 250 firms had adopted it, making it 'the most common system of managerial control in Britain' (Littler, 1982: 114–15), a claim apparently accepted by many commentators (e.g. Gospel, 1983: 102; Lash and Urry, 1987: 180–1). Yet in the absence of any quantitative data beyond the simple number of firms, and given that Littler includes only two of the largest fifty at the time (Hannah, 1983: 101–3, 190–1), one should remain sceptical of the impact of Bedauxism. Certainly the largest single employer of the period, the Post Office, made no significant attempt to adopt Taylorist or Bedauxist policies (Grint, 1986: 298–304), and it is more likely that the (in)significance of Taylorism is demonstrated by Littler's attention to the minimal evidence available (Zeitlin, 1983: 371).

Burawoy's (1979) account of the labour process does go some way in rescuing the Marxist approach by emphasising the way consent is generated by management in its attempt to increase productivity and through the wider social system beyond the factory gates, and also by noting the ways in which workers play games with and against management. Yet the different strategies of control by both managers and workers cannot really be explained within the restricted perspective of class politics, and it is by no means clear that playing games is the quintessence of capital–labour relations either. Edwards (1979) makes another attempt to expand the labour process debate by distinguishing between three phases of capitalist control: simple or hieararchical control, technical control and bureaucratic control. All three are allegedly the result of worker resistance. Simple control is prevalent during the first competitive phase of capitalism, but the capricious nature of such personal systems of authority stimulated wide-scale resistance and control was therefore inscribed into the machinery of production through technical control. Eventually this allowed groups of workers to control the entire production process and hence the switch to a depersonalized system of bureaucratic control complete with hierarchies, rules and careers. Note that not only does the historical evidence not support Edwards (Edwards and Scullion, 1982; P. Thompson, 1984; Batstone et al., 1987), but the assumption is still that 'work' actually means factory employment. Since large numbers of employees have never worked with machines that they could be controlled by, the theoretical significance of technical control must itself be questionable. Paradoxically, Edwards seems to suggest that managerial strategies of control, which are essential to obscure the exploitative nature of the labour process, are themselves a direct response to the patterns and forms of worker resistance rather than assuming that resistance may be one element in the desire for reconstruction. Quite why managers should feel the need to obscure a practice which is hardly newsworthy is unclear. In short, Edwards's account swings the pendulum away from Braverman's lacuna of resistance towards a analysis of managerial strategies based wholly on resistance.

Just as this is inherently limited and delimiting, so too are the general approaches towards technology within this theoretical tradition. This is considered elsewhere (see chapters 4 and 8), but it is worth reinforcing the point in terms of the class analysis. For Marx and the labour process theorists technology is quintessentially a class tool: a machine to oppress and exploit the working class further. But the problem becomes visible when technology appears not to deskill but to enskill, not to degrade but to enhance working experience. It is not necessary to fall into the trap of assuming that all technology enskills and enhances to accept the point that some of it may do. The question then becomes, how can this apparent event best be explained? For Marxists it must be an aberration, forced upon capital for very specific and atypical reasons; possibly concerning the unusual strength of working-class resistance. But the problem is then one of accounting for the very large numbers of aberrations. When aberrations become typical it is time to reconsider the explanation of aberrance and normality.

An alternative is to assume that what drives capitalists along is not the quest for control over the working class but, once again, the desire for profits and the necessity for competing against – not allying with – other capitalists. Thus, whether technology is responsible for deskilling or enskilling, degrading or enhancing is primarily the result of multiple conflicts between capitalists as well as between capitalists and workers, and producers and consumers. What the capitalist is coerced into doing, then, is stitching up alliances where possible and limiting the damage inflicted by foes where necessary. It is, as Latour (1988) has written, as if the contemporary capitalist has become the new Machiavellian Prince; the quest for this Prince is not control over labour through machinery because this is merely a single tactic amongst many in the greater quest for profit or power or whatever. Hence, because labour control is subordinate to, and a derivation of, the greater quest for money or profit it is quite logical to assume that on some occasions the capitalist will seek reduced overt control and enhanced working conditions – provided these facilitate the greater aim in the longer run. The problem, therefore, is not how to explain the atypicality and apparent irrationality of capitalists but to stop perceiving capitalist actions as if they must be explained through the prism of class control.

This brings us to a critical weakness in both Braverman's approach and most Marxist approaches. Unless it can be shown that the labour process is *the* most important arena for explaining social relations, and concomitantly that within the labour process class is the crucial variable, and hence all other social relations are derived from it, then such an approach can only be partially accurate. This does not mean that class is irrelevant or even subordinate to other forms of stratification such as race and gender, and some influential reconstructed approaches to the labour process have been made (Kelly, 1985; Knights et al., 1985; Knights and Willmott, 1988, 1989), though the more they move away from the restrictive concern with the labour process the less overtly Marxist they become. Nor does it mean that class-conscious activity generated at the point of production is impossible: the delimited demonstration of such a phenomenon does not equate with its theoretical disposal to the dustbin of history (cf. Edwards, 1986). Moreover, the alternative approach means that the examination of social relations at the point of production, and their links with other areas of life (especially the domestic), should not be delimited by theoretical closure. As argued in the next chapter, exactly which aspect of stratification is the most important may not be determined other than through empirical examination. Furthermore, one needs to begin to specify not just the top-down constraints and facilities provided by socially structured conditions - such as race, gender and class etc. - but also the way these are aggregated at the level of the individual. That is to say, individuals are not simply, for example, female *and* white *and* working class but a consolidated, if dynamic unity of all three: a white, working-class female for whom her race, class and gender may be of differential significance given the particular situation she is in at the time and the associated interpretations of that situation. Thus the problem of determining the relative importance of class, gender and race necessarily involves examining the experiences as perceived by the individual as well as the material forms present (such as income level, career prospects etc.). Braverman's approach can accommodate neither of these aspects since it ignores the significance of subjective factors and presumes the superiority of class.

Conclusion

This chapter has sought to demonstrate the value and limits of adopting a class-based analysis of work. Although class is critical to any such analysis, to inscribe all forms of industrial action as class action, and all forms of managerial concern as class concerns, remains problematic. The point is not so much that class is merely a fragmentary aspect of individual and collective experience (albeit a large fragment), but that no single social dimension is sufficiently broad to encompass the complexity of social relations at work. What counts as a significant category of social relations at work is not determined by the material structures within which agents act because these structures are themselves the product of agents' interpretations and actions. Thus occupation, craft, family, ethnicity and gender shape different categories of work experience which tends to undermine the solidarity generated solely on class. As we shall consider in the following two chapters, just because employees have similar class backgrounds does not generate any automatic forms of class solidarity; it may well be that these working-class employees consider race or gender or religion or something else as the defining and distinguishing category at work. Similarly, it is a mistake to focus solely upon the labour process itself as if a single slice of work organization holds the key to the totality; it does not. Class control over the labour process is not the sine qua non of capitalism, profit is. And since there are many ways to make a profit there can be no automatic and unmediated connection between class interests and the organization of work. The degradation of labour is not an inevitable result of capitalist work methods because labour is not necessarily critical to the process. Indeed, whether labour is degraded, enskilled, made more autonomous or completely eliminated from production is contingent upon the successful accumulation of profit. Work in capitalist societies does tend to generate conflict given the wage-effort negotiations at the heart of the system, but how that conflict is mediated by the actors involved, and how the result is translated into the organizational forms of work, is not determined by an transcendental need to control the labour *process*. For capitalists and many managers the end product is more important than the process; for many employees the reverse may apply.

6

Gender, Patriarchy and Trade Unions

And thy estimation shall be of the male from twenty years old even unto sixty years old, even thy estimation shall be fifty shekels of silver. . . . And if it be female, then thy estimation shall be thirty shekels.

Leviticus, 27: 3–4

Introduction

Gender inequality is nothing new. Both paid and unpaid forms of work have consistently exhibited patterns of inequality. One of the most persistent aspects of paid labour is that relating to gender-related inequality of rewards. Ignoring all the many problems involved in wage calculations which blur issues of skill, qualifications and hours etc., it is a sobering experience to consider the gendered wage differential. Studies of the sixteenth century calculate that, on average, women earned something between 52 per cent (Roberts, 1979) and 61 per cent (Kussmaul, 1981) of men's average earnings, hardly different from the prescribed differential set down in Leviticus. In 1913 the equivalent figure was 53 per cent (Grint, 1988) and the 1989 figure was about 67 per cent, with women's hourly earnings about 76 per cent of men's (Low Pay Unit, 1989; *Employment Gazette*, April 1990).

Inequality is something which changes both in historical terms and during the life cycle of individuals: at the age of 11 girls' hourly rates of pay are 99 per cent of boys'; by the age of fifteen the differential has changed to 87 per cent (*The Guardian*, 29 November 1989). The greatest gender disparity relates to part-time manual work where women, on average, earn 49 per cent of the hourly rate paid to full-time men on identical work (Equal Opportunities Commission, 1989). At the other end of the scale some 10 per cent of men currently earn over £350 a week in contrast to just 1 per cent of women (Henley, 1989). Inertia is the most appropriate way to describe the inequality of gender-based rewards in this country. Other nations show a considerable disparity: in Sweden women earn, on average, 90 per cent of men's wages, in Japan it is 43 per cent (TURU, 1986: 7). This national diversity is not restricted to wages: roughly twice as many pre-school children are in some form of nursery system in Belgium, the Netherlands and West Germany as in Britain; state support for maternal and paternal rights *vis-à-vis* young children's health and welfare is minimal in Britain; in Sweden parents have the right to 18 months combined leave for pre-school families at 90 per cent of current earnings and the right to work a six-hour day until the child is 8 years old (Meade-King, 1989).

This chapter considers the complex circumstances surrounding women at work by considering three related aspects: first, the various theoretical approaches; second, the post-war era (aspects of the pre-1945 period are discussed in chapter 2); and finally, the influence of trade unions. The approach is one that seeks to explore the alternative perspectives available and then to use the one most heuristic to guide the necessarily brief review of the literature. The essence of the approach is one which perceives the position of women at work to be premised on three axial principles:

First, work patterns are necessarily related to their domestic responsibilities, so that the analysis of 'work' cannot occur in isolation from the analysis of the home – work link. Second, gender, although critical, is not uniquely important in explaining women's work patterns and experiences because individuals are heterogeneous composites: occupationally derived class and ethnicity are also relevant, as may be religion, age, nationality etc. In this particular text attention is restricted primarily to gender, class and ethnicity. Third, the experience of women is not one that can be read off from an 'objective' analysis of social categories but is quintessentially an interpretative process. These social categories influence but do not determine the experience of work. Indeed, what counts as a significant category is an interpretative and therefore contingent phenomenon.

Theoretical Perspectives on Women and Work

The invisibility of gender within the classical perspectives has given way in recent years to a plethora of competing approaches. Although a multitude of positions exists, Walby's (1986a) categorization is the clearest and forms the basis of this review. In sequence, then, the discussion follows the following plan:

1. Classical perspectives of women and work.
2. Gender as irrelevant.
3. Gender as secondary to or derived from class subordination.
4. Patriarchially derived subordination, where gender inequality relates primarily to gender relations.
5. Symbiotically derived subordination, where gender inequality relates to the seamless interleaving of capitalism and patriarchy – capitalist patriarchy.
6. Dualist subordination, where gender inequality relates to the discrete interaction between two autonomous spheres of capitalism and patriarchy.
7. Composite contingent subordination, where gender inequality is derived from the heterogeneous interleaving of gender, ethnicity and class but the connections and their particular influences are both contingently interpreted and constructed and tension-ridden.

In what follows the first six approaches are schematically presented and an alternative formulation, which seeks to overcome some of the main problems of the others, is developed. I then consider the heuristic utility of this alternative 'composite model' in an examination of historical and contemporary gender relations at work. In this instance most of the evidence relates to paid work and a majority applies to paid work outside the home. However, it will become apparent that the relationships between paid and unpaid labour, and between home and work, are so interlaced that the divisions are often merely for analytic purposes. Nevertheless, this chapter will focus, in the main, on paid labour outside the home. Unpaid domestic labour is dealt with in chapter 2.

Classical Perspectives

As noted in chapter 3, the contributions of Marx, Weber and Durkheim to the examination of gender relations at work are less than useful in the main. Certainly they all seemed to assume that gender inequalities were omnipresent in all forms of society, though Marx's collaborator Engels had put forward an argument for the initial existence of a matriarchal society which was undermined by the differentiation between production and reproduction. As production – the sphere of men – began to provide surpluses, so it achieved predominance over reproduction – the sphere of women – and led to the creation of a whole panoply of institutions associated with patriarchal control: private property, social classes and the state. In theory, since patriarchy was derived from private property, and since working men's exploitation of their female partners was a reflection of their own exploited position within capitalism, the elimination of capitaliam and private property would reintroduce sexual equality (Engels, 1968). Engels's anthropological evidence for matriarchy is dubious and the connection between capitalism and patriarchy much more complex than he makes out (Delmar, 1976). That is not to say that there never were any pre-capitalist societies controlled by women: Chinese empresses and Assyrian war queens were as real as Boadicea (Fraser, 1988) or Cleopatra, and certain Pict tribes operated with matrilineal inheritance and descent (Chadwick, 1970: 118). Even though the vast majority of contemporary societies have patriarchal lines of property control some have long traditions of matriarchal control over property, the Reang hill tribe of north-east India being a case in point (*The Guardian*, 25 May 1988).

However sympathetic to certain aspects of the women's emancipation movement in Germany Weber may have been (1948: 26), he regarded the existence of patriarchal domination as 'normal' in the light of 'the normal superiority of the physical and intellectual energies of the male' (1978: 1007). If anything, Durkheim was even more reactionary, though somewhat ambiguous about gender relationships and the relative benefits of marriage to men and women (1933: 57–60; cf. 264–5). In short, the classical theorists have little of substance to add to the debate on gender at work.

Gender as Irrelevant

The concentration upon men within sociology has, until very recently, been so common that it was seldom perceived to require an explanation; there is, as Marx argued, no greater power than when what is actually a sectional interest becomes represented and accepted as a universal interest, as common sense. There is some inconsistency amongst this rather heterogeneous group of approaches to gender, with some using individuals as the unit of study while others use the family, but it is only in conjunction with familially based analysis that theoretical justifications for the exclusion of gender are introduced. Both Goldthorpe (et al., 1980, 1983, 1984b) and Parkin (1972) argue that women's position is dependent upon the class situation of the family, which, in turn, is conditioned by the class position of the head of the family. Naturally, runs their argument, since the head of the family – i.e. the main breadwinner – is male, women's class position is determined by their husband's or partner's class. Of course, some women may have a higher social class than their partner, but they argue that this is unlikely to be a general rule. In fact, logically it cannot be a rule at all, for if women's class is determined by their partner's class then self-evidently the former cannot be different from the latter (Macrae, 1986; Walby, 1986a: 10). Goldthorpe's recent assessment (1984b) suggests that the determination of women's class position by their partners' (obviously single women have their own class) is a manifestation of sexism not within sociology but within society. Thus, he argues, it is because women's life changes *are* dependent upon their partners that sociologists should concentrate upon men.

There are several problems with this kind of approach. First, because it allocates women's class through the family it assumes that income distribution within the family is correlated with class: the higher the class of the male the higher the class of the female. But as pointed out in chapters 1 and 5, and as Brannen and Wilson (1987) and Gershuny (1983) have argued, male monopolization over economic resources makes a mockery of any assumed equality within the family, and it is therefore not possible to assume that women's class is identical to that of their male partners. Indeed, the differentiated control over resources is just one facet of a gendered inequality within the family that also encompasses several areas including domestic labour (see chapter 2) and especially domestic and sexual violence. In Britain only 5 per cent of convictions for violence are made against women (James, 1988), and while women are sometimes violent towards children (as are men), very few women are violent towards other adults – in sharp contrast to men (Rose, 1986: 166–8). The actual extent of domestic violence inflicted on women by men is unknown, though a recent review of the evidence suggests that at least 500,000 women suffer in England and Wales alone (Home Office, 1989). That is not to say that social, or rather societal violence, as opposed to individual violence, does not sometimes allieviate the subordination of women. Societally organized violence, especially in wars of liberation or resistance to foreign oppressors, 'appears to promote citizenship for women more than any other single factor' (Turner, 1986: 71). Violence, then, can both destroy and subjugate women as well as facilitate their partial unshackling.

Second, it is not possible to allocate all class categories to women through male partners because many women are unmarried or do not live with a male partner. A further percentage have a different class from their male partners – or they would have if the criteria for class were individually based, not family based (Stanworth, 1984; Walby, 1986a; McRae, 1986; Leiulfsrud and Woodward, 1987). Third, even the focus upon men as heads of households is inhibited by the exclusion of their female partners, for it assumes that such men are completely unaffected by the resources brought into the family by women. This is markedly influential where analyses of social mobility are made, for although much has been made of the relative mobility of the British 'working class' in the work of Goldthorpe et al. (1980), more recent analysis indicates that although many male workers have been upwardly mobile, many female workers may have suffered a consequential downward mobility (Abbott and Sapsford, 1988). Fourth, in contrast to the above, the emergence of dual-income families within homogamous (same class) marriages may well polarize the experiences of middle- and working-class families. That is, although the rise of cross-class families is important they do not represent the norm. Within that norm almost half of all wives were economically active in 1981 compared to 42 per cent in 1971. But, and this is the crucial point, the disparity between the classes is constantly growing: taking the Registrar General's classification of social classes, wives of professional-class males (class 1) increased their activity rate by 11 per cent over the decade but wives of semi-skilled and unskilled males increased their activity rate only by 3 per cent. The life experiences of British working-class women and middle-class women, therefore, are undergoing qualitatively different, that is polarizing, changes (Bonney, 1988; Truman and Keating, 1988), though American data imply that some form of convergence may be occurring (Treas, 1987).

Finally, Lockwood (1986) has argued that gender cannot be regarded as an explanatory category, not because women derive their class from their male partners but because women do not form a cohesive collectivity, capable of pursuing gender-based issues. This severing of the gender line through alleged political and organizational incompetence not only misrepresents the actions of many women and their organizations over many years (Bouchier, 1983; Boston, 1987), but imbues class-based movements with a coherence they simply do not have. Ironically, despite Lockwood's Weberian approach, such a definition of class is much closer to the 'class for itself' label which Marx introduced as just *one* facet of a class movement.

Gender as Secondary or Derived Subordination

One theoretical solution to the problems posed by a family-based analysis is to consider women both individually, through their occupational status, and collectively through their gender. This opens up a veritable Pandora's box, for women without paid employment, but who are not unemployed, appear to be in the same occupationally defined class. Such a class might well be extremely heterogeneous in terms of life chances, including female members of the 'idle rich' as well as the 'feckless poor', a combination that defies the conventions of stratification theory even if the patterns of life experience within the family *relative* to their male partners may be similar.

Alternatively, although the most orthodox of Marxists have either ignored the gendered dimension to stratification some have regarded it as simply a by-product of class, and therefore of capitalism. Thus Edwards (1979), Braverman (1974) and Rubery (1980) all suggest, though in different ways, that gender plays a part in constraining the supply of labour but is not a central feature of segregation within work. Gender is also influential in so far as it is associated with capitalist strategies for control by 'divide and rule' (Stone, 1974).

A critical aspect of the controversy surrounds the question of exploitation: since domestic labour is not paid, the value it has lies in providing capitalism with a virtually free source of domestic servicing for its employees; capitalists exploit the domestic labour of women by providing wages for men that do not encompass the true costs of producing and reproducing the labour force. One branch of the argument asserts that women's domestic labour is productive in the sense that it is self-evidently labour; without it capitalism would not be viable, and anyway domestic and paid labour are so intertwined as to be mutually productive of value (Seccombe, 1974, 1975). Himmelweit and Mohun (1977) place the emphasis on the consumption undertaken by domestic labour rather than production; a point of some importance to Marxism since only productive labour is deemed to be constructive of value for only this form is exchanged directly with capital.

A second branch is taken by Engels, who argued that a major step outside the boundaries of domestic exploitation for women would come when more women entered the labour force directly through paid employment, but it has to be said that almost the whole of this debate amongst Marxists has been conducted within the confines of the class exploitive nature of capitalism. That is, the issue of gender exploitation by men, and this includes both proletarian and bourgeois men, is either unimportant or relevant only in so far as it illuminates class-based exploitation. As Walby puts it: 'these writers face a serious inconsistency between asserting the derivative nature of women's oppression from capitalism, while recognizing the fact that this oppression pre-dates capitalism. It is illogical to suppose that a social system which arose after patriarchy could be deemed to create social inequalities which pre-date it' (1986a: 20).

A third position is pushed by Gorz whose rather heretical form of Marxism actually has strong resonances with Marx's critique of the commodification of all relations. The evisceration of social relations through the encroachment of economic relations was, according to Marx, an inevitable result of the market imperatives undergirding capitalism. Gorz's argument is that to suggest payment for domestic labour, as a solution to patriarchal and/or capitalist exploitation, is to substitute economic relations for social relations. Thus Gorz charges that although domestic labour is unpaid because it carries associations of servility and subordination to the economically oriented activities of paid labour, it is these associations that should be challenged, not the apparent 'problem' of uncommodified labour (see chapter 1).

A rather different approach, which explains gender exploitation through capitalism, is that associated with the diremption of the home from the central unit of family production through industrialization. Some of the historical evidence on this issue has already been covered above but the issue is theoretically as well as empirically important: the removal of women from paid labour enforces a level of economic dependence by women on men that would, in theory, serve to *exacerbate* patriarchal predominance in the home (Middleton, 1981), or as Zaretsky (1976) argues (though on the basis of inadequate information), to *instigate* patriarchal predominance in the home.

The final interpretation locks into an argument of Marx concerning women's role in the 'reserve army of labour' (Braverman, 1979), that is the pool of unemployed workers who are essential to the smooth functioning of the capitalist economy by providing the extra labour necessary in booms and embodying the deterrent to wage rises and industrial conflict during slumps. Unfortunately, the evidence for this theory is very dubious, primarily because it suggests that men and women are interchangeable in the labour market when in fact the labour market is highly sex-segregated (Alexander, 1976; Beechey, 1986). The argument seems to suggest that the functional utility of women as a cheap, docile labour force explains the development of capitalism; but since patriarchy predates capitalism, and since the reserve army of labour cannot both predate capitalism and be caused by it, the argument appears to suffocate itself in contradictory logic (cf. Barrett, 1980).

Patriarchally Derived Subordination

The third approach to the explanation of gender inequality avers that capitalism is irrelevant, or at best subordinate, to the production and reproduction of male dominance. Since pre-capitalist and non-capitalist social formations manifest patriarchal control, the origins and perpetuating forces must lie in gender relations themselves. One of the earliest and most influential writers in this radical feminist genre is Firestone (1974). She argues that women's subordinate position is directly related to the biological differences between men and women, and, more specifically, to the debilitating consequences for women of sexual reproduction in its various facets: childbirth, pregnancy, breast feeding, childcare and menstruation. Adopting Marx's base/superstructure schema she asserts that reproduction is the base from which everything else follows: hence, again like Marx, she denies the value of tinkering with the superstructure while the reproductive base remains untouched (cf. O'Brien, 1981). Rather, the link between women and reproduction must be severed by the pursuit of a biological solution: only by constructing a reproductive system that does not depend on women can patriarchal power be broken. It is, then, to 'artificial' reproduction that women must look for liberation. However, this really begs the question of technical control. If patriarchy is dependent upon the biological link and, because of this, in control of technical and biological advances, then it would be irrational for patriarchy to allow the development of its own suicide note. Moreover, Firestone's argument seems to slip from the biological aspects of reproduction to the socially constructed aspects of child rearing etc., without much concern for the distinctions; while only women can have children, not all women do, nor does this require that only women are responsible for childcare. Indeed, since many men either do not marry or do not father children it is difficult to explain how these individuals necessarily gain directly from the reproductive activities of most women. Other writers have located the locus of patriarchal power in rape (Brownmiller, 1976) or pornography (Dworkin, 1981). But despite the importance of these two facets of patriarchy in its self-reproduction, it is not self-evident that either or both are the *principal* means for this. It seems unlikely that a society without pornography or rape would necessarily exhibit gender equality, even if it would be a considerably better place to live.

Part of the problem with theoretical evaluations of the superordinate position of patriarchy is the ahistoricism and universalism that often prevails. Not only are men presumed to have been dominant through all time and space but all men are engulfed in the same unidirectional subordination of all women, who in turn have identical experiences. It is also difficult to see how such an invariant and omnipotent system of oppression could be challenged, let alone dissipated. It is problems like this that have encouraged the dismissal of patriarchy as the only independent variable and a return to the possibility of uniting capitalism and patriarchy as symbiotically related twin pillars of gender oppression.

Symbiotically Derived Subordination: Capitalist Patriarchy

If patriarchy alone cannot fully explain gender subordination perhaps the solution is to draw the separate modes of exploitation together: capitalism exploits some women (and some men) economically; patriarchy exploits women politically and socially. This position, most thoroughly argued by Eisenstein (1979, 1984), implies that capitalism and patriarchy are mutually dependent and self-reinforcing. In certain circumstances this may well be true, but there are contradictory forces within both that undermine the alleged mutuality. For example, capitalism is actually composed of discrete capitals whose interests are often incompatible in the sphere of economic exploitation of women, and each discrete capital harbours an inherent antagonism to the requirements of all others: it may be in the interests of one capitalist to exploit his or her employees by providing the lowest possible wages but the consumption of commodities is dependent upon a high level of general income, not a parsimonious one. Furthermore, the interests of men are riven by their contending economic interests as employers and employees (Grint, 1988), and are in no sense universally and congruously patterned by their gender. Capitalist men do not have the same interests as working-class men, even with regard to women workers. The former may consider women as a source of cheap and compliant labour, and prefer them to men as employees; for precisely the same reason working-class men may seek to exclude women from the labour market altogether.

Dualist Approaches: Capitalism and Patriarchy as Autonomous

Given the incompatible aspects of capitalism and patriarchy the final attempt to resolve the problem of gender-based oppression and exploitation is to reunite the two systems in parallel. A variety of routes are proposed in this field: Mitchell (1975) locates ideological control within patriarchy and economic control within capitalism, though this dualism is again one without clear lines of friction between the two. Indeed, the reduction of capitalism to material control, and patriarchy to ideological control, misunderstands the interleaving of each with the other. Thus male workers often fear and resist the encroachment of women not just because they regard 'women's work' as demeaning but because it is perceived as a distinct threat to their material standards of reward (Grint, 1988).

Delphy's (1977) dualism reverts to the conventional Marxist materialist analysis for both spheres: the domestic and capitalist modes of production. Both modes are sites for the exploitation and subordination of women because it is theoretically vacuous to hive off domestic work as unproductive while retaining all work under capitalist exchange as productive. Whatever activities are currently undertaken by women at home as part of their domestic duties are, with very few exceptions, executed for monetary reward outside the home. Indeed, a current estimate of the cost of domestic work puts the total annual figure for 'replacing a wife' in Britain at £19,292, in 1987 prices (the figure is calculated by an insurance group to facilitate 'Family Income Insurance': PLA, 1987: 10). It is, then, not the content of labour that makes it productive or unproductive but the social relations within which it is performed. Nevertheless, according to Delphy, it is the domestic mode which is critical since this prestructures the pattern of gender-related inequalities in the capitalist mode of production.

One of the difficulties with this is that the domestic exploitation of women as a class by men glosses over the gross inequalities between women: both 'idle rich' women and poverty-stricken working women are mutually exploited by their respective male partners. This is not to say that both may well be exploited, but it is to point out the greatly variant forms of exploitation that may exist. Furthermore, we need to be assured that households without men are either non-exploitative, or can isolate themselves from the power of patriarchy derived not from physical manifestations, *qua* men at home, but in its multifarious formations that exist irrespective of adult male presence. For example, the portrayal of women as subordinate in the media or in everyday life in the local neighbourhood or via male children, does not depend upon adult male presence for its viability. Nor do women need to live with a male partner to feel the effects of patriarchy at work. It is because there is no hermetic seal between home and work (unpaid and paid) that they continue to infect each other. If these opaque, and sometimes invisible, links between home and work are ignored, it becomes possible to argue that the under-representation of women amongst senior management has nothing to do with their over-representation at home. As Wolff puts it in her critique of organization theory that ignores the wider social context: 'we can see how long hours and inflexible working time militate against the employment of women with "two roles", but we cannot discuss the basic question of why women have two roles' (Wolff, 1977: 20). We also need to be clear about the exploitation of women by women in the domestic scene. Both white and black South African women may be exploited by men at home but black women servants are also exploited by their female white employers: as Orwell might have argued, under capitalist patriarchy all women are equal – but some are more equal than others.

While Delphy tends to stress the importance of the domestic mode, Hartmann's (1982) account inverts the hierarchy by highlighting the critical role of occupational sex segregation. This patriarchal control of employment opportunities delimits the opportunities for women outside the home and therefore buttresses the ideological pressures on women to remain at home looking after children. One particular feature of this albeit contingent locking of patriarchy and capitalism is apparently demonstrated by the adoption of the family wage as a legitimate trade union principle for collective bargaining acceptable to male workers and capitalists alike. Nevertheless, it is not clear why capitalists should acquiesce to this demand since it keeps wages higher than they need be. Nor, of course, does it gel with claims that capitalism exploits women by *not* paying for domestic services provided by women. It may be that family wages provide an uneasy compromise by balancing the need for quiescent labour with the demands for cheap labour but there is little evidence that employers were anything but unwilling parties to this bargain (Grint, 1988).

The final version of dualism covered here is that of Walby (1986a). She retains the parallel aspects of patriarchy and mode of production but distinguishes between various aspects of patriarchal relations, such as domestic work, paid work, the state, male violence and sexuality, whose relative importance depends upon the nature of the link between patriarchy and the particular mode of production. Thus under capitalism it is paid work and the domestic division of labour which are critical, and they generate both a patriarchal, and essentially privatized, mode of production that exploits 'housewives' or domestic labourers, and a capitalist mode of production that exploits proletarians. These two are correlated through the delimiting of opportunities for women in paid work which effectively renders them economically dependent upon their male partner.

Reconstructing the Theories: a Composite Contingency Model

There is much to be said for Walby's suggestion (especially the more flexible approach developed in her *Theorising Patriarchy* (1990)) because its contingent relationships between the different spheres of patriarchy can be used to explain the variations that exist in time and space; without this flexibility patriarchy becomes so inherently omnipotent as to be incapable of change within or between societies. Nevertheless, the model underlying many other approaches to gender inequality, appears to be, rather ironically, the nuclear family in which the primary breadwinner is a man in full-time employment. The implication of this conventional model (and its typicality is severely restricted in time and space with currently a mere 3 per cent fitting the single male breadwinner and full-time 'housewife and mother' 'ideal' in Britain and 7 per cent in the USA (BMRB, 1988; Kakabadse and McWilliam, 1987; Pahl (ed.), 1988: 12–15) is that women who do not live with men are, by definition, less exploited than all those who do. This may be the empirical norm but it is not an axiomatic principle to be accepted a priori. Families or households where an egalitarian division of domestic labour exists between male and female partners may be atypical but their existence should warn us of the dangers of 'guilt by association'. That is to say that the blanket derivation of oppression by men, the concomitant location of oppression in all women, and the corresponding manichaean distinction between exploiting employers and non-exploiting employees ought to be the subject of empirical investigation rather than theoretical generalization. Nor is it self-evident that the arena of paid work should be prioritized above that of domestic work: it is the case that the limited opportunities for paid work delimit women's freedom within the home but it also clear that women's domestic responsibilities prevent or deter them from seeking certain forms of paid work. It is the seamless web that knits home and 'work', unpaid and paid labour, that confounds the dualist models and the contingent position of individuals within the web.

In fact, while it may be useful for heuristic purposes to separate patriarchy and capitalism, three dangers remain: first, that of slipping from analytic distinctions to empirically discrete explanations; second, in subordinating forms of oppression which are not derived from capitalism or patriarchy; and third, in presuming that analytic models of oppression are the means by which most people understand the world. Hence, in facing empirical reality women do not necessarily confront 'men' or 'capitalists' but particular men who are heterogeneous or composite individuals or representative of such composites. They are white or black; and they are capitalists or supervisors or workers; and they are young or old; and where interpreted as significant they are Catholic or Protestant or Jewish or Muslim etc. Concomitantly, women do not form a homogeneous collective but experience work as middle-class or working-class women; as white or black, and within the ethnic minorities as black or Asian or Mexican etc.; the fact of gender similarity says little about the specific form of oppression or the contradictions between women from different class or ethnic backgrounds (Ramazanoglou, 1989). Indeed, what exist in work situations are individuals and groups whose primary characteristics embody (at least) three distinctive facets of the stratification structure: class, gender and ethnic origin. This is not to deny that other issues are potentially divisive, nor does it deny that non-capitalist societies may be patriarchal and racist but it is to state that social relations are inherently more complex than those implicit in dualist theories.

It is not a question of theoretically unravelling the triple threads that go to make up individuals and groups so that they can be better analysed separately because they only exist as heterogeneous composites. For heuristic purposes, it is important that the threads are identified and most research has followed one such thread at a time (hence the structure of this book), but to postulate discrete hierarchies of influence emanating from each thread is to misunderstand the distinction between the composite as a whole and the sum of its parts. An analytic model may provide a picture in triptych form: for example, of an individual as a worker, as black, and as a women. But the life experiences of this individual are more likely to be refracted through the multiplex network or prism of these social forms: as a black-female-worker. In sum, the analysis, in this instance of women and work, should proceed from the assumption that patriarchy, racism and capitalism form not parallel modes of oppression but a contingent and discordant whole riddled with internal tensions and contradictions.

Perhaps a useful analogy to differentiate this model from dualist models that separate the threads is the distinction between interleaved metals and an alloy: bronze has properties which are distinct from the copper, tin and zinc or lead metals on which it is based. Where the analogy is limited is in the distinction between the tension-ridden and contingent social relationship and the static and stabilized relationship between the metals. This does not mean that there is no utility in considering race, class or gender separately: the material that can be marshalled to cover all these areas is immense, and much of it is constructed from perspectives vastly different from this one, so the process of reconstruction in an introductory text of this sort is an inordinately complex task. And of course many social relationships do not involve all or any of the three aspects: relationships between white middle-class males may or may not involve aspects of gender, race and class: whether they do or not is a contingent aspect subject to empirical investigation. Since those areas where class and race are pre-eminent are covered elsewhere, the next section concentrates on the experiences of women in paid labour outside the home since 1945; unpaid domestic labour and home working are considered in chapter 1, pre-1945 work is covered in chapter 2. Furthermore, from a practical point of view analytic divisions have to be made if we are to avoid paralysing the reader with a morass of unstructured information. Ultimately, of course, to reproduce the divisions is to perpetuate conventions but neither the resources nor the research material to reconstruct the sociology of work afresh are yet available; this chapter can only point towards a future alternative for research.

Women and Paid Labour: The Contemporary Evidence

After the end of the Second World War the experience of women workers was quite different from those in 1919. First, no economic depression followed and, indeed, over two decades of uninterrupted economic growth spanned the period up until the early 1970s. As a result, the opportunities for women, married and single, did not suddenly disappear but rather continued to expand, so that by 1989 53 per cent of women over 16 were employed (in comparison with 76 per cent of men over 16) (*Employment Gazette*, April 1990). Second, and relatedly, the shifts in the economy towards the service sector with its resultant increase in demand for white-collar labour, actually forced some employers into providing unheard-of levels of equality between men and women, most notably in these areas of white-collar shortage (Grint, 1988). Third, the proportion of women working part time continued to increase (to 43 per cent in 1989), partly as a result of wartime experiences of women with domestic responsibilities and partly because it suited employers to use part-timers to soak up fluctuations in demand and yet avoid having to pay National Insurance contributions or involve themselves in the legal aspects of dismissing full-time employees etc. (Beechey, 1986: 28–9). Fourth, women began reappearing in the labour market after their children went to school so that a bimodal distribution was evident from the 1960s, in sharp contrast to the prior pre-1939 pattern (outside the wars themselves) where most women, but especially middle-class women, left the labour market permanently if and when they got married and had children.

Outside the limited areas where some degree of equality prevailed, levels and forms of segregation were and still are very common. The segregation of men and women into different occupations - horizontal segregation - and the distinction between the genders in terms of patterns of authority - vertical segregation - is shown in figure 7. In fact, the relative crudity of the distinctions underestimates the degree of inequality in authority terms and some of the more detailed data are provided later (see also Hakim (1979)). At this point it is just worth noting a few points. First, there are no occupations, as classified here, that are demonstrably equal in gender composition. Second, the genders are distributed in a non-random way: women predominate in education, clerical, catering, cleaning and hairdressing; men dominate in the professions, science and engineering, management, manufacturing, construction and transport. Third, and as a summation of the previous points, there are strong connections between occupations related to the domestic sphere and poorer pay.

Inequality prevails, then, both because of the jobs that women do but also because of the unequal pay they receive when they do similar jobs to men. Most recent reviews would suggest that unequal treatment within jobs, rather than unequal access to particular jobs, is the critical problem for women (Horrell, Rubery and Burchell, 1989), though as figure 7 implies, unequal access is itself commonplace.

British women have, for the most part, never comprised more than a quarter of employers, more than a fifth of managers and more than a tenth of higher professionals throughout this century. Where there has been a considerable expansion in both the absolute and relative numbers of female employees has been in the white-collar and service sector. Very roughly a quarter of all white-collar employees were women at the turn of this century whereas the equivalent figure today is well over half.

One of the changes most often associated with the industrial revolution

Figure 7 Occupations and gender 1989 (UK, millions)

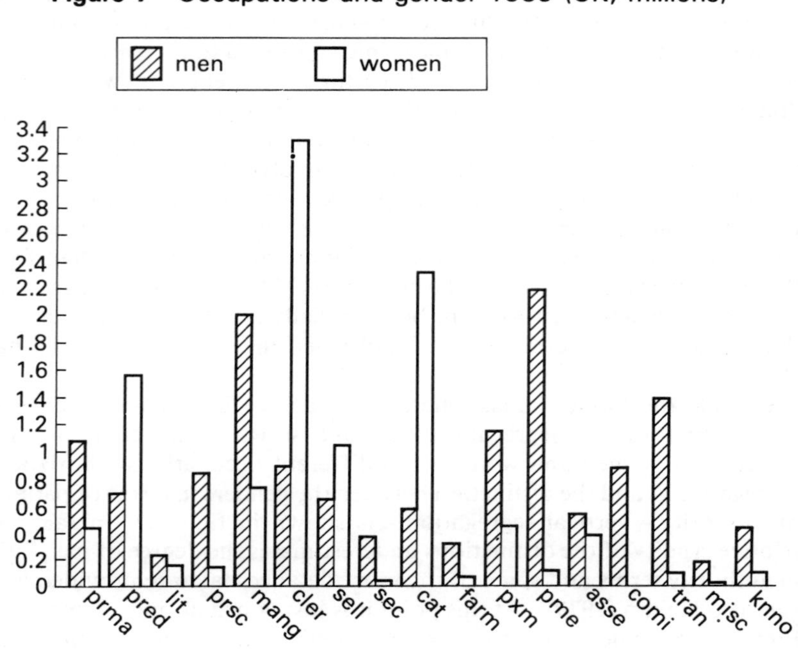

Key:
prma – professional and related supporting management and administration
pred – professional and related in education, welfare and health
lit – literary, artistic and sport
prsc – professional and related in science, engineering, technology and similar fields
mang – management
cler – clerical and related
sell – selling
sec – security and protective service
cat – catering, cleaning, hairdressing and other personal services
farm – farming, fishing and related
pxm – processing, making, repairing and related (excluding metal and electrical)
pme – processing, making, repairing and related (metal and electrical)
asse – painting, repetitive assembling, product inspecting, packaging and related
comi – construction and mining
tran – transport operating, materials moving and storing
misc – miscellaneous
knno – knowledge inadequate

Source: *Employment Gazette*, April 1990

was the gradual eclipse of employment opportunities for married women. The 1851 Census in Britain records that 25 per cent of married women had an 'extraneous occupation' – a label perfectly in keeping with the subsequent Victorian ideology that came to perceive the woman's role as almost wholly encapsulated by the home and family (Alexander, 1976); and, despite the growing significance of factory labour for women from the last quarter of the nineteenth century onwards, the proportion of married women with paid employment dropped to under 10 per cent in the first three decades of the twentieth century before rising steadily to 22 per cent by 1951, just under 50 per cent by 1981 (Joseph, 1983: 6; Beechey, 1986: 13), and 54 per cent in 1989 (*Employment Gazette*, April 1990). Currently over 65 per cent of American mothers with children under 18 are employed (Meade-King, 1988), a midway point between Britain, where 48 per cent of mothers with children under ten are employed (Martin and Roberts, 1984), and Sweden, where 82 per cent of mothers with children under school age are employed (Leiulfsrud and Woodward, 1987). Coincident with a rise in the proportion of married women within the labour force has been a rise in the number of employed women with sole responsibility for dependants. Although the conventional stereotyped male breadwinner may suggest that most men have dependants, in fact only 40 per cent of both men and women have dependents (Beechey, 1986: 9).

The increased rate of employment for married women generally is the most substantial single area of change in occupational activity since the beginning of this century. Generally speaking, since the Second World War, women have tended to adopt either a fragmented work career or a two-phase career with a substantial break of between five and fifteen years whilst they raise their children. Even when children become full-time pupils many women still structure their employment around their continuing domestic responsibilities so that school holidays and early finishing become an essential part of employment arrangements. In 1990 the division between part-time and full-time work amongst married women is roughly half and half (*Employment Gazette*, April 1990). Married women, like the majority of all employees, tend, and indeed have always tended, to regard the monetary rewards of work as critical (Parker, et al., 1967: 53; Roberts, 1985: 241–2; Burnett, 1984), though boredom at home and the need for company also figure prominently in the reasons given for taking up paid work (Hunt, 1968: 77). The pecuniary link is important not just because it delimits assumptions about women's work being for 'pin money' but also because economic rewards are themselves a manifestation of status. That is to say that money is both economically and socially essential, for it provides women with a large number of potential benefits: independent means, a higher familial standard of living, and higher social status etc. But, as we shall see, the experiences of women are not identical, for they are pre-structured through their position as single or with a partner, with or without dependent children, middle-class or working-class, black or white etc.

Equal Pay

Of course, not all occupations are either sex segregated or subject to unequal rewards. For example, the civil services of many countries, along with their associated public sector like education and health etc., often exhibit markedly egalitarian policies. Thus the British Post Office, Civil Service and teaching profession have relatively little in the way of official sexual discrimination, at least in comparison to the private sectors (Grint, 1988). On the contrary, all three areas have provided equal pay in certain areas for decades. That is not to say that equality was ever the primary intention behind the instigators of the policy, nor is it to suggest that these areas currently demonstrate an equality of distribution regarding positions of authority, career structures etc. Equal pay in the teaching profession, first mooted in the NUT referendum of 1919 and achieved by 1961, and a 60 per cent majority of the workforce being female, does not alter the fact that only 15 per cent of female primary school teachers are heads compared to 50 per cent of male primary teachers (NUT, 1988), even though women comprise 80 per cent of primary school teachers (De Lyon and Migniolo, 1989).

Of equal relevance has been the activities of the state, most notably through the 1970 Equal Pay Act and the 1975 Sex Discrimination Act in Britain, and in the USA, for example, the 1963 Equal Pay Act and 1964 Civil Rights Act. This earlier dating of the US Acts should not necessarily be taken to imply a greater concern for justice on the part of the American authorities: Frank Thompson, chairperson of the US House Select Subcommittee on the Equal Pay Bill is reputed to have filed documents relating to women under 'B' for 'Broads' (Randall, 1988), though the liberal ethos of Kennedy's era counteracted this to some extent.

Analyses of the effects of the two British Acts varies quite considerably. Gregory (1982) insists the effects were minimal, though Zabalza and Tannatos (1985), Atkins (1986) and the Labour Research Department (1986), while noting the limited value of both Acts, suggest that some marginal advances were effected, and Marsh (1988b: 55) suggests that women's earnings were raised by about 5 per cent relative to men's to reach the plateau of 67 per cent that they have remained around since. In terms of the individuals who take their case to tribunals only around one quarter are successful (*Employment Gazette*, October 1988) and the actual process itself appears to be very stressful: only 11 per cent of applicants remained with their employers, and continued victimization is common. Given the economic rewards of a successful application (50 per cent of all awards are for less than £300 and 40 per cent of pay increases ordered were for less than £8 a week) it is small wonder that the tribunal option is so little used (Leonard, 1987).

Also important at the time of the original Acts was the Social Contract negotiated between the TUC and the Labour Government between 1974 and 1977 which initially embodied an egalitarian incomes policy and facilitated the erosion of gender-based wage differentials (G. Thompson, 1984). It is noticeable that many ostensibly left-wing unions declined to appreciate the value of this to women and the low paid, and proffered instead 'a cult of militancy which assumed that the low paid would be rewarded by the efforts of the higher paid, without recognizing that this pattern would only reproduce the balance of relativities which were precisely the problem, when what women workers needed was a redistribution within the working class, as much as redistribution between classes' (Campbell, 1982b: 23). Hakim (1981) adds further support to the value of this period, noting a much greater decrease in segregation after the Act than would have been predictable on the basis of historical trends before it. Ultimately, the Equal Pay Act garnered support of one sort or another from many sections of the community, although the TUC had by this time recognized the growing importance of women as union members and begun to support the idea of equal pay for equal value while the CBI still preferred the idea of equal pay for equal work. The latter policy, enacted by the Act, enabled employers to maintain general patterns of gender-based inequality by ensuring that women did not undertake identical duties to men, or, where this proved impossible to maintain, introducing a token man to the 'women's' jobs. However, a series of tribunal cases in 1984 following the Equal Value Regulations (enacted in January 1984 to bring Britain in line with EEC legislation), and Julie Heyward's victory over Cammel Laird, began to undermine the conservative implications of the Act (Hadjifotiou, 1985). The case in favour of equal pay for *equal value* has recently taken a significant step forward with the sequence of judgements supporting Rene Pickstone. Ms Pickstone, a warehouse worker employed by Freemans' mail order company, whose case was supported by the Equal Opportunities Commission, claimed that work of her type was of equivalent value to that undertaken by male warehouse checkers despite the fact that a token male warehouse worker earned the same as his female colleagues. Under the 1970 Equal Pay Act such a case could not be made but the Appeal Court ruled, on 25 March 1987, that Article 119 of the Treaty of Rome and previous European Court rulings were applicable in Ms Pickstone's case, and the Appeal Court judgement was upheld by the Law Lords on 30 June 1988.

Of course, securing the backing of the law is not the equivalent of removing sex discrimination, and many forms of discrimination are beyond the grasp of legal recrimination. Even those within the law are encumbered by the complexities of due process. For example, since the Equal Pay Act was introduced over 3,800 cases have been taken up but only twelve have made it through the fifteen-stage procedure to claim equal pay (Wintour and Tirbutt, 1988). Similarly, the existence of an Equal Opportunities Policy, in and of itself, says little about the effect this may have upon the reality of gender discrimination (Hughes, 1989), and fewer than a third of British companies actually appear to have a written policy (Dickens, 1989: 169). Nevertheless, we should be clear that the limited utility of legal restraint upon employers and employees in purely material or economic terms has also to be supplemented by the symbolic value of legal support for equality and the illegality of certain forms of discrimination (O'Donovan and Szyszczak, 1988). In November 1988 310 Royal Ulster Constabulary women officers were awarded almost £1 million in damages between them in an out of court settlement in Belfast. The political embarrassment of acting illegally, to say nothing of the monetary costs involved, may act as a warning to other employers.

Hours, Workers and Class

Women are also divided by their involvement with paid labour, particularly regarding their status as full-time or part-time workers. Part-time work, in Britain particularly, is overwhelmingly a female experience with fewer than 5 per cent of men undertaking it: eight times less than women (Beechey, 1986: 28; *Employment Gazette*, April 1990). Such work tends to be less skilled and is also concentrated in the white-collar, service and smaller enterprises – all issues which tend to inhibit trade unions and which undermine the likelihood of women furthering their careers.

It is not sufficient to say that women are, in some vague way, exploited by the dual forces of capitalism and patriarchy because a minority of women *are* capitalists and therefore exploit other women and men; yet others have sufficient income or wealth to off-load the most menial tasks on to poorer or less qualified women. Another important element of this is manifested in the means by which men construct career paths for women such that poor rewards actively deter women from seeking careers; the result is a vicious circle of low levels of ambition, commitment and investment in human capital. This is particularly prevalent amongst working-class women, many of whom appear to consider pre-family work in factories and offices as a temporary phenomenon, a short intrusion prior to the 'real' career of marriage and motherhood. Despite the fact that most women will spend three to four times as long in paid work than as a full-time home worker the perception of paid work as temporary continues (Pollert, 1981; Porter, 1982). In contrast, Alban-

Metcalfe and Nicholson's (1984) review of women managers suggests that women are just as committed and ambitious, but with a higher level of qualifications than the equivalently placed male manager.

One important distinction to note here is that of class: the overwhelmingly heteronomous content of many working-class women's jobs with minimal prospects of promotion contrasts sharply with middle-class women's jobs which can combine both greater levels of autonomous activity and career prospects. It is vital, therefore, to retain a grip on both class and gender aspects when considering the evidence of work. Relatedly, although the importance of ethnic divisions is discussed in the following chapter, it should not be taken for granted that women, while united by exploitation from patriarchy and capitalism, form a naturally cohesive unit. It is sufficient to note the sharp fragmentation of attitudes and opinions manifest in Cavendish's (1982) *Women on the Line* to undermine any utopian images of natural sisterhood. In sum, there is no experience which is typical, there are instead a delimited number of compound experiences.

Labour Market Restructuring and Professional Women

Since 1975 of course, the general picture of employment has changed quite considerably in Britain, most notably in terms of mass unemployment and shifts in economic and occupational structure away from the northern-based manufacturing industries towards the south-eastern service-based businesses. Walby (1986a: 222–30) suggests that although employers have tended to discriminate against women, the overall impact has actually been favourable to women, mainly because women have been over-represented in those industries least affected by the economic collapse; a point supported by the wider comparative study of Therborn (1986: 71–3) who suggests that there are links between gender and the patterns of unemployment but they are specific to each country rather than universal. Ironically, then, it has been the segregation of women away from 'men's work' that has protected many of them from the worst effects of the economic slump in Britain, and is currently providing greater opportunities for new employment than those available to, or rather appropriated by, men. Thus, women continue to be barely visible in engineering, particularly within the ranks of technical specialists or management, but also in the manual sectors (C. Smith, 1987: 78–9); whereas clerical work has come to be pre-eminently the area of female predominance with around 75 per cent of the total currently being women (Crompton and Jones, 1982; Routh, 1980).

The current data suggest that 80 per cent of the projected rise in the workforce until 1995 will involve women. Indeed, in the five years between 1983 and 1988 an astonishing inversion of traditional job creation and destruction has been evident. Over that period almost 0.75 million new part-time jobs went to women with just over half a million full-time positions in addition. In contrast, part-time jobs held by men increased by just under 0.25 million while full-time jobs held by men decreased by 100,000 (Gapper, 1989). Yet not all women have managed to survive the collapse of manufacturing unscathed, and women from the ethnic minorities have borne the brunt in some areas. These women have often being unable to find alternative work of equivalent reward within ethnic businesses (Phizacklea, 1987), as the compound threads of capitalism, patriarchy and ethnicity operate in conjunction against them. It is apparent too that in some areas previously associated with the growth of women's employment, such as the financial sector, the introduction of new technology has begun to impinge upon this expansion and, in some circumstances, to reverse it (Mallier and Rosser, 1987).

A more pervasive presence within a particular occupation does not, of course, ensure a greater presence within the hierarchy. For example, British banks have been a major source of employment for women but a minor source of managerial opportunities. About one million women currently work for British clearing banks and comprise 60 per cent of the total staff. Yet in 1986 only 2.5 per cent of Lloyds managers were women, 2.7 per cent of the Midland, and 1.8 per cent at the National Westminster. The most progress made has been at Barclays where the relevant figure stands at 4.3 per cent. How can we account for this, albeit extremely modest, differential? Basically, Barclays have discarded their previously discriminatory recruitment channels (GCSE level entrance for girls, A level entrance for boys) after the Equal Opportunities Commission threatened to investigate the company's recruiting strategy: just as the screening of recruits can delimit the opportunities available to individuals from the ethnic minorities so too are women discriminated against even before they are employed. Of course, where the proportion of women achieving the prerequisite level of professional qualification is increasing, and the proportion of women finalists in the Institute of Banking examinations has increased from 4 per cent in 1975 to 27 per cent in 1988 (Crompton, 1989; Crompton and Sanderson, 1986), then employers are discouraged from selective recruitment, even if it is not prevented. The fact that some progress has been made here suggests that the inertia of tradition is not quite as immovable as many people suspect (Pagano, 1987), even if the cause may have more to do with labour market shortages than concern for implementing equal opportunities policies.

It has also to be remembered, though, that even the suspicion of immobility may be enough to render the attitudes of decision makers, such as recruiters, impermeable to rational critique. As Pearn et al. (1987) argue, in respect of selection tests, even though such tests are not objective measures of ability the fact that recruiters *interpret* them as being objective ensures that they are used in this fashion, often to the detriment of prospective female employees. Career intentions and domestic arrangements are regular questions asked at interviews, but only of women; and the frequency of such events reflects the strength of stereotyping (Collinson, 1987). Some organizations, such as United Biscuits (Pizzaland, Wimpy *inter alia*), Marks and Spencers and John Lewis have even concerned themselves with the regularity of a woman's periods and, in some cases, the details of pregnancies; questions of dubious legality to say nothing of the questionable ethics involved (Macrae, 1988). Again, we have to be clear that such discrimination does not always occur. The study by Chiplin and Grieg (1986) of one Regional Health Authority in the National Health Service suggests that women are not discriminated against, at least not in the process of shortlisting candidates. But the occupational segregation was such that a non-gender-segregated service would require the reallocation of 70 per cent of the existing female employees. Women currently comprise 77 per cent of the NHS staff but only one in seven unit managers is a women. Women do succeed in becoming managers but the majority do not stay within the service and over half of these leave for domestic reasons (Thayer, 1987).

This career break is crucial in explaining the relative absence of senior women managers in the NHS, for the 'golden pathway' to career success is essentially a male path determined by the requirement to be geographically mobile, and to enact a continuous commitment to the NHS, at least until the age of 30. Of course, many women leave to have children prior to this critical point and their domestic responsibilities often impair their geographical mobility; it certainly is not a case of men having superior qualifications, indeed the reality is the reverse. As a direct result the 'golden pathway' appears to be made with patriarchal bricks (Davies and Rosser, 1987).

That the pathway only appears gender-biased in the perspective of women is represented by a recent survey of men in the insurance industry. This indicated that almost half thought women were uninterested in a career – yet three-quarters of the women employed in the same industry said they considered career prospects to be crucial. The insurance industry may be more patriarchal than some but it is by no means unusual: a third of senior male managers from all areas of business in the UK also think that women are inherently unsuitable for managerial jobs (Meade-King, 1986). What is apparent is that male managers seem willing to employ women in subordinate positions but not where they provide future competition for themselves or their male managerial colleagues.

In the USA, women still represent only about 2 per cent of the senior corporate executives, but this is still twice the rate in the UK (Marshall,

1987). Thus although the golden pathways in the USA have some women on them they still tend to hit that all too familiar 'glass ceiling', composed of 'men only' translucent silicates; even those who pass through are wont to reappear within one of the 'triple P departments': purchasing, personnel and public relations (Meade-King, 1988). American women have also been notably successful in establishing their own businesses, currently owning 25 per cent of all US small businesses and starting new ones at five times the rate of men. They are equally well represented within the middle ranks of US corporations, compared to their European colleagues, though they are particularly poorly represented amongst the skilled blue-collar jobs. This higher level of discrimination within manual work is also evident within Britain where female trainees on skilled manual trades often find themselves shunted by their employers back into higher education on the completion of their training rather than taken on as qualified craft workers (YWCA, 1987). This particular problem is present within the British Youth Training Scheme, where segregated training into jobs conventionally associated with specific genders has reinforced the barriers to women, with at least 75 per cent of those on the scheme undertaking sex-stereotyped jobs (Cockburn, 1986, 1987). We should acknowledge that legislative control over discriminatory practices is not a precondition for success. For example, women in France do considerably better than their British counterparts yet France has little of the legislation in place which supposedly prevents discrimination (Dex and Walters, 1989). Here, then, cultural differences should be added to the composite model.

One of the most difficult aspects of this area of inequality is actually establishing the determinate explanations. For example, in 1984 there were only 93 women professors in Britain, accounting for barely 3 per cent of the total, and women comprise 31 per cent of contract researchers but only 7 per cent of tenured staff in 1988 (Bogdanor, 1990). Could this not be explained simply by the differing patterns of life pattern with women academics in part undermining their own promotions by career breaks etc? Well hardly, of the 202 young professors, that is those under 40, only two were women. Unless we assume that an inordinate number of women academics have career breaks this ratio seems capable only of a discriminatory explanation. Furthermore, if there were institutions where women did achieve proportionate levels of professorial posts then the 'normal' pattern of male dominance would no longer be able to rest secure in an argument grounded in the 'inevitable and universal' nature of male dominance. Since Bristol University boasts just one woman professor but University College London has fifteen we can be legitimately sceptical as to the claims of disinterested appointments. The record of Scottish universities is even worse than the overall British record, with a mere 1.5 per cent of Scottish professors being women

(Wojtas, 1989). An American rule of thumb, used by the US courts, is to assume discrimination exists if the success rate of women is less than 80 per cent of that obtained by men. In British universities the method clearly reveals discrimination: only 11 per cent of the total number of academics are women; of these only 17 per cent will be senior lecturers or above, compared to 42 per cent of men. As Donoghue (1988) notes: 'the women seem to be 10 to 15 years behind the men in terms of promotion'.

A depressingly familiar picture emerges from Spencer and Podmore's (1986) survey of the legal profession: more than 14 per cent of solicitors and barristers are women, representing around a fivefold increase since the mid 1950s but there are no female Lords of Appeal, only 3 per cent of Court High Judges are women (all in the Family Division) and a not too dissimilar percentage are Circuit Judges and Recorders. The reasons provided by male solicitors for either not recruiting women or not promoting them when they are recruited typically centre on the issue of child rearing and career breaks. But the level of inequality extends beyond prospective career structures to include current reward levels. In the late 1970s The Royal Commission on Legal Services discovered that the average income of female barristers was some 50–60 per cent of their identically qualified and employed male colleagues. The route between articled clerk and senior position is littered with impediments for women: some involve the channelling of women into specialities that offer low prestige and little prospect of advancement, such as matrimonial and family law; others relate to the social lives of this very small group of professionals which are exclusively constructed around forms of assumed male superiority, notably the macho image of tough, competitive and aggressive courtroom professionals. Yet underlying the gloom is another picture of increasingly embattled senior men confronted by young women undeterred by history or tradition: almost half the current law students in the UK are women and by the mid-1990s over 20 per cent of lawyers should be women; concomitantly, according to the Law Society, more female students currently get 'good' degree (1 or 2:1) results than men and men achieve a disproportionately high number of third-class degrees. Progress at the top end of the occupational ladder may be slow but it is progress, and it goes beyond that achieved in skilled manual jobs.

The medical profession is more open to women than law, though this has not prevented the monopolization of key posts by men, nor has it stanched the apparent influence of the old boy network in maintaining male control. Sponsorship by a patron is one method by which the existing elite reproduce themselves in their own image, most notably within certain specialities. Women comprise 20 per cent of GPs and 13 per cent of hospital consultants, but 98 per cent of general surgeons are men (Allen, 1988). At the level of Medical Laboratory Scientific Officers

(MLSO), the advance of new technology has not loosened up the 'genderarchy', as Harvey (1987) calls it, but actually polarized the career prospects of men and women with the latter increasingly locked into the subordinate career structure. Of course, the 'old boy network' goes far beyond the medical world and it is probably more significant in the fields of business and politics, particularly through the network of male only or male-dominated private clubs (Rogers, 1988), another reason for casting our analytic net wider than necessary just to cover employment organizations.

In engineering, that most archetypical male occupation, there are even fewer women in senior posts than elsewhere. In 1980 22 per cent of the engineering labour force were women, but they only comprised 3 per cent of the managers and under 3 per cent of the scientists, technologists and technicians (Cockburn, 1983b). A substantial part of the explanation for this lies in the cultural attributes of society and its ramifications for the differentiated educational provision at schools which deters girls from taking subjects that are considered male (technical drawing, maths, chemistry and physics etc.). But a less evident causal factor is the recruitment policies of engineering departments in further education establishments. As Newton (1986) remarks, selectors seemed to recruit only those women whom they considered to be androgenous, rather than overtly 'masculine' *or* 'feminine' applicants, either of which would have been perceived as a threat. It is this kind of discrimination which has led to the recent WISE (Women Into Science and Engineering) campaign, which has produced a measured degree of success, boosting the proportion of women on engineering degree courses from 7.8 per cent in 1984 to 10.5 per cent in 1987 (Boseley, 1987).

The evidence relating to the development of computer studies is equally revealing here, for although 25 per cent of the entrants to UK computer courses at universities were women in 1976, by 1987 the percentage had dropped to 15 per cent (Gerver, 1989). Since those schools which delayed the choice of subject specialization until late (primarily Scottish schools), and those which taught computer studies in single-sex classes, did better than the rest, we can assume that the stereotypical notions of 'appropriate' subjects at schools play a large part in dissuading girls and women from such topics, and thus in delimiting their occupational choices. Since it is also the case that female pupils in America, Singapore and France show little of the same kind of gendered lack of interest in computers we can also assume that there is something particularly disadvantageous within the English system: in particular that computers were introduced to English schools through maths departments headed by male teachers and within a system that demanded early specialization. In effect, computer technology became gendered through the process of educational induction.

It is significant that much of the progress that women have made since the Second World War has been in the last decade: one manifestation of this is not just the growing numbers of women within higher education but the age range of female business executives compared to their male counterparts. In 1988 only 24 per cent of British male executives (broadly defined) were under 35, but over 55 per cent of women executives are this young. Similarly, although the percentage of women Assistant Secretaries (current salary up to £29,000) in the British Civil Service remains at a mere 13 per cent this represents a doubling of the proportion since 1982 (Hencke, 1988). However, as we noted in chapter 2, it is the case that the current success of women professionals appears to be restricted, or at least related, to those who consciously decide not to have children. Certainly there is scant evidence that firms are rapidly coming to terms with the demographic changes to encourage women with families back to work (IMS, 1990). The future for women, then, is neither simply opening up generally nor reproducing the exclusions of old; rather, women are being asked to decide between one of two careers: home or work but not both. As Schwartz (1989) has argued, the structures and ideologies of work now force women to consider a twin track future: 'career-primary' or 'career-family'.

As the demographic change gradually alters the ratio of young to old, the situation of one male-based institution that has suffered more than most in the last decade of economic restructuring will become ever more precarious: the trade unions.

Women and Trade Unions

As has already been implied, the position of trade unions on the employment of women and the achievement of equality is less than auspicious. Despite the traditional exclusionary practices of such organizations, which derive their influence through limiting access to employment, the trade unions certainly entered the post Second World War era with an unenviable record of discrimination against women, and, as demonstrated in the next chapter, against ethnic minorities too. As Campbell succinctly put it: 'For most women, trade unions meet at the wrong time in the wrong place about the wrong things. For most trade unions, women are the wrong people in the wrong place at the wrong time going on about the wrong things' (1982). But just as labour market conditions and the influence of the state coerced employers and trade unions alike to acquiesce to some elements of equality in the Post Office and Civil Service, so too the same pressures began mounting up through the 1950s and into the 1960s. An increasing proportion of female labour (especially well educated female labour), an increasing competition between unions for members (especially as manual work declined in importance), and the generation of a reinvigorated feminist political and industrial movement by women for women, all pushed the union movement into reluctant action. Indeed, it has been the historical lack of interest of unions in women that has furthered the survival of a vicious circle of union uninterest stimulating low female density thereby reinforcing the mutual ignorance and hostility of each to the other (Yeandle, 1984: 115–19).

Union density for women has only recently begun to approach the male equivalent. By 1978 the figure was still below 30 per cent but the rapid growth in women's employment has facilitated a jump to the 1987 figure of 41 per cent, representing around 32 per cent of the total number of trade unionists. Union density rates are notoriously difficult to assess but the 1989 Labour Force Survey suggests that 39 per cent of all employees (including the unemployed) are members, encompassing 44 per cent of men and 33 per cent of women. Women, then, comprise 39 per cent of the current union membership (*Employment Gazette*, April, 1990). Since almost 80 per cent of women tend to be employed within the non-manual sector rather than the manual sector the discrepancy is more explicable in occupational rather than gender terms. Indeed, when the larger number of part-time workers are held constant the union density rates for men and women are roughly equivalent (Millward and Stevens, 1986: 54, 61–2; Horne, 1987: 78). Yet despite the fact that over 38 per cent of TUC (Trades Union Congress) affiliated union members are women only around 18 per cent of the delegates to the TUC are women (Trades Unions Congress, 1986).

Concomitantly, different occupations have very different levels of union density: the teaching unions recruit about 70 per cent of women members while unions in the retail sector recruit only 17 per cent of female employees. In fact, the greatest variable is not between manual and non-manual work but between part-time and full-time work, and since women comprise the overwhelming number of part-time workers they are under-represented within the trade unions. (Bruegel, 1983: 159–60; IRRU, 1984; TURU, 1986: 17). This under-representation is bolstered by the traditional difficulties trade unions face in recruiting part-time workers: they are more difficult to recruit because they are geographically dispersed and often work unsocial hours; and the unions have less incentive to recruit them because their turnover rates make membership records difficult to maintain and because unions have a history of hostility to part-timers. The inflexibility of trade unions is also relevant here, for few have proportionately reduced subscriptions for part-time members yet these are usually amongst the least affluent workers of all (Beechey and Perkins, 1987: 150–82). Such is the influence of skilled workers anyway that few unions are controlled by the less skilled and, since many part-timers are considered to be unskilled or at best semi-skilled, it is seldom that their interests prevail (Cockburn, 1987b). None the less, the switch away from full-time male employment in the manufacturing sector towards part-time female employment in the service sector is of some import to the unions, for membership has to follow job creation if the unions are to prosper. With the TGWU (Transport and General Workers' Union), NUT (National Union of Teachers) and CPSA (Civil and Public Servants Association) all losing a third of their respective memberships between 1979 and 1986 (McIlroy, 1988: 29), hostility to part-timers represents organizational suicide.

Given the current belief that at least 66 per cent of all new jobs in Britain in 1990–5 will be taken by women in part-time jobs, and that 90 per cent of the labour force growth over the 1990s will be from women (*Employment Gazette*, April 1989), it is a mute point whether the change of course for unions represents a change of heart or pure self-interest; it is possibly both, but probably the latter. Certainly the labour market developments are serious for the unions: in the first quarter of 1987 only 8 per cent of the new jobs created were filled by the traditional union members: full-time men (Gow, 1987). Of course, the proliferation of policy statements and policies on women need not amount to any material gain but it is important to note that wage differentials based on sex are smaller within unionized enterprises than those without unions. However lethargic and uninterested unions may have been in the past they are least beginning to have some impact upon the levels of gender-based inequalities now (Metcalf, 1988).

By 1984 the TUC had increased the number of women's seats on the General Council to six, it had published a 'Charter for Women' and ensured that every Regional Council in England and Wales had a Women's Advisory Committee. Individual affiliated unions had also begun to make progress: the General, Municipal, and Boilermakers Trade Union (GMBATU) had a national Equal Rights Advisory Committee, and an Equal Rights Officer in each region by 1980; and many, though by no means all, unions had undertaken internal investigations of their treatment of women (Walby, 1986a: 212–30). That said, only five of the TUC's eighty-four affiliated unions have women General Secretaries, and only one (GMBATU) has a quota system to promote the selection of women as Labour Parliamentary candidates. The Manufacturing, Science and Finance union (MSF) and The National Union of Public Employees (NUPE) have reserved seats on the executive for women. It may or may not be coincidental that the three most recent female General Secretaries lead unaffiliated 'associations': the Police Federation, the First Division of Civil Servants, and the Royal College of Nursing. The real disparity becomes evident when we move beyond the national leadership level: of the three thousand officials employed by the largest five unions only seventy-seven are women (Heery and Kelly, 1988), and overall the proportion of full-time officers (FTOs) who are women appears to be about 8 per cent (Heery and Kelly, 1989), though the increase in the number of women full-time officers is three times that of men in the last few years; a movement similar to that amongst professional women. Nevertheless, whether this increase is an effect of union policies or coincidental is a separate issue; although most women FTOs are within the largest unions this merely reflects the more universal connection between size and numbers of FTOs irrespective of gender. Certainly, John Edmonds was vigorously denounced at the GMBATU's 1987 conference when he suggested that 'first class women should replace second class men' (quoted in Gow, 1987), and the vast majority of the FTOs in the Heery and Kelly survey reported that they had been discriminated against both by lay members and fellow male FTOs.

There is still a long way to go: a Labour Research review of the ten unions with the largest proportion of women members shows four unions increasing the number of full-time women officials but four other unions decreasing the number. Over half of these ten unions had fewer than 10 per cent of their full-time officer posts filled by women (Beavis, 1988). Heery and Kelly (1989) suggest from their review, however, that women FTOs are more likely to be within unions with a high proportion of women because this tends to lead to a pool of female activists and because there is a build up of pressure from the rank and file for FTOs which reflect the membership. Women FTOs are also more in evidence in unions which appoint, rather than elect, to such positions, mainly because election is often contingent upon long service which, in turn, is something that not many women members can achieve given their domestic responsibilities and bi-modal working careers.

It is also worth nothing the unintended consequences of government restrictions on unions since 1979. In particular, it would appear that one effect of the 1984 Trade Union Act, which required that all voting members of trade union executives be elected by secret individual ballot, has cut away some of the male predominance in branch and mass meetings and actually facilitated the rise of women within union executives. For example: the National Union of Taylor and Garment Workers now has eleven women out of a fourteen strong executive; the Inland Revenue Staff Association now has seven women out of twenty-seven executive officers; and APEX and ASTMS (Association of Scientific, Technical and Managerial Staffs) have both recorded increases in the proportion of women executive members. All these changes occurred after the Act, and all four witnessed a rapid increase in the proportion of women voting (Hague, 1986).

However, the issue of expanding women's trade unionism is not simply a matter of economic restructuring providing more jobs for women than men (albeit part-time jobs), or of delimiting the effect of patriarchally dominated modes of organization. As Bain (1970) argues, some of the new patterns of work up until 1970 were the very areas which have also exhibited the greatest levels of bureaucratization, particularly in the public sector, and the similarity of conditions engineered by bureaucratization has always proved conducive to trade union development. Of course, the gradual reduction in the public sector in the last decade has interrupted this post-war development, as indeed has the much more hostile attitude of the state itself towards the recognition of unions within its own boundaries. Equally important, since 1970 the number of large plants (employing over 1000 workers) has fallen while the number of small plants (employing fewer than 100 workers) has risen, so that the unions who traditionally recruit best within large plants have been doubly hit (Lash and Urry, 1987: 103–5).

The greater likelihood of men to be found within large organizations, and particularly those within export-oriented manufacturing plants, also partly explains the predominance of men within industrial conflicts. As Purcell (1984) demonstrates, the fact that most women do not appear to be militant trade unionists – defined as those regularly involved in industrial action – obfuscates the point that most men are not militant trade unionists either. It may be more appropriate, then, to assume that certain occupations, and indeed certain regions, rather than specific genders, are militantly oriented (cf. Parkin, 1967; Stead, 1987; Dolby, 1987; Walby, 1988).

This need not, of course, undermine the notion that women are not typically involved in militant activity. Women also tend to be located within the caring professions, though again it may not be the gender of the carer here which is critical but the fact that the individual is in a caring profession whose professional code of conduct and powerful ethical commitment constrain industrial action. Nor is there any exigent connection between industrial involvement and radical consciousness. As Wajcman's (1983) review of the Fakenham women's co-operative concludes, despite the engagement of women with both capitalist economic forces and patriarchal 'co-operatives', the majority retained their conservative beliefs in the sphere of politics and the home. Fatalism, not radicalism or militancy, is the typical reaction of most people, irrespective of gender, to a situation that appears to be beyond the influence of human agents (Purcell, 1984; Cunnison, 1984).

Where you would expect women to be more involved in union activity and industrial action would be where women have returned to work once their children have started school. This return provides several sources of independence that might lead to union membership: an independent source of income; relative independence from children; and direct experience of power relations inherent at work. There is some evidence for this, though little for any direct decanting of resistance at work to supervisors, into resistance at home to men. Watts (1984) suggests that this barrier between industrial radicalism and domestic radicalism reflects the discrete patterning of the two areas of activity with the domestic mode subordinated to the industrial, but a different interpretation would be to substitute the term militancy for radicalism; militancy being concerned with the increased acquisition of economistic rewards within the existing socio-economic structure, radicalism concerned with the restructuring of the system itself. If we assume that woman can be militant at work without being radical at home, not only does this provide a different perspective on the division of ideologies but it actually reflects the normal pattern of most work-based groups: many such groups have long been associated with all manner of economistic militancy, often in defence of privileges retained at the expense of the less well off; few such groups have ever been involved in the promotion of radical measures to restructure the industrial system itself (Grint, 1986: 106–26).

Another important aspect of the gradual increase in women's membership of the trade unions has been the success of the recruitment campaigns by unions themselves as they have struggled to stem the haemorrhaging of members through the collapse of the manufacturing sector. Partly, this has involved recognition of the problems of holding union meetings late at night, or in pubs; issues which reflect and reproduce the conventional patriarchal control over the night and most public arenas. But even the recognition of these kinds of problems and the election of women to official positions in unions does not, in and of itself, secure equality; a women union official interviewed by Imray (Imray and Middleton, 1983) told how the 'Chivalry' of male officials in driving her home or seeing her on the bus turned out to be a scheme by which the 'real' business of the branch could be conducted after she had left. It is not just a case of moving the location and timing of meetings, or even providing crèches, though. Part of the answer has to lie in re-educating the male membership to accept their share of the domestic responsibilities. It is of limited use just providing meetings at more convenient times if women are still held to be solely responsible for children and domestic chores; this not only leaves women with a double workload but ensures that any women with domestic responsibilities, paid employment and an active interest in union affairs has a triple workload (Central London Community Law Centre, 1987). Part of the answer also lies in the acceptance by men that real equality can only be achieved at their expense (Dale, 1987); not all power games are variable-sum ones.

Of course, very few men use whatever spare time they may have to attend their union's meetings anyway, and it has conventionally been understood that the figure for women must be lower. Little research has been undertaken in this area, and the levels of sex segregated occupations always make comparisons difficult, though Harrison's (1979) survey of an ASTMS branch suggests that a higher proportion of women than men attended normal meetings. In many ways this is rather surprising given the conventions of unionism that clearly reflect male lifestyle. As Gill and Whitty argue: 'Without malice or design, but also without concern, men have shaped trade union life to suit those who have no childcare or other domestic responsibilities and on an expectation that every trade union activist has endless evening hours to devote to union work' (quoted in TURU, 1986: 24). Certainly the female FTOs of Heery and Kelly's sample were three times less likely to have children than the average women. Once again, it is the links to the domestic sphere which crucially constrain women in the roles they can undertake. It is this form of discriminatory practice that accounts for one survey that showed over 50 per cent of the female labour force to be either uninterested in or actively hostile to trade unions (Martin and Robert, 1980). Even where trade unions develop non-discriminatory policies this would not necessarily lead to any wide-scale change, at least not immediately; for as Beynon and Blackburn (1984) suggest, even if all the evidence negates all patriarchal assumptions about women in unions the effect of traditions and misinterpretations is to buttress the position of men. Thus, if men *think* that women make poor union members then they will do little to recruit or retain them; as a result women will comprise a small percentage of union members, thereby 'demonstrating' the apparent validity of the patriarchal attitude (Pollert, 1981).

Masculinity, Domestic Labour and Violence

Often underlying some of the patriarchal assumptions about the superiority of men and their work are what appear to women at least rather thinly veiled strategies to protect male egos, though to men they may well seem invisible. Pollert's (1981) account of women factory operatives is a good example here for it reveals how women find security within their poorly paid jobs in part because their income level does not threaten their male partners' egos. Such low self-esteem, ironically premised upon the fragility of masculinity, merely reinforces the perception of work for many working-class women as an interruption between school and having a family, or as a place to secure 'extra' money and social friendship rather than a career in itself. Both of these may further undermine any assumption by women that trade unionism can play any important role in their lives. The analysis of girls at school supports the contention that females both consciously underplay their own abilities so as not to threaten the brittle egos of males (Sharpe, 1976; Horner, 1976) and consider the boredom of both school and employment sufficient to warrant a low level of interest in either. Correspondingly, the assumption that where jobs are short they should be reserved for men is not simply an assumption made by men; as some of the women in Pollert's (1981) study demonstrate, if they had to provide for their husbands or even earned more than them, many of the men would feel 'downgraded' and many of the women would suffer as a result. Even when male unemployment has left women's wages as the main source of income women still perceive their earning power to be auxiliary, rather than primary, within the household (Morris, 1987), and, as suggested in chapter 1, there is little evidence of unemployed men using their 'free' time to take over domestic responsibilities from 'working' wives.

The issue of time is relevant in another sense, for a primary distinguishing feature between male and female employees is the differential use made of 'free' time: men conventionally negotiate a shortening of normal hours to maximize their overtime potential, women prefer to use the extra time at home. In itself, this does not establish autonomously chosen alternatives: it has become a commonplace to acknowledge that men endure, rather than support, their wives' employment activities, and then only on condition that they do not interfere with domestic arrangements (Martin and Roberts, 1984). The real point of value is to note the connection rather than the contradiction between these two apparently dichotomous perspectives on time. It is only because men 'underachieve' at home that they can take advantage of the extra time: the time is made available not by their employers nor by their union's efforts, but by their female partners shouldering most, if not all, of the domestic responsibilites. Thus the model of male work as full-time work, far from being separated from that of women, is intimately dependent upon it.

The issue is one that goes beyond unequal work loads and involves the importance of work and the family to men and women. Crehan (1986: 205–6) argues that many women do not just have obligations to their families, but their family life provides the central meaning of their lives. Crehan further asserts that this is not the case for men, but the evidence is restricted to women and comparative research tends to suggest that men and women both value family life higher than paid work (Feldberg and Glenn, 1984; Dex, 1985: 36–44). The point really is that men are not systematically faced with the dilemma of combining paid work and domestic responsibilities. As Crehan rightly concludes: 'being a conscientious parent and being a conscientious worker should not be competing options that individuals must choose between' (1986: 206).

A further twist in the tail of male egos must be the commensurability of masculinity with militancy. The world of work, in particular the world of male manual work, is one where the pursuit of proletarian maleness – aggression, domination and physical strength – is embodied in many notions of trade union power and working-class resistance. Perhaps the clearest demonstration of this, and the gulf between the prevailing cultures of men and women, is in Willis's (1977) descriptions of working-class boys at school preparing for working-class jobs in factories. It is essentially this preparation for work that carries with it the implicit degradation of women's work and women's worth and the double standards on sexual behaviour that are commonplace. Women also suffer from a more pervasive sexual harassment, that is 'behaviour of a sexual nature which is unwanted, unwelcome and unreciprocated and which might threaten job security or create a stressful or intimidating working environment' (WASH, 1987). The way such harassment is used to control women is another example of the opacity of privilege. That is the way that power often appears almost invisible to the those wielding it but self-evident to those suffering from it. Many men appear to deny their association with discriminatory practices, for such people sexual harassment is 'merely horseplay', and women have long been deterred from complaining about it in the sure knowledge that nothing will be done about an activity that will probably be considered by the (male) managers to be little more than 'fooling around' (Seddon, 1983). That sexual harassment is far from 'horseplay', and far from declining, is demonstrated in a recent survey of US students which revealed that 17 per cent of women were the victims of rape or attempted rape, and 7 per cent of men admitted committing rape or attempting to commit rape in the previous twelve months (*THES*, 9 September 1988).

Currently, the issue of sexual harassment at work is receiving a considerable amount of attention, both in its historical manifestations (Lambertz, 1985), and its contemporary forms (NALGO, 1981; Bularzik, 1978; Gordon, 1981; Hearn and Parkin, 1987; Rubinstein, 1989). The NALGO study is important in exposing the very high levels of harassment that exist; in their study of the Liverpool branch 25 per cent had experienced harassment at their current place of work and 50 per cent at some time in their working lives. Subsequently, several unions have initiated policy statements, including NALGO, NATFHE (National Association of Teachers in Further and Higher Education), ASTMS, CPSA and the National Union of Journalists (NUJ). Even trade union officers themselves appear to be widely involved in such activities: in Heery and Kelly's (1989) survey of 87 women FTOs, 51 per cent complained of sexual harassment from fellow male officers, only marginally less than had complained about harassment from the male rank and file.

Yet some progress is visible. Recently British women have been awarded damages by industrial tribunals when sexual harassment has forced them to resign and, for the first time, this been interpreted as unfair dismissal (Equal Opportunities Commission, 1987). However, the most progressive policies derive from the USA, especially since May 1988 when a district court judge ruled that a female Securities and Exchange Commission attorney was victimized and discriminated against by a 'pervasive sexual atmosphere' in the regional office between 1979 and 1984. This judgement is important because the defendant was not directly involved but argued that the tradition of granting favours and privileges to women employees who consented to managers' sexual advances generated a 'hostile and offensive workplace'. Thus, not only was the complaint upheld against a practice that did not directly involve the defendant but it was upheld against the culture of the organization rather than specific individuals (Hambleton, 1988). As men and women we all bear some responsibility for the perpetuation or elimination of patriarchy.

Conclusion

This chapter has outlined some important contemporary theories that attempt to explain the position and experiences of women at work, and provided a review of the nature of contemporary gender relationships in capitalist society. Self-evidently it has done little more than skim the surface on any of these areas, but that is the nature of such an introductory text as this.

It is important that the major themes are represented here so that their significance is not obscured in the detail. Fundamentally, an analysis of gender at work requires some form of coherent theoretical perspective; a glance at data tables may enlighten you as to how many women are executives but it cannot tell you why this number is as it is, or whether it is capable of alteration. Of the theories discussed earlier I hold little faith in the value of those which ignore gender because the relationships between men and women are crucial in the construction of work ideologies, structures and experiences. Theories which retain either capitalism *or* patriarchy as uniquely critical are inevitably partial and simply cannot explain the gendered work variations that exist in time and space. The symbiotic mutualism theory that presumes capitalist and patriarchal interests are congruent is similarly incapable of accounting for the tension-ridden relationship between these two; and dualist theories that hold the two separated as autonomous forces neglect the qualitative changes that occur when the two are conjoined. The contingent and heterogeneous compound model illustrated here allows the model to encompass the issues of race and ethnicity, and hinges the whole on a respect for the importance of contingency that does not surrender to some of the traditional contingency approaches where everything appears to explain everything. Although the social world of work is inordinately complex the variables of class, race and gender are significantly superordinate in the quest for explanation. Relationships at work are not constructed by the interaction of men and women, workers and bosses, blacks and whites, but by white male bosses, and by black female workers and by all the other possible permutations of this triangular social construct.

The two other significant points that should be drawn from the review of the evidence are the insoluble link between home and work, and the historical patterning of gender relationships. Ultimately, the model of a full-time, single occupation, male breadwinner who worked outside the home and kept his family achieved pre-eminence in the dominant ideology. However, this model is historically atypical and surrounded by so many qualifications that its period of relevance is restricted to between the last third of the nineteenth century and the first third of the twentieth. Equally important, the model was one of a modal representation: there may have been more such male workers around during this period than any other single group, but they did not form an overwhelming majority of the working population. The current pattern of paid work, though still undertaken away from home, has some features resemblant of previous eras, particularly multiple incomes, bimodal employment for women and transient occupations. What also exists today is a permutation of a pattern of gender-differentiated work experiences, occupations and rewards that has prevailed for much longer than the era of industrial capitalism. Thus women are paid less, have less chance of promotion, are less likely to be owners of businesses, are usually found in unskilled or semi-skilled service jobs, and tend to combine paid work with unpaid domestic work. Women are also less likely to be in unions and almost non-existent within union hierarchies. On the other hand, labour market pressures and the force of women's self-organization and commitment to change have begun to restructure their collective experience: they are now less likely than men to be unemployed and more likely to be found in executive positions than before, though still unlikely to be found in skilled manual jobs, especially in the field of engineering. Both employers and trade unions are now seeking to recruit women as never before and, however unimpressive the histories of both these groups have been in their relationships with women, a small but perceptable shift in attitude is developing. Marx was wrong in assuming that history was on the side of the proletariat, history is far more contingently constructed than this; but historically rare opportunities for the advancement of women at work are beginning to appear – whether they mature is another matter.

7

Race, Ethnicity and Labour Markets: Recruitment and the Politics of Exclusion

> I have a dream that one day this nation will rise up, live out the true meaning of its creed: we hold these truths to be self-evident, that all men are created equal.
>
> Martin Luther King, 27 August 1963

Introduction

One of the most important facets of the sociological approach to work relates to the underlying claim that work is a social not an individual activity. In a sense, no one is ever alone at work because of the social structures that underpin, and prevail over, work activities. What appears a freely chosen individual activity may well reflect, at least in part, socially structured constraints and facilitators which are, or appear to be, opaque in nature. For example, white middle-class men may take for granted that their professional career is wholly due to their individual efforts, yet the dearth of ethnic minority women in such careers suggests that the former are facilitated by social forces while the latter are inhibited by them. This relationship between the freedom of individuals to choose their own future and the socially constructed and sustained limitations and opportunities, is a theme which runs through much of the sociology of work, and indeed the social sciences more generally. There are many ways of illustrating this 'problem of agency', though perhaps the three most important socially structured facilitators and constraints existing in contemporary capitalist societies are those of class, gender and race. The first two are dealt with in the two previous chapters and therefore the concentration here is primarily, though not exclusively, on the issue of race and ethnicity at work.

Racism, as suggested in chapter 2, long pre-dates capitalism and has always posed a problem for Marxist accounts: capitalism may be, and indeed has been, able to take advantage of divisions between the work-force on ethnic or racial lines but these divisions were not created by capitalism any more than sexism or patriarchy was. This is not the place to consider the intricacies of the current debates on race and ethnicity and readers unfamiliar with the general debates should consult one or more of the following: Rex (1970, 1986), Banton (1983, 1987), Miles (1982, 1989), Fryer (1984), Sivanandan (1982), Centre for Contemporary Cultural Studies (1982), Brittan and Maynard (1984), Solomos (1989). The term 'race' is infused with political force. Race has become such a pejorative label that many liberal and radically minded researchers have questioned its continued use in social science. After all, since there is no 'scientific' proof that racial groups exist beyond skin colour and minor physical differences, to continue using the term is to fall into the trap of assuming they do exist and thus perpetuate the racism which many such writers disparage. Even the term 'racism' is the subject of considerable debate, but adopting the conventional perspective – that racism involves any suggestion within which humans can be divided into discrete groups in order to legitimate inequality between these groups – physical differences exist within all societies. However, the paramount point is that some features are selected by certain powerful members of such societies as 'ethnically significant'. Conventionally, little attempt is made to ensure that the worst jobs and housing go to those of us with large ears or those who are bald or spotty, but in Europe and North America those with dark skins are often treated just as inequitably (except, of course, in the ironic practices of white racist sunbathers). Racism, therefore, 'categorizes the "other" as inherently different and typically inferior . . . and involves the disadvantageous treatment of the "other", whether intentionally or not' (Jenkins, 1989: 311). What this chapter does is to explain how this racism manifests itself in and at work.

One way of approaching the delicate topic of race is to ignore it altogether and appropriate instead the term 'ethnicity' since this refers to cultural rather than physical or allegedly 'natural' differences between groups. Ethnicity is also significant in so far as many groups are discriminated against because of their cultural attributes rather than their skin colour or apparent racial differences. For example, almost all countries have ethnic minorities within them which remain the butt of discriminatory 'jokes' yet they are often physically identical to the majority population. Of course, not all groups that are discriminated against are minorities – the clearest counter example being South African blacks – but it is more typical within Western capitalist nations at least for the ethnic groups to be minority groups as well. But if the evidence for racial difference, as opposed to ethnic/cultural differences, is marginal at the very best, why persist in the use of such a term? Perhaps the clearest answer relates to the experiences of people who are discriminated against because of their alleged racial distinction: the fact that the distinctions are false does not prevent the discrimination, and ignoring the issue on the grounds of its non-scientific status has seldom proved a resolution to such problems. Nor should the issue of race be reduced to that of ethnicity. As Rex observes: 'The attempt to assimilate racial to ethnic problems, therefore, often led to the interpretation of racial problems not as forms of conflict but as benign phenomena of difference' (1986: 19). That is to say, that racial relationships have been, with few exceptions, conflictual, whereas ethnic relations exhibit a much wider span of reactions from (atypically) mutual admiration to outright hostility. But just as race has a dubious claim to objective existence, so too ethnicity is a socially constructed, and therefore contested, subject. Thus both race and ethnicity may be better conceptualized as a resource which individuals and groups draw upon, and in so doing actively construct, rather than something which exists 'out there'. This does not imply that race is socially constructed only by superordinate groups and that this construct is applied to themselves and imposed upon subordinates, whereas ethnicity is self-constructed. Both constructs are socially constructed and capable of self-application or imposition from outside. Indeed, no categorical distinction can be made between them; rather it is the case that racial constructs are related *primarily* to physical features, while ethnic constructs are related *primarily* to cultural features like common forms of language, location, kinship and customs etc. (Geertz, 1963). In many cases the two will simply be indistinguishable in practice.

Weberian approaches to the general area are represented by reference to exclusionary mechanisms using status as a concept to include race and ethnicity. Just as small-scale social groups and coteries exist and reproduce themselves by excluding those without the necessary characteristics or possessions, so too racial or ethnic groups do the same, as do other social institutions such as trade unions or religious groups (Parkin, 1979). Groups are not restricted simply to rejecting the advances of outsiders, they may also attempt to invade the territory of those by whom they themselves are excluded. Trade unions, for example, may operate with two different forms of exclusionary practice, or 'dual closure': they may attempt 'usurpationary' action against the employers and 'exclusionary' action against minority workers. In principle, exclusionary practices by one group tend to be associated with a priori legitimation of 'inferiority' and 'superiority' by the state (Parkin, 1982: 102), though at the level of the enterprise this need not be so. For example, the exclusion of individuals on the basis of non-possession of familial links, as in the printing or dock trades for many years, has seldom been approved by the state as such, but none the less retains its significance. The opposite method by which groups attempt to wrest control *from* existing exclusivist groups, Parkin's 'usurpationary' strategy, is represented by the Italian cigar makers of Tampa discussed below. The exclusionary line is the one adopted by Gordon (1972), Rubery (1980), Lee (1980), and Craig et al. (1982), but two rather different mechanisms need delineating here: on the one hand there is the conventional market-oriented exclusionary strategy of most groups in positions of power who retain power by excluding the majority irrespective of their characteristics, cultural or social; on the other hand are policies of exclusion focused directly on specific groups, such as women and ethnic minorities (Grint, 1988). In the first case fall the sectionalist methods adopted by many trade unions (Currie, 1979), but most notably craft unions, in which work-based privileges depend upon control over the labour market. The archetypal exclusionary mechanism here is the demand for all labour to be apprenticed, hence 'skilled', and for the number and form of apprenticeships to be controlled by the unions. Printers embody this kind of exclusionary approach and have reaped the benefits of limiting the labour supply for generations in the form of relatively high salary levels (Sisson, 1975; Open University, 1976). Such control has also played a part in the downfall of the printing unions as their strategic influence simultaneously pushed labour costs ever higher, inhibited the adoption of new technology and, therefore, made such technology inevitably more attractive to employers. In the second case fall the activities of unions determined to preserve privileges not just *for* their members but *against* particular out groups, sometimes even those who are members of the same union (Grint, 1988).

The major problem with some exclusionary approaches, and Parkin's approach in particular, is the implication that social life is no more than a network of exclusionary and usurpationary groups. Where Parkin rightly criticizes Marxists for neglecting the existence of non-class issues, he merely inverts the image and denies the existence of all but groups actively excluding others. As many radical critics of putative pluralist societies have demonstrated, to concentrate on what is actively fought over at the level of overt conflict ignores that which embodies inequality of resources but is not revealed in any specific activity (Giddens, 1982a; Lukes, 1974; Clegg, 1989). This is particularly important in explaining institutionalised racism: a group dominated by whites may not adopt overtly racist practices but if it simply recruits in its own image then what appear to be equal opportunities lead to unequal results (Rex, 1986: 108.18; Miles, 1989: 84–7). Few British trade unions, or indeed less progressive institutions, operate with overt exclusionary policies based on race or ethnicity yet the empirical evidence suggests that many are racist. Whether the racism is a reflection of members or institutional practices and policies is a separate issue.

As discussed in chapter 4, the conventional Marxist approach to social stratification is to subordinate aspects such as gender, race and ethnicity to class: the former are derivative of, and therefore subordinate to, the latter. If follows that once class societies are abandoned in favour of socialist and classless societies, sexism and racism will wither spontaneously. The experience of non-capitalist societies, ancient and modern, suggest that nothing of the sort is likely and that discrimination based on gender and race or ethnicity, while it may not be completely autonomous of that derived from social class, is unlikely to disintegrate with the removal of class discrimination. That is not to say that the legitimations of discrimination are constant across time. For example, neither Greek nor Roman slavery was grounded in an ideology of *racial* inferiority. Rather they were both culturally legitimated: free people with political rights (i.e., men) were culturally distinct from the 'barbarians' they enslaved. In turn, this meant that even barbarians, black or white, could become cultured and hence attain equivalent status as the free citizens of Rome or most of the ancient Greek city states (Snowden, 1983). Skin colour as a sign of status, therefore, is a more recent phenomenon associated more directly with the expansion of European powers into Africa and Asia from the fifteenth century, and before this through the development of general hostility between the Islamic and Christian worlds from the twelfth century (Daniel, 1975). Even the slavery system of the West Indies and America operated within an ideological defence of enslavement that sought to justify it rather than simply take it for granted (Curtin, 1972). For example, Africans were deigned particularly suited to work in tropical conditions, in contrast to Europeans; and since the Europeans regarded themselves as culturally superior to Africans, the capture of slaves was sometimes represented as a form of liberation for the slaves from the cultural depravities of their homeland (Barker, 1978; Miles, 1989).

This historical dimension is also important in situating the post-1945 immigrations against previous movements. Since one of the features of capitalism that distinguish it from slavery and prior modes of production is the formal freeing of labour it is likely that emigration and immigration take on a high level of significance. As such we should beware of linking immigration into Britain per se with immigration from the post-war Caribbean and Asian immigration (see Miles, 1990). That the language of immigration still conflates the phenomenon, and persists in labelling ethnic minority Britons as 'immigrants', illustrates the power of certain forms of discourse over others.

Since many ethnic minorities in contemporary Britain still do not occupy positions of equality with the white population it then becomes necessary to consider how various theories explain the persistence of divisions and inequalities. Marxist accounts like Castles and Kosack (1973) imply that the divisions between white and minority workers are representations of a transient hostility derived from competition within the labour market. Over time, the interests of minority and white workers will be perceived as converging and thus white working-class racism will disappear. The critical problem for such accounts lies in the assumption that the temporal dimension is the explanatory variable: workers of different races have *to learn* to combine and, over time, eventually they will do so. It may well be that experience is a significant educative medium, which in itself undermines any deterministic connection between social position and political activity, but the assumption of an inevitable and evolutionary progression, to a point where class interests prevail over racial interests, is premised on very shaky foundation; *when* do these interests coincide and what exactly are the mechanisms that deny the possibility of greater polarization between racial and ethnic groups rather than greater integration?

Marxist accounts often assume that racism is related to distorted or false consciousness: since the interests of the working class, irrespective of race, ethnicity or gender, are constructed through their exploited position, any denial of universal class interests may be explained by reference to misunderstanding or capitalist propaganda designed to divide and rule the working class. Yet racism may form what Miles (1989: 79) calls a 'relatively coherent theory' in so far as it 'explains' the subordinate position of the white working class by reference to the activities of the minorities. What is important here is that an ideology can 'make sense' of the world as interpreted by certain members of the white working class. For example, the construction of the British Empire, and the concomitant destruction of indigenous African and Indian industries and political regimes, is explicable through a complex web of social, economic and especially military developments which the colonized did not have access to. But a simpler explanation, albeit an erroneous one, is that the Empire reflects the innate superiority of the white British 'race': the simple explanation makes sense of a complex phenomena and serves to reproduce racism. The fact that this simpler explanation is empirically wrong does not prevent people from using it to make sense of the world (Miles, 1989: 80–1). Similarly, the fact that competition between different racial or ethnic groups in the labour market is severely limited by the different niches that each group tends to operate within does not debar individuals from explaining their racism by reference to assumed competition. It should be added further that racism cannot simply be related to the work place since so many children, even as young as three and a half, have already recognized, adopted or rejected cultural attitudes concerning race and prejudice (Commission for Racial Equality, 1990).

It is assumed, then, that race or ethnicity is neither subordinate nor superordinate to class, nor indeed to gender. As argued in the previous chapter, the exact significance of any of the three major variables is an empirical question not one that can be settled a priori. Just because the existence and potential importance of ethnic minorities is acknowledged, it cannot be assumed that their ethnicity is the major influence or determinant of their particular position in the social structure or at work. The position of minority working-class women is not equivalent to minority middle-class men, nor are either of these two examples ones which are permanent through space and time. For example, the number of middle-class minorities has grown quite rapidly in the last decade, especially in the USA; fifty years ago few minorities could have aspired to such a position.

The rest of this chapter concentrates on three areas which may be considered pre-eminent in the analysis of race and ethnicity at work. The first section considers the part of the labour market in the perpetuation and elimination of racial discrimination; the second concerns the role played by management in discriminatory recruitment and promotion; the third covers the actions and attitudes of trade unions and workers in Britain and the USA.

Labour Markets and Race

Classical Models

The notion of markets is, of course, central to the machinations of the capitalist economy. In the neo-classical model wages are determined by the direct relationship between the supply and demand of labour. Employers' demands for labour are determined by its marginal productivity and employees' actions are grounded in an equivalent form of economic rationality: the trade off between costs and benefits in any particular job (Wootton, 1955; Marsden, 1986: 19–24). Although most of the work in this area has conventionally been regarded as the preserve of economists, sociological interest has been increasing lately and, in fact, dates back to the rise of functionalist accounts of stratification. Davis and Moore (1945) first developed the approach which asserted that rewards were differentially distributed in order to attract the most capable individuals into the most demanding jobs: without considerable reward those most qualiffied would have little incentive to undertake the most responsible jobs. The theoretical difficulties of functionalism are not the prime consideration here (see Giddens, 1977) but it is important to note how such theoretical limitations undermine the utility of this approach to labour markets. For example, functionalist accounts are unable to provide any criteria for estimating rewards other than that which exactly replicates the status quo: since rewards are functionally distributed, the existing position must be functional. No mental acrobatics in comparing the social value of nurses or teachers with indolent members of the landed gentry or drug dealers are necessary to know that the relationship between worth and reward is less than transparent. Indeed, it is only necessary to demonstrate that the rewards due to identically qualified white men and minority women are divergent to know that the functionalist model simply does not operate as an adequate explanation.

Dual Labour Markets

So how do employers decide what to reward employees? What are the criteria used for assessing the relative merit of individuals? A review of the evidence by Blackburn and Mann suggests that:

> instead of using direct measures of ability, they [employers] use what the economic literature terms "screening devices", that is, they assume that some readily observable characteristic [like race] can serve as an indicator of a certain degree of ability, and select according to that. The most common screening devices are race, sex, previous job history, age, marital status and [in countries where it is appropriate] years of schooling. (1979: 12–13)

This plurality of employment conditions, and its relationship to discrimination and exclusion, has been reduced to a rather starker binary stystem in several approaches of late, all bearing witness to the development of 'dual labour markets'. Dual labour markets are divided between primary and secondary sections. The primary labour market tends to be restricted to large, profitable and capital intensive industries and enterprises which are often unionized, exhibit internal labour market structures of promotion etc., and pay relatively high wages. These organizations are comparatively isolated from the competitive market. The secondary labour market has the reverse characteristics and tends to be related to those with low skills and to women and ethnic minorities, as well as involving much seasonal, part-time and temporary labour. The terms primary and secondary relate to ideal types rather than empirically discrete cases and within both are several tiers so that, for example, the upper tier of the primary labour market comprises professional and managerial jobs whose skills and expertise provide such individuals with considerable chances for inter-firm mobility. The lower tier of this primary labour market still provides better rewards and conditions than those generally available in the secondary market, but the skills and expertise tend to be firm-specific. Beyond these distinctions it is also the case that a number of secondary labour jobs will exist within the primary sector, such as the office cleaners of financial corporations in capital cities. Concomitantly, the directors of firms in the secondary market will probably receive rewards well in excess of those earned by the lower tier of the primary market. Nevertheless, these specific counter-examples confirm, rather than deny, the validity of the general rule.

The growth of this division has been the subject of a number of explanations. First, it may be related to economic concentration, with the more stable and prosperous enterprises controlling higher percentages of the product market and therefore requiring greater levels of staff stability. Second, it may be linked to technical developments and hence to capital intensive firms where investments in training and experience put premiums on worker loyalty: the so called 'golden handcuffs'. The seminal works of Doeringer and Piore (1971), and Berger and Piore (1980) are very influential within this approach, arguing that the emergence of firm-specific skills led inexorably to a segmented market. It is worth reinforcing the point, however, that firm-specific skills not only distil the 'gold' for their bearers but enact the 'handcuffs' too, for such restricted skills operate as controlling mechanisms over their owners since they are, by definition, of limited value outside the firm to which they are specific (Brown, 1982). Third, as Garnsey et al. (1985) have argued, it seems to relate to the pursuit of sectional exclusion as work groups, including trade unions, have sought to protect and advance their own interests, if necessary at the expense of others. But even these explanations, and the model they represent, still have to incorporate the dynamic element of change, for in some countries, especially Italy, once stable primary markets have succumbed to the dispersal effects of peripheralization (Sabel, 1982).

Although ethnic minorities do gravitate towards the secondary labour market the dispersal effects tend to be less salient than those which differentiate between the genders. In fact, ethnic minorities in Britain fair relatively well in comparison to some nations such as Switzerland, where guest workers account for 40 per cent of all factory workers; and in France, where the building trade, for example, is in some areas almost wholly staffed by immigrant workers (Castles and Kosack, 1973). It is, of course, possible to remain within the secondary market and yet derive a high level of earnings from it, though this typically means extremely long hours in rather unsavoury conditions, typically within textile mills or on assembly lines. There is, however, another important feature of secondary markets emphasized by Edwards (1979) amongst others: this is the very high level of insecurity, and in particular the disastrous impact that long-term unemployment can have upon individuals. Workers of ethnic minority origin have consistently suffered a disproportionately high level of unemployment, not merely since the rise of mass unemployment from the late 1970s but right through the 1970s and 1980s (Brown, 1984).

Disaggregating Ethnic Minorities

It is important here to note the differences which do exist between and within the ethnic minorities: to view them as disaggregated rather than aggregated. If the composite contingency model of stratification, which was introduced in the last chapter, is viable then considerable variation between individuals based on the specific and heterogeneous amalgam generated by the inter-relationships between their class, race and gender should be apparent. Inevitably, the data for such an analysis is inadequate, in particular it is not possible to distinguish categories of class properly and for my purposes I have to rely on qualifications as a poor but necessary substitute; there are, after all, strong correlations between class and educational achievement (Halsey, 1986; Burgess, 1986; Reid, I. 1986) and between class, ethnicity and qualifications (Craft and Craft, 1983). A glance at the unemployment rates between 1985 and 1987 in table 8 reveals some suggestive aspects.

Several points are worth raising here, in particular, the contrast between the unemployment rates of whites and ethnic minorities generally with regard to qualifications. For whites, overall, those without qualifications have an unemployment rate 50 per cent higher than for those with some qualifications and almost four times higher than for those with A levels or above. For white males this relationship is even stronger: the unemployment rate for unqualified males is six times higher than for those with A levels or above. The unemployment rate is only just double for the equivalent females. But when comparing whites to ethnic groups the most noticeable thing is the limited relationship between qualifications and unemployment, irrespective of gender. In terms of the ethnic groups themselves it is noticeable that Pakistanis, West Indians and Guyanese do particularly badly, irrespective of their qualifications, while male Indians appear to be the most successful group in terms of using their qualifications to escape unemployment. If some groups do badly in the employment market irrespective of their qualifications then axiomatically the labour market does not operate in a disinterested fashion.

Finally, it is important to note that where sample sizes are too small for statistical analysis the result is often the camouflaging of discrimination and inequality. Thus, minority women in particular tend to be

Table 8 Unemployment rates by ethnic group, gender and highest qualification, 1985–7 (%)

	Highest qualification *A level +*	*Other*	*None*	*All*
Male				
White	3	9	18	11
West Indian/Guyanese	*	24	25	24
Indian	*	13	21	15
Pakistani/Bangladeshi	*	*	31	28
Other	*	18	24	17
Female				
White	5	10	12	10
West Indian/Guyanese	*	24	*	18
Indian	*	19	20	18
Pakistani/Bangladeshi	*	*	*	*
Other	*	20	*	16
All				
White	4	10	15	11
West Indian/Guyanese	8	24	22	21
Indian	*	15	21	16
Pakistani/Bangladeshi	*	19	20	19

* denotes sample too small for reliable estimate
Other include: African, Arab, Chinese, other stated and mixed

Source: *Source Trends*, 1989, table 4.26

omitted from labour market surveys, and consequently their situation at the bottom of the class, race and gender triangle tends to be underplayed if not completely ignored (Bruegel, 1989). Similarly there is considerable disparity between ethnic groups in terms of educational achievements, as represented in table 9, and this may be a pointer towards future employment success, even if the correlations between unemployment and qualifications may be tenuous at best.

What ought to be clear from this table is the dissimilarity between ethnic groups and gender groups and also the complex relationships between these. Those with Indian origins and those from 'other origins' are consistently better qualified than any other minority group, and as well qualified as, if not better qualified than, the white population. The opposite can be said about those from Pakistani or Bangladeshi origins, and it is noticeable that women from these two groups are the least qualified of all. Thus at the extremes there are proportionately twice as many Pakistani and Bangladeshi women as Indian and white men without qualifications. Conversely, there are nearly twice as many highly qualified

Table 9 Qualifications by ethnic group and gender (%)

	All	*White*	*All minorities*	*West Indian/ Guyanese*	*Indian*	*Pakistani/ Bangladeshi*	*Other*
All							
A level +	13	13	14	8	16	7	22
Other	47	48	40	46	41	24	45
None	39	38	43	43	40	66	30
Male							
A level +	14	13	16	*	20	9	25
Other	50	51	41	46	42	27	45
None	35	34	40	46	34	61	27
Female							
A level +	12	12	12	11	12	*	18
Other	44	44	39	45	39	20	45
None	43	43	46	41	46	73	35

* denotes sample too small for reliable estimate

Source: *Employment Gazette*, March 1988, table 6

Indian men as white women. Yet, the unemployment rate for this group of Indian men is higher than that for the well qualified women. In fact, despite the disadvantages facing particular ethnic groups not all suffer proportionately in terms of employment, rather than unemployment. For example, between 1985 and 1987, on average, 88 per cent of the male population in Britain were economically active, and the West Indian and Guyanese population had the highest employment rate for any ethnic group (84 per cent). For women, the average overall rate was 67 per cent, with the West Indian and Guyanese population, at 73 per cent, *more* active than the white population at 68 per cent and considerable higher than the Indian, Pakistani and Bangladeshi population at 42 per cent (*Social Trends*, 1989). The distinctions between ethnic groups are also reproduced in terms of the proportions applying for places at polytechnics and colleges. Ethnic monitoring of applications has only just begun, but the first year's figures suggest that while the ethnic minorities as a whole have a disproportionately high application rate it is really due to applications from black African, Chinese, Indian and Pakistani groups; West Indians and Bangladeshis were lower than or equal to their proportion of the population as a whole (*THES* 26 January 1990). However, since ethnic minorities are also less likely to apply for university places than their white colleagues, it is not axiomatic that their success in the polytechnic and college sector can be taken as proof of general educational success (McGeevor and Brennan, 1990).

In short, neither ethnic origin nor class (manifest, admittedly weakly, in terms of qualifications) nor gender can predict employment status as independent variables. Only when these variables are reconstructed in a compound unity can we begin to make adequate sense of a very complex picture. Even then we need to go beyond the general level of social categories to that of interpretative influences to establish why identically qualified individuals might have very different experiences (see also Bruegel, 1989).

Internal and External Labour Markets

While these macro-level external market data are relatively transparent, many internal labour market constructs appear rather opaque in small and private enterprises, though they do become translucent within large-scale, and most notably public, bureaucracies. Thus, incremental pay scales, promotion by seniority, and internal recruitment to senior posts have long been the hallmark of civil services generally (Weber, 1978), with the British Post Office and British Steel providing particularly 'ideal' types (Grint, 1986; Brannen et al., 1976, Batstone et al., 1983, 1984). Such 'open' systems have often been associated with greater equality simply because discrimination of any sort is rather harder to hide and easier to disclose.

Other, smaller, firms may also be reliant upon their internal labour market, and a classic case is described by Mann (1973a) where a relocating firm takes a large proportion of its workforce with it. So are internal labour markets more appropriate to large stable bureaucracies or to innovative small firms? There is a strong possibility that widely divergent explanations may exist: the internal labour market of the British Post Office developed through the historical importance of its nineteenth-century middle-class clerks, its initial requirement for literate, honest and therefore relatively well rewarded employees, and the need to provide some form of long-term incentive for individual acquiescence and loyalty (Grint, 1986). On the other hand, and despite the contrary arguments of Gordon et al. (1982), the segmentation of the labour market is not a recent phenomenon nor do firms facing rapid technological changes always require long-term loyalty from their employees; indeed, one of the advantages of technological change for employers is that it may well reduce the compunction for firms to retain labour by reducing the training periods associated with technology (Berger and Piore, 1980).

But if some enterprises exhibit clearly defined boundaries between internal and external markets the same cannot be said for all of them. Using the more volatile engineering sector as an illustration, Robinson and Conboy (1970) note how the complex combination, if not confusion, of internal and external markets led to an anarchic wage structure. Freedman's (1984) analysis of US labour markets, on the other hand, concentrates the apparent morass into fourteen more or less coherent segments within which wages are contingently related to variables like size, workers' characteristics and forms of collective bargaining etc. Such apparent pluralism is directly challenged by radical labour market theories (e.g. Stone, 1974) which construe the market pattern as the premeditated outcome of a managerial strategy of control; labour exploitation is achieved through the ancient tactic of divide and rule. But it is not self-evident either why employers should discriminate against the relatively cheap labour of women and ethnic minorities in favour of white male, and therefore expensive, labour. A rather more sophisticated approach has been adopted by Gordon (1972), Lee (1980), Rubery (1980) and Craig et al. (1982). This group emphasizes the part played by strategic groups of workers themselves in rebutting the threat of deskilling, proletarianization and degradation, often at the expense of other less powerful groups. Even this reassessment of the radical conspiratorial approach is denied by the research of Blackburn and Mann (1979) into the labour market for unskilled male manual workers in Peterborough. For them the situation is simply too disorganized for groups to impose their own rational strategies upon the rest. Yet the limitations of the empirical focus, upon a group of unskilled (non-apprenticed) male employees that cannot be regarded as representative of the overall workforce, mean that the results of the study have to be treated with a degree of scepticism. Labour markets, then, are segmented in so far as women and minority groups (and the less skilled) tend to be at the receiving end of many discriminatory practices. Such discrimination is most transparent when immigrant of migrant labour is involved.

Migrant and Immigrant Labour

Piore's (1979) assessment of migrant workers suggests that underlying the apparent confusion of labour markets and most notably the market for migrant labour, where poor wages, conditions and security prevail, is an employers' strategy designed to circumvent a labour shortage. After all, immigration is seldom economically detrimental to the host nation. As Hawkins (1989) has pointed out, the doubling of Australian and Canadian populations through (selective) immigration over the last half century has boosted, not undermined, the wealth creation of these two countries and, because most immigrants tend to be adult and thus immediate potential employees, the host country avoids the social costs involved in their childhood and education. Indeed, there are few, if any, cases where immigration does act as an economic disadvantage to the host country, except perhaps in the very short term; the West German economic decline in 1961, exactly at the time of the Berlin Wall's construction, for example, can hardly be coincidental.

But why do migrant workers accept such terms of employment? Because, argues Piore, they are migrant workers and therefore have few employment rights, little industrial muscle, and even less intention of staying: they work to return home, not to create a new identity for themselves and, as such, approach work in an almost clinically instrumental fashion (Power and Hardman, 1978). Furthermore, what may be low paying and subordinate jobs to indigenous workers in Britain, West Germany or California may well be more attractive than their equivalent opportunities in Pakistan, Turkey or Mexico (Leggett, 1968; Braham, 1980). Piore also asserts that such radical discontinuities in the labour market, which were originally restricted to peripheral areas of the economy, have become increasingly important within the core area. But this implies that the immigrant workers consistently seek the worst kind of jobs available, rather than the best. What is missing here, then, is any concern for the discriminatory practices of the indigenous population who act to keep immigrant workers out of particular jobs. Relatedly, what is critical here is to explain not why immigrant workers accept such poor conditions and rewards but why ethnic minorities, who are citizens of the countries where they work, also suffer similar fates at work. The assessment of the two groups need not begin from radically dichotomous positions. After all, a major difficulty with the neo-classical approach is to assume that shifts in the patterns of labour supply and demand lead to equivalent movements in rewards levels. But the neo-classical approach assumes an inherent scarcity of labour, while in reality alternative sources of labour are often available: immigrant workers, 'full-time' houseworkers, 'retired' or juvenile workers can be, and historically often have been, sucked into the labour market during periods of labour shortage, so that wages of existing employees need not be driven up (Gorz, 1970; Bohning, 1972).

This employer-driven model of labour market control is also relevant to the assessment of power and intent within the labour market because the radical labour market theories not only underestimate the part played by sectionalism in generating internecine struggle within the working class, but they also tend to overestimate the degree of corporate interest underlying employers. Although capital has interests which directly contradict those of labour, the reality, as Marx noted, is one of many capitals not a united capital (Marx, 1973a: 414), and it might be added that it is also one of many parts of labour. Thus, as Garnsey et al. have made clear, in coping with economic uncertainties: 'Wherever possible, employers providing primary employment conditions attempt to pass the costs and burdens of uncertainty on to *smaller firms*', (1985: 21 my emphasis). However imperfect the market for labour may be, it is still market-driven, in part at least, by competive forces of one sort or another. This dispersal of costs is expressly relevant to the way core firms employing indigenous workers tend to push the burden of recession and economic malaise on to those secondary or peripheral firms employing migrant or ethnic minority labour (Piore, 1979); a policy also prevalent within Japan, except that dispersal is contained within the indigenous workforce (Nishikawa, 1980; Hanami, 1979).

Rewarding Labour

It should be clear at this point that although employers are in a competitive situation, and are therefore unlikely to collaborate with each other against general employee interests, this does not imply that delimited collaboration is impossible. Such collaboration may take one of several forms, from the mutual surveillance and avoidance of trade union militants through to corporate resistance to government policies via employers' organizations, but one form of co-operative endeavour recognizably reflecting labour market forces is the setting of minimum wages. Either through the medium of wages councils such as those in Britain, or through mutual consent, firms in direct competition with one another have sometimes agreed to set minimum reward levels so as to remove labour costs from the competitive basket. Whether this provides long-term benefits to either employers or employees is difficult to say, but there is certainly some evidence that it makes firms internationally uncompetitive (Craig et al., 1982). Nevertheless, the removal of minimum wage agreements could prove catastrophic for those employees without the collective support of trade union organization to replace the safety net, and most at risk are the very same employees that appear to be discriminated against from all angles: women, immigrants and ethnic minorities.

Another link between women, immigrant and ethnic minority workers is the patterning of collective rewards. In neo-classical accounts *individuals* are rewarded for their skills but in reality very few employers reward their employees on such a basis and tend, instead, to adopt blanket payment schemes grounded in putative 'going rates'. There are, of course, exceptions to this, either through individual piece rates or in differential schemes where juniors undertaking identical work to seniors are paid considerably less (Grint, 1988), but such patterns are atypical at the moment despite the current trend for individual contracts. Rather more typical is the inertial element of wages which, despite rapid and substantial fluctuations in labour market conditions, tend to remain stable through time (Routh, 1980). This kind of stability poses similar difficulties for a related facet of the labour market in which particular groups are disproportionately funnelled into a narrow band of employment areas, thereby leading to an oversupply of local labour and consequently poor wages and conditions. This 'crowding hypothesis', originally based on the work of Fawcett (1918), Edgeworth (1922) and Robinson (1934), often assumes exclusionary action by male trade unionists. Chiplin and Sloane's (1974) analysis disputes the utility of the overall relationship between crowding and low earnings and it is more reasonable to assume, at least in the case of women, that there is little if any connection between the patterning of labour market fluctuations and the level of collective rewards (Routh, 1980: 123; Grint, 1988).

One attempt to recombine the importance of individual merit with collective reward has been that encapsulated by human capital theory. This seeks to explain differentials between employees on the basis of their variant levels of productivity. In turn, these levels are explained through the degree of investment in training and education. Empirical accounts of this imply that it has some relevance and may be able to explain up to two-thirds of the inequalities of reward between individuals (Mincer and Polachek, 1974; Polachek, 1975). When applied to the differential between minority and white workers, holding qualifications constant, it is patently inappropriate, not just because the wage differentials undermine the theory's relevance (Brown, 1984; *Employment Gazette*, December 1985), but because, as an inquiry into British medical schools suggests, the ability of individuals to achieve qualifications may be dependent upon the colour of their skin (Commission for Racial Equality 1988b). In this case minority students were twice as likely to be refused places as white students (Smith, 1988).

More recent general empirical approaches to wage inequalities have also produced a rather more widely dispersed wage structure (Sloan, 1980; Cohn, 1985) but they have still failed to account for different levels of investment in education and training. In short, it may be that some correlations exist between levels of qualifications and rewards (though even this is severely limited with regard to some ethnic minorities) but why do some groups, and especially women and ethnic minorities, appear to choose this approach and invest relatively little in their human capital? A partial explanation can be given for some women, in so far as they have fragmented and discontinuous careers during their child rearing period (Crompton and Jones, 1984; Garnsey *et al.*, 1985; Walby, 1986a). If such women intend to concentrate upon these activities then it may be that investment in education is considered secondary to their primary role of motherhood. This does not explain why women, rather than women and men, become full-time child rearers, nor does it account for employer discrimination against women without children. Indeed, it self-evidently collapses before the cases where women have a higher level of human investment, but a lower level of reward, than men in comparative jobs (Grint, 1988). Nevertheless, since it is collectivities rather than individuals who tend to set the patterns of reward, there is some evidence that employers operate through stereotypical pictures that regard all women as potential career breakers and reward them disproportionately. Such indiscriminate analysis can also be used to explain why employers continue to reward ethnic minorities as if they were migrant workers (Arrow, 1972). That said, it still is not clear that the correlations between human investment, or assumed human investment, and reward are necessary correlations. That is to say, although women and ethnic minorities may have lower qualifications than men and whites (and it has already been suggested that this does not hold for all groups), since many jobs do not require anything like the levels of skill acquired through training it may well be that qualifications are simply a mechanism for exclusion rather than a necessary precondition for the execution of work-related tasks. As Blackburn and Mann's study of manual workers concludes: 'the *absolute* level of skill of all but the very highest jobs is – to say the least – minimal. Eighty seven per cent of our workers exercise less skill at work than they would if they drove to work. Indeed, most of them expend more mental effort and resourcefulness in getting to work than in doing their jobs' (1979: 280). This artificial relationship between human capital and employment is nicely exposed during times of social crisis, such as war, when apparently unqualified women and juveniles have taken over the jobs of skilled men at the war front with little if any deleterious effect upon levels of efficiency and productivity (Pagnamenta and Overy, 1984; Grint, 1986: 309–10; Boston 1987: 185–218).

Two ramifications flow from this. First, it reinforces the importance of an analysis of the social construction of rewards, rather than an analysis based upon some hypothetical neo-classical account of the labour market. Second, it focuses attention directly upon the way particular groups exploit their market position to promote their own collective interests, at the expense of other, less fortunate, groups if necessary.

The Domestic and the Employment Spheres

It should not be assumed that the constraints under which individuals and collectivities operate are only those derived from economic or political or technological sources outside the home. The exact nature of the link between domestic and wage labour is discussed elsewhere but it is important here to illuminate the difficulty of assuming either that the family operates autonomously from the world of employment or that the actions of agents within the family are somehow free of external constraints generated in and through the labour market. For example, although individuals may deny the ideological relevance of the nuclear family, complete with its mythical two children and full-time houseworker, it is extremely difficult, to attempt to construct alternative lifestyles involving a shared responsibility towards housework and child rearing. It is not difficult simply in the sense of resisting the dominant ideology, but in guaranteeing career advancement or material security for either partner, and therefore for the family as a whole, should housework be shared equally (Freedman, 1984: 59–61). Family ideologies are also important in explaining the restricted employment opportunities of some ethnic minority women. Moreover, it does seem to be the case that the influence of powerful domestic ideologies within some ethnic minorities can undermine what might otherwise be more radical shopfloor systems of resistance by women workers (Westwood and Bhachu, 1989). That is not to say that family relationships are inherently constraining upon the freedom of individuals to move within the labour market. On the contrary, there is much empirical evidence to suggest that social networks grounded in familial and ethnically oriented relationships can play a decisive role in opening up, as well as inhibiting, job opportunities.

Ethnic enclaves are, of course, common in many industrial nations, especially those with large recently immigrant populations where initial language difficulties coupled with native hostility may well encourage new immigrants to seek employment within existing ethnic and family enclaves rather than within the wider labour market (Rimmer, 1972; Ward, 1985; Waldinger, 1985: 213–28; Evans, 1987). For some ethnic minorities the most viable market niche is self-employment in a small business. In Britain the east African Asian and Gujarati communities, in particular, have been remarkably successful in this avenue. The Department of Employment's estimates (*Employment Gazette*, March 1990) put the proportion of Asian self-employed at between 21 per cent and 22 per cent, against the national average of 12 per cent. These figures hide a large gender differential: twice as many Indian men are self-employed as Indian women while the figure for self-employed Pakistani women is too small for a reliable estimate (cf. Huhne, 1988a; Foster, 1987; Brown 1984; *Social Trends* 1989 and Curran and Burrows 1988). The proportion of self-employed Asian women is the same as the white proportion at 4 per cent. The Afro-Caribbean community, however, is markedly less involved in running the conventional stereotypical minority businesses like restaurants, corner shops and clothing ventures, though such stereotypes are very much part of the host mythology rather than an accurate reflection of the diversity of small businesses currently under minorities' control (Wilson and Stanworth, 1988). That said, it is still that case that ethnic minority manufacturing entrepreneurs are disproportionately small in number, and one of the explanations appears to be the racism which such individuals face (Centre for Employment Research, 1990).

A major reason often given for the paucity of Afro-Caribbean small businesses is the allegedly looser family ties which inhibit the initial accumulation of start-up capital, though it does seem that the exclusionary activities of the host society are more important in restricting the employment opportunities for minorities (Jones and McEvoy, 1986). Once a low level of business tradition develops, though, it appears to be self-fulfilling and very detrimental to those seeking to break out of the spiral. A survey of the London borough of Lambeth revealed that 74 per cent of black Britons with Caribbean roots were unsuccessful in gaining start-up capital from banks, while only 13 per cent of those with Asian roots and 6 per cent of native whites were similarly rejected (Smith, 1988). There are (at least) two ways of explaining this differentiation. Either black Britons are simply not economically effective or bank lenders *interpret* them as bad risks. Since the economic activity rate of this group is the highest of all minorities (and for black women it is higher than for white women), the prime responsibility appears to rest with the interpretative activities of discriminatory bank leaders.

Despite the common assumption that minority businesses all tend to be small, family-based enterprises, there is now some evidence of substantial growth in all areas of the economy; though it does seem that while new ventures are aided by family ties they can often only develop properly by disentangling themselves from the family to attract external expertise and capital (Wilson, 1987). Nevertheless, despite the utility of family networks, workers of ethnic minority origin have long provided a substantial part of the secondary labour market with concomitantly poor working conditions, rewards and security.

Anti-Discriminatory Practices

In theory, a free labour market should ensure the efficient allocation of resources such that the only discrimination extant would be that based on the positive projection of efficient employees. As Lewis naively asserts, regarding minority Britons: 'pricisely because it is colour-blind, the free market is their friend' (quoted in Rushdie, *Observer*, 24 July 1988). Of course, the very existence of the British Race Relations Act (1976), which forbids discrimination on racial grounds (defined as colour, race, nationality or ethnic or national origins), and the similar American anti-discriminatory legislation from 1964 implies, amongst other things, that the operations of the 'free' market are systematically flawed. Not only do ethnic minorities find access to organizations difficult, but once inside they generally find themselves discriminated against for reasons that are social rather than economic in origin, and for criteria that include not just skin colour (Doeringer and Piore, 1971) but religious and political affiliation too. For example, the unemployment rate for Catholic workers in Northern Ireland is twice as high as that for Protestant workers (Hearst, 1988; Jenkins, 1988): a manifestation of the troubles in Northern

Ireland that have prompted the British government to enact the Fair Employment policy to halt discrimination against Catholics. This carries penalties far more severe than those liable for discrimination on the grounds of race or gender, though this has yet to prove significant in undermining discriminatory practices.

Even those nations which maintain more general policies of positive discrimination (such as the USA) still exhibit considerable levels of discrimination, as of course do those which do not, such as the UK. The significance of the American system of legislative influence via the Supreme Court is indicative of what can be achieved. For example in 1990, New York's Police Commissioner, Benjamin Ward, is black; as is America's top military individual, Colin Powell, the Chair of the Joint Chiefs of Staff, and David Dinkins, the Mayor of New York. This does not mean that American minorities can expect equal treatment at work, far from it. Boston's (1988) recent review of the empirical evidence suggests that black workers are paid less but work longer hours than white workers across almost all areas of work and in all parts of the USA, though the wage differential is highest in the southern states. Yet some minority groups do seem to succeed within a potentially hostile host society. For example, Gibson's (1988) study of Punjabi Sikhs in America suggests that male, though not female, children, can and do succeed at school and in the labour market, especially in computer sciences and engineering.

However the paucity of such cases suggests their limited generalizability, and the wider perspective throws up a rather different conclusion: between 1970 and 1980 (a decade of positive discrimination in the US educational system) the number of full-time black students enrolled in American colleges rose by almost 100 per cent, while their acquisition of professional, technical and managerial positions rose by 57 per cent between 1973 and 1982 (the comparative figure for the white population in the latter category is 38 per cent) (Macnicol, 1988). However, the material position of young unskilled urban blacks actually worsened during the same period, as the increased opportunities became monopolized by a new black middle class as the economic recession of the late 1970s and early 1980s took effect (Wilson, 1987). Moreover, the Civil Rights Act of 1964, the legal framework upon which the American 'affirmative action' policies of equal opportunity are based, is now under direct threat from the new conservative majority on the US Supreme Court. Three times in 1989 the court has upheld the position of white workers seeking to challenge the affirmative action policies for minorities, and the court has now ruled that the burden of proof in employment discrimination rests with the plaintiff rather than the employer (Walker, 1989).

In short, labour-market-based racism appears to be a universal rather than British phenomenon in contemporary capitalist societies; from France (Linhart, 1981) to Australia (Kriegler, 1982) and the USA (Lash, 1984) it is as commonplace as it is pernicious. But to understand the process through which discrimination is produced and reproduced it is necessary to go beyond the labour market itself and examine several different aspects. Quite clearly, racism and discrimination are engendered and sustained by all manner of different societal forces, including the influence of the state and education (Coates, 1984: 155–91; Rex, 1986; Brittan and Maynard, 1984). But the limitations of space preclude a full analysis, and the next section concentrates upon an issue that is more axiomatically related to issues of work: recruitment.

Recruitment and Racism

Grapevine Recruitment

Among the clearest examples of the intimate links between home and work are the familially-based recruitment procedures, or 'grapevine recruitment, (Grieco, 1987: 33) used by many firms. Grieco's evidence relates to working-class recruitment but the mechanisms, of first constructing a family-based 'vacancy chain' and then solidifying it into the 'capture of opportunity' by a family, are not restricted to class-based exclusionary measures. The implication of this is that even those groups who are not in 'objectively' powerful positions through their skills or control of apprenticeships etc. may still be able to influence the operation of the labour market. This familial base to the control over recruitment is control neither in class terms nor in gender terms but control in the interests of the family network. The ability of apparently weak market groups to intervene in their own future is well demonstrated in the case of Italian migrant labour in the cigar factories of Tampa. Mormino (1982) argues that despite being discriminated against, and notwithstanding the absence of cigar-making craft skills, Italian migrants managed to capture the cigar-making employment from the Hispanics. They did this by a minimalist strategy of secreting tobacco out from the factory, setting up self-help groups to acquire the necessary skills and, eventually, taking over the primary employment opportunities. Not only does this reveal the potential influence of outgroups to transcend their weak market position but, equally important, it shows the limitations of assuming that work practices can be neatly decanted into either class antagonisms or gender antagonisms. It should be reaffirmed here, however, that the ethnic dimension is more powerful in the USA than in most European nations, though the experience of Turkish, Yugoslav or Irish workers etc.

demonstrates that ethnic origin and identity is never an irrelevance. Thus, companies employing predominantly white workers, and those recruiting workers from the ethnic minorities, often tend to reproduce the dominant characteristics of their workforce by recruiting through existing family networks (Jenkins, 1985; Manwaring, 1984; Phizacklea, 1982; Brooks and Singh, 1979), and, originally at least, the isolation of language occasionally played some role in this exclusionary recruitment (Rimmer, 1972). It is not axiomatic, of course, that all individuals will make use of such familial networks to acquire employment. There is evidence of young Afro-Caribbean British workers refusing to accede to the utility of such networks since it implies reproducing the disadvantages suffered by their parents as immigrants. As black Britons their sights are set in line with white workers, not their parents, and as such the familial networks may appear to represent the very institutionalized racism they are trying to avoid (Dex, 1978–9; Jenkins and Parker, 1987). Here the structuring of work experiences through the filters of racism act to buttress the vicious circle of poor jobs, low living standards, and poor education leading back to poor jobs ad infinitum (Ashton, 1986; Braham et al. (eds), 1981).

This should not be taken to imply that grapevine recruitment is the most important method. Quantitative data on recruitment seldom provides sufficient evidence about how different ethnic groups seek employment but that which exists implies that the differences are only sometimes significant and even then seldom crucial. For example, 39 per cent of white and minority workers seek work through Jobcentres and around 20 per cent of each via newspaper adverts or direct to employers; however a higher proportion of whites (28 per cent) than minorities (22 per cent) use the situations vacant columns in newspapers, and more minorities (15 per cent) than whites (10 per cent) use personal contacts (*Employment Gazette*, March 1990). What these data do not tell us, of course, is what happens when different individuals have got past the approach stage and have applied to employers for employment. What role do managers play in perpetuating or undermining discrimination?

Managerial Practice

If the recruitment procedure is designed to reproduce the ethnic homogeneity that already prevails there, then analysis of the gatekeeping role of management may well be irrelevant. Since very few private firms in Britain undertake ethnic monitoring it is also difficult to know just how widespread managerial racism really is; but the refusal of organizations to monitor their ethnic mix, on the grounds that everyone is equal, is akin to the problematic status of the neo-liberal market model: the point is that everyone does not *enter* the market as equal, nor does the market operate along meritocratic principles. Jenkins's (1985, 1988) research suggests that managers involved in the recruiting process have a hierarchy of criteria for acceptability. The primary criteria involve appearance, manner and attitude, and maturity. Secondary criteria relate to 'gut feeling', employment history and experience, the ability to fit in, age, speech style, literacy and marital status. Tertiary criteria concern references and English language competence. In several areas minority workers are likely to face discrimination: they are less likely to fit the stereotypical 'married, two kids and a mortgage' pattern that recruiters seem to seek; their accent may well be regarded by white recruiters as inferior to white speech patterns; and they are less likely to 'fit in' to the existing organization, given the prevailing workgroup racism discussed above. In short, minority workers suffer the ignominies commonly associated with disparaging racial stereotypes. In many ways it seems that a large number of recruiters do not perceive themselves to be racist but prefer white workers on the grounds of expediency: the white workforce is racist, therefore, irrespective of their own liberal notions of 'fairness', white recruiters fear the consequences of recruiting minority workers (Jenkins, 1985). Inevitably, the refusal to challenge assumed racism actually facilitates its reproduction; thus the self-proclaimed liberalism acts merely as a conduit for the perpetuation of racism.

Given the conventional recruitment procedures in many manufacturing firms – word of mouth and social networks – even overtly racist recruiters may never need to execute racial discrimination in any open manner because the method of recruitment preselects ethnic minorities out of the pool through employee screening: a method of some value to US companies too (Rees, 1966). This informal recruitment also implies that surveillance by state agencies is more difficult; even where identically qualified individuals are interviewed the emphasis placed upon the subjective assessment of the interviewer may ensure that the minority interviewee is not selected. A partial solution to this subjectivism is to formalize the procedure, and though this may be not the means to eliminate racial discrimination in the recruitment process, it is seen by Jenkins as a means by which its effects can be reduced (1985).

Ethnicity, Class and Recruitment

Nevertheless, formal recruitment procedures and public sector employment do not axiomatically result in equal opportunity. Ethnic minorities make up about 4.5 per cent of the British population, and 4.8 per cent of the total labour force (with 43 per cent born in Britain) (*Employment*

Gazette, March 1990). Economic activity rates are lower amongst minorities than the white population for those under 24 years old, but higher in terms of self-employment. The greatest level of ethnic differentiation emerges amongst women: the economic activity rate for West Indian or Guyanese women is 73 per cent, for whites it is 69 per cent, for Indians it is 57 per cent and for Pakistani or Bangladeshi women it is 20 per cent. Full-time employment is more prevalent amongst minority than white women (62 per cent minorities to 51 per cent whites), while the white population has a higher proportion in part-time work (26 per cent minorities to 40 per cent whites).

At the broadest level the relationships between gender and ethnic groups are represented in table 10 and figures 8 and 9.

The rather erratic summation of the groups, with several falling under the 100 per cent mark, and the absence of data on Pakistani women because the numbers involved are too small, represents the inadequacy of the existing information we have on such issues. Nevertheless, several aspects of the data are worth commenting on. First, the occupational divisions between white and Indian employees are much smaller than between Indian and other minority groups. This does not mean that Indian employees have achieved equality with the white population but it does reinforce the importance of disaggregating the minorities. Second, the West Indian/Guyanese and Pakistani/Bangladeshi groups

Table 10 Employment by broad occupation, ethnic origin and gender, spring 1986–8 (%)

Employment	*w/m*	*w/f*	*wi/m*	*wi/f*	*i/m*	*i/f*	*p/m*	*p/f*	*r/m*	*r/f*
Managerial & professional	35	26	15	29	42	23	27	*	40	32
Clerical & related	5	30	*	28	7	30	*	*	7	29
Other non-manual	6	10	*	*	6	9	*	*	8	*
Craft etc	25	4	29	*	19	12	17	*	15	*
General labour	1	0	*	*	*	*	*	*	*	*
Other manual	27	30	40	34	26	24	45	*	28	27

key: w/m – white male
w/f – white female
wi/m – West Indian/Guyanese male
wi/f – West Indian/Guyanese female
i/m – Indian male
i/f – Indian female
p/m – Pakistani/Bangladeshi male
p/f – Pakistani/Bangladeshi female
r/m – Rest male
r/f – Rest female
* – Category too small for estimate

Source: *Employment Gazette*, March 1990

Figure 8 Male occupation and ethnic origin 1986–8 (%)

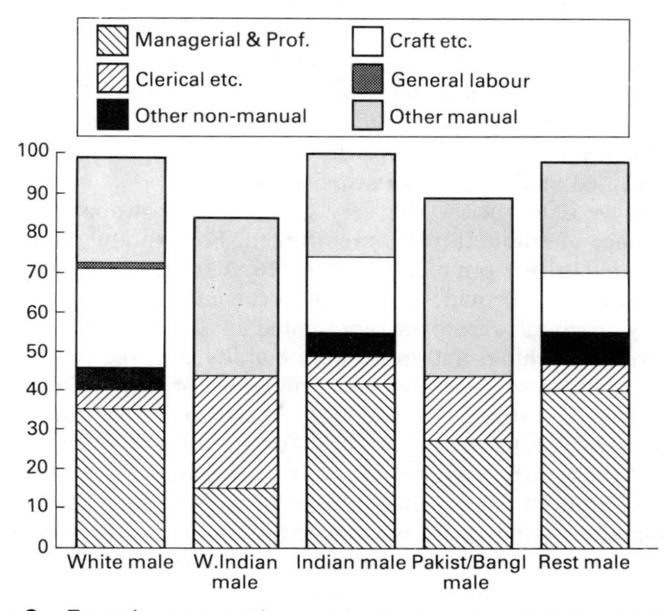

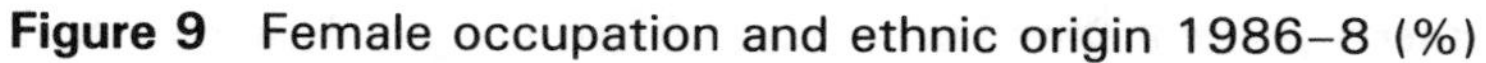

Figure 9 Female occupation and ethnic origin 1986–8 (%)

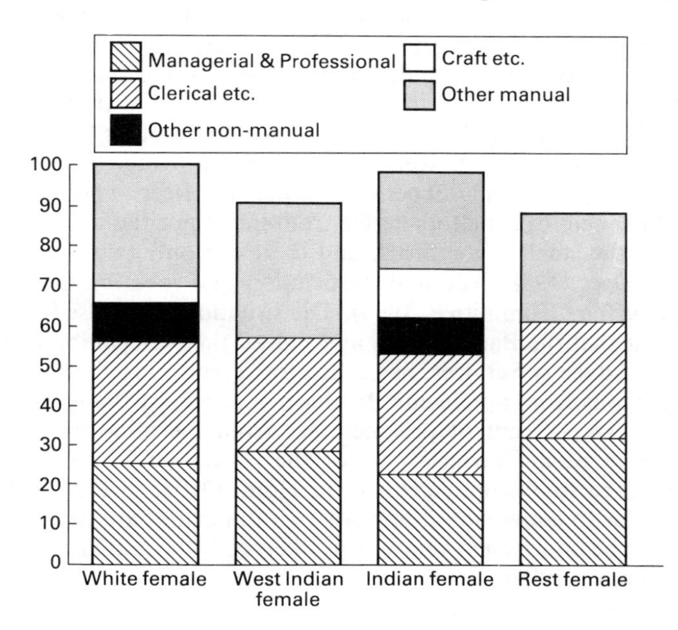

are very similar in occupational structure – with the obvious exclusion of Pakistani/Bangladeshi women. Within these general patterns it is noticeable that the West Indian/Guyanese men have far fewer managers and professionals and, like Pakistani/Bangladeshi men, have a much greater proportion of 'other manual' workers. It may well be that part of the reason is the problematic categorization involved but it may also be the case that these minority groups do fulfil a disproportionate amount of the 'unskilled' and poorly rewarded jobs.

When we delve below the very general occupational categories the significance of ethnic factors is reinforced. For example, although 8 per cent of the British population under 16 is from the ethnic minorities this category only provides 2 per cent of the nation's teachers. Moreover, minority teachers were over-represented in shortage areas, or outside mainstream teaching, and more were employed at the lower end of the salary scale than white teachers (Commission for Racial Equality [CRE], 1988a). Other professions are also likely to reproduce the existing inbalance of employees. There are, for example, no ethnic minorities amongst the top three grades of the British Civil Service, and within the top seven grades there are only 207 out of 18,644 (1 per cent). This is not because ethnic minorities have avoided work in the Civil Service; on the contrary about 4 per cent of the total are minorities (Indians, Pakistanis and Bangladeshis, and West Indians make up about 1 per cent each with a further 1 per cent for all other minorities), marginally higher than the proportion for the total working population (Hencke, 1989).

Another CRE investigation, this time into chartered accountancy, found that members of ethnic minorities were three and a half times less likely to be offered a job than white applicants, and the discriminatory practices occurred at all levels of the screening process (Commission for Racial Equality, 1987). Relatedly, there are a mere 1.9 per cent of probation officers and 0.9 per cent of police officers who are minorities; only 1 per cent of solicitors derive from the minorities and most of these work in the smaller law firms, and there are only two minority circuit judges (Dyer, 1988; National Association of Probation Officers, 1988; Home Affairs Committee, 1989). The situation has caused such embarrassment that the Bar Council, and indeed the Association of Graduate Careers Advisory Services, has called for recruiters to delete requests for photographs from applicants. In sharp contrast, at the receiving end of the law, 14 per cent of prisoners are from the minorities and racism appears to be an intrinsic part of the prison service according to an unpublished study completed for the Home Office in 1986 (BBC, 1988). Even prior to conviction it appears that minorities are twice as likely as whites to be imprisoned yet twice as likely to be acquitted too (*Guardian*, 18 December 1989).

In terms of the general recruitment of non-university graduates it appears that a wide disparity exists between the 70 per cent of white graduates in employment twelve months after graduation compared to less than half the graduates from ethnic minorities (Brennan and McGeevor, 1987). Yet the informality of network recruitment also operates to perpetuate the supply of labour for ethnic businesses, and to ensure that competitors are disadvantaged, as Kim (1981) has demonstrated with regard to Korean businesses in New York, and Light and Bonacich (1988) *vis-à-vis* Korean entrepreneurial success in Los Angeles. Despite the under-representation of minorities in the professional sections of the public sector, it is still here, where recruitment is more often associated with advertising and bureaucratic procedures, that minority workers are generally more likely to receive a greater degree of equality of opportunity; though as the evidence cited above reveals, this may well be a long way short of equality of opportunity. Indeed, since it tends to be those jobs which cannot be filled by word of mouth that end up in the state employment services, and since some of these often tend to be the least attractive jobs, minority workers are provided with fewer and less attractive jobs to choose between. In addition, according to the Manpower Services Commission (MSC), almost half of the Afro-Caribbean people using Jobcentres claimed to have suffered racial discrimination in the search for employment, while almost a quarter of Asian job seekers said the same. The Youth Training Scheme (YTS) has similar overall results: less than 1 per cent of those on YTS schemes were from the minorities in 1987 or 1988, though some companies, such as Dixons, Abbey National and Marks and Spencers were radically more responsive to the needs of minority youths than were most British companies (Sousa, 1988; Hyder, 1989). Similarly, while 69 per cent of all those leaving the YTS found employment, only half of the Afro-Caribbean and Asian youths did so (Manpower Services Commission, 1987). The most recent survey reveals the Stock Exchange, Barclays, Lloyds, IBM and British Airways recruiting well, the major high street retailers, including the Co-op, doing generally badly (*Observer*, 4 March 1990).

It would seem that, under many conditions, it would be rational, that is in their own self-interests, for managers to construct a more formal and less prejudiced approach to recruitment. After all, if discrimination hinders the recruitment of the most qualified and suitable individual for the particular job then it must be against the interests of the company: not just morally but economically too. This is exactly the code of conduct spelled out in numerous Institute of Personnel Management (IPM) (1978) and Confederation of British Industry (CBI) (1970, 1981) reports. In fact, as Jewson and Mason (1986) point out, formality can actually provide the cover for more, rather than less, manipulation of the recruitment procedure. Concomitantly, reducing informal procedures may actually undermine some of the shopfloor patterns of trust between managers and workers. Since there can never be a sufficiently universal rule book to cover all contingencies there clearly is a problem regarding the manipulation or misinterpretation of rules. However, the ordinarily superior record of public employment to private employment regarding ethnic minorities suggests that formality should not be cast aside because of its inevitable problems.

Several studies have demonstrated the disadvantages associated by white employers with ethnic minorities in the recruiting world, but few more vividly than the experiments using fictitious matched pairs of identically qualified white and minority workers. The surveys of Daniel (1968), Jowell and Prescott-Clarke (1970); Smith (1977) and the 1988 BBC documentary series based in Bristol reveal the high levels of racial discrimination that masquerade behind the often liberal façades at work and in the wider community. In some areas, at least until fairly recently, discriminatory policies were much more explicit, bordering on a system not dissimilar to South African apartheid; as a representative of one engineering firm put it, the firm had: 'a policy never to employ a coloured man in a position . . . where in the course of events he would rise to a position where he would give orders to a white man' (Wright, 1968: 75–6). Another method for taking advantage of ethnic differences is that of occupational segregation. This was particularly prevalent in the USA in the early part of this century, when employers both segregated and mixed different ethnic groups with the explicit intention of increasing or decreasing levels of hostility and competition between ethnic groups. The nearest equivalent practice in the UK has been that enacted by employers in Northern Ireland to set Catholics against Protestants (Jenkins, 1988: 316–19). The undermining of any labour solidarity that appeared to be fostering union sympathies appears to have been a primary aim of this divide and rule strategy (Gordon et al., 1982: 141–3). But occupational segregation has more commonly been associated with the sucking in of immigrant labour to replace indigenous workers who refuse to undertake the most arduous and poorly paid jobs. In some circumstances this almost leads to separated labour markets, for example the predominance of minority staff on the London Underground (Rex and Tomlinson, 1979). In other cases it is minority or immigrant workers who undertake specific tasks within enterprises, such as night work and shift work (Smith, 1974). But whatever the division, and however unwilling the white population appears to be to undertake certain jobs, this seldom appears to remove the resistance or discrimination of white workers (Ward, 1978).

In Britain, employers' attitudes towards ethnic minorities even seem to relate to the recognition of trade unions. Recently, union recognition in enterprises where more than 10 per cent of employees are minority shows some degree of decline. Since 1980 even fewer such employers recognize trade unions, irrespective of the general decline in trade union membership and influence. Indeed, ethnic minority workers were employed in substantial numbers in fewer enterprises, primarily because of the collapse of staple industries which employed them and because of the selective shake-out of minority labour mentioned above (Millward and Stevens, 1986: 65–99). Thus, ethnic minorities started out from a position of structured subordination in the labour market, and the economic malaise of the early 1980s has merely served to compound the disadvantages (Smith, 1981; Thomas, 1984). But why should management be concerned about the ethnic content of their workforce when considering union recognition? Are unions, or rather union members and ordinary workers, responsible for the perpetuation of racism or the boosting of reward levels to undermine the economic rationale for employing workers from the ethnic minorities? Answers to these kinds of questions are developed in the final section of this chapter.

Trade Unions, Workers and Racial Discrimination

Trade Unions and Exclusionary Theory

The assumption that class issues, or even just trade union issues, cut across, and are more important than, racial or ethnic issues has a long and ambiguous pedigree. The prioritizing of class above race and gender has already been discussed but it is important to note the continuing relevance of this perspective to the contemporary academic study of work. For example, both Kornblum (1974) and Burawoy (1979) insist that white workers' racism is subordinated to, and generated by, the imperatives of a specifically capitalist mode of production. Since minority wages are usually lower than white workers' wages it might seem paradoxical that capital should provide support for a form of discrimination that delimits the opportunity to maximize profits: if minority labour is cheaper then employers should not accept racism amongst their majority labour force. Three explanations for this paradox are possible. First, it may be that employers are unwilling to risk industrial action on the part of their majority workers by recruiting minority workers. Second, it has been argued that by encouraging racial discrimination within the workforce employers can actually persuade both majority and minority groups to accept rates of reward that are lower than those applicable where non-discriminatory practices operate (Perlo, 1953). Third, it may be taken as a management strategy of divide and rule to ensure that, irrespective of individual rewards, no collective action would occur. Such a strategy has been well documented in the USA over a long period of time (Piven and Cloward, 1977; Gordon et al., 1982).

Whether the exclusionary tactics that do exist, linked to the retention of demarcation boundaries, job allocation and recruitment controls, are beneficial to trade unions in the long run is questionable (Pagnamenta and Overy, 1984: 124–49; Guerin, 1979; Davis, 1985) but not the issue here. At the risk of repetition, what is important is to note how such exclusionary tactics become appropriated for use against specific groups of workers. That is to say that powerful groups of (usually) male, white and skilled workers operate discriminatory bans against (usually) women and ethnic minorities, but retain the camouflage of 'market-based', and therefore avowedly 'legitimate' exclusion. The implications of this for perspectives on the relationship of class of work are covered in chapter 5; this section considers the impact it has on race and work, particularly with regard to Britain and America.

The British Experience

Despite the frequent allocation of left-wing labels to British trade unions, their exclusionary strategies and tactics against ethnic minorities have a long history. Although Elizabeth I seems to have been responsible for the first attempt to repatriate black people from England in 1596, racism within the indigenous British workforce is nothing new (Fryer, 1988). Documented reports of racist attacks by British workers upon Irish workers in the nineteenth century, then Jewish workers at the turn of the century, long pre-date the disparagement of ethnic minorities from the Commonwealth (Miles and Phizacklea) eds, 1979). The TUC has, until very recently, also been prominent in acting against minority workers; for example, as early as 1892 it made a declaration in favour of controlling 'alien' labour. In fact, one of the first black British labour leader appears to have been William Cuffay, a tailor and one of the Chartist leaders (Meade-King, 1986), but the last century and a half has not witnessed the universal 'brotherhood' for which they stood. Black workers had already reached a relatively high number in England by 1830, when a black community of between ten and fifteen thousand existed, and two black men, William Davidson and Robert Wedderburn, were actively involved in the working-class politics of the day (Fryer, 1984). But ethnic conflict was most easily generated where ethnic origin could be coupled with religion: a volatile mix that often disrupted unionism in Ireland, Scotland and the north-west of England as the Protestant orange tinge to trade unionism transformed it into political unionism (Foot, 1965; Neal, 1988).

One of of the earliest cases of offical trade union hostility to their *own* minority members in Britain is that of the National Union of Seamen who were disinclined to support their minority members against the 1925 Special Restrictions (Coloured Alien Seamen) Order (Bhavnani and Bhavnani, 1985: 151–2). Even Ben Tillett, an avowed socialist and radical union leader of the London dockers at the turn of the nineteenth century, was equivocal about the arrival of Jewish immigrants: 'Yes, you are our brothers and we will stand by you. But we wish you had not come' (quoted in Meth, 1973: 5). Similarly, the population as a whole seems to have been at best ambiguous about the status of the Jews. The Boer War was blamed by Keir Hardy and a substantial proportion of trade union leaders on the Army, composed as it allegedly was 'largely [of] Jews and foreigners' (Rhodes James, quoted in Fox (1985: 210). Even during the Second World War indigenous anti-semitism was ever-present amongst the British working class, though they do not seem to have been as anti-semitic as the government feared or the gutter press assumed (Kushner, 1989).

With the influx of migrant labour to Britain at the end of the Second World War it might have been expected that competition for employment would provide the fertile ground for the construction of exclusionary strategies by indigenous workers. In fact, the persistent labour shortage, and funnelling of West Indian immigrants in particular into the unskilled jobs in the public and service sectors that were the most riven by shortages, ensured that there was little direct competition between white and minority workers. In the North and Midlands where many Asian workers found manufacturing jobs, particularly in textiles, the general pattern was one where white employees left, leaving vacancies for Asian workers, rather than one where cheaper Asian workers pushed white workers out of the labour market (Peach, 1968).

This did not deter the production and reproduction of racist attitudes by trade unionists and white workers alike, grounded in the putative threat to white jobs and indigenous culture (LATC, 1984; Mayhew and Addison, 1983: 333), and represented by the likes of Enoch Powell's 'rivers of blood' speech in 1968 on the political right. It should not be forgotten that he was supported by London dockers and (the alleged political left has argued) by the Labour Party – in and out of office – through their support for, and enactment of, various immigration controls based on racial origins (Joshi and Carter, 1984; Bhavnani and Bhavnani, 1985). Nor did it inhibit the General Council of the TUC from adopting policy statements that explicitly linked the existence of immigrant workers to the issue of the 'coloured problem' (TUC, 1958), despite condemning 'all manifestations of racial discrimination' three years earlier. Such racist attitudes were also made manifest in the TUC's support for both Conservative and Labour immigration legislation (Miles and Phizacklea, 1977: 21–39). In fact, the first shift within the TUC from the 'problem of integration' to the 'problem of racism' did not occur until the 1973 Trades Union Congress, when the triple forces of anti-racist rank and file movements, the burgeoning number of strikes against trade union racism by ethnic minorities themselves (Commission for Industrial Relations, 1974; Moore, 1975), and the rise of the neo-fascist National Front coerced the TUC into belated reaction. Since then the TUC has instigated policy documents designed to undercut racism within its own ranks (Trades Union Congress, 1983a, 1983b), but not until the 1989 Trades Union Congress did the anti-racist resolution, originally agreed in 1984, acquire a rule providing for expulsion for 'deliberate acts of unlawful discrimination'. It remains to be seen whether this will have any major impact.

The apparent demise of labour solidarity and collectivism in Britain, most recently associated with the era of Thatcherism, has often been linked to the crumbling of social democratic and liberal 'morality'; in its place has arisen, it is alleged, a harsh Darwinian jungle bereft of morality and, therefore, ill-disposed towards social reforms of all kinds (Hobsbawm, 1981; Offe, 1984). This assumes the existence of prior forms of ideological solidarity that, in fact, seldom seem to have prevailed. Thus neither an entire society, nor the working-class elements of it, appear to have been held in place by unitary ideologies (Mann, 1970; Abercrombie et al., 1980; Held, 1987: 221–42; Marshall et al., 1987). This does not imply that trade unions in Britain or the USA are inherently and irrevocably sectionalist, exclusive and racist; the examples of the Knights of Labor and periods in the UAW's history in the USA (see below), and recent support by some British unions (most notably the National Association of Local Government Officers (NALGO)) for anti-racist policies, suggest that a contradictory amalgam of sectionalism, exclusivity, solidarity and collectivism is a more accurate description of the historical role of the labour movement in most capitalist countries.

Such an amalgam also misrepresents the apparent solidarity of ethnic minorities. Although white assessments tend to assume a solidarity amongst heterogeneous groups like 'Asian' workers and 'black' workers, in reality they are often as disunited as any other apparently homogeneous group. For example, Asian workers are more likely to be organized through their regional and national loyalties than any putative supra-ethnic loyalty: The Indian Workers' Association, the Pakistani Workers' Association and the East Pakistani Welfare Association etc., rather than the Asian Workers Association (Brooks and Singh, 1978–9).

Much of the empirical research suggests that, despite members of ethnic minorities being favourably inclined towards trade unions (Lee, 1987: 145–7), white members of unions are generally less enthusiastic about anti-racist issues than their national officials (Radin, 1966; Commission for Racial Equality, 1981; Miles and Phizacklea, 1978), and, in many instances, racist themselves (CARF, 1981). An example of this appears to be the perpetuation of the 'black problem' attitude of trade union officials. That is to say, just as the early post-war union officials assumed that any problems arising out of racial conflict were 'coloured problems', rather than 'white problems', so it appears that the failure of anti-racist policies is blamed on the failure of minorities to participate in unions. Certainly Lee's (1987) evidence suggests that very few trade union officials regard the involvement of minority members as a union responsibility. Rather, minority workers are defined by their class not their colour; as Vic Feather, a former General Secretary of the TUC, noted in 1968: 'If coloured immigrants are unwilling to integrate or are unable to secure acceptance as they are, we shall have, instead of integration, permanent and weakening division among workpeople' (quoted in Meth, 1973: 23). This is reflected in: the refusal of many white union officials to take issues of racial discrimination seriously; their hostility towards minority caucuses within unions (the most prominent exception to the rule here is NALGO); and the lack of interest which appears to prevail in support of minority officials. Individual minority workers who do make it into the union hierarchy at any level emerge despite, rather than because of, the 'support' from union officialdom (Lee, 1987: 150–3). This is not to disparage the activities of a minority of white shop stewards and union officials, but what evidence does exist suggests that anti-racism in practice is critically dependent upon the existence and actions of a caucus of minority activists, often operating in relative autonomy from the main union (Virdee, 1990).

A useful litmus test for the distinction between anti-racist rhetoric and reality is to compare official pronouncements with public policies. It may be easier for a full-time official to declare her or himself an anti-racist than for the local shop steward because the full-time official may not have to deal with the high level of racism apparent within the British working class. It is worth, therefore, acknowledging the extent to which trade union bureaucracies are themselves staffed by white employees. While there is little systematic evidence on this, because very few unions have adopted ethnic monitoring, it is apparent that where studies do exist they disclose a depressingly conservative picture of grossly under-represented ethnic minorities (National Union of Public Employees, 1985). The situation is worse than appears at first sight because the level of union density amongst ethnic minorities is actually substantially higher than the equivalent figure for white workers (Lee, 1987: 145–6). In 1986 only thirteen of the main thirty-three British unions had any minority officials, and many had only a token minority leader. There are exceptions of course, and Bill Morris, appointed the Deputy General Secretary of the Transport and General Workers Union in 1986, is the most senior minority union offical at the time of writing. But although 56 per cent of minority employees were unionized in 1986, compared to 47 per cent of white employees, only 4 per cent of minority men held elected posts within their unions, compared to 11 per cent of white men. The figures were identical for white and minority women at 2 per cent (Policy Studies Institute, 1986).

Majority group hostility to ethnic minorities in the 1980s is still very evident (Willmott, 1987). Not so much in official discrimination but in the disproportionate levels of material disadvantage experienced (Brown, 1984), and more personal, unofficial, tacit and even unconscious ways, such as the self-allocation of social class: in Lash's study of the USA the vast majority of white respondents placed themselves in an intermediate class above the 'poor', a label which they strongly associated with ethnic minorities (1984: 86), and a manifestation of the absence of labour solidarity. So is the general American experience any better?

The American Experience

In the USA racial conflict between workers was evident through much of the nineteenth century, and while white workers seemed unwilling to support the slavery abolitionists' movement, abolitionists also appeared to denigrate the utility of any labour movement (Guerin, 1979: 144–6). As Du Bois noted: 'the abolitionists did not perceive the new subordination to which the worker was subjected by organized capital, while the workers did not understand that the exclusion from the working class program of four million workers was a fatal omission' (quoted in Guerin, 1979: 145). There were labour leaders who espoused progressive social policies on race, such as William H. Sylvis, leader of the National Labor Union in the 1860s, but the general practice of discrimination remained, buttressed by black support for the Republican 'liberators' from slavery, and white labour antagonism towards the same party perceived to be the representative of big business. This conflict, between the putative exploiters of class and the exploiters of race, is aptly captured by the dichotomous positions taken up by black and white employees of the Pullman Company in the 1894 strike. White workers struck, but their American Railway Union's (ARU) discriminatory policies, in sharp contrast to the more racially liberal policies of the Pullman company, led black workers to resist the strikers. As Eugene Debs, The ARU's leader, so characteristically argued: 'there is no black question independently of the working class question . . . we have nothing special to offer the negro' (quoted in Guerin, 1979: 149).

The Knights of Labor, a progressive general union, did propose anti-racist programmes and recruited up to 60,000 black members by 1896, but they were quickly undermined by the sectionalist traditions of business unionism promulgated by the likes of Gompers and the American Federation of Labour (AFL). Not that the trade unions were sole repositories of racism of course, nor that the discrimination was restricted to blacks; the Irish, Catholics, Jews and women were commonly regarded by the English Protestant male hierarchy in America and England as legitimate scapegoats. Such exclusionary practices, in

America particularly, merely fostered the strike-breaking activities that black workers were often recruited for by white employers, especially during the bitter steel disputes of the early post First World War period. Yet greater levels of discrimination were practised against non-American-born workers; for example, the Arizona Legislature passed the Alien Labor Law which stipulated that 80 per cent of all workers in the state must be American born: a measure explicitly designed to stem the influx of Mexican and Chinese labourers (Hoefer, 1984: 39). Nor was racism restricted to the passing of legislation: in 1919 twenty-five major race riots took place in the USA as mass unemployment greeted many of the black war veterans. Amongst the more than seventy blacks lynched by white mobs during this time several were still wearing their army uniforms (Woodward, 1974).

The National Association for the Advancement of Colored People (NAACP) made several vain attempts to interest the AFL in a multi-racial movement, but the United Mine Workers were almost alone in carrying out such policies in some parts of the country. This progressive platform also framed the original structure of the Committee for Industrial Organization (CIO), set up in 1935 against the background of recruiting conflicts between the craft unions, represented by the leadership of the AFL, and the industrial unions, represented by the rebel CIO. Thus in CIO affiliates, like the United Automobile Workers (UAW), both black and white workers were involved in strike action and social struggles throughout the 1930s and 1940s. Inevitably, perhaps, some employers made attempts to undermine the incipient unity; first, by recruiting black workers instead of white workers because of the formers' traditional antipathy to trade unions, and second, when this failed, to promote the AFL instead of the CIO. Ford, in particular, was an exponent of this tactic.

The fusion of the AFL and CIO in 1957 did little to further the cause of black workers, and, while many unions eventually voiced support for the civil rights movement, only the UAW amongst the large unions pursued this with any vigour. Since US unions have never recruited a majority of white workers, let alone black workers, the continued discrimination against black workers represented by their disproportionate presence amongst the working class (Wright, 1985: 201) is clearly not the sole responsibility of the unions. Exactly how black workers should respond to this situation, which poses the interests of class and race as alternative rather than complementary forms of organization, is not self-evident. Neither integration nor separate organizations have proved overwhelmingly successful and while separate black sections of 'white' organizations may well be a prerequisite to any kind of substantive advance it is also the case that separate organizations can be, and have been, easy to isolate and ignore or have stimulated a white backlash (Wrench, 1985; Virdee, 1990).

Of course, in the USA the great ethnic variety and wave-like periods of immigration brought favourable conditions for the pursuit of trade-union-organized sectionalism (Nelson, 1975), as indeed they have done across the capitalist world ever since (see Cohen, 1988), and the numbers involved were enormous: in 1852 over a thousand people a day were leaving from Britain alone for the USA (Armytage, 1981: 70), and Tranter (1973) estimates that between 1841 and 1939 8.6 million people emigrated from Britain - a third of the natural increase. The importance of the ethnic/family dimension to American patterns of work, particularly during the late nineteenth and early twentieth centuries, should not be underestimated: trade unions and business organizations were just as likely to be marshalled under their ethnic banners as their craft or class banners: thus the United German Trades and the Italian Chamber of Labor were commonplace during this period (Pelling, 1960: 213). Yet the ethnic mix which this generated in the USA, and the exclusionary reaction of American labour, have been considered, by Selig Perlman (1928) for example, as demonstrable proof of the 'maturity' of US unions. These strategies originated, according to Pelling (1960: 212), in attempts to restrict the competition of Chinese labour in California, and there were various methods involved, from constitutional bars on non-white workers to making US citizenship a pre-requisite for membership. In fact, the Chinese immigration into Hawaii's sugar plantations at the end of the last century is a useful example of the problems involved in banning particular groups whilst still requiring immigrant labour. With 50,000 Chinese labourers in Hawaii by 1898 and further immigration banned by an Exclusion Act of 1892, Japanese labourers were encouraged as replacements, at least until they outnumbered the Chinese and were deeply implicated in a rash of labour disputes, whereupon Koreans were sought out to supply the ever-expanding sugar plantations (Patterson, 1988). Where such groups have remained in situ and developed ethnic businesses, they have proved extraordinarily difficult recruiting ground for unions; not just because of the language problem but because ethnic businesses tend to be small, culturally homogeneous units where employer and employee often work side by side and where the class-based claims of union recruiters are devalued both by the ethnic allegiances and the general lack of interest of most unions in aspects of ethnic discrimination. A further problem for unions lies in the essentially ambiguous and often transient status of immigrant workers and those from established ethnic minorities: it is not merely geographic mobility that is common, but social mobility, between employer and employee, is also relatively widespread, a pattern that stretches across national boundaries (Morokvasic, 1987).

It can only be concluded that white workers, trade unions and trade unionists in the USA and the UK bear a major responsibility for not attacking - and by default, therefore, for the preservation of - racism at work, as Phizacklea and Miles argue: 'there remains very little real evidence that organized labour in Britain has seriously confronted the issue of racism within its own ranks and the reality of material disadvantage amongst those who have been the object of racism and discrimination' (1987: 117). Nevertheless, trade unions cannot be isolated from the environment within which they operate. If the environment is racist and the trade unions have to work within it but cannot transcend it, then the responsibility for the perpetuation of racism lies not just at the door of the union movement. Indeed, the most recent evidence suggests that workers with ethnic minority origins are better paid when they work within unionised enterprises than in non-unionized enterprises in so far as wage differentials based on race are narrower (Metcalf, 1988). Trade unions may not have exerted themselves in the fight against racism at work until relatively recently but they have had a measure of success and, given the hostile environment within which they operate, must take at least some credit for positive action.

Conclusion

This chapter has attempted to demonstrate the interleaving of socially structured forces and the influence of agents in the labour market by highlighting several related features of race and ethnicity. It should be apparent that the material position of ethnic minorities, and the associated levels of racial discrimination, cannot be explained simply by reference to a neo-liberal market model where only individuals and the forces of supply and demand exist. Nor can the discriminatory practices of white employers or employees or trade unions be singled out. Rather, the practices of various agents need to be situated within their appropriate socially structured context to illustrate both the contingent openings appropriated by different work groups and the more permanent features of social exclusion that appear to persist in all market-based societies. Racial discrimination in the labour market is not a feature unique to capitalist economies nor to capitalists; nor, it has to be said, are trade unions unambiguous promoters of racial equality or inequality. It is this very fluidity that makes the apportioning of causation and responsibility so difficult. But undergirding the fluidity remains a stability based upon the principle of work as a social phenomenon: neither racism nor racial equality are simply the products of individual attitudes, instead they depend upon a complex web of socially constructed institutions and socially organized agents.

8

Working Technology

People who experience themselves as automata, as robots, as bits of machinery . . . are rightly regarded as crazy. Yet why do we not regard a theory that seeks to transmute persons into automata . . . as equally crazy?

R.D., Laing, *The Divided Self*

Introduction

The nature of the relationship between technology and work is as controversial as the definition of either. As has already been pointed out, 'work' has often been taken to be synonymous with paid labour, though this assumption embodies an enormous variety of evaluative baggage as to the importance of non-domestic labour and economic exchange. Similarly, the definition of technology tends to vary with author: from a delimited concern with machinery through to the entire corpus of organizational features, and all points in between (Winner, 1977: 8–12). Quite often the definition of technology remains implicit and therefore obscure. As a result, technology can become the reserve category which explains all aspects that cannot be explained by other factors, or the bewildering variety of definitions simply confounds any attempted comparisons (see Davis and Taylor, 1976: 390–1). Winner (1977: 8–12) makes an attempt to disentangle the knotty problem by differentiating between the inanimate machinery which he calls 'apparatus', the technical activities of humans which he calls 'technique', and the social arrangements which fuse apparatus and technique, which he calls 'organization'. Ultimately his own analysis tends to conflate these terms and it is striking how difficult it is to separate social and technical aspects. Clearly, the fluidity of definition does inhibit comparative research but does it pose further problems? The critical issue is really one of the explanatory value of the concept. That is, if technology is defined so broadly that it encompasses almost all aspects of the work environment then its explanatory power as an independent variable is minimal: if everything explains everything then nothing can be explained. Relatedly, many sociologists would want to argue that technology, *qua* apparatus, cannot explain anything anyway since technology is itself socially constructed and the effect of technology depends upon the use made of it. Still others would want to deny the apparent neutrality afforded to technology here, for rather than technology being inert it is seen as inherently political in nature: it is not simply a means to any end but a means that already encapsulates particular preferences (Winner, 1985). All these arguments, of course, resurface within that most slippery of agendas, technological determinism versus social determinism. What are considered in the first part of this chapter are both these polar opposite approaches and a third approach which seeks to rescue a limited role for technology where technology does not determine the resultant phenomenon but does affect it as one of several independent variables. Finally, and very briefly because I have already discussed it in chapter 4, I raise again the Actor Network theory which rejects the division between human and non-human actors and conceptualizes the two apparently discrete phenomena as fused elements in a seamless web: a human – technology alloy. This alloy itself is perceived as unstable and inherently contingent – it is constructed through the interpretative processes of actors and does not, therefore, embody any definitive capabilities or 'effects'. This approach, then, denies the 'technicist' perspectives where technology is regarded as an *independent* variable (of whatever significance) on the grounds that no objective account of technical capabilities can be constructed: such accounts are social constructions derived from, and subject to, the interpretative processes of actors. But this does not mean that technology is unimportant; it does mean that what counts as technology and how various rhetorics adopt particular forms of explanation are social constructions not concrete or objective 'facts'. In the second part of this chapter I consider arguments that information technology, amongst other things, has facilitated the construction of a radical new form of work organization: post-Fordism.

Theoretical Approaches to Technology

Technological Determinism

At its simplest, technological determinism considers technology to be an exogenous and autonomous development which coerces and determines social and economic organizations and relationships; it appears to advance spontaneously and inevitably in a manner resemblant of

Darwinian survival, in so far as only the most 'appropriate' innovations survive and only those nations and organizations that adapt to such innovations prosper. This is particularly prescient when information technology is considered, for the march of the microchip appears omnipotent and to deny this is to deny both reality and the future. Whether that future is to be one of Toffler's (1980) utopia or Burnham's (1983) Orwellian dystopia is secondary to the inescapable essence of the future. This perspective also has a long history as well as an apparently radical future, from Saint-Simon and Comte (Kumar, 1978), to the more recent arguments of Leavitt and Whisler (1958), Bell (1960, 1973) and Blauner (1964). While some of the more general discussions concerning technological determinism have sought to highlight the way technological advance tramples all before it, there are some rather more sophisticated résumés which leave a degree of freedom for social groups to manoeuvre (Pool, 1983; Freeman, 1987). Robey (1977), for example, argues that a more contingent relationship between technology and organizations exists in which organizations within unstable environments used computer technology to buttress a decentralized structure while organizations with stable environments used computers to centralized control.

However, technological determinism within the realms of the sociology of work is never quite what it appears to be. For example, although Woodward (1958) and Blauner (1964) are used here to illustrate the principle, neither is a cast iron devotee of the approach: Woodward's later work (1965) certainly shifted away from this perspective towards the middle zone represented in her case by the socio-technical systems theorists (see below). Blauner's argument, despite his attempts to pursue the hard line, actually provides evidence against this and, indeed, he rolls out a disclaimer at the beginning of his book: 'modern factories vary considerably in technology, in division of labour, in economic structure, and in organizational character. These differences produce sociotechnical systems in which the objective conditions and the inner life of employees are strikingly variant' (1964: 5). Nevertheless, he still maintains that 'the most important single factor that gives an industry a distinctive character is its technology' (1964: 6). At the opposite end of the determinist spectrum, social determinism, Gallie similarly slides from a strong anti-technological determinist position into a much softer version. He reports that although technology may not be completely irrelevant 'it is improbable that the characteristics of advanced technology are of any substantial importance in explaining the degree of social integration of workers within the enterprise' (1978: 300). Yet contrast this with his comment earlier that 'There were clear signs in both countries that automation is *conducive* to a certain degree of team autonomy' (1978: 221, my emphasis; see Clark et al., 1988 on this). Accepting, then, that the allocation of author to perspective is a heuristic device not an objective typification, it is apparent that this kind of approach tends to produce 'impact studies' in which the exogenous and determining role of technology produces 'effects' upon work organization and/or worker attitude and behaviour.

For example, Woodward's focus is upon the impact of technology on work organization and control structures, while Blauner's intention is not to explain the impact of technology on work so much as to consider the extent to which feelings of alienation are associated with different types of work situation. In particular, Blauner is interested in operationalizing Marx's concept of alienation and examining the relationship between alienation and the patterning of technological and organizational trends through time. For Blauner alienation is:

> a general syndrome made up of a number of different objective conditions and subjective feelings and states which emerge from certain relationships between workers and the socio-technical settings of employment. Alienation exists when workers are unable to control their immediate work processes, to develop a sense of purpose and function which connects their job to the overall organization of production, to belong to integrated industrial communities and when they fail to become involved in the activity of work as a mode of personal self-expression. In modern, industrial employment, control, purpose, social integration and self-involvement are all problematic. (1964: 15)

Alienation, then, has four related facets: powerlessness, meaninglessness, isolation, and self-estrangement. Each facet expresses a principle of fragmentation; that is, each contributes to the prevention of workers' activities and experiences constituting a wholeness. Given this, Blauner argues that it is possible to locate different work groups on each dimension of alienation and thus to build corporate profiles of experience. The four facets of alienation link directly to technology, or indirectly to it through the division of labour, which he regards as a result of technology. On the basis of secondary survey data on industries in the USA Blauner argues that technology, 'more than any other factor, determines the nature of the job tasks performed by blue collar employees and has an important effect upon a number of aspects of alienation' (1964: 8). For example, technology is alleged to: delimit worker control and freedom; determine the level of interest in a job; affect the size of the plant and the nature of work groups, and thereby influence group cohesion; and finally it patterns the occupational structure and skill distribution.

Moreover, since technology is inherently dynamic so too must be its effects upon alienation.

To map this differential and dynamic impact of technology Blauner focuses upon four organizations that he considers represent the basic phases of technological change over time, but which still persist in one form or another. Hence the original form of technology in the industrialization process was craft technology, represented by the printing industry, which, when the book was published in 1964, had little of the technology currently associated with it. Since the craft workers control much of the process of work directly, and have their considerable degree of freedom buttressed by powerful unions and labour market positions and integrating occupational communities, Blauner argues that this group's technology results in the highest levels of skill and lowest levels of alienation of all groups. In sharp contrast to this group are the textile workers, the machine tenders. Here the minute division of labour engenders a sense of powerlessness and meaninglessness, while the low status of the work is inimicable to any occupational identity. The consequence is a high level of alienation correlated with a low level of skill. Yet Blauner implies that alienation would probably be higher but for the strong community bonds that exist beyond the confines of the factory. The highest levels of alienation exist, according to Blauner, amongst assembly line workers. The technology of the assembly line not only fragments the experience of work into a activity whose only relationship to meaning is through economic reward, it actively stimulates conflict and precludes social integration. Finally, Blauner considers the process work involved in the chemical industry, the technology of which marks the return of skill, autonomy and control to the worker and the related reduction in alienation. Thus Blauner's model of technological development represents an inverted 'U' curve: the early pattern of technology, requiring high levels of skill etc., induced low levels of alienation; the transitional phase where the levels of skill and alienation were inverted; and the final stage where technological developments returned the pattern to its initial formation.

Despite all his protestations to the contrary, then, Blauner certainly appeared to conclude that technological developments, however mediated, generated specific forms of work organization and worker experience. As he sums up his approach: 'the character of the machine system largely determines the degree of control the factory employee exerts over his sociotechnical environment and the range and limitations of his freedom in the work situation' (1964: 170). Yet his analysis has been subject to a cacophony of criticisms. First, his data sources are dubious: they were gathered for other purposes, were already dated, and involved questions of job satisfaction that are notoriously problematic. For example, not only do questions of satisfaction depend upon transient economic and social conditions, but they imply criteria of satisfaction that are seldom explicit and even less grounded in normative consesus. Second, although Blauner's explanations are mobilized through the technology, not all workers in any single industry are engaged in identical operations using equivalent technology. Blauner makes much of the alienation prevalent amongst all workers in automobile plants as a result of the assembly line technology, but admits that only 18 per cent are actually assembly line operatives. Third, although Blauner's conceptualization of alienation involves four facets relating to different areas of control, he argues that the issues of ownership and major decision-making powers are unimportant, not because the subjects of the research say they are unimportant but because Blauner assumes they are unimportant. Even if we accept that Blauner's subjective version of alienation is qualitatively distinct from Marx's objective notion of alienation (i.e., for Marx it is an inherent and undifferentiated element of all capitalist societies and therefore immune to the articulated attitudes of putatively unalienated individuals), Eldridge is surely right to claim that expressions of satisfaction 'are not a sufficient basis for making general statements about the extent to which workers are alienated in industrial societies' (1971: 191). Fourth, Blauner's model of textile workers involves several problems: despite having technology that allegedly induces powerlessness and meaninglessness, the textile workers are represented as having strong integrating tendencies produced in and through the local community - an exogenous feature that Blauner underplays, if not actually disavows, in his theoretical assumptions about the predominant explanatory power of technology. Fifth, one might want to question the ahistorical basis of Blauner's argument which persists despite his concern for the importance of technological developments over time. In particular, it could be argued that to focus upon the *operation* of technology in itself is to ignore the historical introduction of the technology. Thus, what Blauner appears to construe as the 'effects of the technology' might be considered as the effects of management's success in securing control through the technology. For example, although the technology of assembly line production does appear to be inimical to conventional conversations it *need* not be if noise proofing was improved, or workers were provided with radio head sets, or periods on the line were interspersed with jobs away from it.

Nor does assembly line technology mean that group cohesiveness is necessarily undermined (indeed the opposite might apply where the collective experience is one of alienation) and, moreover, the reduction in social interactions may have been one of the intentions anyway: certainly Taylor (1911) was well aware of the problems appertaining to group solidarity and explicitiy designed his approach with this disintegrating effect in mind. Furthermore, the existence of assembly line facilities does not determine who controls its operation: Beynon (1975) recounts how workers could engage in all kinds of activities to reassert a measure of control: sanding the paint off trim lines to impress upon supervisors the folly of authoritarian line control or even organizing a 'rota': 'Eight of them contributed to a pool Every eighth week one of them took the Friday shift off, and got paid a shift's money from the pool' (148). Nor are assembly lines themselves the only way to build mass production vehicles; the Volvo experiments in semi-autonomous work groups clearly deny such a deterministic account (Aguren et al., 1984; Berggren, 1989). Indeed, as mentioned at the beginning, Blauner's data actually tend to contradict the technologically determinist thrust to his argument, and this is particularly evident in his discusion of women workers. His assumption is conventionally patriarchal and simultaneously self-contradictory. Thus, for example, he argues that 'women have, on the average, less physical stamina than men' yet completes the same sentence '[since] working women often double as house wives and mothers, it is to be expected that they would be more fatigued by their work' (p. 71). This is important not just because the double work of women inverts the stamina argument, but because the experiences of women within the textile mill can only be adequately explained by taking into account their domestic labour and relationships and by focusing upon the interpretation that women have of their jobs and technologies. In sum, technologies do not have determinate 'effects': how they are interpreted - and whether actors believe technologies to have determinate effects - is the upshot of contingent interpretations by the actors involved. Blauner actually admits as much, for as he notes: 'Objectively alienating conditions are more pronounced in women's jobs. Yet women are more protected from the self-estranging consequences of alienation because of their more traditional attitudes, their alternative roles, and their secondary commitment to the labor force' (p. 59). The crucial point for the argument here is not Blauner's unsubstantiated assumption that having domestic and non-domestic labour makes alienation less critical but that it undermines any assumption about technologically determined attitudes and behaviour. What needs to considered, then, is how certain groups capture technologies and form an alloy of human and non-human facets to further their own aims: management does not secure control over car workers by dint of personality or role-based authority nor by installing the technology of an assembly line; it secures (temporary) control by secreting its own authority into the assembly line and persuading the workers that managerial definitions of putative technical capabilities and limitations are the only legitimate ones. It therefore becomes impossible to analyse the position without focusing upon the human and technological facets simultaneously. The assembly line without management is as insecure, and indeed as incoherent, as management without an assembly line.

Of course, Blauner's arguments do not fall perfectly into the technological determinist category, and even if they did the weaknesses that undermine many of his assumptions do not, in themselves, eliminate the case for technological determinism; a poor example of a theory in action does not necessarily impoverish the theory, though if a theory consistently failed to provide the basis for adequate empirical accounts we would be justified in resisting the utility of the theory itself. Before we begin to cast further judgement on the theory let us consider another classic account in the same genre: Ely Chinoy's *Automobile Workers and the American Dream*.

Chinoy's account of car assembly workers in post-war America replicates the kind of arguments used by Blauner: the detailed division of labour which is inevitably associated with assembly line technology brings with it the dehumanising consequences of all such technology. Ostensibly, skills are minimal, social relations are almost non-existent, and the possibilities of self-realizing experiences are written out of the work process by virtue of the technology. The result is to create an entire blue-collar workforce without any intrinsic job satisfaction whose reaction to the work is highly instrumental: work is, and can only be in such circumstances, the means to an end. As a direct result the workers focus upon material reward and the consumer products it can be exchanged for; money becomes the only tenuous link between employees and their work experience. In short, the technology prevents self-realization and forces workers to substitute external consumption for intrinsic job satisfaction. There are clear reflections of Marx's claims here about the alienating consequences of work in capitalist society, and there are also ripples emanating from the general Hegelian tradition of work as *the* critical arena of life. Such implicit assumptions are, as has already been discussed in chapter 1, not unique to Chinoy (Offe, 1985: 129–50); undoubtedly, they form the staple diet of most industrial sociology where work is the key category, such that those not in 'satisfying' paid labour are, in effect, prevented from realizing their true humanity. Chinoy, however, systematically fails to provide evidence that the actions of the assembly workers are manifestations of some distorted spirit, rather than the primary intentions of interpretative actors. That is to say, Chinoy just assumes that consumerism is the result of alienation at work, rather than examining whether alienation means the same thing to everyone or whether what count as alienation might be the price individuals may be prepared to accept in order to pursue consumer durables or whatever else individuals prefer to do. Thus cultural pursuits outside formal employment need not be regarded as a response to the shortcomings of work induced by technology or capitalism or whatever, but as a legitimate priority in their own right; in this perspective the search for identity, not the quest for meaningful paid labour, becomes the criteria of satisfaction (Moorhouse, 1984).

So what? one might very well ask. Does the possibility that work may be secondary to identity, or that identity can be constructed beyond work, make any difference to the implications of technological determinism? If the search for personal identity is not inherently focused upon paid labour, and reflects neither the technology of production in isolation, nor simply the social relations of work, then particular attitudes articulated during the experience of paid labour cannot be related directly and solely to the technology of work. Indeed, they may well be derived, to some extent at least, from sources external to the work situation. As far as this particular chapter is concerned this means that we should be wary of assuming that the attitudes of employees in situations where specific forms of technology are present are technologically determined. Indeed, one might question why technology itself appears to reign so highly in research agendas: why do we appear to assume that technology *is* a critical facet of work but the climate or domestic concerns of employees is not?

This is not to say that work cannot be the focus of self-realization, nor that technology is irrelevant to the construction of attitudes; again, while social determinists would deny the latter, the fusion of social and non-social aspects poses inherent problems for either of these deterministic arguments. Neither attitudes, control structures, nor the form and use of technologies are determined, they are all elements in the negotiated order of work. As Woolgar (1989) has demonstrated, the technologies themselves are not stable entities with fixed and determinate 'uses'. Rather the entire design and development process of a technological artefact is socially constructed to the extent that the point at which an artefact is completed is itself subject to stabilization rituals. Technological determinism is seriously flawed, then, but is social determinism, the opposite approach, flawless?

Social Determinism

The opposite form of determinism is the social variety. This approach assumes that technological changes are themselves socially engineered and/or that work relationships are, in any case, derived from, and ultimately determined by, cultural and/or social aspects, rather than technological aspects (Gallie, 1978; Silverman, 1970; Goldthorpe et al., 1968, 1969). The problems of the technological determinist school were, for some authors at least, mere manifestations of a much deeper intellectual malaise. The issue at the heart of the debate was the social construction of knowledge: if the social world was qualitatively different from the natural world because of the essentially interpretative essence of social reality, then the methods and perspectives of the natural sciences were inappropriate to examine the social world. Social reality was produced and reproduced in and through the meaningful actions of subjective individuals to the extent that there could be no direct connection between allegedly objective structures and human actions and attitudes. Rather, all social action was mediated by the subjective and interpretative understandings of individuals, and by the social relationships between individuals. In the context of technology, therefore, what was important was the mediating and subjectivist qualities of actors, not the particular form of technology – the nature of which was in any case the upshot of social constructions. In short, explaining patterns of work relationships and attitudes would be a case of examining individual interpretations and socio-cultural variables not technological variables. As Silverman, the leading authority in the action approach of the time, put it: ' "objective" factors, such as technology and market structure, are literally meaningful only in the sense that is attached by those who are concerned and the end to which they are related' (1970: 37). Ultimately, Silverman's approach moved from what may be called 'mainstream' action theory (for example, Goldthorpe et al., 1968; Bowey, 1976) towards the more radically oriented ethnomethodologists. But between conventional action theory and ethnomethodology lies the intermediate version of Berger and Luckmann (1966) for whom objective factors were socially constructed, but once constructed they became objective and therefore determining. The more radical implications of ethnomethodology, however, were first explored under the mantle of Garfinkel, and represented initially by the works of Bittner (1965) and more recently by the studies of 'scientists' at work (Latour and Woolgar, 1979; Woolgar, 1988). This relativist approach, which denies the intransitive nature of 'objects', focuses upon the shared 'accounting' procedures through which individuals attempt to make sense of the world. Thus technology itself has no objective existence independent of the accounts given to it by individuals. It is, therefore, the practical reasoning which participants engage in that is crucial; the issue of whether technology does or does not have any independent effect upon work and workers is deemed irrelevant since it implies the existence of entities that exist independently of participants' descriptions of them.

Most industrial sociology does not involve this kind of radical relativism and it has had little effective impact upon the mainstream, conventional versions of action theory. One of the most influential early studies was that of Goldthorpe et al.'s *The Affluent Worker* series, which was discussed at some length in chapter 4. The important point here is to note the limited role played by technology as an independent variable in the construction of the typical attitudes of the affluent worker. For Goldthorpe et al., technology influences the level of intrinsic job satisfaction and the patterning of social relationships, but the general attitudinal and behavioural patterns are uncontaminated by technological environments. Instead, they point to the importance of exogenous factors, of orientations and attitudes constructed outside the factory gates, for explaining action inside the factories. As they sum up their approach: 'the orientation which workers have to their employment and the manner, thus, in which they define their work situation can be regarded as *mediating* between features of the work situation objectively considered and the nature of workers' response (1968: 182). 'This mediating, and externally created, set of orientations is self-evidently not the kind of argument put forward by the technological determinism of Blauner and Chinoy where attitudes directly reflect the technology of the labour process (see chapter 1 for further discussion of work orientations).

Perhaps the most useful account based in the action tradition which focuses directly upon the plausibility of technologically determined actions and attitudes is Gallie's comparative study of French and British oil refineries (1978). Since all the refineries were owned by the same company and used technology that was comparable between the two nations (though internally differentiated), technological determinism would imply close parallels between the actions and attitudes of the two groups of employees. Yet as Gallie concludes:

> The principal conclusion of the research is that the nature of the technology per se has, at most, very little importance for the social integration of the workforce. . . . Advanced automation proved perfectly compatible with radically dissimilar levels of social integration and fundamentally different institutions of power. . . . Instead our evidence indicates the critical importance of the wider cultural and social structural patterns of specific societies for determining the nature of social interaction within the advanced sector. (1978: 295)

For example, Gallie's evidence suggests that while almost all the British workers expressed satisfaction with pay levels, two-thirds of the French workers expressed dissatisfaction; while only one strike had occurred in the British refineries between 1963 and 1972, the French refineries had been involved in twenty four strikes; and while most of the British workers regarded their managers as technical experts, French employers were regarded as exploiters by their employees. How does Gallie explain the considerable divergences between French and British workers? Since the technology is similar, this, according to Gallie, rules itself out as an explanatory factor. In fact, Gallie argues that the difference results from three critical features: the more radical and egalitarian traditions of the

French political left; the more autocratic and authoritarian approach of French management; and the more centralized and politicized essence of French wage bargaining.

This, on the face of it at least, seems to seal the fate of the determinist school and of the approach which rescues technology as an independent variable from oblivion. But are there any problems with Gallie's account? Some issues certainly seem worth considering. First, to argue that *national* cultural and political differences override any technologically determined similarities does not necessarily mean that technology is irrelevant, and, as Gallie admits: 'it may nonetheless be the case that technology has some influence within a specific national context' (1978: 300). Yet this still implies an underestimation of the significance of interpretive processes and assumes that the technological and human forces can be separated. But oil refineries are not composed of human-less oil refining technologies any more than technology-less oil workers comprise an oil refinery. Thus, when we compare the oil refineries it is not the case that both British refineries are identical, irrespective of their different technologies, and the same applies to the French examples (the similarities are international rather than intranational, with the Kent and Dunkirk refineries having older technology and the Grangemouth and Lavera having newer technology). As an illustration we could consider the issues of satisfaction at work. Notwithstanding the conceptual and methodological terrors involved in measuring work satisfaction, it is the case that a smaller percentage of workers in the plants using old technology considered themselves 'rather happy at the idea of an interesting day in the refinery'. (The figures are: Laverna, 26 per cent; Dunkirk, 18 per cent; Kent, 34 per cent; and Grangemouth, 43 per cent: p. 86). Now this is not to assume that technology is a determinant of attitudes because the evidence suggests that the national differences are more important than the ostensively technological. But the point here is that the levels of satisfaction are not indentical within either country and, holding the country constant, they appear to correlate with technology. Since what counts as technology is an interpretative process the next step would not be to assume that technology has an independent effect but to investigate the way in which various employees adopt particular forms of explanation and description of the technology, and how such representations of the technology buttress or undermine other aspects of the Actor-Network. Under this umbrella, since we ought not to distinguish between the social and the technical, it is problematic to argue that one or the other has a discrete impact. Instead we need to focus upon the way the Actor Network is brought into play and sustained.

A related case might be the printing industry. For many years this witnessed the capture and holding in place of a network of printing machines and printers, which secured their control over the labour process and provided relatively generous monetary rewards. While this is no longer the case, because the new network of new technology and management displaced the old network, it did exist alongside related machinery processes in other industries where management and 'old' technology prevailed. Without the technology neither side in either industry would have been able to maintain a network of control but neither the technology nor the social group in isolation determined the result. In sum, I would actually concur with Gallie's assessment that technology does not *determine* organizational features or behaviour, and that social variables are important in explaining the differences between France and Britain; this does not, however, mean that technology is irrelevant.

The final example of social determinism is that of 'strategic choice'. This orginated in the criticism of contingency theory (see chapter 4) by Child (1972) for its determinist approach to organizational structure. Without going into detail here it will suffice to note that Child reproved contingency theory for ignoring the critical role played by powerful groups of managers who were in the position to manipulate their own environment. This political hue to the organizational process did much to bring people back in from the cold of structural variables and 'systems needs'. None the less, a stumbling block common to the action approach is the devaluation of socially constructed constraint: some actors may be more powerful than others but the choice of action is still limited by conditions and the power of others, particularly when these others have non-human and relatively intransitive form. That is to say, for example, that the explanation for particular decisions within organizations needs to extend beyond the political machinations of particular groups to encompass the way such groups appropriate and articulate forms of rhetoric about technologies. Whether management's arguments that an assembly line 'needs ' to run at a particular speed or 'determines' the work organization, then, should not be discounted as irrelevant to the actual decision making process because it actually underpins it: if workers can be persuaded by management that the technology determines the labour process, then in effect management control appears encased in steel. That it is actually contingent, that it could be otherwise, is a perspective delegitimated and suppressed by the power of managerial rhetoric.

Let us now turn to the middling theories that attempt 'to rescue the baby of technology without drowning in the technological determinists' bath water' (I. McLoughlin, 1990).

Political Technology and Designer Technology

Somewhere between the polarities of technological determinism and social determinism lies a disparate amalgam of approaches that concede to both technology and socio-cultural forces variant degrees of consequence (Trist and Bamforth, 1951; Winner, 1977, 1985; Noble, 1979; Wilkinson, 1983; Rose et al., 1986; Clark et al., 1988; McLoughlin and Clark, 1988; Pfeffer, 1982). What we have, then, are a variety of different approaches to technology that, suggest that 'the uses and consequences of . . . technology emerge unpredictably from complex social interactions' (Markus and Robey, 1988: 588).

One of the most significant practical advances towards this was the collaborative work of Rice (1963), Trist and Bamforth (1951). The Tavistock approach or socio-technical sysytem theory, as it became known, focused on the links between the technical system of production and the social system of work. The latter was essentially social not individual and, as such, technical production methods which undermined such social activity were necessarily problematic. Although a theoretical model of optimum efficiency could be construed from the technology of production, and a concomitant human model of social efficiency, the combination of social and technical systems inevitably produced a somewhat disjointed amalgam, and, equally significant, a system of disequilibrium. The trick, therefore, was to mesh the two in such a way as to develop an optimum socio-technical system that would, if separated into its component parts, not appear to be the most efficient use of resources, and not retain any long-term equilibrium. There was some disagreement about the significance of the economic system as a potential third leg of the theory, but the general position was that the economic system was a product of the functioning of the other two.

Armed with this composite approach, and an historical appreciation of the need for participatory groups, Trist and Bamforth began investigating the low levels of productivity then experienced by the National Coal Board [NCB]. It had been assumed by the NCB that nationalization, new technology and the production methods familiar to assembly lines would generate huge advances in coal productivity after the war but the opposite appeared to occur. The traditional system of coal getting, the 'single place' or 'composite work role method', involved a small 'marra' group of miners (two to six) in a semi-autonomous relationship to the management: all the miners were multi-skilled, the division of labour was limited and they operated relatively independently of direct supervision. The groups themselves were self-selected and paid as a group, but to ensure the equal distribution of good coal faces a 'cavil' or meeting of management and workers was held every three months to reorganize groups and redistribute coal faces as necessary. Such an organization, in conjunction with the inherent dangers of mining, ensured that managerial control over the actual labour process was minimal; the system was, according to Trist and Bamforth, one of 'responsible autonomy'. However, the introduction of machine cutters and conveyers led to the reoganization of work: the 'single place' system was replaced by the 'longwall method' which, as the name implies, involved a continuous face of coal to be cut by up to fifty miners in a triple shift system: the division of labour was expanded, managerial control was increased and many miners were forced to specialize in one particular facet of mining. The result was not an enormous expansion in productivity but an explosion of wage bargaining, absenteeism and a collapse of morale.

However, one pit had been experimenting with ways of saving some of the benefits of the traditional system of coal getting in a 'composite longwall method' and Bamforth's and Trist's research was conducted at the same pit. In the new system the self-selected group was reintroduced, albeit at a much larger level (around twenty five members), and the division of labour, which was itself restricted, was also the subject of group decision. The result were not just the restoration of morale but the advance of productivity and evidence for the new theoretical approach: socio-technical systems. According to Trist and Bamforth the problems of the longwall system were the result of the disjunction between the technological system and the social system. It may have been the case that an assembly line method of production was *technically* the most efficient but the destruction of the traditional social system and the shaping of the new system to the determining mould of the technology induced severe social problems that became translated as productivity problems.

Two major theoretical conclusions were drawn. First, that the social and technical systems had to be jointly optimized, thereby eliminating at a stroke the pretensions of the technical determinists. Where organizational problems occurred was in the misfit between the characteristics and requirements of the technological system and those of the associated social system. Thus: 'the technological demands place limits on the type of work organization possible, but the work organization has social, psychological properties of its own that are independent of the technology' (quoted in Elliott, 1980). As Heller (1987) recently argued, the problems occur when there is 'an improper application of the technological imperative' (1987: 23). In effect, the issue is that technology does not determine the social system but provides for 'options', that is 'choices based on particular contingencies' which may reconsider the 'impact of technology on people' (1987: 24–5). Given the significance of the interpretative approach to both social *and* technical issues it is evident that the socio-technical approach is gravely weakened by its assumption that technology still has certain determinate needs and objective 'effects' which necessarily constrain the appropriate social system. From the interpretivist perspective it is the contingent interpretation of technologies and their putative constraints and capabilities which is crucial for explaining the relationships to humans. Not only does the technology not determine anything, but the entire system is permanently threatened by instability: no naturally equilibriating organizational systems exist. Heller is right to deny the determinism of technology but to retain the idea that technology still has independent effects is to underestimate the significance of the interpretative component of human–technology interaction.

This also has implications for critics of 'participationists' such as Beirne and Ramsay (1988), for whom even involvement in the (re)design of jobs is of marginal significance and: 'The further into the (design and implementation) process one gets, the more time, money and solidifying thought have already gone into rigidifying the system, and the more residual any participative influences must become' (p. 217). The implication, then, is that managerial control can be built into the technical system through the design and implementation process in an unproblematic way. The point is not that this is irrelevant but that the use of any technology is a contingent issue and is not determined by the design or implementation process. If managerial control could be achieved through monopolizing the design and implementation process (either overtly or through some deceptive scheme of putative participation) then management would be a considerably less equivocal and ambiguous task than it actually is. Moreover, if managerial control could be secured through a duplicitous but invisible mechanism such as semi-autonomous work groups (SAWGs), one wonders why many managers continue to operate the crude and mechanistic forms of control currently in service today.

The second major conclusion of Trist and Bamforth in particular, and the Tavistock group in general was that semi-autonomous groups of workers provided the best structure for maintaining morale, defusing interpersonal frictions and therefore increasing productivity. The ultimate use of many of these ideas may have been overtly managerialist and productivist but it would seem fair to argue that the post-war reconstruction of *homo gregarious* was also an attempt to institutionalize the ideals of justice and equity at work that so many had just died for in the Second World War (See Rose, 1989: 92–3).

After the coal mining study, which was not adopted by the National Coal Board nor supported by the miners' union after a switch to national pay bargaining, a sequence of others was undertaken by the Tavistock researchers. From the study of Ahmedabad weaving sheds (Rice, 1958), it was argued that work ought to involve interdependent tasks and interdependent work groups. From the work in the Norwegian industrial democracy project (Emery and Thorsrud, 1964; Thorsrud et al., 1976), it was argued that optimum work organization would imply: job variety, group organization, worker involvement in decision making, the potential for self-improvement, and some self-evident relationship between jobs and the outside world (see Kelly, 1982 for a useful review).

Whatever the intentions of the Tavistock theorists, their impact, at least in Britain has been limited. Neither the NCB nor any other large industrial concern adopted the ideas. Yet they have had some success elsewhere, particularly in Sweden, Norway and Canada where the initial ideas have now merged into the Quality of Working Life movement that seeks to provide the kind of work experiences for all that are currently the property of the few (Sanderson and Stapenhurst, 1979; Witte, 1980; Zwerdling, 1978). Each have their own forms of participatory work organizations, and arguably the participatory form ranges from the most conservative, in terms of quality circles (Littler, 1985; Robson, 1982; Batstone, 1988a) which are primarily concerned with expanding forms of consultation, through to the radical end, probably the best known examples of which are the semi-autonomous work groups, some of which have consciously attempted to redesign technology in line with the social aspects of production.

Winner's (1977, 1985) argument, that 'technical things have political qualities' is a interesting example of this 'designer technology' approach. It starts out as an apparent emergent argument but is ultimately a form of technological determinism (1985: 26). What Winner is anxious to attack is the assumption that technology is neutral and, therefore, that the impact and importance of thechnology depends upon the use we put it to. In the context of this debate we could represent this argument, which Winner considers to be naive, as the assumption that the technology of the assembly line need not lead to repetitious and alienating work experiences. Part of the explanation for the rise of this naive view, in Winner's mind, is the distate for technological determinism: since it is not the case that social developments are driven by technological developments, it has become a commonplace to assume that technology has no impact in and of itself. Rather, technology is socially constructed. Yet this underlines their inherently political nature, for if technology is not the product of autonomous creation then it must become entrammelled in the political ribbons of its designers and users; and it almost certainly carries with it the unintended consequences that so often manifest themselves. One of Winner's own examples (1985) relates how the New York architect Robert Moses designed bridges so low that buses, and therefore the black and poorer white sections of New York, could not gain access to Jones Beach. What appears, therefore, to be the result of 'neutral' technological developments actually embodies the political preferences of the designer. Here, technological determinism reappears as 'designer determinism': control over the design and construction process of the artefact ensures the required result; or does it?

Contrary to the implications of 'designer determinism' - whether the poor are kept away from Jones Beach, and if they are whether that is determined by Moses's low bridges or something else - is also open to interpretation (Woolgar, 1990). At its most banal one might want to question *whether* the poor were deterred, and if they were *what* deterred them? Might it be that they had no desire to go there, or that the bridges were only interpreted as a minor impediment in a whole system or network of human and non-human obtacles? I might not end up at the Queen's Garden Party this year but it will not be just because the gates will deter me. Contrary to Winner's assumption, and others of 'technicist' inclinations, the preferences of designers, makers and users do not lead in any unmediated way to particular outcomes, for the position and power of current users mediate between design and outcome and are channelled in part by the unintended consequences of social life. What is crucial, then, is to retain the ambiguity of technology in the sense that organizations and social relations are determined neither by technology nor by social agency; organizations are the contingent result of a permanently unstable network of human and non-human actors. Technology and its properties are not fixed or determinate but contingent.

This is reflected in analyses that consider the relationship between gender and technology. Since this general approach incorporates the politics of technology it it also supports notions of gendered technology. Such concerns range from rescuing the role of women in the field of technological invention (Karpf, 1987) through to the links between technology and male domination on the shop floor. Perhaps the clearest example of the latter is Cockburn's (1983a) study of the British printing industry where, for example, the creation and retention of 50 lb printing blocks was regarded as effective in preventing women from entering the hand compositors, craft. Even the linotype machine, introduced towards the end of the nineteenth century, which eliminated many of the skills of hand compositing, failed to open up the craft to women as shopfloor control by male trade unionists prevented the entry of women. A similar pattern emerges in studies on new technology. In theory the expansion of keyboard skills through word processing and computer-based developments might be considered as providing an opportunity for women to break free from their subordinate position within offices and factories, but most of the case studies suggest that technological advance tends to buttress or even exacerbate gender-based discrimination (Barker and Downing, 1980; Liff, 1988; Webster, 1990). One area of overtly patriarchal dominance where women have made some headway, despite the predominance of technology normally associated with men, is engineering. Yet the efforts of the WISE campaign (Women into Science and Engineering) still face enormous difficulties in persuading women to take up such a challenge and persuading men to cease discriminating against women in general and female scientists and engineers in particular (Harding (ed.), 1986). In all these cases the crucial explanations illuminate the patriarchal, and therefore political, skin of technology. However, the texture of the skin is not a fixed feature: to continue the animal analogy, it is an unfortunate consequence for many animals that their skin can be reshaped to a variety of human related forms.

Wilkinson's (1983) case studies, while not concerned with issues of gender, detail the introduction of new technology in a variety of work situations. He not only attacks the 'impacts of innovation' or determinist approaches for their failure to account for variable adoptions and effects of technology, but suggests that technical features constrain but do not determine the possible options open to management. Particularly relevant for this form of approach is the 'technicist' notion that, irrespective of the social construction of technology, once the technology is constructed its technical capacity is to a large extent inscribed or encased into its fabric such that it operates as an independent variable. This, nevertheless, is still subject to two conditional assumptions: first, that the technology remains political; second, that its effects are still mediated by social action, structures and unintended consequences.

The most recent attempt to articulate a perspective bearing some resemblance to this ideal has been that of Rose et al., (1986), Clark et al., (1988) and McLoughlin and Clark (1988). Their studies of technological change in the telecommunications industry suggests that one form of exchange equipment facilitates individual working patterns while another lends itself more to team approaches, and that the relative impact of technological and social forces tends to alter the further away individuals are from the immediate work task. Technology in this perspective, therefore, becomes conceptualised as politically impregnated, as historically encumbered and as one among many potentially independent variables. But 'once the stages leading to the choice of a particular system are accomplished, then social choices become frozen in a given technology' (Clark et al., 1988: 32). This approach, I would suggest, which limits the social aspects of technology to the design process, underestimates the significance of the alloyed nature of technology. Inasmuch as technology embodies social aspects it is not a stable and determinate object (albeit one with political preferences inscribed into it), but an unstable and indeterminate artefact whose precise significance is negotiated but never settled. For example, telephone systems themselves were used originally to broadcast concert music and it was not axiomatic that the telephone would first be restricted primarily to a two-way personal communication system and now adopted to transmit digital communications between computers (Finnegan and Heap, 1988). Its use originally, and indeed its use now, was and is the result of negotiations, not determinations derived from the embodied politics of the artefact.

Actor Networks and Contingent Technology

Finally, let me briefly run back through the Actor Network model (see chapter 4 for a longer review) which has been adopted principally as a way of explaining the development and stabilization of forms of technology. Fundamentally, the approach suggests that power depends upon the construction and maintenance of a network of actors; these networks involve both human and non-human 'actors' and we should not distinguish between human and non-human elements but should talk instead of the 'heterogeneous entities that constitute a network' (Bijker et al., 1987: 11). That is, we should consider the unity of human and non-human actors in terms of a 'seamless web' as Hughes (1979) calls it or 'heteogeneous engineering' in Law's (1986) case. Actor Networks do not automatically maintain themselves, even though a viable method of extending the time span of a network is to inscribe it into material form. Rather, they, and their associated technologies, are inherently contingent and require constant reproduction and reaffirmation by the actors involved. For example, one of the ways the East German state managed to stem the haemorrhage of its population to the West in the 1950s was by building the Berlin Wall and persuading its citizens that the system was permanent and beyond challenge. This Actor Network linking the Communist Party, the armed forces, the Wall and associated border fences, and a proliferation of bureaucratic controls, was indeed interpreted by many as impermeable and its power appeared complete. The point that the Actor Network remained so solid for almost four decades but collapsed within a four-month spell in 1989–90 highlights the significance of the interpretative act: neither the political technology of the wall not the 'objective' power of the communist regime determined the state of East German society. When a large proportion of the population's interpretation of the power of that network altered so did the 'reality'.

Summary

Let me summarize this theoretical approches section not by regurgitating the essence of each of the perspectives considered but by linking the alternatives to the perennial debate on human agency reconstructed through a theatrical metaphor. The issue of technology and its importance for work and organizational change mirrors a much larger concern within social science on the importance that should be attached to human agency in any explanatory framework. In many ways the very essence of sociology is an attempt to grapple with this knotty conundrum: do people choose their circumstances or are they chosen for them? Are we simply players on a stage mechanically reproducing our various roles or is the perfomance really developed in a much more unpredictable manner through the interpretative skills of the actors? Relatedly, what part do the technical sets play – do they determine the production? do they just affect it? are they irrelevant? or is their importance again a result of the actors' interpretations and therefore a contingent issue?

The technological determinist school reflects the structural approaches that were prevalent during the 1950s and early 1960s, most notably in the guise of systems theories (Dunlop, 1958), and later the ideas of Blauner and Chinoy considered above. Here, humans simply reflect their structural position in some form or another, and the effect of autonomous humans is non-existent or minimal. Humans are merely role playing, and these roles are determined by the technologies of the stage. The reaction of many sociologists to this human automaton approach was first to push back the limits of structural determinism in all its forms and reconstruct a moral individualist approach to institutionalized individuals (Goffman, 1959), and then to draw the debate closer to organizational analysis through an alternative action approach (Silverman, 1970). Through the ideas of Goldthorpe, Gallie and Child this action approach not merely pulled humans back on stage to take their role amongst the structure of sets but actually began to suggest that the sets themselves were relatively unimportant given the significance of the performers. As such the technology itself tended to disappear from view into the proverbial black box. The third approach covered here, designer and political technology, is technicist in that it drags technology back on stage, but this time as one amongst a number of elements. It implies that although the sets on stage are socially constructed, once completed or frozen they have specific and identifiable effects upon the actors. The fourth approach, Actor Networks and contingent technologies, keeps the technical sets on stage but not as a determinant of organizations or change, rather as a critical element in an unstable and permanently negotiated network of human and non-human actors. For this approach what is important is not what the technology *is*, because this is always the subject of interpretations, but what difference such interpretations make to the eventual perfomance as a whole.

In the next section I want to pursue the analysis of technology at work by considering one archetypal form, the assembly line, in some detail. I will also assess the current proclamations of its untimely death at the hands of new technologies represented in post-Fordism.

Flexible Specialization, Fordism, Neo-Fordism, Post-Fordism

Although the assembly line is probably most closely associated with Chaplin's film *Modern Times* (1936), its roots actually lie in the Chicago meat industry of the 1890s. But the first assembly line production system was Ford's Detroit plant, set up in 1913. As with the earliest factories (see chapter 2), the original assembly line technology was not innovative at all. What was new was the organizational development in which the work was brought by a conveyor belt to the worker so the speed of task completion could be controlled by management through the technology itself (Gartman, 1979). Note again that the Detroit plant would not have been viable without the juxtapositon of Ford's managerial style and the technology. In conjunction with these organizational changes the division of labour was radically expanded along the lines proposed by individuals like Taylor. Whatever the success of Taylorist assembly line production, there were three inherent, and in some ways ironic, limitations inscribed into the very system itself: variable consumer demand, the counter-productive effects upon employees, and declining improvements to marginal efficiency. As far as Taylor and Ford were concerned the system appeared to be a virtuous circle: first, as long as consumers wanted, or more probably could be persuaded, to buy invariant products, represented most typically by Ford's single-colour single-model mass-produced model T, then assembly lines were ideal. They took a long time to set up and were expensive in technological investment which took advantage of the very high division of labour and associated cheap labour, but once running they appeared to churn out identikit products ad infinitum. Second, the assumption was that since workers were only really motivated by high wages then providing startlingly high wages would solve all labour problems associated with the deskilling and degradation of jobs so clearly described by Braverman. Third, as long as a scientific approach to work organization was adopted gigantic improvements in technical efficiency were feasible.

However, Ford found to his own cost that the division of labour, and what his employees regarded as the alienating conditions associated with such a production method, took a heavy toll of employee morale: labour turnover rate rose to 380 per cent in 1913 and the revolutionary Industrial Workers of the World moved in to organize the workers. Ford's response was radical: wages leaped up to the magic 'five-dollar day' in 1914, though even this ultimately failed to provide a permanent solution to labour problems. A second problem was that if work processes could be scientifically assessed and improved then there was a finite limit to, or at least a declining return from, the extent to which time and motion studies etc. could increase productivity. Third, 'Fordism', as this method of mass production for a mass market became known, also had limitations in so far as consumer demand was concerned: it was all very well persuading everyone to buy a car or even two, but a saturated market would require some form of dehydration if it was not to choke off demand and hence production and profit.

One part of the solution was and still is to stimulate variable demand, but variable demand requires variable production systems – hence the adoption of new technology to provide a quicker response to consumer demand and to generate different consumer demands. This new technology also required a more flexible and probably, therefore, a more skilled workforce. Again, what we have is a technological and a social form which are interdependent: flexible technology with an inflexible workforce does not lead to flexible production.

Neo-Fordism is often regarded as representing the alternative production system in which the stultifying rigidities of Fordism were eased apart to allow some degree of flexible production using new technologies to expand the range of products without modifying the tight managerial control structures (Sabel, 1982; Smith, 1989). However, this neo-Fordist solution to the problems of Fordism may be a transient one, or it may be a solution for particular forms of work in particular regions at particular times. After all, it is far from clear, and actually very doubtful, whether we can define all pre-neo-Fordist production methods as Fordist, hence it is not axiomatic either that neo-Fordism should be regarded as a solution to pre-existing problems or that it is prevalent in itself. Even where it does exist, and it is certainly the case that neo-Fordist calls for 'flexibility' and 'quality' are now vogue terms of the lexicon of business, there are many who doubt that neo-Fordism is the solution to the problem. For these people the problems lie much deeper than simply at the level of technology and reflect rather the very nature of Fordism as an organizational form, replete with its large-scale and cumbersome bureaucracies, its over-concentrated control structures and its over-centralized decision making.

The apparent long-term solution to the assembly line blues, post-Fordism or flexible specialization, implies that at the level of the organization it is necessary to decentralize, to become more flexible and to specialize. The solution at the level of the work place is to do away with the assembly line, to increase the skill levels and flexibility of the workforce, to provide team work structures, and to seek out specialized niche markets for high quality, high value products and services. Flexibility, then, is a critical component of the new models of working technology, but flexibility itself tends to combine two rather different forms: numerical/external flexibility and functional/internal flexibility (Atkinson, 1985; Streek, 1987). The former couplet refers to a company's ability to adjust labour supply to product demand and relates to the use of internal and external labour markets in association with the polarizing of labour use, as critical, and thus privileged 'core', workers are divorced from non-critical and hence disadvantaged 'peripheral' workers. The latter couplet, of functional/internal flexibility, refers to the company's ability to assign work irrespective of the labour involved: the more multi-skilled or polyvalent the workforce is, and the more they are itinerant, that is free from attachments to particular job, task or area territories, the more flexible labour is.

Post-Fordism or 'flexible specialization', which implies the use of new technologies to produce smaller batch, 'customized' products in contrast to the standardized products of the first two-thirds of this century, first made its physical appeareance in the late 1960s and its academic debut at the hands of Piore and Sabel (1984), though the same argument had been made by Reich (1983) slightly earlier under the term 'flexible system'. Whatever the term used, the notion marks the point of change both from 'Fordism' and 'neo-Fordism'. Post-Fordism or flexible specialization represents a rather ungainly mixture of craft-based work using new technologies within specific politico-industrial regions (such as the Tuscany region of Italy), combined with the more generalized adoption of new technologies within mass production industries to tailor products much closer to particular niches within the market. Thus the ultimate destination of this apparent transition between production systems is one which combines the flexible worker (polyvalent and itinerant) and the flexible production method (computer assisted, robotized etc.) both geared towards the flexible demands of the modern consumer.

As ever, there is a considerable degree of confusion and overlap between different terms involved in the debates but I shall retain the distinctions set out above: Fordism represents the archetypal assembly line production system with extensive division of labour and isolated workers using limited skills; Neo-Fordism represents a transitional form in which workers are required to become flexible through the use of multiple skills and multiple tasks; Post-Fordism, or flexible specialization, occurs when these multiply-skilled and flexible workers are engaged in production system which depend upon teamworking rather than isolated individuals, and involve a reduction in the division of labour and some flattening of hierarchical authority, that is, devolved responsibility for decision making (e.g. semi-autonomous work groups). The division between neo-Fordism and post-Fordism extends beyond the work place to encompass producer–customer relations, such that neo-Fordism is still premised upon Fordist mass production for international mass markets whereas post-Fordism implies a large degree of product specialization for specialized, and often localized, markets.

As so often appears to happen, the roots of these changes do not actually lie within the last decade but much deeper. For example, the quest to *develop* the consumption of manufactured artefacts, rather than rationalize the production process as Taylor suggested or simply *respond* to consumer demands, has a history that stretches back at least over fifty years just in the car manufacturing industry (Veblen, 1904; Sloan, 1965; Robins and Webster, 1989; Harvey, 1989: 126).

For example, just before the outbreak of the Second World War the British car producers (Morris, Austin, Ford, Vauxhall, Rootes and Standard) produced almost four times as many models as the American producers, but they exported twelve time less (Pagnamenta and Overy, 1984: 227). Unless we assume that British consumers were fifty years ahead of their time in terms of expanding consumer choice it is probably safer to assert that the market is actively created by producers rather than producers simply responding to consumer demand. That is not to deny the influence of the consumer but it is to rescue the significance of producer-generated consumer demand from the dustbin of preflexible production systems.

Relatedly, Smith (et al.'s, 1989) historical review of Cadbury's suggests that while flexibility of labour is a contemporary managerial ideal, there is little or no attempt to imbue labour with greater skills nor to extend the product range in line with apparently more sophisticated consumer demand. Yet Smith's own claim that the flexible specialization thesis is a variant of technological determinism is misplaced since Piore and Sabel (1984) are quite specific that product markets not technological determinism are at the centre of the paradigm shift. Nor does Smith's (1989) review of mass production in the food industry confirm that mass producers everywhere are cutting products and concentrating on a small number of items; they may be in food production but a glance through car magazines should be enough to persuade anyone that a multiplicity of options in body shape, engine size and performance, options packs, colours, ABS brakes, power steering, four wheel drive, four wheel steering etc., is the current trend. Perhaps the point is that different industries operate in quite different ways and a sectoral analysis is required. Similarly, Harvey (1989: 156) notes the declining half-life of products as neo-Fordist methods lock into rapidly changing fashions. Again, we have to be careful here. Motor cars have had their life expectancy increased considerably recently through the greater use of galvanized steel and plastics etc: the era of the rust-bucket in five years is gradually being replaced by the 'lifetime guarantee' already provided by Volvo, for example, using post-Fordist production techniques associated with semi-autonomous work groups. What we have, then, is not the replacement of one form of production by another but the development of parallel and juxtaposed systems operating for different kinds of markets. Diversity not uniformity is the more likely pattern because the market system is anarchic, because labour is recalcitrant and unpredictable, and because the Actor Network is unstable. Indeed, it is because capitalism is inherently unstable that such diversity is typical and it is this very diveristy which makes attempts to straitjacket the entire corpus into one pattern, Fordist, neo-Fordist or whatever, such a dubious procedure: what appears to be happening in one place at a particular time need not be read off from alterations in another place at the same time.

The three models, in so far as they are discrete, are often assumed to be evolutionary in pattern, with Fordism predominating until the late 1960s and early 1970s since when neo-Fordist inroads have been made which are themselves now being challenged by the post-Fordist approaches. Yet it has never been adequately demonstrated that Fordist technologies and organizational methods were ever predominant, and some countries such as Sweden and Japan in particular, have experimented with non-Fordist methods for many years. As argued in chapter 2 many British unions have a pre-Fordist tradition of single skills (monovalence) and demarcated territories (territoriality) which have protected them from the vicissitudes of managerial rationalization but tended to make British companies less flexible than, for example, the Japanese workforce. In fact, the Japanese system of sub-contracting adds another dimension to the flexible firm since sub-contracting allows fluctuations in demand to be displaced and dispersed away from the core firm towards its peripheral satellites. As the economy and industrial organization become progressively less stable and more dynamic, so, it is alleged, firms which are more flexible in a variety of ways will be better placed to ride out the economic storm.

The displacing strategy also implies that Fordist, neo-Fordist and post-Fordist models of work may continue in parallel form. Thus, the core groups and processes may develop multiple skills and flexible non-assembly-line production methods, possible in semi-autonomous work groups, while the periphery continues with the Fordist system. Certainly a dualist approach combining core and periphery groups has some support (Goldthorpe, 1984a; Harrison and Bluestone, 1988). But what may appear to be a rational and strategic long-term plan at the level of the economy more probably involves individual firms in ad hoc and very variable approaches to such a dualist strategy, at least in Britain (Batstone and Gourlay, 1986; Batstone et al, 1987). Indeed, one might question the extent to which concern for flexibility in any form has been translated into effective procedures and practices: all enterprises may be interested in achieving a polyvalent, non-territorial and committed workforce producing high quality products and services – but assertions of good intentions are not evidence of achievement.

The humanitarian implications of taking assembly lines out of commission and replacing them with more flexible, skill-oriented and computer-aided production systems are, however, supported by Piore and Sabel (1984), Reich (1983), Katz and Sabel (1985) and Piore (1986), who relate the changes directly to the fragmentation of the product market, and relate the work process changes to a wider decentralized and generally fragmenting socio-economic system. Of course the flexibility allegedly induced by neo-Fordism is not simply related to the freeing of labour restrictions in the form of demarcation disputes etc. Indeed, a complete corpus of literature has sprung up to contest the claims about the way firms have developed their labour market through expanding reliance upon peripheral labour in secondary labour markets (see chapter 7). Thus most of the recent growth in jobs in Britain has been in temporary or part-time work, primarily filled by women (see Hakim, 1990 for a review of core – periphery arguments)

It is worth noting just how such buzzwords as Fordism and 'managerial control' take on a life of their own within the pages of academic and business texts: for labour process theorists, 'managerial control, appeared to be the quintessence of all capitalism to the extent that profits appeared to be subordinate to managerial control over the labour process. Chapter 5 argues that the opposite is the case, that is that control over the labour process is subordinate to profit making, and the development of new working practices such as the semi-autonomous work groups in several Volvo plants could be taken as an example of both post-Fordism and the subordination of control to profit. For adherents to labour process approaches the critical question is what do such technological and organizational developments imply for managerial control over labour and the labour process? By definition, since the exploitation of labour can only be increased by the securement of more effective mechanisms of labour control, all such developments must be simply more sophisticated versions of control, as indeed are all aspects of neo-human relations or neo-Fordism. This approach to human labour, what Doray (1988) calls 'a rational madness', axiomatically indicates that labour is inherently problematic and in consequent need of coercive control by management (Kern and Schumann, 1987).

It is not coincidental, as discussed in chapters 2 and 4, that where systems of labour regulation are enacted which are premised upon recalcitrant labour the end result is often to generate precisely this kind of reaction amongst the workforce. If one of the causes of factory development was the lack of control over homeworkers then the organization of the initial factory was likely to embody strict coercive routines. The disciplinary mechanism of nineteenth-century factories are not, however, necessarily the most rational for a situation where employees do not have an alternative method of work to go to, and have already become accustomed to, if not exactly compliant with, forms of hierarchical authority. Concomitantly, when competition increases and flexibility of demand in the product market requires an equivalent flexibility within the labour market, that is a co-operative rather than an obdurate workforce, such Fordist systems become increasingly ineffective and inefficient. The problem, however, is that switching from one form of production to another is not simply a question of replacing the technology and altering the organizational fabric. Technologies of production incorporate histories, and one such as Fordism embodies the very traces of coercion and distrust that the more flexible systems attempt to transcend. Thus any company which announces that 'as from tomorrow morning everything will be different' is unlikely to impress a workforce with generations of experience that suggests nothing changes expect the siren calls of management.

This does not mean that Taylorist or Fordist methods were the only ones appropriate for the first two-thirds of this century, but they are no longer. Instead there are always alternatives available, as the Japanese systems of flexible working have shown since their industrialization in the nineteenth century: a pre-Fordist post-Fordism, one might say. But once systems are in place they accumulate patterns of routine and institutional privilege that make it increasingly difficult to change them. As Olson (1982) has argued, the longer an organizational system survives, the more sclerotic it becomes as privileged agents and groups surround themselves with material and symbolic forms of protection. Only when such organizations or system are shocked into reorganization, through war, revolution or plummeting membership or profits etc., are they in a position to change radically. In effect, then, Fordist technologies and their associated organizations of managers and trade unions grounded in the extreme divisions of labour are all locked together in the corporate system, and under such circumstances the intractable nature of Fordism becomes more understandable. Moreover, since trade unions, in Britain particularly, have conventionally tended to take a reactive stance towards management they have little experience or interest in work organization restructuring. The likely result therefore, at least where Fordist regimes exist and are being reconstructed, will be the construction of new working practices which further the objectives of capital without building in various practices to protect labour. If unions take no proactive role in designing work and its associated technology, no responsibility for ensuring the work practices operate properly, and are not the first point of reference for semi-autonomous work groups, it is not difficult to see that they may well find themselves, rather than their members, at the periphery of whatever post-Fordist developments might occur.

What semi-autonomous work groups and the like embody are methods of increasing profits and/or efficiency by increasing worker autonomy from management. Now self-evidently not all movements in this direction will be successful, nor will all enterprises want to go in this direction, but then neither are they forced into the opposite direction of decreased worker autonomy mirrored in Braverman's analysis. Nor, and this point is critical, need we assume that management is enamoured of production methods such as semi-autonomous work groups. Where worker autonomy is increased, albeit in the interests of, and dependent upon, higher productivity and profits, then we may well expect to discover resistance from line managers whose status, power and possibly even security, are threatened by such developments. The crucial issue is that most first and middle level managers probably derive little direct material or symbolic benefits from this form of production but this may be considerably less important to senior managers, board members and share holders than increased profitability. Some managers may be interested in managerial control, but they are a very heterogeneous group (Reed, 1989), and anyway, capitalism is driven by the quest for profits not the quest for managerial control.

The general argument also implies that flexibility is itself a disparate approach with some forms of work organization and their associated technologies, such as semi-autonomous work groups, considerably more autonomous and participative than others. Workers who are polyvalent can just as easily find themselves doing a number of different forms of work they regard as tedious without any increase in skill or rewards, as they may find themselves within jobs perceived as relatively meaningful, skilled and rewarded; the choices are constructed and executed through the Actor Network of human and non-human forms, they are not technically determined. This also implies that technical developments or social developments are unlikely, in and of themselves, to alter the nature of relations at work – in short, that class, gender and ethnic relations are, *ceteris paribus*, likely to remain and possibly even become strengthened under newer production systems (Walby, 1989; Jenson, 1989). Thus women may tend to make up the majority of any peripheralized work force while men continue to monopolize what counts as skilled work.

The emphasis on definition should also alert us to the social construction of categories like neo-Fordism etc. For the current band of neologist disciples it would seem that the reverential repetition of 'neo-Fordism' or 'flexibility' is endowed with magical properties: since the terms are so prevalent amongst the academic and business literature surely this merely reflects the explosion of interest amongst business enterprise? I have severe reservations about this: most businesses appear to be much less coherently structured than such concepts imply and much more intractable than business consultants might admit. We cannot easily resolve the problems by reference to the empirical data since so little exists and since the criteria by which flexible specialization is deemed to exist are inherently flexible. No study has yet marshalled sufficient evidence to show that the movement towards flexibility is an inevitable and universal process but then there were few attempts to do the same for Fordism either. For example, even those forms of work which we might categorize as most clearly Fordist, such as the assembly of cars, seldom involves a majority of the workforce actually on the assembly line itself (Marsden et al., 1985: 68–70). It is quite plausible, then, to argue that within the archetypal Fordist organization, only a minority of the workforce are subject to Fordist systems of labour control. This is important because so much of the debate is constructed around the polarizing axis of Fordism – neo-Fordism and post-Fordism. Yet if the most Fordist of industries neither represents the typical industry of its time, nor do a majority of its own workers operate under Fordist conditions, then we have to ask whether the debate should remain constrained by an axis that is simply atypical. Once we reject the basis of the debate, that is once we move beyond such a simplistic and erroneous axis of work organizations, then we can begin to assess where new patterns of work fit in. If we do not have to situate them either as Fordist, neo-Fordist or post-Fordist then we have freed ourselves from the tyranny of what may turn out to be a false, or at least, partial, typology. It way be simpler to operate *as if* the history of production could be compressed into one of three moulds but if the excess extruding from the moulds is greater than the material within the moulds then we should think about changing their size and shape.

As far as industrial production is concerned the debate over flexibility tends to concentrate upon the impact of skills. Since Taylor the orthodoxy, promulgated by Braverman amongst others, has been that only through greater extension of the division of labour will the economies of scale, the cheapening and controlling of labour, and the specialization of skills be achieved. However, the advocates of flexible specialization (such as Sabel and Piore), which involves inverting the division of labour, decentralizing production and seeking higher value added products, have argued nor merely that Taylor and Braverman were wrong in their belief that production could not be organized in any other way, but that the flexible specialization path offered up the opportunity to restore dignity and control to the workforce. Thus the interpretative position on flexibility and Fordism often expresses more fundamental political paradigms. For those supporting the flexibility option it seems that new market forces, new technology and the self-limiting features of Fordism have offered up the opportunity to restructure work patterns in quite radical ways (Mathews, 1989). For those who disavow the appearance of flexibility and who retain the Fordist perspective, albeit with neo-Fordist trappings, the changes are either irrelevant or merely another sequence in capitalism's permanent quest for profits. Naturally, not all who accept the Fordist or flexibilist ideas are Marxists or pluralists, respectively; there are many radicals and conservatives in both camps but nevertheless the tendency has been for the debaters to split along the radical/pluralist divide. A rather different approach is encapsulated by the so-called regulation approach.

The 'regulation school' (Aglietta, 1979; de Vroey, 1984) sought out the links between various facets of capitalism, including norms, habits and laws etc. (Lipietz, 1987), in order to analyse its patterns of stability or regulation. Where the social relations of the labour process were deemed 'appropriate' for the technology involved, which, in turn, comformed to the consumption patterns and social institutions, then the fabric of the whole network was held secure through this symmetrical and symbiotic form of regulation or 'regimes of accumulation' (Lipietz, 1987).

> A regime of accumulation describes the stabilization over a long period of the allocation of the net product between consumption and accumulation; it implies some correspondence between the transformation of both the conditions of production and the conditions of reproduction of wage earners. A particular system of accumulation can exist because its schema of reproduction is coherent. (quoted in Harvey, 1989 121)

Neo-Fordism was one such regime, deriving from the accumulating problems of Fordism in different levels of society. At the national economic level most capitalist countries ran into severe economic, and particularly monetary, problems in the early 1970s as inflation began to eat away at confidence and material wealth, and the various welfare systems looked increasingly precarious and deeply implicated in problems facing the capitalist states. At the level of the shop floor there were different manifestations of the same problem, especially increasing alienation amongst the workforce and the limitations of monovalent and territorial employees. These limitations are, under the regulation approach, derived not so much from the failings of the Fordist system as from the successes. Taylorist quests for the most systematic and scientific way of ensuring production have been followed to the extent that little more can be achieved by pursuit of such strategies: they are, so the theory goes, already as efficient as possible.

Harvey (1989) argues that Fordism failed to penetrate deeply into capitalism between the wars because it was so dependent upon the development of a new worker whose concerns were pecuniary and externally directed, and because Fordism was premised upon a level of stability and general affluence that did not arrive until the end of the Second World War. Certainly the New Deal, and the equivalent but radically reactionary policies in Germany and Italy, had been developed to transcend the problems of capitalist regulation during the 1930s but only the post-war boom provided the basis for the Fordist system of regul-tion, which also included a self-disciplining mechanism provided by the trade unions (1989: 125–34). This, in itself, may seem paradoxical since the capitalists of most nations had shown little enthusiasm for the regulatory value of unions. Indeed, the argument bears more than a passing resemblance to functionalist Marxist accounts through which all manner of phenomena that appear to disrupt the system of accumulation within capitalism are apparently essential to its long-term stability. Nevertheless, the significance of a regulation approach is that it highlights the symmetry between production and consumption: mass production delivers and depends upon mass consumption.

Quite by what criteria we judge a culture or production system to be 'mass' as opposed to 'individualist' is never clear. Certainly consumption patterns change, but this is a necessary corollary of a successful capitalist system of production and consumption and entails little about the direction in which it changes. After all, to take a paltry but perhaps symbolic example, the arrival of the electronic organizer and its predecessor, the personal organizer, may originally have been a mark of individualism but it is those without such contraptions that appear to be the individualists now. Products may be marketed as individualizing but profits are generated by massaging the consumers' individualism so that it exactly replicates as many other individualists as possible. Equally important, we have to question the assumption that the changes which have occurred actually do represent a radical break with previous production and consumption systems. As Kumar (1978) points out, the belief that a particular period marks out a radical discontinuity from the past is hardly new, with the assumption that automation marked a qualitative new era in the early 1960s being just one in a long line.

The response to the problems of Fordism was also at different levels. States began to cut back on their welfare systems and to introduce market forces into all areas of public institutions. At the level of the firm and economic sector, new products, new services and new methods of production were all attempted; some of which involved relatively minor adaptations of the labour process to suit the new technologies: job enrichment, quality circles and semi-autonomous work groups became popular, though for the regulation schools' approach these were merely attempts to patch up and reinvigorate the capitalist system of control rather than qualitative advances towards more humane conditions of work (Palloix, 1976; Coriat, 1980). Also important were heavy and repeated doses of market discipline for the labour force to induce some degree of flexibility as well as shaking out labour itself through mass unemployment.

None of this means that nothing is new. The development of information technologies and the closer integration of financial markets through the compression of time and space are self-evident alterations to the prior system, though the undermining of national sovereignty and the ever-closer networking of national economies, especially through integrated systems of financial credit, are probably more significant than the generation of new forms of profitable enterprise (Harvey, 1989; Held, 1989). What is important is to avoid the tidal wave arguments of Sabel and Piore without resorting to the Canute-like position represented by Pollert (1988). The point is not that everything has changed or that nothing has changed but that capitalism is inherently dynamic and fragmented in make up. Thus Fordist, neo-Fordist, and even an occasional post-Fordist technique, exist side by side, sometimes within the same product market such as motor cars. This clearly poses problems for regulation theory, which suggests patterns of symmetry between production and consumption, labour control and public policy. But the reality is never likely to be one where symmetry exists and always more likely to manifest disharmony, tension and contradiction in conjunction with their opposites.

Conclusion

This chapter has sought to illustrate two separate aspects of working technology: the theoretical problems of monistic accounts of technology at work and an explanation and critique of the current trend towards post-Fordism. At the theoretical level I have argued against both monistic forms of argument, social and technical determinism, which imply social or technological factors in isolation from each other can operate as determining variables. There are few if any forms of work that do not require a combination of human and non-human aspects to transform or create anything, and to separate the two out is not simply problematic but illogical. It is the forms of adhesion between social and technical facets in work, not the methods of division, which should be the focus of explanation. In the post-Fordist debate I argued that however tempting such simplifying and reductionist models might appear to be, the world of work was and is considerably more complex than any of these models suggests. This is not just because the empirical data for vertification is inadequate (though it most certainly is), but because the data are usually constructed through either of the monistic perspectives which I have already rejected as inadequate to the task. It is because we cannot read off developments at work through isolating the technological or social variables that the data are misconstructed. Only if we assume that the quintessence of the debate is the interpreted, negotiated, alloyed and contingent nature of social and technological elements can we even begin to account for the diversity of experiences of workers at work.

Bibliography

Abbott, P. and Sapsford, R. 1988: *Women and Social Class*. London: Tavistock.
Abercrombie, N., Hill. S. and Turner, B. S. 1980: *The Dominant Ideology Thesis*. London: Allen & Unwin.
Abercrombie, N. and Urry, J. 1983: *Capital, Labour and the New Middle Class*. London: Allen & Unwin.
Abercrombie, N., Warde, A., Soothill, K., Urry, J., and Walby, S. 1988: *Contemporary British Society*. Cambridge: Polity Press.
Aglietta, M. 1979: *A Theory of Capitalist Regulation*. London: New Left Books.
Aguren, S., Bredbacka, C., Hansson, R., Ihregren, K., and Karlsson, K. G. 1984: *Volvo Kalmar Revisited: Ten Years of Experience*. Stockholm: Efficiency and Participation Development Council.
Alban-Metcalfe, B. and Nicholson, N. 1984: *The Career Development of British Managers*. London: British Institute of Management.
Albrow, M. 1970: *Bureaucracy*. London: Macmillan.
Aldrich, H. E. 1972: 'Technology and Organizational Structure: a Re-examination of the findings of the Aston Group', *Administrative Science Quarterly*, Vol. 17, pp. 26–43.
Aldrich, H. E. 1979: *Organizations and Environments*. Eaglewood Cliffs, New Jersey: Prentice Hall.
Alexander, S. 1976: 'Women's work in Nineteenth Century London' in Open University (ed.), *The Changing Experience of Women*. Oxford: Martin Robertson.
Allen, I. 1988: *Doctors and Their Careers*. London: PSI.
Allen, V. L. 1981: *The Militancy of the British Miners*. Shipley: The Moor Press.
Alvesson, M. 1987: *Organization Theory and Technocratic Consciousness*. Berlin: De Gruyter.
Anderson, G. L. 1976: *Victorian Clerks*. Manchester: Manchester University Press.

Anderson, G. L. 1977: 'The Social Economy of Late Victorian Clerks', in Crossick, G. (ed.), *The Lower Middle Class in Britain 1870–1914*. London: Croom Helm.

Anderson, P. 1974: *Lineages of the Absolutist State*. London: New Left Review Editions.

Anderson, P. 1977: 'The Limits and Possibilities of Trade Union Action', in Clarke, T. and Clements, L. (eds), *Trade Unions Under Capitalism*. London: Fontana.

Andrle, V. 1989: *Workers in Stalin's Russia: Industrialization and Social Change in a Planned Economy*. Brighton: Wheatsheaf.

Anthony, P. D. 1977: *The Ideology of Work*. London: Tavistock.

Arber, S. and Gilbert, N. 1989: 'Men: the Forgotten Carers', *Sociology*, Vol. 23, No. 1, pp. 111–18.

Archer, J. and Rhodes, V. 1987: 'Bereavement and Reactions to Job Loss: a Comparative Review', *British Journal of Social Psychology*, Vol. 26, No. 3, pp. 211–24.

Arendt, H. 1958: *The Human Condition*. Chicago: The University of Chicago Press.

Argyris, C. 1957: *Personality and Organization*. New York: Harper & Row.

Argyris, C. 1964: *Integrating the Individual and the Organization*. New York: Wiley.

Aries, P. 1973: *Centuries of Childhood*. Harmondsworth: Penguin.

Armytage, W. H. G. 1981: 'Population and Bio-Social Background', in Roderick, G. and Stevens, M. (eds), *Where did we go Wrong?* Brighton: Falmer Press.

Arneson, R. J. 1987: 'Meaningful Work and Socialism', *Ethics*, Vol. 97, No. 3, pp. 517–45.

Arrow, K. 1972: 'Models of Job Discrimination', in Pascall, A. H. (ed.), *Racial Discrimination in the Labor Market*. Lexington, Mass.: D.C. Heath.

Ashton, D. N. 1986: *Unemployment under Capitalism: the Sociology of British and American Labour Markets*. Brighton: Wheatsheaf.

Atkins, S. 1986: 'The Sex Discrimination Act 1975: the End of a Decade', *Feminist Review*, No. 24, pp. 57–70.

Atkinson, J. 1985: 'Flexibility: Planning for an Uncertain Future', *Manpower Policy and Practice*, Vol. 1, (summer), pp. 26–9.

Avineri, S. 1968: *The Social and Political Thought of Karl Marx*. Cambridge: Cambridge University Press.

Ayres, G. E. 1988: *Social Conditions and Welfare Legislation 1800–1930*. London: Macmillan.

Bagwell, P. S. 1974: *Industrial Relations in 19th Century Britain*. Irish University Press.

Bain, G. S. 1970: *The Growth of White Collar Unionism*. Oxford: Clarendon.

Bain, G. S. and Price, R. 1980: *Profiles of Union Growth*. Oxford: Blackwell.

Baldamus, W. 1961: *Efficiency and Effort*. London: Tavistock.

Banton, M. 1983: *Racial and Ethnic Competition*. Cambridge: Cambridge University Press.

Banton, M. 1987: *Racial Theories*. Cambridge: Cambridge University Press.

Baran, P. A. and Sweezy, P. M. 1966: *Monopoly Capital*. New York: Monthly Review Press.

Barker, A. J. 1978: *The African Link: British Attitudes to the Negro in the Era of the Atlantic Slave Trade, 1550–1807*. London: Frank Cass.

Barker, J. and Downing, H. 1980: 'Word Processing and the Transformation of Patriarchal Relations of Control in the Office', *Capital and Class*, Vol. 10, pp. 64–99.

Barrett, M. 1980: *Women's Oppression Today: Problems in Marxist Feminist Analysis*. London: Verso.

Barrett, M. and McIntosh, M. 1980: 'The "Family Wage": Some Problems for Socialists and Feminists', *Capital and Class*, No. 11, pp. 51–72.

Bartos, J. 1989: *Marketing to Women – a Global Perspective* London: Heinemann.

Basoux, J. L. 1987: 'Women's Intuition and the New Vogue', *Times Higher Educational Supplement*, 17 July.

Batstone, E. 1979: 'Systems of Domination, Accommodation and Industrial Enterprise', in Burns, T. (ed.), *Work and Power*. London: Sage.

Batstone, E. 1985: 'International Variations in Strike Activity', *European Sociological Review* Vol. 1, No. 1, pp. 46–64.

Batstone, E. 1988a: *The Reform of Workplace Industrial Relations: Theory, Myth and Evidence*. Oxford: Clarendon.

Batstone, E. 1988b: 'The Frontier of Control', in Gallie, D. (ed.), *Employment in Britain*. Oxford: Blackwell.

Batstone, E., Boraston, I. and Frenkel, S. 1977: *Shop Stewards in Action*. Oxford: Blackwell.

Batstone, E., Boraston, I. and Frenkel, S. 1978: *The Social Organization of Strikes*. Oxford: Blackwell.

Batstone, E., Ferner, A. and Terry, M. 1983: *Unions on the Board*. Oxford: Blackwell.

Batstone, E., Ferner, A. and Terry, M. 1984: *Consent and Efficiency*. Oxford: Blackwell.

Batstone, E. and Gourlay, S. 1986: *Unions, Unemployment and Innovation*. Oxford: Blackwell.

Batstone, E., Gourlay, S., Levie, H. and Moore, R. 1987: *New Technology and the Process of Labour Regulation*. Oxford: Clarendon.

Baumgartner, T., Burns, T. R. and DeVille, P. 1979: 'Work, Politics and Social Structuring Under Capitalism', in Burns, T., Karlsson, L. A. and Rus, V. (eds), *Work and Power*. London: Sage.

BBC. 1988: *Newsnight*, 21 September.

Bean, R. and Stoney, P. 1986: 'Strikes on Merseyside', *Industrial Relations Journal*, Vol. 17, No. 1, pp. 9–23.

Beavis, S. 1988: *The Guardian*, 4 March.

Beavis, S. 1989: *The Guardian*, 12 May.

Becker, G. 1985: 'Human Capital, Effort, and the Sexual Division of Labour', *Journal of Labour Economics* Vol. 3, pp. 33–58.

Beechey, V. 1986: *Women and Employment*. Milton Keynes: Open University Press.

Beechey, V. and Perkins, T. 1987: *A Matter of Hours: Women, Part-time Work and the Labour Market*. Cambridge: Polity Press.

Beetham, D. 1987: *Bureaucracy*. Milton Keynes: Open University Press.

Behagg, C. 1990: *Politics and Production in the Early Nineteenth Century*. London: Routledge.

Beirne, M. and Ramsay, H. 1988: 'Computer Redesign and Labour Process Theory', in Knights, D. and Willmott, H. (eds), *New Technology and the Labour Process*. London: Macmillan.

Bell, D. 1960: *The End of Ideology*. Glencoe, Ill.: The Free Press.

Bell, D. 1973: *The Coming of Post-Industrial Society*. New York: Basic Books.

Bentham, J. 1977: 'Labour and Repose', in Clayre, A. (ed.), *Nature and Industrialization*. Oxford: Oxford University Press.

Berg, M. 1980: *The Machinery Question and the Making of Political Economy 1815–1848*. Cambridge: Cambridge University Press.

Berg, M. 1985: *The Age of Manufactures 1700–1820*. London: Fontana.

Berg, M. 1987: 'Women's Work and Mechanization', in Joyce, P. (ed.), *The Historical Meanings of Work*. Cambridge: Cambridge University Press.

Berg, M. 1988a: 'Workers and Machinery in Eighteenth Century England', in Rule, J. (ed.), *British Trade Unionism 1750–1850*. London: Longman.

Berg, M. 1988b: 'Women's Work, Mechanization and Early Industrialization', in Pahl, R.E. (ed.), *On Work*. Oxford: Blackwell.

Berger, P. and Luckmann, T. 1966: *The Social Construction of Reality*. New York: Doubleday.

Berger, S. and Piore, M. 1980: *Dualism and Discontinuity in Industrial Societies*. Cambridge: Cambridge University Press.

Berggren, C. 1989: 'New Production Concepts in Final Assembly - the Swedish Experience' in Wood, S. (ed.), *The Transformation of Work*? London: Unwin Hyman.

Berk, R. and Berk, S. F. 1979: *Labour and Leisure at Home*. London: Sage.

Berle, A. A. and Means, G. C. 1968: *The Modern Corporation and Private Property*. New York: Macmillan.

Bernstein, R. J. 1983: *Beyond Objectivism and Relativism*. Oxford: Blackwell.

Bertalanffy, L. 1981: 'General Systems Theory – a Critical Review', in Open Systems Group (eds), *Systems Behaviour*. London: Harper & Row.

Best, G. 1979: *Mid-Victorian Britain 1851–75*. London: Fontana.

Beynon, H. 1975: *Working for Ford*. Wakefield: EP Publishing.

Beynon, H. and Blackburn, R. 1984: 'Unions: the Men's Affair?', in Siltanen, J. and Stanworth, M. (eds), *Women and the Public Sphere*. London: Hutchinson.

Bhavnani, K. K. and Bhavnani, R. 1985: 'Racism and Resistance in Britain', in Coates, D., Johnston, G. and Bush, R. (eds), *A Socialist Anatomy of Britain*. Cambridge: Polity Press.

Bijker, W. E., Hughes, T. P. and Pinch, T. (eds), 1987: *The Social Construction of Technological Systems*. Cambridge, Mass.: MIT Press.

Bittner, E. 1965: 'The Concept of Organization', *Social Research*, Vol. 32, No. 3, pp. 239–55.

Blackburn, R. and Mann, M. 1979: *The Working Class in the Labour Market*. London: Macmillan.
Blauner, R. 1964: *Alienation and Freedom*. Chicago: Chicago University Press.
Blumberg, P. 1968: *Industrial Democracy*. London: Constable.
Blythe, R. 1969: *Akenfield*. Harmondsworth: Penguin.
BMRB (British Market Research Bureau) 1988: *Target Group Index Survey*. London: BMRB.
Bogdanor, V. 1990: *Women at the Top*. London: Hansard Society.
Bohning, W. 1972: *The Migration of Workers in the United Kingdom and the European Community*. Oxford: Oxford University Press/Institute of Race Relations.
Bonnell, V.E. 1984: *Roots of Rebellion: Workers' Politics and Organization in St. Petersburg and Moscow 1900–1914*. Berkeley: University of California Press.
Bonney, N. 1988: 'Dual Earning Couples: Trends of Change in Great Britain', *Work, Employment and Society*, Vol. 2, No. 1, pp. 89–102.
Boseley, S. 1987: *The Guardian*, 27 June.
Boston, S. 1987: *Women Workers and the Trade Unions*. London: Lawrence & Wishart.
Boston, T.D. 1988: *Race, Class and Conservatism*. London: Unwin Hyman.
Bostyn, A. and Wight, D. 1987: 'Inside a Community: Values Associated with Money and Time', in Fineman, S. (ed.), *Unemployment: Personal and Social Consequences*. London: Tavistock.
Bott, E. 1971: *Family and Social Network*. London: Tavistock.
Bouchier, D. 1983: *The Feminist Challenge: the Movement for Women's Liberation in Britain and the United States*. London: Macmillan.
Bourdieu, P. 1979: *Algeria 1960*. Cambridge: Cambridge University Press.
Bowey, A. 1976: *The Sociology of Organizations*. London: Hodder & Stoughton.
Bowles, M.L. 1989: 'Myth, Meaning and Work Organization', *Organization Studies*, Vol. 10, No. 3, pp. 405–21.
Braham, P. 1980: *Class, Race and Immigration*. Milton Keynes: Open University Press.
Braham, P., Rhodes, E. and Pearn, M. (eds), 1981: *Discrimination and Disadvantage in Employment*. London: Harper & Row.
Brannen, J. and Wilson, G. 1987: *Give and Take in Families*. London: Allen & Unwin.
Brannen, P., Batstone, E. V., Fatchett, D. and White, P. 1976: *The Worker Directors: a Sociology of Participation*. London: Hutchinson.
Braverman, H. 1974: *Labor and Monopoly Capital*. New York: Monthly Review Press.
Braybon, G. 1981: *Women Workers in the First World War*. London: Croom Helm.
Brennan, J. and McGeevor, P. 1987: *Employment of Graduates from Ethnic Minorities*. London: CRE.
Briggs, A. 1955: *Victorian People*. Harmondsworth: Penguin.
Brighton Labour Process Group. 1977: 'The Capitalist Labour Process', *Capital and Class*, Vol. 1, pp. 3–42.
Brindle, D. 1989: *The Guardian*, 27 November.

Brittan, A. and Maynard, M. 1984: *Sexism, Racism and Oppression*. Oxford: Blackwell.

Brooks, D. and Singh, K. 1978–9: 'Ethnic Commitment Versus Structural Reality: South Asian Immigrant Workers in Britain', *New Community*, Vol. 8, No. 1, pp. 19–30.

Brooks, D. and Singh, K. 1979: 'Pivots and Presents: Asian Brokers in British Foundries', in Wallman, S. (ed.), *Ethnicity of Work*. London: Macmillan.

Brown, C. 1984: *Black and White Britain: the Third PSI Survey*. London: Heinemann/PSI.

Brown, D. and Harrison, M. J. 1978: *A Sociology of Industrialization*. London: Macmillan.

Brown, G. 1988: *The Guardian*, 17 March.

Brown, P. 1977: *Sabotage*. Nottingham: Spokesman.

Brown, R. 1973: 'Sources of Objectives in Work and Employment', in Child, J. (ed.), *Man and Organization*. London: Allen & Unwin.

Brown, R. 1974: 'The Attitude to Work, Expectations and Social Perspectives of Shipbuilding Apprentices', in Leggatt, T. (ed.), *Sociological Theory and Survey Research*. London: Sage.

Brown, R. 1978: 'Work', in Abrams, P. (ed.), *Work, Urbanism and Inequality*. London: Weidenfeld & Nicolson.

Brown, R. 1982: 'Work Histories, Career Strategies and the Class Structure,' in Giddens, A. and Mackenzie, G. (eds), *Social Class and the Division of Labour*. Cambridge: Cambridge University Press.

Brown, R. 1988: 'The Employment Relationship in Sociological Theory', in Gallie, D. (ed.), *Employment in Britain*. Oxford: Blackwell.

Brown, S. and Clayre, A. 1978: *Work, Morality and Human Nature*. Milton Keynes: Open University Press.

Brown, W. (ed.), 1981: *The Changing Contours of British Industrial Relations*. Oxford: Blackwell.

Brown, W. and Wadhwani, S. 1990: 'The Economic Effects of Industrial Relations Legislation since 1979', *National Institute Economic Review*, Feb., pp. 57–70.

Brownmiller, S. 1976: *Against Our Will: Men, Women and Rape*. Harmondsworth: Penguin.

Bruegel, I. 1983: 'Women's employment, legislation and the labour market', in Lewis, J. (ed.), *Women's Welfare, Women's Rights*. London: Croom Helm.

Bruegel, I. 1989: 'Sex and Race in the Labour Market', *Feminist Review*, No. 32 (summer) pp. 47–68.

Bruland, T. 1982: 'Industrial Conflict as a Source of Technical Innovation', *Economy and Society*, Vol. 11, pp. 91–121.

Buchanan, D. A. and Boddy, D. 1983: *Organizations in the Computer Age: Technological Imperatives and Strategic Choice*. Aldershot: Gower.

Buchanan, D. A. and Huczynski, A. A. 1985: *Organizational Behaviour: an Introductory Text*. London: Prentice Hall.

Buckland, S. and MacGregor, S. 1987: 'Discouraged Workers? The Long Term Unemployed and the Search for Work', in Fineman, S. (ed.), *Unemployment: Personal and Social Consequences*. London: Tavistock.

Buick, A. and Crump, J. 1986: *State Capitalism: the Wages System under New Management*. London: Macmillan.
Bularzik, M. 1978: 'Sexual Harassment at the Workplace', *Radical America*, Vol. 12, pp. 25–43.
Burawoy, M. 1979: *Manufacturing Consent*. Chicago: University of Chicago Press.
Burawoy, M. 1985: *The Politics of Production*. London: Verso.
Burawoy, M. and Lukacs, J. 1989: 'What is Socialist about Socialist Production?: Autonomy and Control in a Hungarian Steel Mill', in Wood, S. (ed.), *The Transformation of Work?* London: Unwin Hyman.
Burgess, K. 1980: *The Challenge of Labour*. London: Croom Helm.
Burgess, R. G. 1986: *Sociology, Education and Schools*. London: Batsford.
Burnett, J. (ed.) 1984: *Useful Toil: Autobiographies of Working People from the 1820s to the 1920s*. London: Allen Lane.
Burnett, J. 1990: Personal communication.
Burnham, D. 1983: *The Rise of the Computer State*. London: Wiedenfeld & Nicolson.
Burnham, J. 1962: *The Managerial Revolution*. London: Macmillan.
Burns; T. and Stalker, G. M. 1961: *The Management of Innovation*. London: Tavistock.
Burrell, G. 1988: 'Modernism, Postmodernism and Organizational Analysis 2: the Contribution of Michel Foucault', *Organization Studies*, Vol. 9, No. 2, pp. 221–35.
Burrell, G. and Morgan, G. 1979: *Sociological Paradigms and Organizational Analysis*. Aldershot: Gower.
Burris, B. H. 1989: 'Technocratic organization and control', *Organization Studies*, Vol. 10, No. 1, pp. 1–22.
Callinicos, A. 1983: *The Revolutionary Ideas of Marx*. London: Bookmarks.
Callon, M. 1986: 'The Sociology of an Actor Network', in Callon, M., Law, J. and Rip, A. (eds), *Mapping the Dynamics of Science and Technology*. London: Macmillan.
Campbell, B. 1982a: 'Power not Pin Money', *New Socialist*, July–August.
Campbell, B. 1982b: 'Women: Not What they Bargained For', *Marxism Today*, March.
Carey, A. no date. *A Sociological Critique of Industrial Psychology and Sociology*. mimeo., University of New South Wales.
CARF (Campaign Against Racism and Fascism). 1981: *Southhall: the Birth of a Black Community*. London: Institute of Race Relations.
Carlyle, T. 1977: 'The Mechanical Age', in Clayre, A. (ed.), *Nature and Civilization*. Oxford: Oxford University Press.
Carroll, D. T. 1983: 'A Disappointing Search for Excellence', *Harvard Business Review*, Nov.-Dec.
Castles, S. and Kosack, G. 1973: *Immigrant Workers and Class Structure in Western Europe*. London: Oxford University Press.
Cavendish, R. 1982: *Women on the Line*. London: Routledge.
Central London Community Law Centre. 1987: *Organizing as Women Trade Unionists*. London: CLCLC.

Centre for Contemporary Cultural Studies. 1982: *The Empire Strikes Back*. London: Hutchinson.

Centre for Employment Research. 1990: *Ethnic Minority Businesses and Employment in Greater Manchester*. Manchester Polytechnic.

Chadwick, E. 1842: 'Report on the Sanitary Condition of the Labouring Population', in Ward, J. T. (ed.), 1970: *The Factory System*. Newton Abbot: David & Charles.

Chadwick, N. 1970: *The Celts*. Harmondsworth: Penguin.

Chandler, A. D. 1962: *Strategy and Structure: Chapters in the History of the American Industrial Enterprise*. Cambridge, Mass.: MIT Press.

Channon, D. 1973: *The Strategy and Structure of British Enterprise*. Cambridge, Mass.: Harvard University Press.

Chapman, S. D. 1972: *The Cotton Industry in the Industrial Revolution*. London: Macmillan.

Child, J. 1969: *British Management Thought*. London: Allen & Unwin.

Child, J. 1972: 'Organizational Structure, Environment and Performance', *Sociology*, Vol. 6, No. 1, pp. 1–22.

Chinoy, E. 1955: *Automobile Workers and the American Dream*. New York: Doubleday.

Chiplin, B. and Grieg, N. 1986: *Equality of Opportunity for Women in the NHS*. London: DHSS mimeo.

Chiplin, B. and Sloane, P. J. 1974: 'Sexual Discrimination in the Labour Market', *British Journal of Industrial Relations*, Vol. 12, No. 3, pp. 371–402.

Christie, I. R. 1984: *Stress and Stability in Late Eighteenth Century Britain*. Oxford: Clarendon.

Clark, A. 1982: *Working Life of Women in the Seventeenth Century*. London: Routledge.

Clark, D. Y. 1987: 'Families Facing Redundancy', in Fineman, S. (ed.), *Unemployment: Personal and Social Consequences*. London: Tavistock.

Clark, J., Mcloughlin, I., Rose, H. and King, R. 1988: *The Process of Technological Change: New Technology and Social Choice in the Workplace*. Cambridge: Cambridge University Press.

Clayre, A. (ed.) 1977: *Nature and Industrialization*. Oxford: Oxford University Press.

Clegg, H. A. 1976: *Trade Unionism Under Collective Bargaining*. Oxford: Blackwell.

Clegg, H. A. 1979: *The Changing System of Industrial Relations in Great Britain*. Oxford: Blackwell.

Clegg, S. 1989: *Frameworks of Power*. London: Sage.

Clegg, S. and Dunkerley, D. 1980: *Organization, Class and Control*. London Routledge.

Clutterbuck, D. and Crainer, S. 1989: *Men and Women who Changed Management*. London: Macmillan.

Coates, D. 1984: *The Context of British Politics*. London: Hutchinson.

Coates, D. and Johnston, G. (eds). 1983: *Socialist Strategies*. Oxford: Martin Robertson.

Cockburn, C. 1983a: *Brothers: Male Dominance and Technological Change*. London: Pluto.

Cockburn, C. 1983b: 'Caught in the Wheels', *Marxism Today*, pp. 16–20. November.
Cockburn, C. 1986: *Training for Her Job and for His*. London: EOC.
Cockburn, C. 1987a: *Two-Track Training: Sex Inequalities and the YTS*. London: Macmillan.
Cockburn, C. 1987b: *Women, Trade Unions and Political Parties*. London: Fabian Research Series, No. 349.
Cohen, A. P. 1979: 'The Whalsey Croft', in Wallman, S. (ed.), *Social Anthropology of Work*. Cambridge: Cambridge University Press.
Cohen, I. J. 1989: *Structuration Theory: Anthony Giddens and the Constitution of Social Life*. London: Macmillan.
Cohen, R. 1988: *The New Helots: Migrants in the International Division of Labour*. Aldershot: Gower.
Cohn, S. 1985: *The Process of Occupational Sex-Typing*. Philadelphia: Temple University Press.
Cole, G. D. H. 1955: Miscellaneous Documents on Guild Socialism, *The Cole Collection*, Nuffield College, Boxes B/3/3/E; B/3/5/B.
Cole, G. D. H. and Postgate, R. 1938: *The Common People*. London: Methuen.
Coleman, D. C. 1975: *Industry in Tudor and Stuart England*. London: Macmillan.
Collinson, D. L. 1987: *Barriers to Fair Selection*. London: EOC/HMSO.
Commission for Industrial Relations. 1974: *Mansfield Hosiery Mills Ltd*. Report No. 76. London: HMSO.
Commission for Racial Equality. 1981: *BL Cars Ltd . . . Report of a Formal Investigation*. London: CRE.
Commission for Racial Equality. 1987: *Chartered Accountancy Training Contracts*. London: CRE.
Commission for Racial Equality. 1988a: *Ethnic Minority School Teachers*. London: CRE.
Commission for Racial Equality. 1988b: *Learning in Terror: a Survey of Racial Harassment in Schools and Colleges*. London: CRE.
Commission for Racial Equality. 1990: *From Cradle to Grave*. London: CRE.
Confederation of British Industry. 1970: *Race Relations in Employment: Advice to Employers*. London: CBI.
Confederation of British Industry. 1981: 'Statement and Guide on General Principles and Practice', in Braham, P. et al., *Discrimination and Disadvantage in Employment*. London: Harper & Row.
Cooley, M. 1980: 'Computerization: Taylor's Latest Disguise', *Economic and Industrial Democracy*, Vol. 1, pp. 523–39.
Cooper, R. 1986: 'Organization Disorganization', *Social Science Information*, Vol. 25, No. 2, pp. 299–335.
Cooper, R. 1989: 'Modernism, Post Modernism and Organizational Analysis 3: the Contribution of Jaques Derrida', *Organization Studies*, Vol. 10, No. 4, pp. 479–502.
Cooper, R. and Burrell, G. 1988: 'Modernism, Postmodernism and Organizational Analysis', *Organization Studies*, Vol. 9, No. 1, pp. 91–112.
Coriat, B. 1980: 'The Restructuring of the Assembly Line', *Capital and Class*, Vol. 11, pp. 34–43.

Cornelius, A. *The Guardian*, 27 October.

Cotgrove, S. and Box, S. 1970: *Science, Industry and Society*. London: Allen & Unwin.

Cowan, R. S. 1983: *More Work for Mother: the Ironies of Household Technology from the Open Hearth to the Microwave*. New York: Basic Books.

Craft, M. and Craft, A. 1983: 'The Participation of Ethnic Minority Pupils in Further and Higher Education', *Educational Review*, Vol. 25, No. 1, pp. 10–19.

Crafts, N. F. R. 1985: *British Economic Growth During the Industrial Revolution*. Oxford: Oxford University Press.

Craib, I. 1984: *Modern Social Theory*. Brighton: Wheatsheaf.

Craig, C., Rubery, J. Tarling, R. and Wilkinson, F. 1982: *Labour Market Structure, Industrial Organization and Low Pay*. Cambridge: Cambridge University Press.

Crehan, K. 1986: 'How the Other Half Works', in Epstein, T. S., Crehan, K., Gerzer, A. and Sass, J. (eds), *Women Work and the Family in Britain and Germany*. London: Croom Helm.

Cressey, P. and McInnes, J. 1980: 'Voting for Ford: Industrial Democracy and the Control of Labour', *Capital and Class*, Vol. 11, pp. 5–33.

Crompton, R. 1989: 'Women in Banking: Continuity and Change since the Second World War', *Work, Employment and Society*, Vol. 3, No. 2, pp. 141–56.

Crompton, R. and Jones, G. 1982: *White Collar Proletariat: Deskilling and Gender in Clerical Work*. London: Macmillan.

Crompton, R. and Sanderson, K. 1986: 'Credentials and Careers: Some Implications of the Increase in Professional Qualifications amongst Women', *Sociology*, Vol. 20, No. 1, pp. 25–42.

Cronin, J. E. 1979: *Industrial Conflict in Modern Britain*. London: Croom Helm.

Cronin, J. E. 1984: *Labour and Society in Britain 1918–79*. London: Batsford.

Crouch, C. 1982: *Trade Unions: the Logic of Collective Action*. London: Fontana.

Croucher, R. 1986: *We Refuse to Starve in Silence: a History of the National Unemployed Workers' Movement 1920*–46. London: Lawrence & Wishart.

Crowley-Bainton, T. 1987: 'Discriminating Employers', *New Society*, 27 November.

Crozier, M. 1964: *The Bureaucratic Phenomenon*. London: Tavistock.

Crozier, M. 1983: 'Implications for the Organization', in Otway, H. J. and Peltu, M. (eds), *New Office Technology*. London: Ablex.

Cunningham, H. 1980: *Leisure in the Industrial Revolution*. London: Croom Helm.

Cunnison, S. 1984: 'Participation in Local Union Organization. School Meals Staff: A Case Study', in Garminikow, E., Morgan, D., Purvis, J. and Taylorson, D. (eds), *Gender, Class and Work*. London: Heinemann.

Curran, J. and Burrows, R. 1988: *Enterprise in Britain: a National Profile of Small Business Owners and the Self-Employed*. London: Small Business Research Trust.

Currie, R. 1979: *Industrial Politics*. Oxford: Clarendon.

Curtin, P. D. 1972: 'British Images of Africans in the Nineteenth Century', in Baxter, P. and Sansom, B. (eds), *Race and Social Difference*. Harmondsworth: Penguin.

Cutler, A. 1978: 'The Romance of Labour', *Economy and Society*, Vol. 7, No. 1, pp. 74–9.

Dabscheck, B. and Niland, J. 1981: *Industrial Relations in Australia*. London: Allen & Unwin.

Dahrendorf, R. 1959: *Class and Class Conflict in an Industrial Society*. London: Routledge.

Daito, E. 1979: 'Summary of Discussions of the 4th International Conference on Business History', in Nakagawa, K. (ed.), *Labor and Management*. Tokyo: University of Tokyo.

Dale, A. 1987: 'Occupational Inequality, Gender and Life Cycle', *Work, Employment and Society*, Vol. 1, No. 3, pp. 326–51.

Daniel, M. 1975: *The Arabs and Medieval Europe*. London: Longman.

Daniel, W. L. 1968: *Racial Discrimination in England, Based on the PEP Report*. Harmondsworth: Penguin.

Davidoff, L. and Hall, C. 1987: *Family Fortunes: Men and Women of the English Middle Class, 1780*–1850. London: Hutchinson.

Davies, C. and Rosser, J. 1987: 'Women's Career Paths: a Male Pathway unwilling to Bend', *The Health Service Journal*, 5 February.

Davies, R. J. 1979: 'Economic Activity, Incomes Policy and Strikes: a Quantitative Analysis', *BJIR*, Vol. 17, pp. 205–23.

Davis, K. and Moore, W. E. 1945: 'Some principles of stratification', *American Sociological Review*, Vol. 10, No. 2, pp. 242–9.

Davis, L. E. and Taylor, J. C. 1976: 'Technology, Organization and Job Structure', in Dubin, R. (ed.), *Handbook of Work, Organization and Society*. Chicago: McNally.

Davis, M. 1985: *Prisoners of the American Dream: Politics and Economy in the History of the US Working Class*. London: Verso.

Deaton, D. 1983: 'Unemployment', in Bains, G.S. (ed.), *Industrial Relations in Britain*. Oxford: Blackwell.

Deem, R. 1985: 'Work and the Family', Unit 14 Part 1, *Work and Society*. Milton Keynes: Open University Press.

Delmar, R. 1976: 'Looking again at Engels's "Origins of the Family, Private Property and the State"', in Mitchell, J. and Oakley, A. (eds), *The Rights and Wrongs of Women*. Harmondsworth: Penguin.

Delphy, C. 1977: *The Main Enemy*. London: Women's Research and Resources Centre.

De Lyon, H. and Migniolo, F. 1989: *Women Teachers*. Milton Keynes: Open University Press.

Derrida, J. 1973: *Speech and Phenomena*. Evanston: Northwestern University Press.

Derrida, J. 1978: *Writing and Difference*. London: Tavistock.

De Vroey, M. 1984: 'A Regulation Approach Interpretation of the Contemporary Crisis', *Capital and Class*, Vol. 23, pp. 45–66.

Dex, S. 1978–9: 'Job Search Methods and Ethnic Discrimination', *New Community*, Vol. 7, No. 1, pp. 31–9.

Dex, S. 1985: *The Sexual Division of Work: Conceptual Revolutions in the Social Sciences*. Brighton: Wheatsheaf.

Dex, S. 1988: *Women's Attitudes towards Work*. London: Macmillan.

Dex, S. and Walters, P. 1989: 'Women's Occupational Status in Britain; France and the USA: Explaining the Difference', *Industrial Relations Journal*, Vol. 20, No. 3, pp. 203–10.

Dickens, L. 1989: 'Women – a Rediscovered Resource?', *Industrial Relations Journal*, Vol. 20, No. 3, pp. 167–75.

Dobson, C. R. *Masters and Journeymen: a Prehistory of Industrial Relations 1717-1800*. London: Croom Helm.

DOE (Department of Employment). 1971: *British Labour Statistics*. London: HMSO.

Doeringer, P. and Piore, M. 1971: *Internal Labour Markets and Manpower Analysis*. Lexington, Mass.: D. C. Heath.

Dolby, N. 1987: *Norma Dolby's Diary*. London: Verso.

Donaldson, L. 1985: *In Defence of Organization Theory*. Cambridge: Cambridge University Press.

Donoghue, H. 1988: 'University Statistical Records: Age Patterns', *AUT Woman*, No. 13, spring.

Donovan Commission, 1968: *Report of the Royal Commission on Trade Unions and Employers' Associations*. London: HMSO.

Doray, B. 1988: *From Taylorism to Fordism*. London: Free Association Books.

Dore, R. P. 1973: *British Factory–Japanese Factory*. London: Allen & Unwin.

Drucker, P. 1951: *The New Society*. London: Heinemann.

Dubin, R. 1962: 'Industrial Workers' Worlds', in Rose, A. M. (ed.), *Human Behaviour and Social Processes*. London: Routliege.

Dubois, P. 1979: *Sabotage in Industry*. Harmondsworth: Penguin.

Dumont, L. 1977: *From Mandeville to Marx: the Genesis and Triumph of Economic Ideology*. Chicago: University of Chicago Press.

Dunlop, J. T. 1958: *Industrial Relations Systems*. New York: Holt.

Durcan, J. W. and McCarthy, W. E. J. 1974: 'The State Subsidy Theory of Strikes', *BJIR*, March, pp. 26–47.

Durcan, J. W., McCarthy, W. E. J. and Redman, G. P. 1983: *Strikes in Post War Britain*. London: Allen & Unwin.

Durkheim, E. 1933: *The Division of Labour in Society*. New York: Free Press.

Dutton, W. H. 1987: 'Decision Making in the Information Age: Computer Models and Public Policy', in Finnegan, R. et al., *Information Technology: Social Issues*. London: Hodder & Stoughton.

Dutton, W. H. 1988: 'The Automation of Bias', in Open University, *An Introduction to Information Technology: Social and Technological Issues*. Milton Keynes: Open University.

Dworkin, A. 1981: *Pornography: Men Possessing Women*. London: Women's Press.

Dyer, C. 1988: *The Guardian*, 10 October.

Earle, P. 1989: *The Making of the English Middle Classes: Business, Society and Family Life in London. 1660–1730*. London: Methuen.

Edgell, S. 1980: *Middle Class Couples*. London: Allen & Unwin.

Edgeworth, F. Y. 1922: 'Equal Pay to Men and Women for Equal Work', *Economic Journal*, Vol. 32, pp. 431–57.
Edwards, I. 1983: 'The Art of Shovelling', in Richards, V. (ed.), *Why Work?* London: Free Press.
Edwards, P. K. 1978: 'Time-Series Regression Models of Strike Activity: a reconsideration with American Data', *British Journal of Industrial Relations*, Vol. 16, pp. 320–34.
Edwards, P. K. 1981: *Strikes in the United States 1881–1974*. Oxford: Blackwell.
Edwards, P. K. 1983a: 'The End of American Strike Statistics', *British Journal of Industrial Relations*, Vol. 31, pp. 392–4.
Edwards, P. K. 1983b: 'The Pattern of Collective Industrial Action', in Bain, G. S. (ed.), *Industrial Relations in Britain*. Oxford: Blackwell.
Edwards, P. K. 1986: *Conflict at work: a Materialist Analysis of Workplace Relations*. Oxford: Blackwell.
Edwards, P. K. and Scullion, H. 1982: *The Social Organization of Industrial Conflict*. Oxford: Blackwell.
Edwards, R. 1979: *Contested Terrain*. London: Heinemann.
Ehrenreich, B. and English, D. 1979: *For Her Own Good*. London: Pluto.
Eisenberg, P. and Lazarsfeld, P. F. 1938: 'The Psychological Effects of Unemployment', *Psychological Bulletin*, pp. 335–90.
Eisenstein, Z. R. 1979: 'Developing a Theory of Capitalist Patriarchy and Socialist Feminism', in Eisenstein , Z. R. (ed.), *Capitalist Patriarchy*. New York: Monthly Review Press.
Eisenstein, Z. R. 1984: *Feminism and Sexual Equality: Crisis in Liberal America*. New York: Monthly Review Press.
Elbaum, B. and Lazonick, W. (eds). 1986: *The Decline of the British Economy*. Oxford: Oxford University Press.
Eldridge, J. E. T. 1968: *Industrial Disputes*. London: Routledge.
Eldridge, J. E. T. 1971: *Sociology and Industrial Life*. London: Michael Joseph.
Elger, T. 1982: 'Braverman, Capital Accumulation and Deskilling', in Wood, S. (ed.), *The Degradation of Work?* London: Hutchinson.
Elliott, D. 1980: 'The Organization as a System', in Salaman, G. and Thompson, K. (eds), *Control and Ideology in Organizations*. Milton Keynes: Open University Press.
Ellison, J. 1989: *The Guardian*, 2 March.
Elster, J. 1985: *Making Sense of Marx*. Cambridge: Cambridge University Press.
Emery, E. F. and Thorsrud, E. 1964: *Form and Content in Industrial Democracy*. London: Tavistock.
Employment Dept. *Employment Gazette*. London: HMSO.
Engels, F. 1968: 'Origins of the Family, Private Property and the State', in Marx, K. and Engels, F., *Selected Works in One Volume*. London: Lawrence and Wishart.
Engels, F. 1969a: *The Condition of the Working Class in England*. London: Panther.
Engels, F. 1969b: 'Preface' in Marx's *Theories of Surplus Value*. London: Lawrence & Wishart.
Equal Opportunities Commission. 1987: *Sex Discrimination Decisions*. No. 16. Manchester EOC.

Equal Opportunities Commission. 1989: *Women and Men in Britain 1989.* London: EOC.

Evans, M. D. R. 1987: 'Language Skill, Language Usage, and Opportunity: Immigrants in the Australian Labour Market', *Sociology*, Vol. 21, No. 2, pp. 253–74.

Fairbairns, Z. 1988: 'Wages for Housework', *New Internationalist*, March.

Fawcett, M. G. 1918: 'Equal Pay for Equal Work', *Economic Journal*, Vol. 28, pp. 1–6.

Feldberg, R. and Glenn, E. N. 1984: 'Male and Female: Job versus Gender Models in the Sociology of Work', in Siltanen, J. and Stanworth, M. (eds), *Women and the Public Sphere: a Critique of Sociology and Politics*. London: Hutchinson.

Ferguson, M. 1987: *The History of Mary Prince, a West Indian Slave*. London: Pandora.

Fildes, V. 1988: *Wet Nursing: a History from Antiquity to the Present*. Oxford: Blackwell.

Fineman, S. 1983: *White Collar Unemployment: Impact and Stress*. London: John Wiley.

Fineman, S. 1987: 'The Middle Class: Unemployed and Underemployed', in Fineman, S. (ed.), *Unemployment: Personal and Social Consequences* London: Tavistock.

Finnegan, R. and Heap, N. 1988: *Information Technology and its Implications*. Milton Keynes: Open University Press.

Firestone, S. 1974: *The Dialectic of Sex: the Case for Feminist Revolution*. New York: Morrow.

Flanders, A. 1965: *Industrial Relations: What is Wrong with the System?* London: Faber.

Flanders, A. 1970: 'Industrial Relations: What is Wrong with the System?', in Flanders, A., *Management and Unions*. London: Faber.

Fletcher, C. 1973: 'The End of Management', in Child, J. (ed.), *Man and Organization*. London: Allen & Unwin.

Foot, P. 1965: *Immigration and Race in British Politics*. Harmondsworth: Penguin.

Form, W. 1987: 'On the Degradation of Skills', *Annual Review of Sociology*, Vol. 13, pp. 29–47.

Forrester, K. and Ward, K. 1986: 'Organising the Unemployed? The TUC and the Unemployed Workers Centres', *Industrial Relations Journal*, Vol. 17, No. 1, pp. 46–56.

Foster, A. 1987: 'The Invisible Men', *Management Today*, November.

Foster, J. 1974: *Class Struggles in the Industrial Revolution*. London: Weidenfeld & Nicolson.

Foucault, M. 1977: *Madness and Civilization*. New York: Vintage.

Foucault, M. 1979: *The History of Sexuality, Vol. 1*. Harmondsworth: Penguin.

Foucault, M. 1980: *Power/Knowledge*. Brighton: Harvester.

Fox, A. 1971: *The Sociology of Work in Industry*. London: Collier Macmillan.

Fox, A. 1974: *Beyond Contract*. London: Faber.

Fox, A. 1976: 'The Meaning of Work', Unit 6, *People and Work*. Milton Keynes: Open University Press.

Fox, A. 1985: *History and Heritage: the Social Origins of the British Industrial Relations System*. London: Allen & Unwin.
Fox, A. and Flanders, A. 1969: 'The Reform of Collective Bargaining: From Donovan to Durkheim', *British Journal of Industrial Relations*, Vol. 2, pp. 151–80.
Francis, A. 1986: *New Technology at Work*. Oxford: Oxford University Press.
Fraser, A. 1988: *Boadicea's Chariot: the Warrior Queens*. London: Weidenfeld & Nicolson.
Fraser, R. (ed.). 1968: *Work: Twenty Personal Accounts*. Harmondsworth: Penguin.
Fraser, R. 1979: *Blood of Spain: the Experience of Civil War 1936–1939*. London: Allen Lane.
Freedman, M. 1984: 'The Search for Shelters', in Thompson, K. (ed.), *Work, Employment and Unemployment*. Milton Keynes: Open University Press.
Freeman, C. 1987: 'The Case for Technological Determinism', in Finnegan, R. et al. (eds), *Information Technology: Social Issues*. Milton Keynes: Open University Press.
Frenkel, S. (ed.). 1980: *Industrial Action*. London: Allen & Unwin.
Friedman, A. L. 1977: *Industry and Labour: Class Struggle at Work and Monopoly Capitalism*. London: Macmillan.
Friedman, H. and Meredeen, S. 1980: *The Dynamics of Industrial Conflict*. London: Croom Helm.
Fryer, D. and McKenna, S. 1987: 'The Laying Off of Hands – Unemployment and the Experience of Time', in Fineman, S. (ed.), *Unemployment: Personal and Social Consequences*. London; Tavistock.
Fryer, P. 1984: *Staying Power: the History of Black People in Britain*. London: Pluto.
Fryer, P. 1988: *Black People in the British Empire*. London: Pluto.
Gale, S. 1985: 'The Housewife', in Littler, C. R. (ed.), *The Experience of Work*. Aldershot: Gower.
Gallie, D. 1978: *In Search of the New Working Class*. Cambridge: Cambridge University Press.
Gallie, D. 1983: *Social Inequality and Class Radicalism in France and Britain*. Cambridge: Cambridge University Press.
Gallie, D. 1989: 'Employment, Unemployment and Social Stratification', in Gallie, D. (ed.), *Employment in Britain*. Oxford: Blackwell.
Gapper, J. 1989: *Financial Times*, 20 February.
Garen, J. and Krislov, J. 1988: 'An Examination of the New American Strike Statistics in Analyzing Strike Incidence', *BJIR*, Vol. 26, pp. 75–84.
Garfinkel, H. 1984: *Studies in Ethnomethodology*. Oxford: Blackwell.
Garnsey, E., Rubery, J. and Wilkinson, F. 1985: *Labour Market Structure and Workforce Divisions*. Milton Keynes: Open University Press.
Gartman, D. 1979: 'Origins of the Assembly Line and Capitalist Control of Work at Ford', in Zimbalist, A. (ed.), *Case Studies on the Labor Process*. New York: Monthly Review.
Gavron, H. 1968: *The Captive Wife*. Harmondsworth: Penguin.
Geary, D. 1984: *European Labour Protest 1848–1939*. London: Methuen.
Geary, D. 1987: 'Working class Culture in Imperial Germany', in Fletcher, R.

(ed.), *Bernstein to Brandt: a Short History of German Social Democracy*. London: Edward Arnold.

Geertz, C. 1963: *Old Societies and New States* – the Quest for Modernity in Asia and Africa. Glencoe, Ill.: Free Press.

Gennard, J. 1977: *Financing Strikers*. London: Macmillan.

George, D. 1931: *England in Transition*. Harmondsworth: Penguin.

George, M. D. 1965: *London Life in the Eighteenth Century*. Harmondsworth: Penguin.

Gershuny, J. I. 1983: *Social Innovation and the Division of Labour*. Oxford: Oxford University Press.

Gershuny, J. I. and Thomas, G. S. 1980: *Changing Patterns of Time Use*. Brighton: SPRU.

Gerver, E. 1989: 'The Gender of Informatics', lecture quoted in *Times Higher Education Supplement*, 24 February.

Gibson, M. A. 1988: *Accommodation without Assimilation: Sikh Immigrants in an American High School*. Ithaca, N. Y.: Cornell University Press.

Giddens, A. 1971: *Capitalism and Modern Social Theory*. Cambridge: Cambridge University Press.

Giddens, A. 1973: *The Class Structure of the Advanced Societies*. London: Hutchinson.

Giddens, A. 1977: 'Functionalism après la lutte', in Giddens, A., *Studies in Social and Political Theory*. London: Hutchinson.

Giddens, A. 1979: *Central Problems in Social Theory: Action, Structure and Contradictions in Social Analysis*. London: Macmillan.

Giddens, A. 1981: *A Contemporary Critique of Historical Materialism*. London: Macmillan.

Giddens, A. 1982a: *Profiles and Critiques in Social Theory*. London: Macmillan.

Giddens, A. 1982b: 'Labour and Interaction', in Thompson, J. B. and Held, D. (eds), *Habermas: Critical Debates*. London: Macmillan.

Giddens, A. 1984: *The Constitution of Society*. Cambridge: Polity Press.

Glendinning, C. and Millar, J. (ed.). 1988: *Women and Poverty in Britain*. Brighton: Wheatsheaf.

Gluckstein, D. 1985: *The Western Soviets: Workers' Councils Versus Parliament 1915–1920*. London: Bookmarks.

Godelier, M. 1980: 'Work: the Words used to represent Work and Workers', *History Workshop*, No. 10, autumn, pp. 164–74.

Goffman, E. 1959: *The Presentation of Self in Everyday Life*. New York: Doubleday.

Goffman, E. 1961: *Asylums*. Harmondsworth: Penguin.

Goldman, P. and Van Houten, D. R. 1980: 'Bureaucracy and Domination: Managerial Strategy in turn-of-the-century American Industry', in Dunkerley, D. and Salaman, G. (eds), *The International Yearbook of Organizational Studies, 1979*. London: Routledge.

Goldschmidt-Clermont, L. 1987: *Unpaid Work in the Household*. Geneva: International Labour Office.

Goldthorpe, J. H. 1980: *Social Mobility and Class Structure in Modern Britain*. Oxford: Clarendon.

Goldthorpe, J. H. 1983: 'Women and Class Analysis: in Defence of the Conventional View', *Sociology*, Vol. 17, pp. 465–88.

Goldthorpe, J. H. 1984b: 'Women and Class Analysis: a Reply to the Critics', *Sociology*, Vol. 18, pp. 491–9.
Goldthorpe, J. H. 1984a: 'The End of Convergence: Corporatist and Dualist Tendencies in Modern Western Societies', in Goldthorpe, J. (ed.), *Order and Conflict in Contemporary Capitalism*. Oxford: Clarendon.
Goldthorpe, J. H., Llewellyn, C. and Payne, C. 1980: *Social Mobility and Class Structure in Modern Britain*. Oxford: Clarendon.
Goldthorpe, J. H., Lockwood, D., Bechhofer, F. and Platt, J. 1968: *The Affluent Worker: Industrial Attitudes and Behaviour*. London: Cambridge University Press.
Goldthorpe, J. H., Lockwood, D., Bechhofer, F. and Platt, J. 1969: *The Affluent Worker in the Class Structure*. London: Cambridge University Press.
Goldthorpe, J. H. and Payne, C. 1986: 'Trends in Intergenerational Class Mobility in England and Wales 1972–1983', *Sociology*, Vol. 20, No. 1, pp. 1–24.
Goodman, G. 1985: *The Miner's Strike*. London: Pluto.
Gordon, D. M. 1972: *Theories of Poverty and Underdevelopment*. Lexington, Mass.: D. C. Heath.
Gordon, D. M., Edwards, R. and Reich, M. 1982: *Segmented Work, Divided Workers: The Historical Transformation of Labor in the United States*. Cambridge: Cambridge University Press.
Gordon, L. 1981: 'The Politics of Sexual Harrassment', *Radical America*, Vol. 15, pp. 7–14.
Gorz, A. 1970: 'Immigrant Labour', *New Left Review*, Vol. 1
Gorz, A. 1982: *Farewell to the Working Class*. London: Pluto.
Gorz, A. 1985: *Paths to Paradise: On the Liberation From Work*. London: Pluto.
Gorz, A. 1989: *Critique of Economic Reason*. London: Verso.
Gospel, H. 1983: 'The Development of Management Organization in Industrial Relations: an Historical Perspective', in Thurley, K. and Wood, S. (eds), *Industrial Relations and Management Strategy*. Cambridge: Cambridge University Press.
Gouldner, A. W. 1954: *Patterns of Industrial Bureaucracy*. New York: Free Press.
Gouldner, A. W. 1965: *Wildcat Strike*. New York: Antioch Press.
Gow, D. 1987: *The Guardian*, 3 September.
Gramsci, A. 1971: *Selections from Prison Notebooks*. London: Lawrence & Wishart.
Gramsci, A. 1978: *Selections from Political Writings 1921–1926* London: Lawrence & Wishart.
Gray, R. 1981: *The Aristocracy of Labour in Nineteenth Century Britain*. London: Macmillan.
Gray, R. 1987: 'Languages of Factory Reform', in Joyce, P. (ed.), *The Historical Meanings of Work*. Cambridge: Cambridge University Press.
Gregory, J. 1982: 'Some Cases that Never Reached the Tribunal', *Feminist Review*, No. 10, pp. 75–89.
Grieco, M. 1987: 'Family Networks and the Closure of Employment', in Lee, G. and Loveridge, R. (eds), *The Manufacture of Disadvantage: Stigma and Social Closure*. Milton Keynes: Open University Press.

Grint, K. 1986: 'Bureaucracy and Democracy: the Quest for Industrial Control in the British Postal Business 1918–1939.' D.Phil Thesis. Oxford University.

Grint, K. 1988: 'Women and Equality: the Acquisition of Equal Pay in the Post Office 1870-1961', *Sociology*, Vol. 22, No. 1, pp. 87-108.

Guerin, D. 1979: *100 years of Labor in the USA*. London: Ink Links.

Habermas, J. 1970: *Towards a Rational Society*. London: Heinemann.

Habermas, J. 1971: *Knowledge and Human Interests*. London: Heinemann.

Habermas, J. 1974: *Theory and Practice*. London: Heinemann.

Hadjifotiou, N. 1985: 'Rate for the Job', *Marxism Today*, June.

Hague, H. 1986: 'Women and Unions', *Marxism Today*, June.

Hain, P. 1986: *Political Strikes: the State and Trade Unionism in Britain*. Harmondsworth: Penguin.

Hakim, C. 1979: *Occupational Segregation, a Comparative Study of the Degree and Pattern of the Differentiation between Men and Women's Work in Britain, the United States, and Other Countries*. Research Paper, No. 9. London: Dept. of Employment.

Hakim, C. 1981: 'Job Segregation: Trends in the 1970s', *Employment Gazette*, December, pp. 521-9.

Hakim, C. 1990: 'Core and Periphery in Employers' Workforce Strategies: Evidence from the 1987 ELUS Survey', *Work, Employment and Society*, Vol. 4, No. 2, pp. 157-88.

Halsey, A. H. 1986: *Change in British Society*. Oxford: Oxford University Press.

Hambleton, R. 1988: 'The American Gender Gap', *Times Higher Education Supplement*, 12 August.

Hammond, J. L. and B. 1949: *The Town Labourer 1760-1832, Vol. II* London: Guild Books.

Hanami, T. 1979: *Labor Relations in Japan Today*. London: John Martin.

Handy, C. B. 1985: *Understanding Organizations*. Harmondsworth: Penguin.

Hannah, L. 1983: *The Rise of the Corporate Economy*. London: Methuen.

Haraszti, M. 1977: *A Worker in a Worker's State*. Harmondsworth: Penguin.

Harding, J. (ed.). 1986: *Perspectives on Science and Gender*. Brighton: Falmer Press.

Harding, P. and Jenkins, R. 1989: *The Myth of the Hidden Economy*. Milton Keynes: Open University Press.

Hardy, D. 1979: *Alternative Communities in Nineteenth Century England*. London: Longman.

Harman, C. 1982: *The lost Revolution: Germany 1918-23*. London: Pluto.

Harper, K. 1990: *The Guardian*, 8 June.

Harris, M. 1990: 'Working in the UK Voluntary Sector', *Work, Employment and Society*, Vol. 4, No. 1, pp. 125-40.

Harrison, B. and Bluestone, B. 1988: *The Great U-Turn*. New York: Basic Books.

Harrison, J. F. C. 1984: *The Common People: a History from the Norman Conquest to the Present*. London: Flamingo.

Harrison, M. 1979: 'Participation of Women in Trade Union Activities', *Industrial Relations Journal*, Vol. 10, pp. 41-55.

Hartley, J. 1987: 'Managerial Unemployment: the Wife's Perspective and Role',

in Fineman, S. (ed.), *Unemployment: Personal and Social Consequences*. London: Tavistock.
Hartmann, H. 1982: 'Capitalism, Patriarchy, and Job Segregation by Sex', in Giddens, A. and Held, D. (eds), *Classes, Power and Conflict: Classical and Contemporary Debates*. London: Macmillan.
Harvey, D. 1989: *The Condition of Postmodernity*. Oxford: Blackwell.
Harvey, J. 1987: 'New Technology and the Gender Divisions of Labour', in Lee, G. and Loveridge, R. (eds), *The Manufacture of Disadvantage*. Milton Keynes: Open University Press.
Harvie, C. 1978: *The Experience of Industrialization*. Milton Keynes: Open University Press.
Hassard, J. and Sharifi, S. 1989: 'Corporate Culture and Strategic Change', *Journal of General Management*, Vol. 15, No. 2, pp. 4–19.
Hawkins, F. 1989: *Critical Years in Immigration*. Montreal: McGill-Queens University Press.
Haynes, M. 1988: 'Employers and Trade Unions, 1824–1850', in Rule, J. (ed.), *British Trade Unionism 1750–1850*. London: Longman.
Hearn, J. and Parkin, W. 1987: *'Sex' at 'Work': the Power and Paradox of Organization Sexuality*. Brighton: Wheatsheaf.
Hearst, D. 1988: *The Guardian*, 25 May.
Heath, A. 1981: *Social Mobility*. London: Fontana.
Heery, E. and Kelly, J. 1988: 'Union Women: a Survey of Women Full Time Officials'. London: LSE, Dept. of Industrial Relations. mimeo.
Heery, E. and Kelly, J. 1989: ' "A Cracking Job for a Woman" – a Profile of Women Trade Union Officers', *Industrial Relations Journal*, Vol. 20, No. 3, pp. 192–202.
Held, D. 1980: *Introduction to Critical Theory*. London: Hutchinson.
Held, D. 1984: 'Power and Legitimacy in Contemporary Britain', in McLennan, G., Held, D. and Hall, S. (eds), *State and Society in Contemporary Britain*. Cambridge: Cambridge University Press.
Held, D. 1987: *Models of Democracy*. Cambridge: Polity Press.
Held, D. 1989: *Political Theory and the Modern State*. Cambridge: Polity Press.
Held, D. and Thompson, J. B. (eds). 1989: *Social Theory of Modern Societies: Anthony Giddens and his Critics*. Cambridge: Polity Press.
Heller, F. 1987: 'The Technological Imperative and the Quality of Employment', *New Technology, Work and Employment*, Vol. 2, No. 1, pp. 19–26.
Hencke, D. 1988: *The Guardian*, 5 May.
Hencke, D. 1989: *The Guardian*, 26 September.
Henley Centre of Forecasting. 1989: *The Women's Decade*. Henley.
Herding, R. 1972: *Job Control and Union Structure*. Rotterdam: Rotterdam University Press.
Herzberg, F. 1966: *Work and the Nature of Man*. New York: Staples Press.
Heyderbrand, W. V. 1985: 'Technarchy and neo-Corporatism: Toward a Theory of Organizational Change under Advanced Capitalism and Early State Socialism', *Current Perspectives in Social Theory*, Vol. 6, pp. 71–128.
Heywood, C. 1989: *Childhood in Nineteenth Century France: Work, Health and Education among the 'classes populaires'*. Cambridge: Cambridge University Press.

Hill, B. 1989: *Women, Work and Sexual Politics in Eighteenth Century England*. Oxford: Blackwell.
Hill, C. 1969: *Reformation to Industrial Revolution*. Harmondsworth: Penguin.
Hill, J. 1978: 'The Psychological Impact of Unemployment', *New Society*, 19 January.
Hill, S. 1981: *Competition and Control at Work*. London: Heinemann.
Himmelweit, S. and Mohun, S. 1977: 'Domestic Labour and Capital', *Cambridge Journal of Economics*, Vol. 1, No. 1, pp. 15–31.
Hinton, J. 1973: *The First Shop Stewards' Movement*. London: Allen & Unwin.
Hinton, J. 1983: *Labour and Socialism: a History of the British Labour Movement*. Brighton: Wheatsheaf.
Hirschhorn, L. 1984: *Beyond Mechanization*. Cambridge, Mass.: MIT Press.
Hobsbawm, E. J. 1964a: *Labouring Men*. London: Weidenfeld & Nicolson.
Hobsbawm, E. J. 1964b: 'Custom, Wages and Work-load', in Hobsbawm, E. J., *Labouring Men: Studies in the History of Labour*. London: Weidenfeld and Nicolson.
Hobsbawm, E. J. 1969: *Industry and Empire*. Harmondsworth: Pelican.
Hobsbawm, E. J. 1981: 'The Forward March of Labour Halted?', in Jacques, M. and Mulhearn, F. (eds), *The Forward March of Labour Halted?* London: New Left Books.
Hobsbawm, E. J. 1984: *Worlds of Labour Revisited*. London: Wiedenfeld & Nicolson.
Hobsbawm, E. J. and Rudé, G. 1973: *Captain Swing*. Harmondsworth: Penguin.
Hochschild, A. 1989: *The Second Shift*. New York: Viking Press.
Hoefer, H. J. 1984: *American Southwest*. London: Harrap.
Holley, J. C. 1981: 'The Two Family Economies of Industrialism: Factory Workers in Victorian Scotland', *Journal of Family History*, Vol. 6, No. 1.
Holton, B. 1976: *British Syndicalism 1910–1914*. London:Pluto.
Home Affairs Committee. 1989: *Racial Attacks and Harassment*. London: HMSO.
Home Office. 1989: *Domestic Violence: an Overview of the Literature*. London: HMSO.
Hopkins, E. 1979: *A Social History of the English Working Classes 1815–1945*. London: Edward Arnold.
Hopkins, E. 1988: *Birmingham: the First Manufacturing Town in the World, 1760–1840*. London: Weidenfeld & Nicolson.
Horne, J. 1987: *Work and Unemployment*. London: Longman.
Horner, M. 1976: 'Towards an Understanding of Achievement Related Conflict in Women', in Stacey, J., Beraud, S. and Daniels, J. (eds), *And Jill Came Tumbling After: Sexism in American Education*. New York: Dell Publishing.
Horrell, S., Rubery, J. and Burchell, B. 1989: 'Unequal Jobs or Unequal Pay?', *Industrial Relations Journal*, Vol. 20, No. 3, pp. 176–91.
Horrie, C. 1989: *The Observer*, 17 December.
Houghton, W. E. 1957: *The Victorian Frame of Mind 1820–1870*. New Haven, Conn.: Yale University Press.
Howkins, A. 1985: *Poor Labouring Men: Rural Radicalism in Norfolk 1870–1923*. London: Routledge.

Hudson, K. 1970: *Working to Rule. Railway Workshop Rules: a Study of Industrial Discipline*. Bath: Adams & Dart.
Hughes, P. 1989: 'Evaluating an Equal Opportunities Initiative', *Gender and Education*, Vol. 1, No. 1, pp. 5–14.
Hughes, T. 1979: 'The Electrification of America: the Systems Builders', *Technology and Culture*, Vol. 20, No. 1, pp. 124–62.
Huhne, C. 1988a: *The Guardian*, 10 March.
Huhne, C. 1988b: *The Guardian*, 30 June.
Huhne, C. 1988c: *The Guardian*, 13 January.
Humphries, J. 1988: 'Protective Law, the State, and Working Class Men', in Pahl, R. E. (ed.), *On Work*. Oxford: Blackwell.
Hundley, G. 1988: 'Taxation and Strikes', *BJIR*, Vol. 26, pp. 57–62.
Hunt, A. 1968: *A Survey of Women's Employment*, Vol. 1. London: HMSO.
Hunt, E. 1981: 'Stamp out Women', extract from *British Labour History: 1815–1914*. London: Weidenfeld and Nicolson.
Hutson, S. and Jenkins, R. 1989: *Taking the Strain: Families, Unemployment and the Transition to Adulthood*. Milton Keynes: Open University Press.
Hyder, K. 1989: *The Observer*, 21 May.
Hyman, R. 1971: *Marxism and the Sociology of Trade Unionism*. London: Pluto.
Hyman, R. 1972: *Strikes*. London: Fontana.
Hyman, R. 1979: 'The Politics of Workplace Trade Unionism', *Capital and Class*, No. 8, pp. 54–67.
Hyman, R. 1989: *The Political Economy of Industrial Relations* London: Macmillan.
Imray, L. and Middleton, A. 1983: 'Public and Private: Marking the Boundaries', in Garminikow, E., Morgan, D., Purvis, J. and Taylorson, D. (eds), *The Public and the Private*. London: Heinemann.
IMS (Institute of Manpower Studies). 1990: *Good Practices in the Employment of Women Returners*. Report No. 183. Brighton: IMS.
Ingham, G. K. 1970: *Size of Industrial Organization and Worker Behaviour*. Cambridge: Cambridge University Press.
Ingham, G. K. 1974: *Strikes and Industrial Conflict*. London: Macmillan.
Institute of Personnel Management. 1978: *Towards Fairer Selection: a Code for Non-discrimination*. London: IPM.
IRRU (Industrial Relations Review and Report), 1984: 'Part-time Work: a Survey', May.
Jaccoby, S. M. 1988: 'Employee Attitude Surveys in Historical Perspective', *Industrial Relations*, Vol. 27, No. 1, pp. 74–93.
Jackson, M. P. 1977: *Industrial Relations*. London: Croom Helm.
Jackson, M. P. 1987: *Strikes: Industrial Conflict in Britain, USA and Australia*. Brighton: Wheatsheaf.
Jacobs, E., Orwell, S., Paterson, P. and Weltz, F. 1978: *The Approach to Industrial Change*. London: Anglo-German Foundation for the Study of Industrial Society.
Jacques, E. 1967: *Equitable Payment*. Harmondsworth: Penguin.
Jacques, M. and Mulhearn, F. (eds), 1981: *The Forward March of Labour Halted?* London: Verso.
Jahoda, M. 1979: 'The Impact of Unemployment in the 1930s and 1970s', *Bulletin*

of the British Psychological Society, Vol. 32, pp. 309–14.

James, O. 1988: *The Observer*, 17 July.

Jay, M. 1973: *The Dialectical Imagination: a History of the Frankfurt School and the Institute of Social Research, 1923–1950*. Boston, Mass.: Little Brown.

Jehoel-Gijsbers, G. and Groot, W. 1989: 'Unemployed Youth: a Lost Generation?', *Work, Employment and Society*, Vol. 3, No. 4, pp. 491–508.

Jenkins, R. 1985: 'Black Workers in the Labour Market: the Price of Recession', in Roberts, B., Finnegan, R. and Gallie, D. (eds), *New Approaches to Economic Life*. Manchester: Manchester University Press.

Jenkins, R. 1988: 'Discrimination and Equal Opportunity in Employment: Ethnicity and "Race" in the United Kingdom', in Gallie, D. (ed.), *Employment in Britain*. Oxford: Blackwell.

Jenkins, R. and Parker, G. 1987: 'Organizational Politics and the Recruitment of Black Workers', in Lee, G. and Loveridge, R. (eds), *The Manufacture of Disadvantage: Stigma and Social Closure*. Milton Keynes: Open University Press.

Jenson, J. 1989: 'The Talents of Women, the Skills of Men: Flexible Specialization and Women', in Wood, S. (ed.), *The Transformation of Work?* London: Unwin Hyman.

Jewson, N. and Mason, D. 1986: 'Modes of Discrimination in the Recruitment Process', *Sociology*, Vol. 20, No. 1, pp. 43–63.

Johnson, T. 1972: *Professions and Power*. London: Macmillan.

Johnson, W. 1986: 'Worshipping Work', *New Internationalist*, No. 166, December.

Johnston, L. 1986: *Marxism, Class Analysis and Socialist Pluralism*. London: Allen & Unwin.

Joll, J. 1979: *The Anarchists*. London: Methuen.

Jones, G.S. 1983: *Languages of Class: Studies in English Working Class History 1832–1982*. Cambridge: Cambridge University Press.

Jones, T. and McEvoy, D. 1986: 'Ethnic Enterprise: the Popular Image', in Curran, J. et al. (eds), *The Survival of the Small Firm*, Vol. 1. Aldershot: Gower.

Joseph, G. 1983: *Women at Work*. London: Philip Allan.

Joshi, H. 1986: 'Gender Inequality in the Labour Market and the Domestic Division of Labour', in Nolan, P. and Paine, S., *Rethinking Socialist Economics*. Cambridge: Polity Press.

Joshi, S. and Carter, B. 1984: 'The Role of Labour in the Creation of a Racist Britain', *Race and Class*, Vol. 25, No. 3, pp. 53–70.

Jowell, R. and Prescott-Clarke, P. 1970: 'Discrimination against White Collar Workers in Britain', *Race*, Vol. 11, No. 4, April.

Jowell, R., Witherspoon, S. and Brook, L. (eds), 1989: *British Social Attitudes Special International Report*. Aldershot: Gower.

Joyce, P. 1980: *Work, Society and Politics*. London: Methuen.

Joyce, P. 1987: 'The Historical Meanings of Work: an Introduction', in Joyce, P. (ed.), *The Historical Meaning of Work*. Cambridge: Cambridge University Press.

Kakabadse, A. and McWilliam, G. 1987: 'Superpowers' Superwomen', *Management Today*. September.

Karlsen, C. F. 1988: *The Devil in the Shape of a Women: Witchcraft in Colonial New England*. New York: W. W. Norton.
Karpf, A. 1987: 'Recent Feminist Approaches to Women and Technology', in McNeil, M. (ed.), *Gender and Expertise*. London: Free Association Books.
Katz, H. C. and Sabel, C. F. 1985: 'Industrial Relations and Industrial Adjustment in the Car Industry', *Industrial Relations*, Vol. 24, No. 2, pp. 295–315.
Kelly, A. and Brannick, T. 1988: 'Explaining the Strike-proneness of British Companies in Ireland', *BJIR* Vol. 26, pp. 37–56.
Kelly, J. 1982: *Scientific Management, Job Redesign and Work Performance*. London: Academic Press.
Kelly, J. 1985: 'Management's Redesign of Work', in Knights, D., Willmott, H. and Collinson, D. (eds), *Job Redesign*. Aldershot: Gower.
Kelly, J. 1988: *Trade Unions and Socialist Politics*. London: Verso.
Kemp, R. 1989: 'How to Tame the Wildcats', *Management Today*, August.
Kendall, W. 1969: *The Revolutionary Movement in Britain 1900–21*. London: Weidenfeld & Nicolson.
Kern, H. and Schumann, M. 1987: 'Limits of the Division of Labour: New Production and Employment Concepts in West German Industry', *Economic and Industrial Democracy*, Vol. 8, No. 2, pp. 151–70.
Kerr, C., Dunlop, J. T., Harbison, F. and Myers, C. A. 1960: *Industrialism and Industrial Man*. Cambridge, Mass.: Harvard University Press.
Kerr, C. and Siegel, A. J. 1954: 'The Inter-Industry Propensity to Strike', in Kornhauser, A. et al. (eds), *Industrial Conflict*. New York: McGraw-Hill.
Kieser, A. 1989: 'Organizational, Institutional and Social Evolution: Medieval Craft Guilds and the Genesis of Formal Organizations', *Administrative Science Quarterly*, Vol. 34, pp. 540–64.
Kim, I. 1981: *The New Urban Immigrants: Korean Immigrants in New York City*. Princeton, N. J.: Princeton University Press.
Kitching, G. 1983: *Rethinking Socialism*. London: Methuen.
Knights, D. 1989: 'Culture, Control and Competition', paper presented at the PICT workshop on Culture and Information Technology' March, UMIST.
Knights, D. and Willmott, H. (eds), 1988: *New Technology and the Labour Process*. London: Macmillan.
Knights, D. and Willmott, H. 1989: 'Power and Subjectivity at Work', *Sociology*, Vol. 23, No. 4, pp. 535–58.
Knights, D., Willmott, H. and Collinson, D. (eds) 1985: *Job Redesign*. Aldershot: Gower.
Knowles, K. G. J. C. 1952. *Strikes: a Study in Industrial Conflict*. Oxford: Blackwell.
Kochan, T. A., Katz, H. C. and McKersie, R. B. 1986: *The Transformation of American Industrial relations*. New York: Basic Books.
Kogevinas, E. 1990: *Sociodemographic Differences in Cancer Survival*. London: HMSO.
Kolakowski, L. 1978: *Main Currents of Marxism*, Vol. 2. Oxford: Oxford University Press.
Kornblum, W. 1974: *Blue Collar Community*. Chicago: Chicago University Press.

Kornhauser, A. 1965: *The Mental Health of the Industrial Worker*. New York: John Wiley.
Korpi, W. and Shalev, M. 1979: 'Industrial Relations and Class Conflict in Capitalist Societies', *British Journal of Sociology*, Vol. 30, pp. 164–87.
Korpi, W. and Shalev, M. 1980: 'Strikes, Power and Politics in Western Nations 1900–76', *Political Power and Social Theory*, Vol. 1, pp. 301–34.
Kossler, R. and Muchie, M. 1990: 'American Dreams and Soviet Realities: Socialism and Taylorism', *Capital and Class*, No. 40, pp. 61–88.
Krieger, J. 1984: *Undermining Capitalism: State Ownership and the Dialectic of Control in the British Coal Industry*. London: Pluto.
Kriegler, R. J. 1982: *Working for the Company*. Oxford: Oxford University Press.
Kropotkin, P. 1983: 'The Wage System', in Richards, V. (ed.), *Why Work?* London: Aldgate.
Kumar, K. 1978: *Prophecy and Progress: the Sociology of Industrial and Post-Industrial Society*. London: Penguin.
Kumar, K. 1984: 'The Social Culture of Work', in Thompson, K. (ed.), *Work, Employment and Unemployment*. Milton Keynes: Open University Press.
Kushner, T. 1989: *The Persistence of Prejudice: Antisemitism in British Society during the Second World War*. Manchester: Manchester University Press.
Kussmaul, A. 1981: *Servants in Husbandry in Early Modern England*. Cambridge: Cambridge University Press.
Kusterer, K. C. 1978: *Know-How on the Job*. Boulder, Col.: Westview Press.
Kynaston, D. 1976: *King Labour*. London: Allen & Unwin.
Labour Research Department. 1986: *Women's Pay: Claiming Equal Value*. London: LRD.
Labriola, A. 1931: *Beyond Capitalism and Socialism*. Paris.
Lal, D. 1989: *The Hindu Equilibrium*, Vol. 2: *Aspects of Indian Labour*. Oxford: Oxford University Press.
Lambertz, J. 1985: 'Sexual Harassment in the Nineteenth Century English Cotton Industry', *History Workshop Journal*, Vol. 19, pp. 29–61.
Landes, D. 1972: *The Unbound Prometheus*. Cambridge: Cambridge University Press.
Landes, D. 1986: 'What do Bosses Really Do?', *Journal of Economic History*, Vol. 46, No. 3, pp. 585–623.
Lane, T. 1974: *The Union Makes Us Strong*. London: Arrow.
Lane, T. and Roberts, K. 1971: *Strike at Pilkingtons*. London: Fontana.
Larson, M. S. 1977: *The Rise of Professionalism*. Berkeley, Cal.: University of California Press.
Lash, S. 1984: *The Militant Worker: Class and Radicalism in France and America*. London: Heinemann.
Lash, S. and Urry, J. 1987: *The End of Organized Capitalism*. Cambridge: Polity Press.
LATC (Lancashire Association of Trades Councils), 1984: *Lancashire United?* Report given at LATC conference.
Latour, B. 1986: 'The Powers of Association', in Law, J. (ed.), *Power, Action and Belief: a New Sociology of Knowledge?* London: Routledge.
Latour, B. 1987: *Science in Action*. Milton Keynes: Open University Press.

Latour, B. 1988: '*The Prince* for Machines as well as for machinations', in Elliott, B. (ed.), *Technology and Social Process*. Edinburgh: Edinburgh University Press.
Latour, B. and Woolgar, S. 1979: *The Social Construction of Scientific Facts*. London: Sage.
Law, J. 1986: 'On the Methods of Long Distance Control: Vessels, Navigation and the Portuguese route to India', in Law, J. (ed.), *Power, Action and Belief: a New Sociology of Knowledge?* Keele: Sociological Review Monograph.
Law, J. 1988: 'The Anatomy of a Socio-technical Struggle', in Elliott, B. (ed.), *Technology and Social Process*. Edinburgh: Edinburgh University Press.
Lawler, E. 1973: 'Satisfaction and Behaviour', in Straw, B. (ed.), *Psychological Foundations of Organizational Behaviour*. Santa Monica: Goodyear.
Lawrence, P. R. and Lorsch, J. W. 1967: *Organization and Environment: Managing Differentiation and Integration*. Cambridge, Mass.: Harvard University Press.
Lawson, N. 1985: 'Britain's Economy: a Mid-term Report', in Coates, D. and Hillard, J. (eds), *The Economic Revival of Modern Britain*. Aldershot: Edward Elgar.
Lazonick, W. H. 1979: 'Industrial Relations and Technical Change: the Case of the Self-Acting Mule', *Cambridge Journal of Economics*, Vol. 3, No. 3, pp. 231–62.
Leavitt, H. J. and Whisler, T. L. 1958: 'Management in the 1980s', *Harvard Business Review*, Vol. 36, pp. 41–8.
Lee, D. 1980: 'Skill, Craft and Class: a Theoretical Critique and a Critical Case', *Sociology*, Vol. 15, pp. 57–78.
Lee, D. 1982: 'Beyond Deskilling: Skill, Craft and Class', in Wood, S. (ed.), *The Degradation of Work?* London: Hutchinson.
Lee, G. 1987: 'Black Members and their Unions', in Lee, G. and Loveridge, R. (eds), *The Manufacture of Disadvantage: Stigma and Social Closure*. Milton Keynes: Open University Press.
Lee, R. and Lawrence, P. 1985: *Organizational Behaviour: Politics at Work*. London: Hutchinson.
Leeson, R. A. 1980: *Travelling Brothers*. St Albans: Paladin.
Leggett, J. 1968: *Class, Race and labour*. New York: Cambridge University Press.
Leghorn, L. and Parker, K. 1981: *Woman's Worth*. London: Routledge.
Leiulfsrud, H. and Woodward, A. 1987: 'Women at Class Crossroads', *Sociology*, Vol. 21, No. 3, pp. 393–412.
Lenin, V. I. 1968a: *Selected Works*. Moscow: Progress Publishers.
Lenin, V. I. 1968b: 'The State and Revolution', *Collected Works*. Moscow: Progress Publishers.
Lenin, V. I. 1968c: 'The Immediate Tasks of the Soviet Government', *Selected Works*. Moscow: Progress Publishers.
Lenin, V. I. 1970: *What Is To Be Done?* London: Panther.
Lenin, V. I. 1978: *Imperialism: the Highest Stage of Capitalism*. Moscow: Progress Publishers.
Leonard, A. 1987: *Pyrrhic Victories*. London: EOC/HMSO.

Lewenhak, S. 1977: *Women and Trade Unions: an Outline History of Women in the British Trade Union Movement*. London: Ernest Benn.
Lewin, K. 1958: 'Group Decision and Social Change', in Maccoby, E. E. Newcomb, T., Hartley, E. I. (eds), *Readings in Social Psychology*. New York: Holt, Rinehart and Winston.
Libetta, L. 1988: 'Implications of Tacit Skills: Evidence for Theory and Research', paper delivered at the PICT/WICT conference, Bath, 26 March.
Liff, S. 1988: 'Gender, Office Work and Technological Change', paper delivered to the PICT/WICT Workshop, Bath, 26 March.
Light, I. and Bonacich, E. 1988: *Immigrant Entrepreneurs: Koreans in Los Angeles, 1965–1982*. Los Angeles: University of California Press.
Lindert, P. H. and Williamson, J. G. 1982: 'Revising England's Social Tables 1688–1812', *Explorations in Economic History*, Vol. 19, pp. 94–109.
Lindhert, P. H. 1980: 'English Occupations 1670–1811', *Journal of Economic History*, Vol. 40, No. 4, pp. 685–712.
Linhart, R. 1981: *The Assembly Line*. London: John Calder.
Lipietz, A. 1987: *Mirages and Miracles: the Crisis of Global Fordism*. London: Verso.
Littler, C. R. 1982: *The Development of the Labour Process in Capitalist Societies*. London: Heinemann.
Littler, C. R. 1985: 'The Design of Jobs', in Littler, C. R. (ed.), *The Experience of Work*. Aldershot: Gower.
Locke, J. 1960: *Two Treatises of Government*. Cambridge: Cambridge University Press.
Lockwood, D. 1958: *The Blackcoated Worker*. London: Allen & Unwin.
Lockwood, D. 1966: 'Sources of Variation in Working Class Images of Society', *Sociological Review*, Vol. 4, No. 2, pp. 249–67.
Lockwood, D. 1986: 'Class, Status and Gender', in Crompton, R. and Mann, M. (eds), *Gender and Stratification*. Cambridge: Polity Press.
Lorsch, J. 1986: 'Managing Culture: the Invisible Barrier to Change', California Management Review, Vol. 28, No. 2, pp. 95–109.
Loscocco, K. A. 1989: 'The Instrumentally Oriented Factory Worker: Myth or Reality?', *Work and Occupations*, Vol. 16, No. 1, pp. 3–25.
Loudon, J. B. 1979: 'Workers, Lords and Masters' in Wallman, S. (ed.), *Social Anthropology of Work*. London: Academic Press.
Low Pay Unit. 1989: *Getting it Right for Women*. London: LPU.
Lukács, G. 1971: *History and Class Consciousness*. London: Merlin.
Lukes, S. 1974: *Power: a Radical View*. London: Macmillan.
Luthra, M., Oakley, R., Austin, R. and Fitzgerald, M. 1988: *Racial Harassment*. London: Dept. of Environment.
McClelland, K. 1987: 'Time To Work, Time to Live', in Joyce, P. (ed.), *The Historical Meanings of Work*. Cambridge: Cambridge University Press.
McGeevor, P. and Brennan, J. 1990: *Ethnic Minorities and the Graduate Labour Market*. London: CRE.
McGregor, D. 1960: *The Human Side of Enterprise*. New York: McGraw-Hill.
McGregor, D. 1984: 'Theory X and Theory Y', in Pugh, D. (ed.), *Organization Theory*. Harmondsworth: Penguin.

McIlroy, J. 1988: *Trade Unions in Britain Today*. Manchester: Manchester University Press.

McLellan, D. 1980: *Marxism After Marx*. London: Macmillan.

McLoughlin, I. 1990: 'Technological Change at Work', paper presented at the Centre for Research into Innovation, Culture and Technology (CRICT), Brunel University, 2 May.

McLoughlin, I. and Clark, J. 1988: *Technological Change at Work*. Milton Keynes: Open University Press.

Macnicol, J. 1988: 'Lumpen Proles', in *Times Higher Education Supplement*, 11 March.

Macrae, C. 1988: *Observer*, 21 August.

Macrae, S. 1986: *Cross Class Families*. Oxford: Clarendon.

Malcomson, R. W. 1981: *Life and Labour in England 1700–1780*. London: Hutchinson.

Malcomson, R. W. 1988: 'Ways of Getting a Living in Eighteenth-Century England' in Pahl, R. E. (ed.), *On Work*. Oxford: Blackwell.

Malinowski, B. 1984: 'The Primitive Economics of the Trobriand Islanders', in Littler, C. R. (ed.), *The Experience of Work*. London: Heinemann.

Mallet, S. 1975: *The New Working Class*. Nottingham: Spokesman.

Mallier, A. T. and Rosser, M. J. 1987: 'Changes in the Industrial Distribution of Female Employment in Great Britain, 1951–1981', *Work, Employment and Society*, Vol. 1, No. 4, pp. 463–86.

Mann, M. 1970: 'The Social Cohesion of Liberal Democracy', *American Sociological Review*, Vol. 35, No. 3, pp. 423–39.

Mann, M. 1973a: *Consciousness and Action among the Western Working Class*. London: Macmillan.

Mann, M. 1973b: *Workers on the Move*. Cambridge: Cambridge University Press.

Mann, M. 1986: *The Sources of Social Power*, Vol. 1. Cambridge: Cambridge University Press.

Mannheim, K. 1951: *Freedom, Power and Democratic Planning*. London: Routledge.

Manpower Services Commission. 1987: *Ethnic Minorities and Job Centres*. Sheffield: MSC.

Manwaring, T. 1984: 'The Extended Internal Labour Market', *Cambridge Journal of Economics*, Vol. 8, No. 2, pp. 161–87.

Marceau, J. 1989: *A Family Business? the Making of an International Business Elite*. Cambridge: Cambridge University Press.

Marcuse, H. 1964: *One Dimensional Man*. Boston, Mass.: Beacon Press.

Marcuse, H. 1969: *An Essay on Liberation*. Boston, Mass.: Beacon Press.

Marglin, S. 1982: 'What do the Bosses do? The Origins and Functions of Hierarchy in Capitalist Production', in Giddens, A. and Held, D. (eds), *Classes, Power and Conflict*. London: Macmillan.

Markus, M. L. and Robey, D. 1988: 'Information Technology and Organizational Change: Causal Structure in Theory and Research', *Management Science*, Vol. 34, No. 5, pp. 583–98.

Marlow, J. 1985: *The Tolpuddle Martyrs*. London: Grafton.

Marsden, D. 1986: *The End of Economic Man: Custom and Competition in Labour Markets*. Brighton: Wheatsheaf.
Marsden, D., Morris, T., Willman, P. and Wood, S. 1985: *The Car Industry: Labour Relations and Industrial Adjustment*. London: Tavistock.
Marsh, A. I. 1982: *Employee Relations Policy and Decision Making*. Aldershot: Gower.
Marsh, A. and Ryan, V. 1989: *The Seamen: a History of the National Union of Seamen*. Oxford: Malthouse Press.
Marsh, C. 1988a: 'Unemployment in Britain', in Gallie, D. (ed.), *Employment in Britain*. Oxford: Blackwell.
Marsh, C. 1988b: *Exploring Data: an Introduction to Data Analysis for Social Scientists*. Cambridge: Polity Press.
Marshall, G. 1982: *In Search of the Spirit of Capitalism: an Essay on Max Weber's Protestant Ethic Thesis*. London: Hutchinson.
Marshall, G., Newby, H., Rose, D. and Vogler, C. 1988: *Social Class in Modern Britain*. London: Hutchinson.
Marshall, G., Vogler, C., Rose, D. and Newby, H. 1987: 'Distributional Struggle and Moral Order in a Market Society', *Sociology*, Vol. 21, No. 1, pp. 55–74.
Marshall, J. 1987: 'Less Equal than Others', *Times Higher Education Supplement*, 17 April.
Martin, J. and Roberts, C. 1980: *Women and Employment*. London: HMSO.
Martin, J. and Roberts, C. 1984: *Women and Employment: a Lifetime Perspective*. London: Dept. of Employment.
Martin, P. 'The Concept of Class', in Anderson, R. J., Hughes, J. A. and Sharrock, W. W. (eds), 1987: *Classic Disputes in Sociology*. London: Allen & Unwin.
Martin, R. 1969: *Communism and British Trade Unionism 1924–1933*. Oxford: Clarendon.
Marx, K. 1954: *Capital, Volume 1*. London: Lawrence & Wishart.
Marx, K. 1968: 'The Eighteenth Brumaire of Louis Bonaparte', in *Selected Works in One Volume*. London: Lawrence & Wishart.
Marx, K. 1969: *Theories of Surplus Value*. London: Lawrence & Wishart.
Marx, K. 1970: *The German Ideology*. London: Lawrence & Wishart.
Marx, K. 1973a: *Selected Works in Three Volumes*, Vol. 1. Moscow: Progress Publishers.
Marx, K. 1973b: *Grundrisse*. Harmondsworth: Penguin.
Marx, K. 1975: *Early Writings*. Harmondsworth: Penguin.
Marx, K. 1981: *Capital, Volume 3*. Harmondsworth: Penguin.
Marx, K. and Engels, F. 1968: 'The Communist Manifesto', *Selected Works in One Volume*. London: Lawrence & Wishart.
Maslow, A. 1943: 'A Theory of Human Motivation', *Psychological Review*, Vol. 50, pp. 370–96.
Mass Observation. 1943: *War Factory*. London: Hutchinson.
Mathews, J. 1989: *Tools of Change: New Technology and the Democratization of Work*: London: Pluto.
Mathias, P. 1969: *The First Industrial Nation: an Economic History of Britain 1700–1914*. London: Methuen.
Matthews, J. 1972: *Ford Strike*. London: Panther.

Mayhew, K. and Addison, J. 1983: 'Discrimination in the Labour Market', in Bain, G. S. (ed.), *Industrial Relations in Britain*. Oxford: Blackwell.

Maynard, M. 1985: 'Housework', Unit 3 part 2, *Work and Society*. Milton Keynes: Open University Press.

Maynard, M. 1988: 'Gender at Work', *Times Higher Education Supplement*, 26 August.

Meade-King, M. 1986: *The Guardian*, 11 November.

Meade-King, M. 1988: *The Guardian*, 8 September.

Meade-King, M. 1989: *The Guardian*, 17 October.

Merton, R. K. 1957: *Social Theory and Social Structure*. New York: Free Press.

Metcalf, D. 1989: 'Water Notes Dry Up', *British Journal of Industrial Relations*, Vol. 27, No. 1, pp. 1-32.

Meth, M. 1973: *Brothers of All Men?* London: Runnymede Industrial Unit.

Michels, R. 1949: *Political Parties*. New York: Free Press.

Middleton, C. 1981: 'Peasants, Patriarchy and the Feudal Mode of Production in England: a Marxist Appraisal', *Sociological Review*, Vol. 29, No. 1, pp. 105–54.

Middleton, C. 1988: 'The Familiar Fate of the Famulae', in Pahl, R. E. (ed.), *On Work: Historical, Comparative and Theoretical Approaches*. Oxford: Blackwell.

Miles, I. 1983: 'Adaptation to Unemployment?', Occasional Paper No. 20. Brighton: Science Policy Review Unit.

Miles, J. 1850: *Chapters in the Life of a Dundee factory Boy*, in Ward, J. T. (ed.), 1970: *The Factory System*, Vol. 2. Newton Abbot: David & Charles.

Miles, R. 1982: *Racism and Migrant Labour*. London: Routledge.

Miles, R. 1989: *Racism*. London: Routledge.

Miles, R. 1990: 'Whatever Happened to the Sociology of Migration?', *Work, Employment and Society*, Vol. 4, No. 2, pp. 281–98.

Miles, R. and Phizacklea, A. 1977: 'The TUC, Black Workers and New Commonwealth Immigration, 1954–1973', CRER Working Papers. Coventry: University of Warwick.

Miles, R. and Phizacklea, A. 1978: 'The TUC and Black Workers, 1974–76', *British Journal of Industrial Relations*, Vol. 16, pp. 195–207.

Miles, R. and Phizacklea, A. (eds), 1979: *Racism and Political Action in Britain*. London: Routledge.

Miliband, R. 1972: *Parliamentary Socialism*. London: Merlin.

Miller, D. 1984: *Anarchism*. London: Macmillan.

Millward, N. and Stevens, M. 1986: *British Workplace Industrial Relations 1980–1984*. Aldershot: Gower.

Milne, S. 1989: *The Guardian*, 9 September.

Mincer, J. and Polachek, S. 1974: 'Family Investment in Human Capital: Earnings of Women', *Journal of Political Economy*. Vol. 82, No. 2, pp. 76–108.

Mintzberg, H. 1979: *The Structuring of Organizations*. Englewood Cliffs, N. J.: Prentice Hall.

Mintzberg, H. 1989: 'Strategic Force', *Management Today*, April.

Mitchell, J. 1975: *Psychoanalysis and Feminism*. Harmondsworth: Penguin.

Mitchell, J. and Parris, H. 1983: *The Politics and Government of Britain*. Milton Keynes: Open University Press.

Moher, J. 1988: 'From Suppression to Containment: Roots of Trade Union Law to 1825', in Rule, J. (ed.), *British Trade Unionism 1750–1850: the Formative Years*. London: Longman.

Moore, R. 1975: *Racism and Black Resistance in Britain*. London: Pluto Press.

Moore, B. Jnr. 1967: *Social Origins of Dictatorship and Democracy*. Harmondsworth: Penguin.

Moore Campbell, B. 1988: *Successful Women, Angry Men*. London: Arrow.

Moorhouse, H. F. 1984: 'American Automobiles and Workers' Dreams', in Thompson, K. (ed.), *Work, Employmen and Unemployment: Perspectives on Work and Society*. Milton Keynes: Open University Press.

Moorhouse, H. F. 1987: 'The 'Work Ethic' and 'Leisure' Activity: the Hot Rod in Post-war America', in Joyce, P. (ed.), *The Historical Meanings of Work*. Cambridge: Cambridge University Press.

More, C. 1980: *Skill and the English Working Class: 1870–1914*. London: Croom Helm.

Morgan, G. 1986: *Images of Organization*. London: Sage.

Mormino, G. 1982: 'We Worked Hard and We Took Care of Our Own: Oral History and Italians in Tampa', *Labor History*, Vol. 23, No. 3, pp. 395–415.

Morokvasic, M. 1987: 'Immigrants in the Parisian Garment Industry', *Work, Employment and Society*, Vol. 1, No. 4, pp. 441–62.

Morris, L. 1987: 'Constraints on Gender: the Family Wage, Social Security and the Labour market', *Work, Employment and Society*, Vol. 1, No. 1, pp. 85–106.

Morris, L. 1990: *The Workings of the Household: a US-UK Comparison*. Oxford: Polity Press.

Morris, W. 1983: 'Useful Work and Useless Toil', in Richards, V. (ed.), *Why Work?* London: Freedom Press.

Morton, A. L. 1962: *The Life and Ideas of Robert Owen*. London: Lawrence & Wishart.

Mouffe, C. 1979: 'Hegemony and Ideology in Gramsci', in Mouffe, C. (ed.), *Gramsci and Marxist Theory*. London: Routledge.

Musgrave, P. W. 1981: 'The Labour Force: Some Relevant Attitudes', in Roderick, G. and Stevens, M. (eds), *Where Did We Go Wrong?* Brighton: Falmer Press.

Nadworny, M. J. 1955: *Scientific Management and the Unions, 1900–32*. Cambridge, Mass.: Harvard University Press.

Nakase, T. 1979: 'The Introduction of Scientific Management in Japan and its Characteristics', in Nakagawa, K. (ed.), *Labor and Management*. Tokyo: University of Tokyo Press.

NALGO, 1981: *Sexual Harassment is a Trade Union Issue*. London: NALGO.

National Association of Probation Officers. 1988: *Black People in the Criminal Justice System*. London: NAPO.

National Union of Public Employees (NUPE). 1985: *The Report of the Race Equality Working Party*. London: NUPE.

National Union of Teachers, 1988: *Women* – what does the NUT offer you? London: NUT.

Naughtie, J. 1988: *The Guardian*, 10 May.

NBPA (National Back Pain Association). 1989: Radio 3, 16 October.

Neal, F. 1988: *Sectarian Violence: the Liverpool Experience, 1819–1914*. Manchester: Manchester University Press.
Nelson. D. 1974: 'Scientific Management, Systematic Management and labor, 1880–1915', *Business History Review*, Vol. 28, pp. 479–500.
Nelson, D. 1975: *Managers and Workers: Origins of the New Factory System in the United States, 1880–1920*. Madison, Wis.: University of Wisconsin Press.
New Internationalist, 1988: 'Housework: the Facts', March.
Newton, P. 1986: 'Female Engineers: Femininity Redefined?', in Harding, J. (ed.), *Perspectives on Gender and Science*. Brighton: Falmer Press.
Ng, I. and Maki, D. 1988: 'Strike Activity of US Institutions in Canada', *BJIR*, Vol. 26, pp. 63–74.
Nichols, T. 1969: *Ownership, Control and Ideology*. London: Allen & Unwin.
Nicols, T. and Armstrong, P. 1976: *Workers Divided*. London: Fontana.
Nishikawa, S. (ed.). 1980: *The Labour Market in Japan: Selected Readings*. Tokyo: University of Tokyo Press.
Noble, D. F. 1974: *America by Design*. New York: Oxford University Press.
Noble, D. F. 1979: 'Social Choice in Machine Design: the Case of Automatically Controlled Machine Tools', in Zimbalist, A. (ed.), *Case Studies on the Labour Process*. New York: Monthly Review Press.
North, D. C. and Thomas, R. P. 1973: *The Rise of the Western World*. Cambridge: Cambridge University Press.
Northcott, J. and Rogers, P. 1982: *Microelectronics in Industry*. London: Policy Studies Institute.
Nyland, C. 1987: 'Scientific Planning and Management', *Capital and Class*, No. 33, pp. 55–83.
Oakley, A. 1974: *Housewife*. London: Allen Lane.
O'Brien, M. 1981: *The Politics of Reproduction*. London: Routledge.
O'Brien, M. 1982: 'The Working Father', in Beail, N. and McGuire, J. (eds), *Fathers: Psychological Perspectives*. London: Junction Books.
O'Donovan, K. and Szyszczak, E. 1988: *Equality and Sex Discrimination Law*. Oxford: Blackwell.
Offe, C. 1984: *Contradictions of the Welfare State*. London: Hutchinson.
Offe, C. 1985: *Disorganized Capitalism*. Cambridge: Polity Press.
Olson, M. 1982: *The Rise and Decline of Nations: Economic Growth, Stagflation, and Social Rigidities*. New Haven, Conn.: Yale University Press.
Open Systems Group. 1981: *Systems Behaviour*. London: Harper & Row.
Open University, 1976: *Press, Papers and Print*. Milton Keynes: Open University Press.
Orlikowski, W. 1988: 'Computer Technology in Organizations: Some Critical Notes', in Knights, D. and Willmott, H. (eds), *New Technology and the Labour Process*. London: Macmillan.
Orth, J. V. 1980: 'The Legal Status of English Trade Unions', in Harding, A. (ed.), *Law Making and Law Makers in British History*. London: Royal Historical Society.
Orwell, G. 1984: *The Penguin Essays of George Orwell*. Harmondsworth: Penguin.
Ouchi, W. A. 1981: *Theory Z: How American Business can meet the Japanese Challenge*. Reading, Ma.: Addison-Wesley.

Owen, S. J. 1987: 'Household Production and Economic Efficiency: Arguments for and against domestic specialization', *Work, Employment and Society*, Vol. 1, No. 2, pp. 157–78.
Ozanne, R. 1979: 'United States Labor-Management Relations 1860–1930', in Nakagawa, N. (ed.), *Labor and Management*. Tokyo: University of Tokyo Press.
Pagano, M. 1987: *The Guardian*, 1 September.
Pagnamenta, R. and Overy, R. 1984: *All Our Working Lives*. London: BBC.
Pahl, R. E. 1984: *Divisions of Labour*. Oxford: Blackwell.
Pahl, R. E. (ed.). 1988: *On Work: Historical, Comparative and Theoretical Approaches*. Oxford: Blackwell.
Palloix, C. 1976: 'The Labour Process: From Fordism to Neo-Fordism', in Conference of Socialist Economists (eds), *The Labour Process and Class Strategies*. London: Stage One.
Parker, S. R., Brown, R. K., Child, J. and Smith, M. A. 1967: *The Sociology of Industry*. London: Allen & Unwin.
Parkin, F. 1967: 'Working Class Conservatives', *British Journal of Sociology*, Vol. 18, pp. 278–90.
Parkin, F. 1972: *Class Inequality and Political Order: Social Stratification in Capitalist and Communist Countries*. New York: Holt, Reinhart and Winston.
Parkin, F. 1979: *Marxism and Class Theory: a Bourgeois Critique*. London: Tavistock.
Parkin, F. 1982: *Max Weber*. London: Tavistock.
Patterson, W. 1988: *The Korean Frontier in America: Immigration in Hawaii, 1896–1910*. Honolulu: University of Hawaii Press.
Payne, J. 1987: 'Does Unemployment Run in Families?', *Sociology*, Vol. 21, No. 2, pp. 199–214.
Payne, J. 1989: 'Unemployment and Family Formation among Young Men', *Sociology*, Vol. 23, No. 2, pp. 171–92.
Peach, C. 1968: *West Indian Migration to Britain*. Oxford: Oxford University Press.
Pearn, M. A., Kandola, R. S. and Mottram, R. D. 1987: *Selection Tests and Sex Bias*. London: EOC/HMSO.
Pelling, H. 1960: *American Labor*. Chicago: University of Chicago Press.
Pelling, H. 1968: 'The Concept of the Labour Aristocracy', in Pelling, H., *Popular Politics and Society in Late Victorian England*. London: Macmillan.
Pelling, H. 1976: *A History of British Trade Unionism*. Harmondsworth: Penguin.
Penn, R. 1982: 'Skilled Manual Workers in the Labour Process', in Wood, S. (ed.), *The Degradation of Work?* London: Hutchinson.
Perkin, H. 1969: *The Origins of Modern English Society 1780–1880*. London: Routledge.
Perkin, H. 1989: *The Rise of Professional Society: England since 1880*. London: Routledge.
Perlman, J. 1976: *The Myth of Marginality*. Berkeley, Cal.: University of California Press.
Perlman, S. 1928: *A Theory of the Labor Movement*. New York: Kelley.

Perlo, V. 1953: *The Negro in Southern Agriculture*. New York: International Publishers.

Pfeffer, J. 1982: *Organizations and Organization Theory*. Marshfield, MA.: Pitman.

Pfeffer, R. 1979: *Working for Capitalism*. New York: Columbia University Press.

Phillips, A. and Taylor, B. 1980: 'Sex and Skill: Notes Towards a Feminist Economics', *Feminist Review*, No. 6, pp. 79–88.

Phizacklea, A. 1982: 'Migrant Women and Wage Labour: the Case of West Indian Women in Britain', in West, J. (ed.), *Work, Women and the Labour Market*. London: Routledge.

Phizacklea, A. 1987: 'Minority Women and Economic Restructuring: the Case of Britain and the Federal Republic of Germany', *Work, Employment and Society*, Vol. 1, No. 3, pp. 309–25.

Phizacklea, A. and Miles, M. 1987: 'The British Trade Union Movement and Racism', in Lee, G. and Loveridge, R. (eds), *The Manufacture of Disadvantage*. Milton Keynes: Open University Press.

Piore, M. J. 1979: *Birds of Passage: Migrant Labor and Industrial Societies*. Cambridge: Cambridge University Press.

Piore, M. J. 1986: 'Perspectives on Labour Market Flexibility', *Industrial Relations*, Vol. 25, No. 2, pp. 146–66.

Piore, M. J. and Sabel, C. F. 1984: *The Second Industrial Divide*. New York: Basic Books.

Piven, F. F. and Cloward, R. A. 1977: *Poor People's Movements: How They Succeed, How They Fail*. New York: Pantheon Books.

PLA (Provident Life Assurance). 1987: 'Life after Death: Putting a Price on your Wife', *Lifelines*, No. 3. London: PLA.

Polachek, S. 1975: 'Discontinuities in Labor Force Participation and its Effects on Women's Market Earnings', in Lloyd, C. B. (ed.), *Sex, Discrimination and the Division of Labor*. New York: Columbia University Press.

Polan, A. J. 1984: *Lenin and the End of Politics*. London: Methuen.

Policy Studies Institute (PSI). 1986: *Black and White Britain*. London: PSI.

Pollard, S. 1965: *The Genesis of Modern Management*. London: Edward Arnold.

Pollert, A. 1981: *Girls, Wives, Factory Lives*. London: Macmillan.

Pollert, A. 1988: 'The Flexible Firm: Fact or Fiction?', *Work, Employment and Society*, Vol. 2, No. 3, pp. 281–316.

Pollitt, C. 1986: 'Democracy and bureaucracy', in Held, D. and Pollitt, C. (eds), *New Forms of Democracy*. London: Sage.

Pool, I. de S. 1983: *Technologies of Freedom*. Cambridge, Mass: Belknap Press.

Porter, M. 1982: 'Standing on the Edge: Working Class Housewives and the World of Work', in West, J. (ed.), *Women, Work and the Labour Market*. London: Routledge.

Postan, M. M. 1972: *The Medieval Economy and Society*. Harmondsworth: Penguin.

Poulantzas, N. 1978: *Classes in Contemporary Capitalism*. London: Verso.

Power, J. and Hardman, A. 1978: *Western Europe's Migrant Workers*. London: Minority Rights Group.

Pretty, D. A. 1989: *The Rural Revolt that Failed: Farm Workers' Trade Unions in Wales, 1889–1950*. Cardiff: University of Wales Press.
Pugh, D. S. and Hickson, D. J. 1976: *Organizational Structure in its Context*. Farnborough: Saxon House.
Purcell, K. 1984: 'Militancy and Acquiescence among Women Workers', in Siltanen, J. and Stanworth, M. (eds), *Women and the Public Sphere: a Critique of Sociology and Politics*. London: Hutchinson.
Radin, B. 1966: 'Coloured Workers and British Trade Unions', *Race*, Vol. 8, No. 2.
Rainnie, A. 1989: *Industrial Relations in Small Firms: Small Isn't Beautiful*. London: Routledge.
Ramazanoglou, C. 1989: *Feminism and the Contradictions of Oppression*. London: Routledge.
Randall, A. 1988: 'The Industrial Moral Economy of the Gloucestershire Weavers in the Eighteenth Century', in Rule, J. (ed.), *British Trade Unionism 1750–1850*. London: Longman.
Randall, V. 1988: 'In whose interest?', *Times Higher Education Supplement*, 12 August.
Rattansi, A. 1981: *Marx and the Division of Labour*. London: Macmillan.
Rattansi, A. 1982: 'Marx and the Abolition of the Division of Labour' in Giddens, A. and Mackenzie, G. (eds), *Social Class and the Division of Labour*. Cambridge: Cambridge University Press.
Ray, L. 1987: 'The Protestant Ethic Debate', in Anderson, R. J., Hughes, J. A. and Sharrock, W. W. (eds), *Classic Disputes in Sociology*. London: Allen & Unwin.
Redding, D. and Leydon, W. 1990: *The Guardian*, 7 June.
Reddy, W. 1985: *The Rise of Market Culture*. Cambridge: Cambridge University Press.
Reed, M. 1985: *Redirections in Organizational Analysis*. London: Tavistock.
Reed, M. 1989: *The Sociology of Management*. Brighton: Harvester.
Rees, A. 1966: 'Information Networks in labor markets', *American Economic Review*, Vol. 56, pp. 559–66.
Reich, R. B. 1983: *The Next American Frontier*. New York: Times Books.
Reid, I. 1986: *The Sociology of School and Education*. London: Fontana.
Reid, R. 1986: *Land of Lost Content*. London: Cardinal.
Rex, J. 1970: *Race Relations in Sociological Theory*. London: Weidenfeld Nicolson.
Rex, J. 1986: *Race and Ethnicity*. Milton Keynes: Open University Press.
Rex, J. and Tomlinson, S. 1979: *Colonial Immigrants in a British City* – a Class Analysis. London: Routledge.
Ricardo, D. 1951: *The Principles of Political Economy and Taxation*. Cambridge: Cambridge University Press.
Rice, A. K. 1958: *Productivity and Social Organization*. London: Tavistock.
Rice, A. K. 1963: *The Enterprise and its Environment*. London: Tavistock.
Rimmer, M. 1972: *Race and Industrial Conflict*. London: Heinemann.
Roberts, C. 1985: 'Research on Women in the Labour Market: the Context and Scope of the Women and Employment Survey', in Roberts, B., Finnegan,

R. and Gallie, D. (eds), *New Approaches to Economic Life*. Manchester: Manchester University Press.

Roberts, D. 1979: *Paternalism in Early Victorian England*. London: Croom Helm.

Roberts, E. 1982: 'Working Wives and their Families', in Barker, T. and Drake, M. (eds), *Population and Society in Britain 1850–1980*. London: Batsford.

Roberts, M. 1979: 'Sickles and Scythes', *History Workshop Journal*, No. 7, pp. 3–28.

Robey, D. 1977: 'Computers and Management Structures: Some Empirical Findings Re-examined', *Human Relations*, Vol. 30, pp. 963–76.

Robins, K. and Webster, F. 1989: *The Technical Fix*. London: Macmillan.

Robinson, D. and Conboy, W. M. 1970: 'Wage Structures and Internal Labour Markets', in Robinson, D. (ed.), *Local Labour Markets and Wage Structures*. London: Gower.

Robinson, J. 1934: *The Economics of Imperfect Competition*. London: Macmillan.

Robson, M. 1982: *Quality Circles: a Practical Guide*. Aldershot: Gower.

Roche, W. 1983: 'Status, Economism and Wage Practices: Fox's Theory of Trust Dynamics', paper read to Nuffield College Industrial Sociology Workshop, 8 November.

Roche, W. K. 1986: 'Systems Analysis and Industrial Relations', *Economic and Industrial Democracy*, Vol. 7, No. 3, pp. 3–28.

Roderick, G. and Stephens, M. (eds), 1981: *Where Did We Go Wrong?* Brighton: Falmer Press.

Rodger, N. A. M. 1986: *The Wooden World: An Anatomy of the Georgian Navy*. London: Fontana.

Roemer, J. (ed.), 1986: *Analytic Marxism*. Cambridge: Cambridge University Press.

Roethlisberger, F. J. and Dickson, W. J. 1939: *Management and the Worker*. Cambridge, Mass.: Harvard University Press.

Rogers, B. 1988: *Men Only*. London: Pandora.

Rose, H. 1986: 'Women's Work: Women's Knowledge', in Mitchell, J. and Oakley, A. (eds), *What is Feminism?* Oxford: Blackwell.

Rose, H., McLoughlin, I., King, R., Clark, J. 1986: 'Opening the Black Box: the Relation Between Technology and Work', *New Technology, Work and Employment*, Vol. 1, No. 1, pp. 18–26.

Rose, M. 1975: *Industrial Behaviour: Theoretical Developments Since Taylor*. London: Allen Lane.

Rose, M. and Jones, R. 1985: 'Managerial Strategy and Trade Union Responses in Work Reorganization Schemes at Establishment Level', in Knights, D., Willmont, H. and Collinson, D. (eds), *Job Redesign: Critical Perspectives on the Labour Process*. Aldershot: Gower.

Rose, N. 1989: *The Productive Subject*. London: Routledge.

Rose, R. 1983: *Getting by in Three Economies*. Glasgow: Centre for the Study of Public Policy.

Rosenberg, H. 1986: *Surviving in the City*. Toronto: Oxfam.

Rosenbrock, H. 1988: 'Engineers and the Work that People do', in Finnegan, R.,

Salaman, G. and Thompson, K. (eds), *Information Technology: Social Issues*. London: Hodder Stoughton.
Rosenburg, N. 1979: *Perspectives on Technology*. Cambridge: Cambridge University Press.
Ross, A. M. and Hartmann, P. T. 1960: *Changing Patterns of Industrial Conflict*. New York: Wiley.
Routh, G. 1980: *Occupations and Pay in Great Britain 1906–1979*. London: Macmillan.
Roy, D. 1954: 'Efficiency and the Fix', *American Journal of Sociology*, Vol. 60, pp. 427–42.
Roy, D. 1973: 'Banana Time', in Salaman, G. and Thompson, K. (eds), *People and Organizations*. London: Longman.
Rubery, J. 1980: 'Structured Labour Markets, Worker Organization and Low Pay', in Amsden, A. (ed.), *The Economics of Women and Work*. Harmondsworth: Penguin.
Rubinstein, M. 1989: 'Preventing Sexual Harassment at Work', *Industrial Relations Journal*, Vol. 20, No. 3, pp. 226–36.
Rubinstein, W. D. 1988: *Elites and Wealthy in Modern British History*. Brighton: Harvester.
Rueschemeyer, D. 1986: *Power and the Division of Labour*. Cambridge: Polity Press.
Rule, J. 1987: 'The Property of Skill' in Joyce, P. (ed.), *The Historical Meanings of Work*. Cambridge: Cambridge University Press.
Rule, J. 1988: 'The Formative Years of British Trade Unionism', in Rule, J. (ed.), *British Trade Unionism 1750–1850*. London: Longman.
Russell, B. 1984: 'In Praise of Idleness', in Richards, V. (ed.), *Why Work?* London: Freedom Press.
Russell, G. 1983: *The Changing Role of Fathers*. Milton Keynes: Open University Press.
Rustow, D. A. 1970: 'How does a democracy come into existence?', *Comparative Politics*, No. 2.
Sabel, C. F. 1982: *Work and Politics: the Division of Labour in Industry*. Cambridge: Cambridge University Press.
Sahlins, M. 1972: *Stone Age Economics*. London: Tavistock.
Saint-Simon, H. 1964: *Social Organization, the Science of Man, and Other Writings* (ed. Markham, F.). New York: Harper Torch Books.
Salaman, G. 1979: *Work Organizations, Resistance and Control*. London: Longman.
Salaman, G. 1984: *Working*. London: Ellis Horwood/Tavistock.
Salamon, M. 1987: *Industrial Relations: Theory and Practice*. London: Prentice Hall International.
Salway, P. 1981: *Roman Britain*. Oxford: Clarendon.
Samuel, R. 1983a: 'The Middle Class Between the Wars: part one', *New Socialist*, Jan./Feb.
Samuel, R. 1983b: 'The Middle Class Between the Wars: part two', *New Socialist*, Mar./April.
Sanderson, G, and Stapenhurst, F. (eds), 1979: *Industrial Democracy Today*. New York: McGraw-Hill.

Saville, J. 1973: 'The Ideology of Labourism', in Benewick, R., Berki, R. N. and Parekh, B. (eds), *Knowledge and Belief in Politics*. London: Allen & Unwin.

Sayers, S. 1988: 'The Need to Work', in Pahl, R. (ed.), *On Work*. Oxford: Blackwell.

Schwartz, F. N. 1989: 'Management Women and the New Facts of Life', *Harvard Business Review*, Jan./Feb.

Schwimmer, E. 1979: 'The Self and the Product' in Wallman, S. (ed.), *Social Anthropology of Work*. London: Academic Press.

Scott, J. 1979: *Corporations, Classes and Capitalism*. London: Macmillan.

Scott, J. F. and Homans, G. C. 1947: 'Reflections on the Wildcat Strikes', *American Sociological Review*, Vol. 12, pp. 278–87.

Searle-Chatterjee, M. 1979: 'The Polluted Identity of Work: a Study of Benares Sweepers', in Wallman, S. (ed.), *Social Anthropology of Work*. Cambridge: Cambridge University Press.

Seccombe, W. 1974: 'The Housewife and her Labour under Capitalism', *New Left Review*, No. 83, pp. 3–24.

Seccombe, W. 1975: 'Domestic Labour – Reply to Critics', *New Left Review*, No. 94, pp. 84–96.

Seddon, V. 1983: 'Keeping Women in their Place', *Marxism Today*, July.

Segalen, M. 1983: *Love and Power in the Peasant Family*. Oxford: Blackwell.

Seglow, P. 1983: 'Organizational Survival as an Act of Faith: the Case of the BBC', in Thurley, K. and Wood, S. (eds), *Industrial Relations and Management Strategy*. Cambridge: Cambridge University Press.

Selbourne, D. 1985: *Against Socialist Illusion*. London: Macmillan.

Sennett, R. and Cobb, J. 1977: *The Hidden Injuries of Class*. Cambridge: Cambridge University Press.

Sharpe, S. 1976: *Just like a Girl*. London: Penguin.

Sharrock, W. and Anderson, B. 1986: *The Ethnomethodologists*. London: Tavistock.

Sheridan, A. 1980: *Michel Foucault: the Will to Power*. London: Tavistock.

Shields, A. 1986: *On the Battle Lines 1919–1939*. New York: International Publishers.

Shoard, M. 1987: 'Pursuit of the Gentry', *Times Higher Education Supplement*, 7 July.

Shorter, E. and Tilly, C. 1974: *Strikes in France 1830–1968*. Cambridge: Cambridge University Press.

Sievers, B. 1984: 'Motivation as a Surrogate for Meaning', Arbeitspapiere des Fachbereichs Wirtschaftswissenschaft, No. 81. Wuppertal Bergische Universität. Quoted in Alvesson, M. 1987: *Organization Theory and Technocratic Consciousness*. Berlin: De Gruyter.

Silver, M. 1973: 'Recent British Strike Trends: a Factual Analysis', *BJIR*, Vol. 11, pp. 66–104.

Silverman, D. 1970: *The Theory of Organizations*. London: Heinemann.

Simmel, G. 1971: 'The Metropolis and Mental Life', in Thompson, K. and Tunstall, J. (eds), *Sociological Perspectives*. Harmondsworth: Penguin.

Sinfield, A. 1981: *What Unemployment Means*. Oxford: Martin Robertson.

Sinfield, A. 1985: 'Being out of Work', in Littler, C. R. (ed.), *The Experience of Work*. Aldershot: Gower.

Sirianni, C. 1982: *Workers' Control and Socialist Democracy: the Soviet Experience*. London: Verso.
Sisson, K. 1975: *Industrial Relations in Fleet Street*. Oxford: Blackwell.
Sivanandan, A. 1982: *A Different Hunger: Writings on Black Resistance*. London: Pluto.
Skeels, J. W. 1971: 'Measures of US Strike Activity', *Industrial and Labour Relation, Review*, Vol. 24, pp. 515–25.
Sloan, A. P. 1965: *My Years with General Motors*. London: Sidgwick & Jackson.
Sloan, P. J. (ed.). 1980: *Women and Low Pay*. London: Macmillan.
Sloan, R. P., Gruman, J. C. and Allegrante, J. P. 1987: *Investing in Employee Healthcare: a Guide to Effective Health Promotion in the Workplace*. San Francisco: Jossey Bass.
Smith, C. 1987: *Technical Workers: Class, Labour and Trade Unionism*. London: Macmillan.
Smith, C. 1989: 'Flexible Specialization, Automation and Mass Production', *Work, Employment and Society*, Vol. 3, No. 2, pp. 203–20.
Smith, C., Child, J. and Rowlinson, M. 1989: *Innovation in Work Organization: Cadbury Ltd. 1900–1985*. Cambridge: Cambridge University Press.
Smith, D. J. 1974: *Racial Disadvantage in Employment*. London: Political and Economic Policy/Social Science Institute.
Smith, D. J. 1977: *Racial Disadvantage in Britain: the PEP Report*. Harmondsworth: Penguin.
Smith, D. J. 1981: *Unemployment and Racial Minorities*. London: Policy Studies Institute.
Smith, H. L. 1984 'The Womenpower Problem in Britain during the Second World War', *The Historical Journal*, Vol. 27, No. 4, pp. 925–45.
Smith, J. H. 1987: 'Elton Mayo and the hidden Hawthorne', *Work, Employment and Society*, Vol. 1, No. 1, pp. 107–20.
Smith, S. 1981: 'Craft Consiousness and Class Consciousness', *History Workshop*, No. 11, pp. 33–56.
Smith, S. 1988: *The Observer*, 20 March.
Snell, K. D. M. 1985: *Annals of the Labouring Poor: Social Change and Agrarian England 1660–1900*. Cambridge: Cambridge University Press.
Snowden, F. M. 1983: *Before Colour Prejudice: the Ancient View of Blacks*. Cambridge, Mass.: Harvard University Press.
Social Trends. 1988. 1989. 1990. London: HMSO.
Solomos, J. 1989: *Race and Racism in Contemporary Britain*. London: Macmillan.
Sonenscher, M. 1989: *Work and Wages: Natural Law, Politics and the Eighteenth Century French Trades*. Cambridge: Cambridge University Press.
Sousa, de E. 1988: *The Firms That Like To Say No!* Birmingham: BTURC Publishing.
Spencer, A. and Podmore, D. 1986: *In a Man's World: Essays on Women in Male Dominated Professions*. London: Tavistock.
Spencer, H. 1971: 'The Study of Sociology', in Thompson, K. and Tunstall, J. (eds), *Sociological Perspectives*. Harmondsworth: Penguin.
Spretnak, C. and Capra, F. 1985: *Green Politics: the Global Promise*. London: Paladin.

Spriano, D. 1975: *The Occupation of the Factories: Italy 1920*. London: Pluto.
Stalker, P. 1986: 'Street Wise', *New Internationalist*, No. 166, December.
Stanworth, M. 1984: 'Women and Class Analysis: a Reply to John Goldthorpe', *Sociology*, Vol. 18, No. 2, pp. 159–70.
Stark, T. 1988: *Income and Wealth in the 1980's*. London: Fabian Society Papers.
Stead, J. 1987: *Never the Same Again: Women and the Miners' Strike*. London: Women's Press.
Stevenson, J. 1984: *British Society 1914–45*. Harmondsworth: Pelican.
Stewart, M. L. 1989: *Women, Work and the French State*. McGill-Queens University Press.
Stinchcombe, A. L. 1965: 'Social Structure and Organizations', in March, J. G. (ed.), *Hand Book of Organizations*. Chicago: McNally.
Stone, K. 1974: 'The Origin of the Structures in the Steel Industry', in Edwards, R., Reich. M. and Gordon, D. (eds), *Labor Market Segmentation*. Lexington, Mass.: D. C. Heath.
Strauss, A. et al. 1963: 'The Hospital and its Negotiated Order', in Freidson, E. (ed.), *The Hospital in Modern Society*. New York: Free Press.
Streek, W. 1987: 'The Uncertainties of Management in the Management of Uncertainty', *Work, Employment and Society*, Vol. 1, No. 3, pp. 281–308.
Summerfield, P. 1985: *Women Workers in the Second World War: Production and Patriarchy in Conflict*. London: Croom Helm.
Sweezy, P. M. 1942: *The Theory of Capitalist Development*. New York: Monthly Review Press.
Sykes, R. 1988: 'Trade Unions and Class Consciousness: the Revolutionary Period of General Unionism, 1829–1834', in Rule, J. (ed.), *British Trade Unionism 1750–1850*. London: Longman.
Taylor, A. J. 1972: *Laissez Faire and State Intervention in Nineteenth Century Britain*. London: Macmillan.
Taylor, C. 1979: *Hegel and Modern Society*. Cambridge: Cambridge University Press.
Taylor, D. 1988: 'Life Sentence: the Politics of Housework', *New Internationalist*, March.
Taylor, F. W. 1903: 'Shop Management' reprinted in Taylor, F. W. 1964: *Scientific Management*. New York: Harper & Row.
Taylor, F. W. 1911: *The Principles of Scientific Management*. New York: Harper & Row.
Taylor, R. 1982: *Workers and the New Depression*. London: Macmillan.
Thayer, C. 1987: 'Retraining Women', *The Health Service Journal*, 5 February.
Therborn, G. 1977: 'The Rule of Capital and the Rise of Democracy', *New Left Review*, 103.
Therborn, G. 1986: *Why Some People are More Unemployed than Others*. London: Verso.
Thomas, D. N. 1984: *White Bolts, Black Locks: Participation in the Inner City*. London: Allen & Unwin.
Thompson, E. P. 1968: *The Making of the English Working Class*. Harmondsworth: Penguin.
Thompson, E. P. 1971: 'The Moral Economy of the English Crowd in the Eighteenth Century', *Past and Present*, Vol. 50, pp. 76–136.

Thompson, E. P. 1982: 'Time, Work Discipline and Industrial Capitalism', in Giddens, A. and Held, D. (eds), *Classes, Power and Conflict*. London: Macmillan.

Thompson, G. 1984: 'Economic Intervention in the Post-war Economy', in Mclennan, G., Held, D. and Hall, S. (eds), *State and Society in Contemporary Britain: a Critical Introduction*. Cambridge: Polity Press.

Thompson, K. 1988: *Under Siege: Racism and Violence in Britain*. Harmondsworth: Penguin.

Thompson, P. 1984: *The Nature of Work: an Introduction to Debates on the Labour Process*. London: Macmillan.

Thorsrud, E., Sorenson, B. A. and Gustavsen, B. 1976: 'Sociotechnical Approaches to Industrial Democracy in Norway', in Dubin, R. (ed.), *Handbook of Work, Organization and Society*. Chicago: Rand McNally.

Toffler, A. 1980: *The Third Wave*. London: Collins.

Tomlinson, J. 1982: *The Unequal Struggle: British Socialism and the Capitalist Enterprise*. London: Methuen.

Tonnies, F. 1955: *Community and Society, Gemeinschaft und Gesellschaft*. London: Routledge.

Touraine, A. 1971: *The Post Industrial Society*. London: Wildwood House.

Trades Union Congress. 1983a: *Race Relations at work*. London: TUC.

Trades Union Congress. 1983b: *TUC Workbook on Racism*. London: TUC.

Trades Union Congress. 1986: *Statistical Statement and List of Delegates*. London: TUC.

Tranter, N. L. 1973: *Population since the Industrial Revolution*. London: Croom Helm.

Traub, R. 1978: 'Lenin and Taylor: the Fate of "Scientific Management" in the early Soviet Union', *Telos*, Vol. 37, pp. 82–92.

Treas, J. 1987: 'The Effect of Women's Labor Force Participation on the Distribution of Income in the United States', *Annual Review of Sociology*, Vol. 13, pp. 259–88.

Trist, E. L. and Bamforth, K. W. 1951: 'Some Social and Psychological Consequences of the Longwall Method of Coal Getting', *Human Relations*, 4, No. 1, pp. 3–38.

Trist, E. L., Higgin, G. W., Murray, H. and Pollock, A. B. 1963: *Organizational Choice*. London: Tavistock.

Truman, C. and Keating, J. 1988: 'Technology, Markets and the Design of Women's Jobs', *New Technology, Work and Employment*, Vol. 3, No. 1, pp. 21–9.

Turnbull, P. J. 1988: 'Leaner and Possibly Fitter: the Management of Redundancy in Britain', *Industrial Relations Journal*, Vol. 19, No. 3, pp. 201–13.

Turner, B. S. 1986: *Citizenship and Capitalism: the Debate over Reformism*. London: Allen & Unwin.

Turner, H. A. 1962: *Trade Union Growth, Structure and Policy: a Comparative Study of the Cotton Unions*. London: Allen & Unwin.

Turner, H. A. 1963: *The Trend of Strikes*. Leeds: Leeds University Press.

Turner, H. A. 1969: *Is Britain Really Strike Prone?* London: Cambridge University Press.

TURU (Trade Union Research Unit). 1986: *Women and Trade Unions*, Technical Note No. 100. Oxford: Ruskin College.

Vanek, J. 1974: 'Time spent in Housework', *Scientific American*, November.

Veblen, T. 1899: *The Theory of the Leisure Class*. London: Macmillan.

Veblen, T. 1904: *The Theory of Business Enterprise*. New York.

Veblen, T. 1921: *The Engineers and the Price System*. New York.

Virdee, S. 1990: 'Trade Unions and Racism: the Case of Independent Black Caucuses'. Unpublished Master's Thesis, Brunel University.

Wajcman, J. 1982: 'Working Women', *Capital and Class*, Vol. 18, pp. 135–81.

Wajcman, J. 1983: *Women in Control: Dilemmas of a Workers' Cooperative*. Milton Keynes: Open University Press.

Walby, S. 1986a: *Patriarchy at Work: Patriarchal and Capitalist Relations in Employment*. Cambridge: Polity Press.

Walby, S. 1986b: 'Gender, Class and Stratification', in Crompton, R. and Mann, M. (eds) *Gender and Stratification*. Cambridge: Polity Press.

Walby, S. 1988: 'Gender Politics and Social Theory', *Sociology*, Vol. 22, No. 2, pp. 215–32.

Walby, S. 1989: 'Flexibility and the Changing Sexual Division of Labour' in Wood, S. (ed.), *The Transformation of work?* London: Unwin Hyman.

Waldinger, R. 1985: 'Immigrant Enterprise and the Structure of the Labour Market', in Roberts, B., Finnegan, R. and Gallie, D. (eds), *New Perspectives on Economic Life*. Manchester: Manchester University Press.

Walker, C. R. and Guest, R. H. 1952: *The Man on the Assembly Line*. Cambridge, Mass.: Harvard University Press.

Walker, C. R., Guest, R. H. and Turner, A. N. 1956: *The Foreman on the Assembly Line*. Cambridge Mass.: Harvard University Press.

Walker, K. E. and Woods, M. 1976: *Time Use: a Measure of Household Production of Family Goods and Services*. American Home Economics Association.

Walker, M. 1989: *The Guardian*, 14 June.

Wallace, A. 1978: *Rockdale: the Growth of an American Village in the Early Industrial Revolution*. New York: Knopf.

Wallerstein, I. 1974: *The Modern World System*. New York: Academic Press.

Wallerstein, I. 1979: *The Capitalist World Economy*. Cambridge: Cambridge University Press.

Ward, R. 1978: 'Race Relations in Britain', *British Journal of Sociology*, Vol. 29, No. 4.

Ward, R. 1985: 'Minority Settlement and the Local Economy', in Roberts, B., Finnegan, R. and Gallie, D. (eds), *New Perspectives on Economic Life*. Manchester: Manchester University Press.

Warner, W. L. and Low, J. O. 1947: *The Social System of the Modern Factory* New Haven, Conn.: Yale University Press.

Warr, P. 1983: 'Work and Unemployment', in Drenth, P. J. D., Thierry, H., Willems, D. J. and de Wolff, C. J. (eds), *Handbook of Work and Organizational Psychology*. London: John Wiley.

Warr, P. B. 1987: *Work, Unemployment and Mental Health*. Oxford: Clarendon.

WASH. 1987: 'Women Against Sexual Harassment', London: WASH.

Watson, T. J. 1986: *Management, Organization and Employment Strategy*. London: Routledge.
Watts, I. 1984: 'Industrial Radicalism and the Domestic Division of Labour', in Siltanen, J. and Stanworth, M. (eds), *Women and the Public Sphere*. London: Hutchinson.
Webb, S. and Webb. B. 1919: *The History of Trade Unionism, 1666–1920*. London: Webb & Webb.
Webb, S. and Webb. B. 1920: *Industrial Democracy*. London: Longman.
Weber, M. 1948: *From Max Weber* (Gerth. H. H. and Mills, C. W. , eds). London: Routledge.
Weber, M. 1976: *The Protestant Ethic and the Spirit of Capitalism*. London: Allen & Unwin.
Weber, M. 1978: *Economy and Society*. Berkeley, Cal.: University of California Press.
Webster, J. 1990: *Office Automation: the Labour Process and Women's Work in Britain*. London: Harvester Wheatsheaf.
Weissbach, L. S. 1989: *Child Labor Reform in Nineteenth Century France*. Baton Rouge: Louisiana State University Press.
Westwood, S. and Bhachu, P. (eds), 1989: *Enterprising Women: Ethnicity, Economy and Gender Relations*. London: Routledge.
Whipp, R. 1987: 'A Time to every Purpose: an Essay on Time and Work' in Joyce, P. (ed.), *The Historical Meanings of Work*. Cambridge: Cambridge University Press.
Whipp, R. and Grieco, M. 1983: 'Family and Workplace: the Social Organization of Work', paper given at the SSRC workshop on 'Work Organization', July.
White, M. 1983: *Long Term Unemployment and Labour Markets*. London: Policy Studies Institute.
Wiener, M. J. 1981: *English Culture and the Decline of the Industrial Spirit 1850–1980*. Cambridge: Cambridge University Press.
Wilkinson, B. 1983: *The Shopfloor Politics of New Technology*. London: Heinemann.
Willis, P. 1977: *Learning to Labour: How Working Class Kids Get Working Class Jobs*. Aldershot: Gower.
Willmott, H. 1987: 'Racism, Politics and Employment Relations', in Lee, G. and Loveridge, R. (eds), *The Manufacture of Disadvantage: Stigma and Social Closure*. Milton Keynes: Open University Press.
Wilson, P. and Stanworth, J. 1988: 'Growth Strategies in Small Asian and Caribbean Businesses', *Employment Gazette*, January.
Wilson, W. J. 1987: *The Truly Disadvantaged: the Inner City, the Underclass and Public Policy*. Chicago: Chicago University Press.
Winn, M. 1983: *Children Without Childhood*. New York: Pantheon.
Winner, L. 1977: *Autonomous Technology*. Cambridge, Mass.: MIT Press.
Winner, L. 1985: 'Do Artefacts have Politics?', In Mackenzie, D. and Wajcman, J. (eds), *The Social Shaping of Technology*. Milton Keynes: Open University Press.
Wintour, P. and Tirbutt, S. 1988: *The Guardian*, 26 October.
Witte, J. F. 1980: *Democracy, Authority and Alienation in Work*. Chicago: Chicago University Press.

Wojtas, O. 1989: 'Forced off Career Ladder', *Times Higher Education Supplement*, 10 March.

Wolff, E. N. (ed.). 1987: *International Comparisons of the Distribution of Household Wealth*. Oxford: Clarendon.

Wolff, J. 1977: 'Women in Organizations', in Clegg, S. and Dunkerley, D. (eds), *Critical Issues in Organizations*. London: Routledge.

Wood, E. 1981: 'Marxism and Ancient Greece', *History Workshop*, No. 11, pp. 3–22.

Wood, E. M. 1986: *The Retreat from Class: a New True Socialism*. London: Verso.

Wood, S. (ed.). 1982: *The Degradation of Work*. London: Hutchinson.

Woodburn, J. 1980: 'Hunters and Gatherers Today and Reconstruction of the Past', in Gellner, E. (ed.), *Soviet and Western Anthropology*. London: Duckworth.

Woodward, C. Vann. 1974: *The Strange Career of Jim Crow*. New York: Oxford University Press.

Woodward, J. 1958: *Management and Technology*. London: HMSO.

Woodward, J. 1965: *Industrial Organization*. Oxford: Oxford University Press.

Woodward, J. (ed.). 1970: *Industrial Organization: Behaviour and Control*. Oxford: Oxford University Press.

Woolgar, J. 1989: Personal Communication.

Woolgar, S. 1988: *Science: the Very Idea*. London: Ellis Horwood/Tavistock.

Woolgar, S. 1989a: 'Stabilization Rituals: Steps in the Socialization of a New Machine', paper presented at the PICT conference, Brunel University, May.

Woolgar, S. 1989b: 'Designing Users and Selling Futures', paper presented at the PICT conference, CRICT, Brunel University, May.

Woolgar, S. 1990: Personal communication.

Wootton, B. 1955: *The Social Foundations of Wage Policy*. London: Allen & Unwin.

Wrench, J. 1985: 'Unequal Comrades: Trade Unions, Equal Opportunity and Anti-Racism', mimeo, RUER. Coventry: University of Warwick.

Wright, E. O. 1978: *Class, Crisis and the State*. London: New Left Books.

Wright, E. O. 1985: *Classes*. London: Verso.

Wright, P. 1968: *The Coloured Worker in British Industry*. Oxford: Oxford University Press/Institute for Race Relations.

Wright, T. 1867: *Some Habits and Customs of the Working Classes by a Journeyman Engineer*. London: Tinsley Brothers. Republished 1967 by Augustus M. Kelley Publishers.

Wright Mills, C. 1951: *White Collar*. Oxford: Oxford University Press.

Wright Mills, C. 1970: *The Sociological Imagination*. Harmondsworth: Penguin.

Wyatt, S. 1989: 'Networking the State: the Story of the Government Data Network', paper delivered at CRICT, Brunel University, 22 November.

Yeandle, S. 1984: *Women's Working Lives: Patterns and Strategies*. London: Tavistock.

YWCA. 1987: *Girls in 'Male' Jobs: a Research Report*. London: YWCA.

Zabalza, A. and Tzannatos, Z. 1985: *Women and Equal Pay*. Cambridge: Cambridge University Press.

Zaleznik, A. 1989: 'Real Work', *Harvard Business Review*, Jan./Feb.
Zaretsky, E. 1976: *Capitalism, the Family and Personal Life.* London: Pluto.
Zeitlin, J. 1982: 'Trade Unions and Job Control: a Critique of Rank and Filism', paper to The Society for the Study of Labour History at Birkbeck College, London, 27 November.
Zeitlin, J. 1983: 'Social Theory and the History of Work', *Social History*, 8, pp. 365–74.
Zeitlin, J. 1985: 'Engineers and Compositors: a Comparison', in Harrison, R. and Zeitlin, J. (eds), *Divisions of Labour: Skilled Workers and Technological Change in Nineteenth Century England.* Brighton: Harvester.
Zwerdling, D. 1978: *Democracy at Work*. Washington D. C.: Association for Self Management.

Index